ST PAUL
Sunday Missal
2009

GW00730196

Texts a[
Ireland, England & Wales and Scotland

ST PAULS

Imprimatur:
✠ Michael Smith
Bishop of Meath
10 July 2008

Introductions and Reflections by Gearard Ó Floinn

ST PAULS
Moyglare Road, Maynooth, Co. Kildare, Ireland.
187 Battersea Bridge Road, London SW11 3AS, U.K.

ISBN 9780854397440
© ST PAULS, 2008

Printed by AGAM, Madonna dell'Olmo (CN), Italy.

ST PAULS is an activity of the Priests and Brothers of the Society of St Paul who proclaim the Gospel through the media of social communication.

CONTENTS

Epiphany: celebrated in England, Wales and Scotland — *4 January*

THE ORDER OF MASS

INTRODUCTORY RITES

ENTRANCE ANTIPHON — *see Mass of the day*

GREETING

In the name of the Father, and of the Son, and of the Holy Spirit.
Amen.

The grace of our Lord Jesus Christ and the love of God and the
fellowship of the Holy Spirit be with you all.
And also with you.

or

The grace and peace of God our Father and the Lord Jesus Christ
be with you.
Blessed be God, the Father of our Lord Jesus Christ.

or

And also with you.

or

The Lord be with you.
And also with you.

The celebrant may briefly introduce the Mass of the day.

RITE OF BLESSING AND SPRINKLING HOLY WATER

*This rite may be used instead of the penitential rite at the beginning of
Mass. The Kyrie is also omitted.*

*The celebrant greets the people. A vessel containing the water to be blessed
is placed before him.*

Dear friends,
this water will be used
to remind us of our baptism.
Let us ask God to bless it
and to keep us faithful
to the Spirit he has given us.

After a brief silence, he joins his hands and continues:

1. God our Father,
    your gift of water
    brings life and freshness to the earth;

it washes away our sins
and brings us eternal life.

We ask you now
to bless ✠ this water,
and to give us your protection on this day
which you have made your own.
Renew the living spring of your life within us
and protect us in spirit and body,
that we may be free from sin
and come into your presence
to receive your gift of salvation.

We ask this through Christ our Lord.

or

2. Lord God almighty,
   creator of all life,
   of body and soul,
   we ask you to bless ✠ this water:
   as we use it in faith
   forgive our sins
   and save us from all illness
   and the power of evil.

   Lord,
   in your mercy
   give us living water,
   always springing up as a fountain of salvation:
   free us, body and soul, from every danger,
   and admit us to your presence
   in purity of heart.

   Grant this through Christ our Lord.

or (during the Easter season)

3. Lord God almighty,
   hear the prayers of your people:
   we celebrate our creation and redemption.
   Hear our prayers and bless ✠ this water
   which gives fruitfulness to the fields,
   and refreshment and cleansing to man.
   You chose water to show your goodness
   when you led your people to freedom
   through the Red Sea
   and satisfied their thirst in the desert

with water from the rock.
Water was the symbol used by the prophets
to foretell your new covenant with man.
You made the water of baptism holy
by Christ's baptism in the Jordan:
by it you give us a new birth
and renew us in holiness.
May this water remind us of our baptism
and let us share the joy
of all who have been baptised at Easter.
We ask this through Christ our Lord.

Where it is customary, salt may be mixed with the holy water. The priest blesses the salt, saying:

Almighty God,
we ask you to bless ✠ this salt
as once you blessed the salt scattered over the water
by the prophet Elisha.
Wherever this salt and water are sprinkled,
drive away the power of evil,
and protect us always
by the presence of your Holy Spirit.
We ask this through Christ our Lord.

The priest sprinkles himself, his ministers, and the people. Meanwhile, an antiphon or an appropriate song is sung.

When he returns to his place, the priest says:

May almighty God cleanse us of our sins,
and through the eucharist we celebrate
make us worthy to sit at his table
in his heavenly kingdom.
Amen.

When it is prescribed, the GLORIA is then sung or said, and the Mass continues.

PENITENTIAL RITE

The celebrant invites the people to repent of their sins. He may use the following or similar words:

My brothers and sisters,
to prepare ourselves to celebrate the sacred mysteries,
let us call to mind our sins.

or

As we prepare to celebrate the mystery of Christ's love,
let us acknowledge our failures
and ask the Lord for pardon and strength.

or

Coming together as God's family,
with confidence let us ask the Father's forgiveness,
for he is full of gentleness and compassion.

A pause for silent reflection follows. After a brief silence all say:

A

**I confess to almighty God,
and to you, my brothers and sisters,
that I have sinned through my own fault**

(All strike their breast)

**in my thoughts and in my words,
in what I have done,
and in what I have failed to do;
and I ask blessed Mary, ever virgin,
all the angels and saints,
and you, my brothers and sisters,
to pray for me to the Lord our God.**

May almighty God have mercy on us,
forgive us our sins,
and bring us to everlasting life.
Amen.

Lord, have mercy.
Lord, have mercy.
Christ, have mercy.
Christ, have mercy.
Lord, have mercy.
Lord, have mercy.

or B

Lord, we have sinned against you:
Lord, have mercy.
Lord, have mercy.
Lord, show us your mercy and love.
And grant us your salvation.
May almighty God have mercy on us,
forgive us our sins,

and bring us to everlasting life.
Amen.

or C (1)

You were sent to heal the contrite:
Lord, have mercy.
Lord, have mercy.
You came to call sinners:
Christ, have mercy.
Christ, have mercy.
You plead for us at the right hand of the Father:
Lord, have mercy.
Lord, have mercy.

May almighty God have mercy on us,
forgive us our sins,
and bring us to everlasting life.
Amen.

or (2)

Lord Jesus, you came to gather the nations
into the peace of God's kingdom:
Lord, have mercy.
Lord, have mercy.
You come in word and sacrament to strengthen us in holiness:
Christ, have mercy.
Christ, have mercy.
You will come in glory with salvation for your people:
Lord, have mercy.
Lord, have mercy.

May almighty God have mercy on us,
forgive us our sins,
and bring us to everlasting life.
Amen.

or (3)

Lord Jesus, you are mighty God and Prince of peace:
Lord, have mercy.
Lord, have mercy.

Lord Jesus, you are Son of God and Son of Mary:
Christ, have mercy.
Christ, have mercy.

Lord Jesus, you are Word made flesh and splendour of the Father:

Lord, have mercy.
Lord, have mercy.

May almighty God have mercy on us,
forgive us our sins,
and bring us to everlasting life.
Amen.

or (4)

Lord Jesus, you came to reconcile us
    to one another and to the Father:
Lord, have mercy.
Lord, have mercy.

Lord Jesus, you heal the wounds of sin and division:
Christ, have mercy.
Christ, have mercy.

Lord Jesus, you intercede for us with your Father:
Lord, have mercy.
Lord, have mercy.

May almighty God have mercy on us,
forgive us our sins,
and bring us to everlasting life.
Amen.

or (5)

You raise the dead to life in the Spirit:
Lord, have mercy.
Lord, have mercy.

You bring pardon and peace to the sinner:
Christ, have mercy.
Christ, have mercy.

You bring light to those in darkness:
Lord, have mercy.
Lord, have mercy.

May almighty God have mercy on us,
forgive us our sins,
and bring us to everlasting life.
Amen.

or (6)

Lord Jesus, you raise us to new life:
Lord, have mercy.
Lord, have mercy.

Lord Jesus, you forgive us our sins:
Christ, have mercy.
Christ, have mercy.

Lord Jesus, you feed us with your body and blood:
Lord, have mercy.
Lord, have mercy.

May almighty God have mercy on us,
forgive us our sins,
and bring us to everlasting life.
Amen.

or (7)

Lord Jesus, you have shown us the way to the Father:
Lord, have mercy.
Lord, have mercy.

Lord Jesus, you have given us the consolation of the truth:
Christ, have mercy.
Christ, have mercy.

Lord Jesus, you are the Good Shepherd,
    leading us into everlasting life:
Lord, have mercy.
Lord, have mercy.

May almighty God have mercy on us,
forgive us our sins,
and bring us to everlasting life.
Amen.

or (8)

Lord Jesus, you healed the sick:
Lord, have mercy.
Lord, have mercy.

Lord Jesus, you forgave sinners:
Christ, have mercy.
Christ, have mercy.

Lord Jesus, you give us yourself to heal us and bring us strength:
Lord, have mercy.
Lord, have mercy.

May almighty God have mercy on us,
forgive us our sins,
and bring us to everlasting life.
Amen.

GLORIA

Glory to God in the highest,
   and peace to his people on earth.

Lord God, heavenly King,
almighty God and Father,
   we worship you, we give you thanks,
   we praise you for your glory.

Lord Jesus Christ, only Son of the Father,
Lord God, Lamb of God,
you take away the sin of the world:
   have mercy on us;
you are seated at the right hand of the Father:
   receive our prayer.

For you alone are the Holy One,
you alone are the Lord,
you alone are the Most High,
   Jesus Christ,
   with the Holy Spirit,
   in the glory of God the Father. Amen.

OPENING PRAYER

(Turn to the Mass of the day)

LITURGY OF THE WORD

READINGS, RESPONSORIAL PSALM,
GOSPEL ACCLAMATION
(Turn to the Mass of the day)

PROFESSION OF FAITH *(Nicene Creed)*

We believe in one God,
   the Father, the Almighty,
   maker of heaven and earth,
   of all that is, seen and unseen.

We believe in one Lord, Jesus Christ,
   the only Son of God,
   eternally begotten of the Father,
   God from God, Light from Light,
   true God from true God,
   begotten, not made,
   of one Being with the Father.
   Through him all things were made.
   For us men and for our salvation
     he came down from heaven:

   (All bow during these three lines)

   by the power of the Holy Spirit
     he became incarnate from the Virgin Mary,
     and was made man.

For our sake he was crucified under Pontius Pilate;
   he suffered death and was buried.
On the third day he rose again
   in accordance with the Scriptures;
he ascended into heaven
   and is seated at the right hand of the Father.
He will come again in glory to judge the living and the
      dead,
   and his kingdom will have no end.

We believe in the Holy Spirit, the Lord, the giver of life,
   who proceeds from the Father and the Son.
   With the Father and the Son he is worshipped and
     glorified.
   He has spoken through the Prophets.
   We believe in one holy catholic and apostolic Church.
   We acknowledge one baptism for the forgiveness of sins.
   We look for the resurrection of the dead,
     and the life of the world to come. Amen.

PROFESSION OF FAITH   *(Apostles' Creed)*

I believe in God, the Father almighty,
  creator of heaven and earth.

I believe in Jesus Christ, his only Son, our Lord.
  He was conceived by the power of the Holy Spirit
    and born of the Virgin Mary.
  He suffered under Pontius Pilate,
    was crucified, died, and was buried.
  He descended to the dead.
  On the third day he rose again.
  He ascended into heaven,
    and is seated at the right hand of the Father.
  He will come again to judge the living and the dead.

I believe in the Holy Spirit,
  the holy catholic Church,
  the communion of saints,
  the forgiveness of sins,
  the resurrection of the body,
  and the life everlasting. Amen.

PRAYER OF THE FAITHFUL

LITURGY OF THE EUCHARIST

PREPARATION OF THE GIFTS

Blessed are you, Lord, God of all creation.
Through your goodness we have this bread to offer,
which earth has given and human hands have made.
It will become for us the bread of life.
Blessed be God for ever.

By the mystery of this water and wine
may we come to share in the divinity of Christ,
who humbled himself to share in our humanity.

Blessed are you, Lord, God of all creation.
Through your goodness we have this wine to offer,
fruit of the vine and work of human hands.
It will become our spiritual drink.
Blessed be God for ever.

Lord God, we ask you to receive us
and be pleased with the sacrifice we offer you
with humble and contrite hearts.

Lord, wash away my iniquity; cleanse me from my sin.

The priest says these or similar words:
Pray, brothers and sisters, that our sacrifice
may be acceptable to God, the almighty Father.

**May the Lord accept the sacrifice at your hands
for the praise and glory of his name,
for our good, and the good of all his Church.**

PRAYER OVER THE GIFTS
(Turn to the Mass of the day)

EUCHARISTIC PRAYER

The Lord be with you
And also with you.
Lift up your hearts.
We lift them up to the Lord.
Let us give thanks to the Lord our God.
It is right to give him thanks and praise.

The celebrant continues alone.

PREFACES

PREFACE OF ADVENT I
(From the First Sunday of Advent until 16 December)

Father, all-powerful and ever-living God,
we do well always and everywhere to give you thanks
through Jesus Christ our Lord.

When he humbled himself to come among us as a man,
he fulfilled the plan you formed long ago
and opened for us the way to salvation.

Now we watch for the day,
hoping that the salvation promised us will be ours
when Christ our Lord will come again in his glory.

And so, with all the choirs of angels in heaven
we proclaim your glory
and join in their unending hymn of praise:

**Holy, holy, holy Lord, God of power and might,
heaven and earth are full of your glory.**
    Hosanna in the highest.
Blessed is he who comes in the name of the Lord.
    Hosanna in the highest.

PREFACE OF ADVENT II
(17-24 December)

Father, all-powerful and ever-living God,
we do well always and everywhere to give you thanks
through Jesus Christ our Lord.

His future coming was proclaimed by all the prophets.
The virgin mother bore him in her womb with love beyond all
    telling.
John the Baptist was his herald
and made him know when at last he came.

In his love Christ has filled us with joy
as we prepare to celebrate his birth,
so that when he comes he may find us watching in prayer,
our hearts filled with wonder and praise.

And so, with all the choirs of angels in heaven
we proclaim your glory
and join in their unending hymn of praise:

Holy, holy, holy…

PREFACE OF CHRISTMAS I

Father, all-powerful and ever-living God,
we do well always and everywhere to give you thanks
through Jesus Christ our Lord.

In the wonder of the incarnation
your eternal Word has brought to the eyes of faith
a new and radiant vision of your glory.
In him we see our God made visible
and so are caught up in love of the God we cannot see.

And so, with all the choirs of angels in heaven
we proclaim your glory
and join in their unending hymn of praise:

Holy, holy, holy…

PREFACE OF CHRISTMAS II

Father, all-powerful and ever-living God,
we do well always and everywhere to give you thanks
through Jesus Christ our Lord.

Today you fill our hearts with joy
as we recognise in Christ the revelation of your love.
No eye can see his glory as our God,
yet now he is seen as one like us.

Christ is your Son before all ages,
yet now he is born in time.
He has come to lift up all things to himself,
to restore unity to creation,
and to lead mankind from exile into your heavenly kingdom.

With all the angels of heaven
we sing our joyful hymn of praise:

Holy, holy, holy…

PREFACE OF CHRISTMAS III

Father, all-powerful and ever-living God,
we do well always and everywhere to give you thanks
through Jesus Christ our Lord.

Today in him a new light has dawned upon the world:
God has become one with man,
and man has become one again with God.

Your eternal Word has taken upon himself our human weak-
    ness,
giving our mortal nature immortal value.
So marvellous is this oneness between God and man
that in Christ man restores to man the gift of everlasting life.

In our joy we sing to your glory
with all the choirs of angels:

Holy, holy, holy...

PREFACE OF LENT I

Father, all-powerful and ever-living God,
we do well always and everywhere to give you thanks
through Jesus Christ our Lord.

Each year you give us this joyful season
when we prepare to celebrate the paschal mystery
with mind and heart renewed.
You give us a spirit of loving reverence for you, our Father,
and of willing service to our neighbour.

As we recall the great events that gave us new life in Christ,
you bring the image of your Son to perfection within us.

Now, with angels and archangels,
and the whole company of heaven,
we sing the unending hymn of your praise:

Holy, holy, holy...

PREFACE OF LENT II

Father, all-powerful and ever-living God,
we do well always and everywhere to give you thanks.

This great season of grace is your gift to your family
to renew us in spirit.
You give us strength to purify our hearts,
to control our desires,
and so to serve you in freedom.
You teach us how to live in this passing world,
with our heart set on the world that will never end.

Now, with all the saints and angels,
we praise you for ever:

Holy, holy, holy...

PREFACE OF EASTER II

Father, all-powerful and ever-living God,
we do well always and everywhere to give you thanks
through Jesus Christ our Lord.

We praise you with greater joy than ever in this Easter season,
when Christ became our paschal sacrifice.

He has made us children of the light,
rising to new and everlasting life.
He has opened the gates of heaven
to receive his faithful people.
His death is our ransom from death;
his resurrection is our rising to life.

The joy of the resurrection renews the whole world,
while the choirs of heaven sing for ever to your glory:

Holy, holy, holy...

PREFACE OF EASTER III

Father, all-powerful and ever-living God,
we do well always and everywhere to give you thanks
through Jesus Christ our Lord.

We praise you with greater joy than ever in this Easter season,
when Christ became our paschal sacrifice.

He is still our priest,
our advocate who always pleads our cause.
Christ is the victim who dies no more,
the Lamb, once slain, who lives for ever.

The joy of the resurrection renews the whole world,
while the choirs of heaven sing for ever to your glory:

Holy, holy, holy...

PREFACE OF EASTER IV

Father, all-powerful and ever-living God,
we do well always and everywhere to give you thanks
through Jesus Christ our Lord.

We praise you with greater joy than ever in this Easter season,
when Christ became our paschal sacrifice.

In him a new age has dawned,
the long reign of sin is ended,

a broken world has been renewed,
and man is once again made whole.

The joy of the resurrection renews the whole world,
while the choirs of heaven sing for ever to your glory:

Holy, holy, holy…

PREFACE OF EASTER V

Father, all-powerful and ever-living God,
we do well always and everywhere to give you thanks
through Jesus Christ our Lord.

We praise you with greater joy than ever in this Easter season,
when Christ became our paschal sacrifice.

As he offered his body on the cross,
his perfect sacrifice fulfilled all others.
As he gave himself into your hands for our salvation,
he showed himself to be the priest, the altar, and the lamb of
    sacrifice.

The joy of the resurrection renews the whole world,
while the choirs of heaven sing for ever to your glory:

Holy, holy, holy…

PREFACE OF SUNDAYS IN ORDINARY TIME I

Father, all-powerful and ever-living God,
we do well always and everywhere to give you thanks
through Jesus Christ our Lord.

Through his cross and resurrection
he freed us from sin and death
and called us to the glory that has made us
a chosen race, a royal priesthood,
a holy nation, a people set apart.

Everywhere we proclaim your mighty works
for you have called us out of darkness
into your own wonderful light.

And so, with all the choirs of angels in heaven
we proclaim your glory
and join in their unending hymn of praise:

Holy, holy, holy…

PREFACE OF SUNDAYS IN ORDINARY TIME II

Father, all-powerful and ever-living God,
we do well always and everywhere to give you thanks
through Jesus Christ our Lord.

Out of love for sinful man,
he humbled himself to be born of the Virgin.

By suffering on the cross
he freed us from unending death,
and by rising from the dead
he gave us eternal life.

And so, with all the choirs of angels in heaven
we proclaim your glory
and join in their unending hymn of praise:

Holy, holy, holy...

PREFACE OF SUNDAYS IN ORDINARY TIME III

Father, all-powerful and ever-living God,
we do well always and everywhere to give you thanks.

We see your infinite power
in your loving plan of salvation.
You came to our rescue by your power as God,
but you wanted us to be saved by one like us.
Man refused your friendship,
but man himself was to restore it
through Jesus Christ our Lord.

Through him the angels of heaven offer their prayer of
    adoration
as they rejoice in your presence for ever.
May our voices be one with theirs
in their triumphant hymn of praise:

Holy, holy, holy...

PREFACE OF SUNDAYS IN ORDINARY TIME IV

Father, all-powerful and ever-living God,
we do well always and everywhere to give you thanks
through Jesus Christ our Lord.

By his birth we are reborn.
In his suffering we are freed from sin.

By his rising from the dead we rise to everlasting life.
In his return to you in glory
we enter into your heavenly kingdom.

And so, we join the angels and the saints
as they sing their unending hymn of praise:

Holy, holy, holy...

PREFACE OF SUNDAYS IN ORDINARY TIME V

Father, all-powerful and ever-living God,
we do well always and everywhere to give you thanks.

All things are of your making,
all times and seasons obey your laws,
but you chose to create man in your own image,
setting him over the whole world in all its wonder.
You made man the steward of creation,
to praise you day by day for the marvels of your wisdom and
    power,
through Jesus Christ our Lord.

We praise you, Lord, with all the angels and saints
in their song of joy:

Holy, holy, holy...

PREFACE OF SUNDAYS IN ORDINARY TIME VI

Father, all-powerful and ever-living God,
we do well always and everywhere to give you thanks.

In you we live and move and have our being.
Each day you show us a Father's love;
your Holy Spirit, dwelling within us,
gives us on earth the hope of unending joy.

Your gift of the Spirit,
who raised Jesus from the dead,
is the foretaste and promise
of the paschal feast of heaven.

With thankful praise,
in company with the angels,
we glorify the wonders of your power:

Holy, holy, holy...

PREFACE OF SUNDAYS IN ORDINARY TIME VII

Father, all-powerful and ever-living God,
we do well always and everywhere to give you thanks.

So great was your love
that you gave us your Son as our Redeemer.
You sent him as one like ourselves,
though free from sin,
that you might see and love in us
what you see and love in Christ.
Your gifts of grace, lost by disobedience,
are now restored by the obedience of your Son.

We praise you, Lord, with all the angels and saints
in their song of joy:

Holy, holy, holy...

PREFACE OF SUNDAYS IN ORDINARY TIME VIII

Father, all-powerful and ever-living God,
we do well always and everywhere to give you thanks.

When your children sinned
and wandered far from your friendship,
you reunited them with yourself
through the blood of your Son
and the power of the Holy Spirit.

You gather them into your Church,
to be one as you, Father, are one
with your Son and the Holy Spirit.
You call them to be your people,
to praise your wisdom in all your works.
You make them the body of Christ
and the dwelling-place of the Holy Spirit.

In our joy we sing to your glory
with all the choirs of angels:

Holy, holy, holy...

EUCHARISTIC PRAYERS

EUCHARISTIC PRAYER I

We come to you, Father,
with praise and thanksgiving,
through Jesus Christ your Son.
Through him we ask you to accept and bless ✠
these gifts we offer you in sacrifice.

We offer them for your holy catholic Church,
watch over it, Lord, and guide it;
grant it peace and unity throughout the world.
We offer them for N., our Pope,
for N., our bishop,
and for all who hold and teach the catholic faith
that comes to us from the apostles.

Remember, Lord, your people,
especially those for whom we now pray, N. and N.
Remember all of us gathered here before you.
You know how firmly we believe in you
and dedicate ourselves to you.
We offer you this sacrifice of praise
for ourselves and those who are dear to us.
We pray to you, our living and true God,
for our well-being and redemption.

In union with the whole Church
we honour Mary,
*the ever-virgin mother of Jesus Christ our Lord and God.
We honour Joseph, her husband,
the apostles and martyrs

Special form of In union with the whole Church

Christmas and during the octave

In union with the whole Church
we celebrate that day [night]
when Mary without loss of her virginity
gave the world its Saviour.
We honour her, *

Epiphany

In union with the whole Church
we celebrate that day
when your only Son,

sharing your eternal glory,
showed himself in a human body.
We honour Mary,*

Holy Thursday

In union with the whole Church
we celebrate that day
when Jesus Christ, our Lord,
was betrayed for us.
We honour Mary,*

From the Easter Vigil to the Second Sunday of Easter inclusive

In union with the whole Church
we celebrate that day [night]
when Jesus Christ, our Lord,
rose from the dead in his human body.
We honour Mary,*

Ascension

In union with the whole Church
we celebrate that day
when your only Son, our Lord,
took his place with you
and raised our frail human nature to glory.
We honour Mary,*

Pentecost

In union with the whole Church
we celebrate the day of Pentecost
when the Holy Spirit appeared to the apostles
in the form of countless tongues.
We honour Mary,*

Peter and Paul, Andrew,
[James, John, Thomas,
James, Philip,
Bartholomew, Matthew, Simon and Jude;
we honour Linus, Cletus, Clement, Sixtus,
Cornelius, Cyprian, Lawrence, Chrysogonus,
John and Paul, Cosmas and Damian]
and all the saints.
May their merits and prayers
gain us your constant help and protection.
[Through Christ our Lord. Amen.]

Father, accept this offering *
from your whole family.
Grant us your peace in this life,
save us from final damnation,
and count us among those you have chosen.
[Through Christ our Lord. Amen.]

* *From the Easter Vigil to the Second Sunday of Easter*

Father, accept this offering
from your whole family
and from those born into the new life
of water and the Holy Spirit,
with all their sins forgiven.
Grant us your peace in this life,
save us from final damnation,
and count us among those you have chosen.
[Through Christ our Lord. Amen.]

Bless and approve our offering;
make it acceptable to you,
an offering in spirit and in truth.
Let it become for us
the body and blood of Jesus Christ,
your only Son, our Lord.

The day before he suffered
he took bread in his sacred hands
and looking up to heaven,
to you, his almighty Father,
he gave you thanks and praise.
He broke the bread,
gave it to his disciples, and said:

TAKE THIS, ALL OF YOU, AND EAT IT:
THIS IS MY BODY WHICH WILL BE GIVEN UP FOR YOU.

When supper was ended,
he took the cup.
Again he gave you thanks and praise,
gave the cup to his disciples, and said:

TAKE THIS, ALL OF YOU, AND DRINK FROM IT:
THIS IS THE CUP OF MY BLOOD,
THE BLOOD OF THE NEW AND EVERLASTING COVENANT.
IT WILL BE SHED FOR YOU AND FOR ALL

SO THAT SINS MAY BE FORGIVEN.
DO THIS IN MEMORY OF ME.

Let us proclaim the mystery of faith:

1. **Christ has died,**
   Christ is risen,
   Christ will come again.

2. **Dying you destroyed our death,**
   rising you restored our life.
   Lord Jesus, come in glory.

3. **When we eat this bread and drink this cup,**
   we proclaim your death, Lord Jesus,
   until you come in glory.

4. **Lord, by your cross and resurrection**
   you have set us free.
   You are the Saviour of the world.

5. **My Lord and my God.** *(for Ireland only)*

Father, we celebrate the memory of Christ, your Son.
We, your people and your ministers,
recall his passion,
his resurrection from the dead,
and his ascension into glory;
and from the many gifts you have given us
we offer to you, God of glory and majesty,
this holy and perfect sacrifice:
the bread of life
and the cup of eternal salvation.

Look with favour on these offerings
and accept them as once you accepted
the gifts of your servant Abel,
the sacrifice of Abraham, our father in faith,
and the bread and wine offered by your priest Melchisedech.

Almighty God,
we pray that your angel may take this sacrifice
to your altar in heaven.
Then, as we receive from this altar
the sacred body and blood of your Son,
let us be filled with every grace and blessing.
[Through Christ our Lord. Amen.]

Remember, Lord, those who have died
and have gone before us marked with the sign of faith,
especially those for whom we now pray, N. and N.
May these, and all who sleep in Christ,
find in your presence
light, happiness, and peace.
[Through Christ our Lord. Amen.]

For ourselves, too, we ask
some share in the fellowship of your apostles and martyrs,
with John the Baptist, Stephen, Matthias, Barnabas,
[Ignatius, Alexander, Marcellinus, Peter,
Felicity, Perpetua, Agatha, Lucy,
Agnes, Cecilia, Anastasia]
and all the saints.
Though we are sinners,
we trust in your mercy and love.
Do not consider what we truly deserve,
but grant us your forgiveness.

Through Christ our Lord
you give us all these gifts.
You fill them with life and goodness,
you bless them and make them holy.

Through him,
with him,
in him,
in the unity of the Holy Spirit,
all glory and honour is yours,
almighty Father,
for ever and ever.
Amen.

(Turn to page 54)

EUCHARISTIC PRAYER II

PREFACE *(may be substituted by another)*

Father, it is our duty and our salvation,
always and everywhere
to give you thanks
through your beloved Son, Jesus Christ.

He is the Word through whom you made the universe,
the Saviour you sent to redeem us.
By the power of the Holy Spirit
he took flesh and was born of the Virgin Mary.

For our sake he opened his arms on the cross;
he put an end to death
and revealed the resurrection.
In this he fulfilled your will
and won for you a holy people.

And so we join the angels and the saints
in proclaiming your glory
as we sing (say):

**Holy, holy, holy Lord, God of power and might,
heaven and earth are full of your glory.**
> **Hosanna in the highest.**

Blessed is he who comes in the name of the Lord.
> **Hosanna in the highest.**

Lord, you are holy indeed,
the fountain of all holiness.
Let your Spirit come upon these gifts to make them holy,
so that they may become for us
the body ✠ and blood of our Lord, Jesus Christ.

Before he was given up to death,
a death he freely accepted,
he took bread and gave you thanks.
He broke the bread,
gave it to his disciples, and said:

TAKE THIS, ALL OF YOU, AND EAT IT:
THIS IS MY BODY WHICH WILL BE GIVEN UP FOR YOU.

When supper was ended, he took the cup.
Again he gave you thanks and praise,
gave the cup to his disciples, and said:

TAKE THIS, ALL OF YOU, AND DRINK FROM IT:
THIS IS THE CUP OF MY BLOOD,
THE BLOOD OF THE NEW AND EVERLASTING COVENANT.
IT WILL BE SHED FOR YOU AND FOR ALL
SO THAT SINS MAY BE FORGIVEN.
DO THIS IN MEMORY OF ME.

Let us proclaim the mystery of faith:

1.   **Christ has died,**
     Christ is risen,
     Christ will come again.

2.   **Dying you destroyed our death,**
     rising you restored our life.
     Lord Jesus, come in glory.

3.   **When we eat this bread and drink this cup,**
     we proclaim your death, Lord Jesus,
     until you come in glory.

4.   **Lord, by your cross and resurrection**
     you have set us free.
     You are the Saviour of the world.

5.   **My Lord and my God.** *(for Ireland only)*

In memory of his death and resurrection,
we offer you, Father, this life-giving bread,
this saving cup.
We thank you for counting us worthy
to stand in your presence and serve you.
May all of us who share in the body and blood of Christ
be brought together in unity by the Holy Spirit.

Lord, remember your Church throughout the world;
make us grow in love,
together with N., our Pope,
N., our bishop, and all the clergy.

In Masses for the dead the following may be added:

Remember N., whom you have called from this life.
In baptism he (she) died with Christ:
may he (she) also share his resurrection.

Remember our brothers and sisters
who have gone to their rest
in the hope of rising again;

bring them and all the departed
into the light of your presence.

Have mercy on us all;
make us worthy to share eternal life
with Mary, the virgin Mother of God,
with the apostles, and with all the saints
who have done your will throughout the ages.
May we praise you in union with them,
and give you glory
through your Son, Jesus Christ.

Through him,
with him,
in him,
in the unity of the Holy Spirit,
all glory and honour is yours,
almighty Father,
for ever and ever.
Amen.

(Turn to page 54)

EUCHARISTIC PRAYER III

Father, you are holy indeed,
and all creation rightly gives you praise.
All life, all holiness comes from you
through your Son, Jesus Christ our Lord,
by the working of the Holy Spirit.
From age to age you gather a people to yourself,
so that from east to west
a perfect offering may be made
to the glory of your name.

And so, Father, we bring you these gifts.
We ask you to make them holy by the power of your Spirit,
that they may become the body ✠ and blood
of your Son, our Lord Jesus Christ,
at whose command we celebrate this eucharist.

On the night he was betrayed,
he took bread and gave you thanks and praise.
He broke the bread, gave it to his disciples, and said:

TAKE THIS, ALL OF YOU, AND EAT IT:
THIS IS MY BODY WHICH WILL BE GIVEN UP FOR YOU.

When supper was ended, he took the cup.
Again he gave you thanks and praise,
gave the cup to his disciples, and said:

TAKE THIS, ALL OF YOU, AND DRINK FROM IT:
THIS IS THE CUP OF MY BLOOD,
THE BLOOD OF THE NEW AND EVERLASTING COVENANT.
IT WILL BE SHED FOR YOU AND FOR ALL
SO THAT SINS MAY BE FORGIVEN.
DO THIS IN MEMORY OF ME.

Let us proclaim the mystery of faith:

1. **Christ has died,**
    Christ is risen,
    Christ will come again.

2. **Dying you destroyed our death,**
    rising you restored our life.
    Lord Jesus, come in glory.

3. **When we eat this bread and drink this cup,**
    we proclaim your death, Lord Jesus,
    until you come in glory.

4. **Lord, by your cross and resurrection**
    you have set us free.
    You are the Saviour of the world.

5. **My Lord and my God.** *(for Ireland only)*

Father, calling to mind the death your Son endured for our
      salvation,
his glorious resurrection and ascension into heaven,
and ready to greet him when he comes again,
we offer you in thanksgiving this holy and living sacrifice.

Look with favour on your Church's offering,
and see the Victim whose death has reconciled us to yourself.
Grant that we, who are nourished by his body and blood,
may be filled with his Holy Spirit,
and become one body, one spirit in Christ.

May he make us an everlasting gift to you
and enable us to share in the inheritance of your saints,
with Mary, the virgin Mother of God;
with the apostles, the martyrs,

(Saint N.) and all your saints,
on whose constant intercession we rely for help.

Lord, may this sacrifice,
which has made our peace with you,
advance the peace and salvation of all the world.
Strengthen in faith and love your pilgrim Church on earth;
your servant, Pope N., our bishop N.,
and all the bishops,
with the clergy and the entire people your Son has gained
    for you.
Father, hear the prayers of the family you have gathered here
    before you.
In mercy and love unite all your children wherever they may be.*
Welcome into your kingdom our departed brothers and sisters,
and all who have left this world in your friendship.
We hope to enjoy for ever the vision of your glory,
through Christ our Lord, from whom all good things come.

In Masses for the dead, the following may be said:

Remember N.
In baptism he (she) died with Christ:
may he (she) share his resurrection,
when Christ will raise our mortal bodies
and make them like his own in glory.
Welcome into your kingdom our departed brothers and sisters,
and all who have left this world in your friendship.
There we hope to share in your glory
when every tear will be wiped away.
On that day we shall see you, our God, as you are.
We shall become like you
and praise you for ever through Christ our Lord,
from whom all good things come.

Through him,
with him,
in him,
in the unity of the Holy Spirit,
all glory and honour is yours,
almighty Father,
for ever and ever.
Amen.

(Turn to page 54)

EUCHARISTIC PRAYER IV

PREFACE

Father in heaven,
it is right that we should give you thanks and glory:
you are the one God, living and true.
Through all eternity you live in unapproachable light.
Source of life and goodness, you have created all things,
to fill your creatures with every blessing
and lead all men to the joyful vision of your light.
Countless hosts of angels stand before you to do your will;
they look upon your splendour
and praise you, night and day.
United with them,
and in the name of every creature under heaven,
we too praise your glory as we sing (say):

**Holy, holy, holy Lord, God of power and might,
heaven and earth are full of your glory.**
    Hosanna in the highest.
Blessed is he who comes in the name of the Lord.
    Hosanna in the highest.

Father, we acknowledge your greatness:
all your actions show your wisdom and love.
You formed man in your own likeness
and set him over the whole world
to serve you, his creator,
and to rule over all creatures.
Even when he disobeyed you and lost your friendship
you did not abandon him to the power of death,
but helped all men to seek and find you.
Again and again you offered a covenant to man,
and through the prophets taught him to hope for salvation.
Father, you so loved the world
that in the fullness of time you sent your only Son to be
    our Saviour.

He was conceived through the power of the Holy Spirit,
and born of the Virgin Mary,
a man like us in all things but sin.
To the poor he proclaimed the good news of salvation,
to prisoners, freedom,
and to those in sorrow, joy.
In fulfilment of your will

he gave himself up to death;
but by rising from the dead,
he destroyed death and restored life.
And that we might live no longer for ourselves but for him,
he sent the Holy Spirit from you, Father,
as his first gift to those who believe,
to complete his work on earth
and bring us the fullness of grace.

Father, may this Holy Spirit sanctify these offerings.
Let them become the body ✠ and blood of Jesus Christ our Lord
as we celebrate the great mystery
which he left us as an everlasting covenant.

He always loved those who were his own in the world.
When the time came for him to be glorified by you,
        his heavenly Father,
he showed the depth of his love.

While they were at supper,
he took bread, said the blessing, broke the bread,
and gave it to his disciples, saying:
TAKE THIS, ALL OF YOU, AND EAT IT:
THIS IS MY BODY WHICH WILL BE GIVEN UP FOR YOU.

In the same way, he took the cup, filled with wine.
He gave you thanks, and giving the cup to his disciples, said:
TAKE THIS, ALL OF YOU, AND DRINK FROM IT:
THIS IS THE CUP OF MY BLOOD,
THE BLOOD OF THE NEW AND EVERLASTING COVENANT.
IT WILL BE SHED FOR YOU AND FOR ALL
SO THAT SINS MAY BE FORGIVEN.
DO THIS IN MEMORY OF ME.

Let us proclaim the mystery of faith:

1. **Christ has died,**
   Christ is risen,
   Christ will come again.

2. **Dying you destroyed our death,**
   rising you restored our life.
   Lord Jesus, come in glory.

3. **When we eat this bread and drink this cup,**
   we proclaim your death, Lord Jesus,
   until you come in glory.

4.   **Lord, by your cross and resurrection**
     you have set us free.
     You are the Saviour of the world.

5.   **My Lord and my God.** *(for Ireland only)*

Father, we now celebrate this memorial of our redemption.
We recall Christ's death, his descent among the dead,
his resurrection, and his ascension to your right hand;
and, looking forward to his coming in glory,
we offer you his body and blood,
the acceptable sacrifice
which brings salvation to the whole world.

Lord, look upon this sacrifice which you have given to your
     Church;
and by your Holy Spirit, gather all who share this one bread and
     one cup
into the one body of Christ, a living sacrifice of praise.

Lord, remember those for whom we offer this sacrifice,
especially N., our Pope,
N., our bishop, and bishops and clergy everywhere.
Remember those who take part in this offering,
those here present and all your people,
and all who seek you with a sincere heart.

Remember those who have died in the peace of Christ
and all the dead whose faith is known to you alone.
Father, in your mercy grant also to us, your children,
to enter into our heavenly inheritance
in the company of the Virgin Mary, the Mother of God,
and your apostles and saints.
Then, in your kingdom, freed from the corruption of sin and death,
we shall sing your glory with every creature through Christ our
     Lord,
through whom you give us everything that is good.

Through him,
with him,
in him,
in the unity of the Holy Spirit,
all glory and honour is yours,
almighty Father,
for ever and ever. **Amen.**

(Turn to page 54)

EUCHARISTIC PRAYER
FOR MASSES OF RECONCILIATION I

PREFACE

Father, all-powerful and ever-living God,
we do well always and everywhere to give you thanks and praise.
You never cease to call us
to a new and more abundant life.
God of love and mercy,
you are always ready to forgive;
we are sinners
and you invite us
to trust in your mercy.

Time and time again
we broke your covenant,
but you did not abandon us.
Instead, through your Son, Jesus our Lord,
you bound yourself even more closely to the human family
by a bond that can never be broken.

Now is the time
for your people to turn back to you
and to be renewed in Christ your Son,
a time of grace and reconciliation.

You invite us
to serve the family of mankind
by opening our hearts
to the fullness of your Holy Spirit.

In wonder and gratitude,
we join our voices with the choirs of heaven
to proclaim the power of your love
and to sing of our salvation in Christ:
Holy, holy, holy…

Father, from the beginning of time
you have always done what is good for man
so that we may be holy as you are holy.

Look with kindness on your people
gathered here before you:
send forth the power of your Spirit
so that these gifts may become for us
the body ✠ and blood of your beloved Son, Jesus the Christ,
in whom we have become your sons and daughters.

When we were lost
and could not find the way to you,
you loved us more than ever:
Jesus, your Son, innocent and without sin,
gave himself into our hands
and was nailed to a cross.
Yet before he stretched out his arms between heaven and earth
in the everlasting sign of your covenant,
he desired to celebrate the Paschal feast
in the company of his disciples.

While they were at supper,
he took bread and gave you thanks and praise.
He broke the bread, gave it to his disciples, and said:
TAKE THIS, ALL OF YOU, AND EAT IT:
THIS IS MY BODY WHICH WILL BE GIVEN UP FOR YOU.

At the end of the meal,
knowing that he was to reconcile all things in himself
by the blood of his cross,
he took the cup, filled with wine.
Again he gave you thanks, handed the cup to his friends,
    and said:
TAKE THIS, ALL OF YOU, AND DRINK FROM IT:
THIS IS THE CUP OF MY BLOOD,
THE BLOOD OF THE NEW AND EVERLASTING COVENANT.
IT WILL BE SHED FOR YOU AND FOR ALL
SO THAT SINS MAY BE FORGIVEN.
DO THIS IN MEMORY OF ME.

Let us proclaim the mystery of faith:

1. **Christ has died,**
   Christ is risen,
   Christ will come again.

2. **Dying you destroyed our death,**
   rising you restored our life.
   Lord Jesus, come in glory.

3. **When we eat this bread and drink this cup,**
   we proclaim your death, Lord Jesus,
   until you come in glory.

4. **Lord, by your cross and resurrection**
   you have set us free.
   You are the Saviour of the world.

5. **My Lord and my God.** *(for Ireland only)*

We do this in memory of Jesus Christ,
our Passover and our lasting peace.
We celebrate his death and resurrection
and look for the coming of that day
when he will return to give us the fullness of joy.
Therefore we offer you, God ever faithful and true,
the sacrifice which restores man to your friendship.

Father,
look with love
on those you have called
to share in the one sacrifice of Christ.
By the power of your Holy Spirit
make them one body,
healed of all division.

Keep us all
in communion of mind and heart
with N., our Pope, and N., our bishop.
Help us to work together
for the coming of your kingdom,
until at last we stand in your presence
to share the life of the saints,
in the company of the Virgin Mary and the apostles,
and of our departed brothers and sisters
whom we commend to your mercy.

Then, freed from every shadow of death,
we shall take our place in the new creation
and give you thanks
with Christ, our risen Lord.

Through him,
with him,
in him,
in the unity of the Holy Spirit,
all glory and honour is yours,
almighty Father,
for ever and ever.
Amen.

(Turn to page 54)

EUCHARISTIC PRAYER
FOR MASSES OF RECONCILIATION II

PREFACE

Father, all-powerful and ever-living God,
we praise and thank you through Jesus Christ our Lord
for your presence and action in the world.

In the midst of conflict and division,
we know it is you
who turn our minds to thoughts of peace.
Your Spirit changes our hearts:
enemies begin to speak to one another,
those who were estranged join hands in friendship,
and nations seek the way of peace together.

Your Spirit is at work
when understanding puts an end to strife,
when hatred is quenched by mercy,
and vengeance gives way to forgiveness.

For this we should never cease
to thank and praise you.
We join with all the choirs of heaven
as they sing for ever to your glory:
Holy, holy, holy...

God of power and might,
we praise you through your Son, Jesus Christ,
who comes in your name.
He is the Word that brings salvation.
He is the hand you stretch out to sinners.
He is the way that leads to your peace.

God our Father,
we had wandered far from you,
but through your Son you have brought us back.
You gave him up to death
so that we might turn again to you
and find our way to one another.

Therefore we celebrate the reconciliation
Christ has gained for us.
We ask you to sanctify these gifts
by the power of your Spirit,
as we now fulfil your Son's ✠ command.

While he was at supper
on the night before he died for us,
he took bread in his hands,
and gave you thanks and praise.
He broke the bread,
gave it to his disciples, and said:

TAKE THIS, ALL OF YOU, AND EAT IT:
THIS IS MY BODY WHICH WILL BE GIVEN UP FOR YOU.

At the end of the meal he took the cup.
Again he praised you for your goodness,
gave the cup to his disciples, and said:

TAKE THIS, ALL OF YOU, AND DRINK FROM IT:
THIS IS THE CUP OF MY BLOOD,
THE BLOOD OF THE NEW AND EVERLASTING COVENANT.
IT WILL BE SHED FOR YOU AND FOR ALL
SO THAT SINS MAY BE FORGIVEN.
DO THIS IN MEMORY OF ME.

Let us proclaim the mystery of faith:

1. **Christ has died,**
   Christ is risen,
   Christ will come again.

2. **Dying you destroyed our death,**
   rising you restored our life.
   Lord Jesus, come in glory.

3. **When we eat this bread and drink this cup,**
   we proclaim your death, Lord Jesus,
   until you come in glory.

4. **Lord, by your cross and resurrection**
   you have set us free.
   You are the Saviour of the world.

5. **My Lord and my God.** *(for Ireland only)*

Lord our God,
your Son has entrusted to us
this pledge of his love.
We celebrate the memory of his death and resurrection
and bring you the gift you have given us,
the sacrifice of reconciliation.
Therefore, we ask you, Father,
to accept us, together with your Son.

Fill us with his Spirit
through our sharing in this meal.
May he take away all that divides us.

May this Spirit keep us always in communion
with N., our Pope, N., our bishop,
with all the bishops and all your people.
Father, make your Church throughout the world
a sign of unity and an instrument of your peace.

You have gathered us here
around the table of your Son,
in fellowship with the Virgin Mary, Mother of God,
    and all the saints.
In that new world where the fullness of your peace will be
    revealed,
gather people of every race, language, and way of life
to share in the one eternal banquet
with Jesus Christ the Lord.

Through him,
with him,
in him,
in the unity of the Holy Spirit,
all glory and honour is yours,
almighty Father,
for ever and ever.
Amen.

(Turn to page 54)

EUCHARISTIC PRAYER
FOR MASSES WITH CHILDREN I

PREFACE
God our Father,
you have brought us here together
so that we can give you thanks and praise
for all the wonderful things you have done.
We thank you for all that is beautiful in the world
and for the happiness you have given us.
We praise you for daylight
and for your word which lights up our minds.

We praise you for the earth,
and all the people who live on it,
and for our life which comes from you.

We know that you are good.
You love us and do great things for us.
So we all sing (say) together:

**Holy, holy, holy Lord, God of power and might,
heaven and earth are full of your glory.**
    Hosanna in the highest.

Father,
you are always thinking about your people;
you never forget us.
You sent us your Son Jesus,
who gave his life for us
and who came to save us.
He cured sick people;
he cared for those who were poor
and wept with those who were sad.
He forgave sinners
and taught us to forgive each other.
He loved everyone
and showed us how to be kind.
He took children in his arms and blessed them.
So we are glad to sing (say):

Blessed is he who comes in the name of the Lord.
    Hosanna in the highest.

God our Father,
all over the world your people praise you.
So now we pray with the whole Church:
with N, our Pope and N, our bishop.
In heaven the blessed Virgin Mary,
the apostles and all the saints
always sing your praise.
Now we join with them and with the angels
to adore you as we sing (say):

**Holy, holy, holy Lord, God of power and might,
heaven and earth are full of your glory.**
    Hosanna in the highest.
Blessed is he who comes in the name of the Lord.
    Hosanna in the highest.

God our Father,
you are most holy
and we want to show you that we are grateful.
We bring you bread and wine
and ask you to send your Holy Spirit to make these gifts
the body ✠ and blood of Jesus your Son.
Then we can offer to you
what you have given to us.

On the night before he died,
Jesus was having supper with his apostles.
He took bread from the table.
He gave you thanks and praise.
Then he broke the bread,
gave it to his friends, and said:
TAKE THIS, ALL OF YOU, AND EAT IT:
THIS IS MY BODY WHICH WILL BE GIVEN UP FOR YOU.

When supper was ended,
Jesus took the cup that was filled with wine.
He thanked you, gave it to his friends, and said:
TAKE THIS, ALL OF YOU, AND DRINK FROM IT:
THIS IS THE CUP OF MY BLOOD,
THE BLOOD OF THE NEW AND EVERLASTING COVENANT.
IT WILL BE SHED FOR YOU AND FOR ALL
SO THAT SINS MAY BE FORGIVEN.
DO THIS IN MEMORY OF ME.

We do now what Jesus told us to do.
We remember his death and his resurrection
and we offer you, Father, the bread that gives us life,
and the cup that saves us.
Jesus brings us to you;
welcome us as you welcome him.

Let us proclaim the mystery of faith:

1. **Christ has died,**
    Christ is risen,
    Christ will come again.

2. **Dying you destroyed our death,**
    rising you restored our life.
    Lord Jesus, come in glory.

3. **When we eat this bread and drink this cup,**
    we proclaim your death, Lord Jesus,
    until you come in glory.

4. **Lord, by your cross and resurrection
    you have set us free.
    You are the Saviour of the world.**

5. **My Lord and my God.** *(for Ireland only)*

Father,
because you love us,
you invite us to come to your table.
Fill us with the joy of the Holy Spirit
as we receive the body and blood of your Son.

Lord,
you never forget any of your children.
We ask you to take care of those we love,
especially of N. and N.,
and we pray for those who have died.
Remember everyone who is suffering from pain or sorrow.

Remember Christians everywhere
and all other people in the world.
We are filled with wonder and praise
when we see what you do for us
through Jesus your Son,
and so we sing:

Through him,
with him,
in him,
in the unity of the Holy Spirit,
all glory and honour is yours,
almighty Father,
for ever and ever.
Amen.

(Turn to page 54)

EUCHARISTIC PRAYER
FOR MASSES WITH CHILDREN II

PREFACE
God our loving Father,
we are glad to give you thanks and praise
because you love us.
With Jesus we sing your praise:

Glory to God in the highest.

or

Hosanna in the highest.

Because you love us,
you gave us this great and beautiful world.
With Jesus we sing your praise:

Glory to God in the highest.

or

Hosanna in the highest.

Because you love us,
you sent Jesus your Son
to bring us to you
and to gather us around him
as the children of one family.
With Jesus we sing your praise:

Glory to God in the highest.

or

Hosanna in the highest.

For such great love
we thank you with the angels and saints
as they praise you and sing:

**Holy, holy, holy Lord, God of power and might,
heaven and earth are full of your glory.**
    Hosanna in the highest.
Blessed is he who comes in the name of the Lord.
    Hosanna in the highest.

Blessed be Jesus, whom you sent
to be the friend of children and of the poor.
He came to show us
how we can love you, Father,
by loving one another.

He came to take away sin,
which keeps us from being friends,
and hate, which makes us all unhappy.

He promised to send the Holy Spirit,
to be with us always
so that we can live as your children.
Blessed is he who comes in the name of the Lord.
Hosanna in the highest.

God our Father,
we now ask you
to send your Holy Spirit
to change these gifts of bread and wine
into the body ✠ and blood
of Jesus Christ, our Lord.

The night before he died,
Jesus your Son showed us how much you love us.
When he was at supper with his disciples,
he took bread,
and gave you thanks and praise.
Then he broke the bread,
gave it to his friends, and said:
TAKE THIS, ALL OF YOU, AND EAT IT:
THIS IS MY BODY WHICH WILL BE GIVEN UP FOR YOU.
Jesus has given his life for us.

When supper was ended,
Jesus took the cup that was filled with wine.
He thanked you, gave it to his friends, and said:
TAKE THIS, ALL OF YOU, AND DRINK FROM IT:
THIS IS THE CUP OF MY BLOOD,
THE BLOOD OF THE NEW AND EVERLASTING COVENANT.
IT WILL BE SHED FOR YOU AND FOR ALL
SO THAT SINS MAY BE FORGIVEN.
Jesus has given his life for us.

Then he said to them:
DO THIS IN MEMORY OF ME.

And so, loving Father,
we remember that Jesus died and rose again
to save the world.
He put himself into our hands
to be the sacrifice we offer you.
We praise you, we bless you, we thank you.

Lord our God,
listen to our prayer.
Send the Holy Spirit
to all of us who share in this meal.
May this Spirit bring us closer together
in the family of the Church,
with N., our Pope,
N., our bishop,
all other bishops,
and all who serve your people.

We praise you, we bless you, we thank you.

Remember, Father, our families and friends (N.)
and all those we do not love as we should.
Remember those who have died (N.)
Bring them home to you
to be with you for ever.

We praise you, we bless you, we thank you.

Gather us all together into your kingdom.
There we shall be happy for ever
with the Virgin Mary, Mother of God and our mother.
There all the friends
of Jesus the Lord will sing a song of joy.

We praise you, we bless you, we thank you.

Through him,
with him,
in him,
in the unity of the Holy Spirit,
all glory and honour is yours,
almighty Father,
for ever and ever.
Amen.

(Turn to page 54)

EUCHARISTIC PRAYER
FOR MASSES WITH CHILDREN III

PREFACE

* We thank you,
God our Father.
You made us to live for you and for each other.
We can see and speak to one another,
and become friends,
and share our joys and sorrows.

* During Easter season

We thank you,
God our Father.
You are the living God;
you have called us to share in your life,
and to be happy with you for ever.
You raised up Jesus, your Son,
the first among us to rise from the dead,
and gave him new life.
You have promised to give us new life also,
a life that will never end,
a life with no more anxiety and suffering.

And so, Father, we gladly thank you
with everyone who believes in you;
with the saints and the angels,
we rejoice and praise you, saying:

Holy, holy, holy…

Yes, Lord, you are holy;
you are kind to us and to all.
For this we thank you.
We thank you above all for your Son, Jesus Christ.

† You sent him into this world
because people had turned away from you
and no longer loved each other.
He opened our eyes and our hearts
to understand that we are brothers and sisters
and that you are Father of us all.

† During Easter season

He brought us the Good News
of life to be lived with you for ever in heaven.

He showed us the way to that life,
the way of love.
He himself has gone that way before us.

He now brings us together to one table
and asks us to do what he did.

Father,
we ask you to bless these gifts of bread and wine
and make them holy.
Change them for us into the body ✠ and blood of Jesus Christ,
     your Son.
On the night before he died for us,
he had supper for the last time with his disciples.
He took bread and gave you thanks.
He broke the bread
and gave it to his friends, saying:
TAKE THIS, ALL OF YOU, AND EAT IT:
THIS IS MY BODY WHICH WILL BE GIVEN UP FOR YOU.

In the same way he took a cup of wine.
He gave you thanks
and handed the cup to his disciples, saying:
TAKE THIS, ALL OF YOU, AND DRINK FROM IT:
THIS IS THE CUP OF MY BLOOD,
THE BLOOD OF THE NEW AND EVERLASTING COVENANT.
IT WILL BE SHED FOR YOU AND FOR ALL
SO THAT SINS MAY BE FORGIVEN.

Then he said to them:
DO THIS IN MEMORY OF ME.

God our Father,
we remember with joy
all that Jesus did to save us.
In this holy sacrifice,
which he gave as a gift to his Church,
we remember his death and resurrection.

Father in heaven,
accept us together with your beloved Son.
He willingly died for us,
but you raised him to life again.
We thank you and say:

Glory to God in the highest.

Jesus now lives with you in glory,
but he is also here on earth, among us.
We thank you and say:

Glory to God in the highest.

One day he will come in glory
and in his kingdom
there will be no more suffering,
no more tears, no more sadness.
We thank you and say:

Glory to God in the highest.

Father in heaven,
you have called us
to receive the body and blood of Christ at this table
and to be filled with the joy of the Holy Spirit.
Through this sacred meal
give us strength to please you more and more.

Lord, our God,
remember N., our Pope,
N., our bishop, and all other bishops.

* Help all who follow Jesus
to work for peace
and to bring happiness to others.

*During Easter season:

Fill all Christians with the gladness of Easter.
Help us to bring this joy
to all who are sorrowful.

Bring us all at last
together with Mary, the Mother of God,
and all the saints,
to live with you
and to be one with Christ in heaven.

Through him,
with him,
in him,
in the unity of the Holy Spirit,
all glory and honour is yours,
almighty Father,
for ever and ever. **Amen.**

COMMUNION RITE

Let us pray with confidence to the Father
in the words our Saviour gave us:

or

Jesus taught us to call God our Father,
and so we have the courage to say:

or

Let us ask our Father to forgive our sins
and to bring us to forgive those who sin against us:

or

Let us pray for the coming of the kingdom
as Jesus taught us:

At the priest's invitation all sing or say the Lord's Prayer.

Our Father, who art in heaven,
hallowed be thy name.
Thy kingdom come.
Thy will be done on earth as it is in heaven.
Give us this day our daily bread,
and forgive us our trespasses,
as we forgive those who trespass against us,
and lead us not into temptation,
but deliver us from evil.

Deliver us, Lord, from every evil,
and grant us peace in our day.
In your mercy keep us free from sin
and protect us from all anxiety
as we wait in joyful hope
for the coming of our Saviour, Jesus Christ.

For the kingdom, the power, and the glory
are yours, now and for ever.

Lord Jesus Christ, you said to your apostles:
I leave you peace, my peace I give you.
Look not on our sins, but on the faith of your Church,
and grant us the peace and unity of your kingdom
where you live for ever and ever. **Amen.**

The peace of the Lord be with you always.

And also with you.

Let us offer each other the sign of peace.

All make a sign of peace according to local custom.

May this mingling of the body and blood of our Lord Jesus Christ bring eternal life to us who receive it.

Lamb of God, you take away the sins of the world:
have mercy on us.
Lamb of God, you take away the sins of the world:
have mercy on us.
Lamb of God, you take away the sins of the world:
grant us peace.

The priest says quietly:

Lord Jesus Christ, Son of the living God,
by the will of the Father and the work of the Holy Spirit
your death brought life to the world.
By your holy body and blood
free me from all my sins and from every evil.
Keep me faithful to your teaching,
and never let me be parted from you.

or

Lord Jesus Christ,
with faith in your love and mercy
I eat your body and drink your blood.
Let it not bring me condemnation,
but health in mind and body.

Showing the Host to the people, the priest says:

This is the Lamb of God
who takes away the sins of the world.
Happy are those who are called to his supper.

Lord, I am not worthy to receive you,
but only say the word and I shall be healed.

COMMUNION ANTIPHON

(Turn to the Mass of the day)

The communicant is offered the host:

The body of Christ.
Amen.

When the communicant is offered the chalice:

The blood of Christ.
Amen.

PRAYER AFTER COMMUNION

(Turn to the Mass of the day)

CONCLUDING RITE

The Lord be with you.
And also with you.

May almighty God bless you,
the Father, and the Son, ✠ and the Holy Spirit.
Amen.

Go in the peace of Christ.

or

The Mass is ended, go in peace.

or

Go in peace to love and serve the Lord.
Thanks be to God.

SOLEMN BLESSINGS

ADVENT

You believe that the Son of God once came to us;
you look for him to come again.
May his coming bring you the light of his holiness
and free you with his blessing.
Amen.

May God make you steadfast in faith,
joyful in hope, and untiring in love
all the days of your life.
Amen.

You rejoice that our Redeemer came to live with us as man.
When he comes again in glory,
may he reward you with endless life.
Amen.

May almighty God bless you,
the Father, and the Son, ✠ and the Holy Spirit.
Amen.

EASTER SEASON

Through the resurrection of his Son
God has redeemed you and made you his children.
May he bless you with joy.
Amen.

The Redeemer has given you lasting freedom.
May you inherit his everlasting life.
Amen.

By faith you rose with him in baptism.
May your lives be holy,
so that you will be united with him for ever.
Amen.

May almighty God bless you,
the Father, and the Son, ✠ and the Holy Spirit.
Amen.

ORDINARY TIME I: Blessing of Aaron (Numbers 6:24-26)
May the Lord bless you and keep you.
Amen.

May his face shine upon you,
and be gracious to you.
Amen.

May he look upon you with kindness,
and give you his peace.
Amen.

May almighty God bless you,
the Father, and the Son, ✠ and the Holy Spirit.
Amen.

ORDINARY TIME II (Philippians 4:7)
May the peace of God
which is beyond all understanding
keep your hearts and minds
in the knowledge and love of God
and of his Son, our Lord Jesus Christ.
Amen.

May almighty God bless you,
the Father, and the Son, ✠ and the Holy Spirit.
Amen.

ORDINARY TIME III
May almighty God bless you in his mercy,
and make you always aware of his saving wisdom.
Amen.

May he strengthen your faith with proofs of his love,
so that you will persevere in good works. **Amen**.

May he direct your steps to himself,
and show you how to walk in charity and peace.
Amen.

May almighty God bless you,
the Father, and the Son, ✠ and the Holy Spirit.
Amen.

ORDINARY TIME IV

May the God of all consolation
bless you in every way
and grant you peace all the days of your life.
Amen.

May he free you from all anxiety
and strengthen your hearts in his love.
Amen.

May he enrich you with his gifts of faith, hope, and love,
so that what you do in this life
will bring you to the happiness of everlasting life.
Amen.

May almighty God bless you,
the Father, and the Son, ✠ and the Holy Spirit.
Amen.

ORDINARY TIME V

May almighty God keep you from all harm
and bless you with every good gift.
Amen.

May he set his Word in your heart
and fill you with lasting joy.
Amen.

May you walk in his ways,
always knowing what is right and good,
until you enter your heavenly inheritance.
Amen.

May almighty God bless you,
the Father, and the Son, ✠ and the Holy Spirit.
Amen.

LATIN TEXTS

(PEOPLE'S PARTS)

INTRODUCTORY RITES

In nómine Patris, et Fílii, et Spíritus Sancti.
Amen.

or

Dóminus vobíscum.
(or another greeting)
Et cum spíritu tuo.

CONFITEOR

Confíteor Deo omnipoténti et vobis, fratres,
quia peccávi nimis
cogitatióne, verbo, ópere et omissióne:
(All strike their breast)
mea culpa, mea culpa, mea máxima culpa.
Ideo precor beátam Maríam semper Vírginem,
omnes Angelos et Sanctos,
et vos, fratres, oráre pro me
ad Dóminum Deum nostrum.

KYRIE

Kyrie, eléison. **Kyrie, eléison.**
Christe, eléison. **Christe, eléison.**
Kyrie, eléison. **Kyrie, eléison.**

GLORIA

Glória in excélsis Deo
et in terra pax homínibus bonæ voluntátis.
Laudámus te, benedícimus te,
adorámus te, glorificámus te,
grátias ágimus tibi propter magnam glóriam tuam,
Dómine Deus, Rex cæléstis,
Deus Pater omnípotens.
Dómine Fili unigénite, Iesu Christe,
Dómine Deus, Agnus Dei, Fílius Patris,
qui tollis peccáta mundi, miserére nobis;
qui tollis peccáta mundi,
    súscipe deprecatiónem nostram.
Qui sedes ad déxteram Patris, miserére nobis.
Quóniam tu solus Sanctus, tu solus Dóminus,
    tu solus Altíssimus,

Iesu Christe, cum Sancto Spíritu:
  in glória Dei Patris. Amen.

After the first and second readings
Deo grátias.

Before the Gospel
Dóminus vobíscum.
Et cum spíritu tuo.

Léctio sancti Evangélii secúndum N.
Glória tibi, Dómine.

At the end of the Gospel
Verbum Dómini.
Laus tibi, Christe.

CREDO

Credo in unum Deum,
Patrem omnipoténtem, factórem cæli et terræ,
visibílium ómnium et invisibílium.
Et in unum Dóminum Iesum Christum,
Fílium Dei unigénitum,
et ex Patre natum ante ómnia sæcula.
Deum de Deo, lumen de lúmine,
  Deum verum de Deo vero,
génitum, non factum, consubstantiálem Patri:
per quem ómnia facta sunt.
Qui propter nos hómines
  et propter nostram salútem
descéndit de cælis.

(All bow during the next two lines)

Et incarnátus est de Spíritu Sancto
ex María Vírgine, et homo factus est.
Crucifíxus étiam pro nobis sub Póntio Piláto;
passus et sepúltus est,
et resurréxit tértia die, secúndum Scriptúras,
et ascéndit in cælum, sedet ad déxteram Patris.
Et íterum ventúrus est cum glória,
  iudicáre vivos et mórtuos,
cuius regni non erit finis.
Et in Spíritum Sanctum, Dóminum et vivificántem:
qui ex Patre Filióque procédit.
Qui cum Patre et Fílio simul adorátur
  et conglorificátur:

qui locútus est per prophétas.
Et unam, sanctam, cathólicam et apostólicam Ecclésiam.
Confíteor unum baptísma in remissiónem peccatórum.
Et exspécto resurrectiónem mortuórum,
et vítam ventúri sǽculi. Amen.

Response to offertory prayers
Benedíctus Deus in sǽcula.

Response to the Orate Fratres
**Suscípiat Dóminus sacrifícium de mánibus tuis
ad laudem et glóriam nóminis sui,
ad utilitátem quoque nostram
totiúsque Ecclésiæ suæ sanctæ.**

Dialogue before the Preface
Dóminus vobíscum.
Et cum spíritu tuo.

Sursum corda.
Habémus ad Dóminum.

Grátias agámus Dómino Deo nostro.
Dignum et iustum est.

SANCTUS
**Sanctus, Sanctus, Sanctus Dóminus Deus Sábaoth.
Pleni sunt cæli et terra glória tua.
        Hosánna in excélsis.
Benedíctus qui venit in nómine Dómini.
        Hosánna in excélsis.**

After the Consecration
Mystérium fidei.

1. **Mortem tuam annuntiámus, Dómine,
        et tuam resurrectiónem confitémur, donec vénias.**

2. **Quotiescúmque manducámus panem hunc
        et cálicem bíbimus,
        mortem tuam annuntiámus, Dómine, donec vénias.**

3. **Salvátor mundi, salva nos,
        qui per crucem et resurrectiónem tuam liberásti nos.**

PATER NOSTER
Præcéptis salutáribus móniti,
et divína institutióne formáti,
audémus dicere:

Pater noster, qui es in cælis:
sanctificétur nomen tuum;
advéniat regnum tuum;
fiat volúntas tua, sicut in cælo, et in terra.
Panem nostrum cotidiánum da nobis hódie;
et dimítte nobis débita nostra,
sicut et nos dimíttimus debitóribus nostris;
et ne nos indúcas in tentatiónem;
sed líbera nos a malo.

Acclamation after the Líbera nos

Quia tuum est regnum,
et potéstas, et glória
in sæcula.

At the Pax

Pax Dómini sit semper vobíscum.
Et cum spíritu tuo.

AGNUS DEI

Agnus Dei, qui tollis peccáta mundi:
    miserére nobis.
Agnus Dei, qui tollis peccáta mundi:
    miserére nobis.
Agnus Dei, qui tollis peccáta mundi:
    dona nobis pacem.

Lord, I am not worthy

Domine, non sum dignus ut intres sub tectum meum:
sed tantum dic verbo, et sanabitur ánima mea.

CONCLUSION

Dóminus vobíscum.
Et cum spíritu tuo.

Benedícat vos omnípotens Deus
Pater, et Fílius, ✠ et Spíritus Sanctus.
Amen.

Ite, missa est.
Deo grátias.

1 JANUARY

SOLEMNITY OF MARY, MOTHER OF GOD

The title 'Mother of God' is the equivalent in the Western or Latin branch of Christianity of the earlier Eastern or Greek title of *Theotokos* which literally means 'God-bearer'. This word was used of Mary from at least the time of the theologian Origin (died c. 254). It was the cause of some controversy on the basis that its meaning failed to reflect the humanity of Jesus over against his divinity, but it was upheld by the great Councils of Ephesus (431) and Chalcedon (451).

ENTRANCE ANTIPHON   *(cf. Is 9:2.6; Lk 1:33)*

A light will shine on us this day, the Lord is born for us: he shall be called Wonderful God, Prince of Peace, Father of the world to come; and his kingship will never end.

or

Hail, holy Mother! The child to whom you gave birth is the King of heaven and earth for ever.

GREETING, PENITENTIAL RITE, GLORIA — *pages 7-14*

OPENING PRAYER

Let us pray
    [that Mary, the mother of the Lord,
    will help us by her prayers]

God our Father,
may we always profit by the prayers
of the Virgin Mother Mary,
for you bring us life and salvation
through Jesus Christ her Son
who lives and reigns with you and the Holy Spirit,
one God, for ever and ever.

or

Let us pray
    [in the name of Jesus,
    born of a virgin and Son of God]

Father,
source of light in every age,
the virgin conceived and bore your Son
who is called Wonderful God, Prince of peace.

May her prayer, the gift of a mother's love,
be your people's joy through all ages.

May her response, born of a humble heart,
draw your Spirit to rest on your people.

FIRST READING   (Nb 6:22-27)

A reading from the book of Numbers.

They are to call down my name on the sons of Israel, and I will bless them.

The Lord spoke to Moses and said, 'Say this to Aaron and his
sons: "This is how you are to bless the sons of Israel. You shall
say to them:

May the Lord bless you and keep you.
May the Lord let his face shine on you and be gracious to you.
May the Lord uncover his face to you and bring you peace."

This is how they are to call down my name on the sons of
Israel, and I will bless them.'

This is the word of the Lord.

RESPONSORIAL PSALM   (Ps 66:2-3.5.6.8)

℟   **O God, be gracious and bless us.**

1.   God, be gracious and bless us
     and let your face shed its light upon us.
     So will your ways be known upon earth
     and all nations learn your saving help. ℟

2.   Let the nations be glad and exult
     for you rule the world with justice.
     With fairness you rule the peoples,
     you guide the nations on earth. ℟

3.   Let the peoples praise you, O God;
     let all the peoples praise you.
     May God still give us his blessing
     till the ends of the earth revere him. ℟

SECOND READING   (Gal 4:4-7)

A reading from the letter of St Paul to the Galatians.

God sent his Son, born of a woman.

When the appointed time came, God sent his Son, born of a
woman, born a subject of the Law, to redeem the subjects of
the Law and to enable us to be adopted as sons. The proof that
you are sons is that God has sent the Spirit of his Son into our
hearts: the Spirit that cries, 'Abba, Father', and it is this that
makes you a son, you are not a slave any more; and if God has
made you son, then he has made you heir.

This is the word of the Lord.

GOSPEL ACCLAMATION   *(Heb 1:1-2)*

Alleluia, alleluia!
At various times in the past
and in various different ways,
God spoke to our ancestors through the prophets;
but in our own time, the last days,
he has spoken to us through his Son.
Alleluia!

GOSPEL   *(Lk 2:16-21)*

A reading from the holy Gospel according to Luke.

They found Mary and Joseph and the baby... When the eighth day came, they gave him the name Jesus.

The shepherds hurried away to Bethlehem and found Mary and Joseph, and the baby lying in the manger. When they saw the child they repeated what they had been told about him, and everyone who heard it was astonished at what the shepherds had to say. As for Mary, she treasured all these things and pondered them in her heart. And the shepherds went back glorifying and praising God for all they had heard and seen; it was exactly as they had been told.

When the eighth day came and the child was to be circumcised, they gave him the name Jesus, the name the angel had given him before his conception.

This is the Gospel of the Lord.

PROFESSION OF FAITH — *pages 15-16*

PRAYER OVER THE GIFTS

God our Father,
we celebrate at this season
the beginning of our salvation.
On this feast of Mary, the Mother of God,
we ask that our salvation
will be brought to its fulfilment.

PREFACE OF THE BLESSED VIRGIN MARY

Father, all-powerful and ever-living God,
we do well always and everywhere to give you thanks
as we celebrate the motherhood of the Blessed Virgin Mary.

Through the power of the Holy Spirit,
she became the virgin mother of your only Son,
our Lord Jesus Christ,
who is for ever the light of the world.

Through him the choirs of angels
and all the powers of heaven
praise and worship your glory.
May our voices blend with theirs
as we join in their unending hymn:
Holy, holy, holy…

COMMUNION ANTIPHON   (Heb 13:8)
Jesus Christ is the same yesterday, today, and for ever.

PRAYER AFTER COMMUNION
Father,
as we proclaim the Virgin Mary
to be the mother of Christ and the mother of the Church,
may our communion with her Son
bring us to salvation.

SOLEMN BLESSING
Every good gift comes from the Father of light.
May he grant you his grace and every blessing,
and keep you safe throughout the coming year.
Amen.

May he grant you unwavering faith,
constant hope, and love that endures to the end.
Amen.

May he order your days and work in his peace,
hear your every prayer,
and lead you to everlasting life and joy.
Amen.

May almighty God bless you,
the Father, and the Son, ✠ and the Holy Spirit.
Amen.

REFLECTION
The title of today's *feast* draws attention to two aspects of the
incarnation. First, Mary. As always in the liturgy her person
and role never stand alone but appear alongside the person
and role of her Son. Her part in the drama of salvation is to
the fore today. Second, Mother of God. Because the human
being Jesus is God also Mary is the bearer of God, *Theotokos*,
which we usually render as Mother of God.

4 JANUARY

SECOND SUNDAY AFTER CHRISTMAS

(In England, Scotland and Wales the Epiphany *is celebrated on this Sunday — see page 71)*

Today's celebration, coming as it does between Christmas Day and the Epiphany contains themes which are connected to these feasts. Though Christmas Day and the Epiphany form part of the Church's season of Christmas tide, there is a difference of emphasis. Christmas Day celebrates the coming of the Son of God as a human being and the Epiphany highlights the revealing of this truth to all the nations of the earth. Both themes are echoed in today's prayers.

ENTRANCE ANTIPHON *(Ws 18:14-15)*

When peaceful silence lay over all, and night had run half of her swift course, your all-powerful word, O Lord, leaped down from heaven, from the royal throne.

GREETING, PENITENTIAL RITE, GLORIA — *pages 7-14*

OPENING PRAYER

Let us pray
    [that all humankind may be enlightened by the gospel]

God of power and life,
glory of all who believe in you,
fill the world with your splendour
and show the nations the light of your truth.

or

Let us pray
    [aware of the dignity to which we are called
    by the love of Christ]

Father of our Lord Jesus Christ,
our glory is to stand before the world
as your own sons and daughters.

May the simple beauty of Jesus' birth
summon us always to love what is most deeply human,
and to see your Word made flesh
reflected in those whose lives we touch.

FIRST READING *(Si 24:1-2.8-12)*

A reading from the book of Ecclesiasticus.

The wisdom of God has pitched her tent among the chosen people.

Wisdom speaks her own praises,
in the midst of her people she glories in herself.
She opens her mouth in the assembly of the Most High,
she glories in herself in the presence of the Mighty One.

'Then the creator of all things instructed me,
and he who created me fixed a place for my tent.
He said, "Pitch your tent in Jacob,
make Israel your inheritance."
From eternity, in the beginning, he created me,
and for eternity I shall remain.
I ministered before him in the holy tabernacle,
and thus was I established on Zion.
In the beloved city he has given me rest,
and in Jerusalem I wield my authority.
I have taken root in a privileged people
in the Lord's property, in his inheritance.'
This is the word of the Lord.

RESPONSORIAL PSALM   (Ps 147:12-15.19-20)

℟   **The Word was made flesh, and lived among us.**
or **Alleluia!**

1. O praise the Lord, Jerusalem!
    Zion, praise your God!
    He has strengthened the bars of your gates,
    he has blessed the children within you. ℟

2. He established peace on your borders,
    he feeds you with finest wheat.
    He sends out his word to the earth
    and swiftly runs his command. ℟

3. He makes his word known to Jacob,
    to Israel his laws and decrees.
    He has not dealt thus with other nations;
    he has not taught them his decrees. ℟

SECOND READING   (Eph 1:3-6.15-18)

A reading from the letter of St Paul to the Ephesians.

He determined that we should become his adopted sons through Jesus.

Blessed be God the Father of our Lord Jesus Christ, who has
blessed us with all the spiritual blessings of heaven in Christ.
Before the world was made, he chose us, chose us in Christ, to
be holy and spotless, and to live through love in his presence,
determining that we should become his adopted sons, through

Jesus Christ, for his own kind purposes, to make us praise the glory of his grace, his free gift to us in the Beloved.

That will explain why I, having once heard about your faith in the Lord Jesus, and the love that you show towards all the saints, have never failed to remember you in my prayers and to thank God for you. May the God of our Lord Jesus Christ, the Father of glory, give you a spirit of wisdom and perception of what is revealed, to bring you to full knowledge of him. May he enlighten the eyes of your mind so that you can see what hope his call holds for you, what rich glories he has promised the saints will inherit.

This is the word of the Lord.

GOSPEL ACCLAMATION   (cf. 1 Tm 3:16)
Alleluia, alleluia!
Glory be to you, O Christ, proclaimed to the pagans;
Glory be to you, O Christ, believed in by the world.
Alleluia!

GOSPEL   (Jn 1:1-18)
(For Shorter Form, *read between* ◗ ◖*)*
A reading from the holy Gospel according to John.
The Word was made flesh, and lived among us.

◗In the beginning was the Word:
the Word was with God
and the Word was God.
He was with God in the beginning.
Through him all things came to be,
not one thing had its being but through him.
All that came to be had life in him
and that life was the light of men,
a light that shines in the dark,
a light that darkness could not overpower.◖

A man came, sent by God.
His name was John.
He came as a witness,
as a witness to speak for the light,
so that everyone might believe through him.
He was not the light,
only a witness to speak for the light.

◗The Word was the true light
that enlightens all men;
and he was coming into the world.

He was in the world
that had its being through him,
and the world did not know him.
He came to his own domain
and his own people did not accept him.
But to all who did accept him
he gave power to become children of God,
to all who believe in the name of him
who was born not out of human stock
or urge of the flesh
or will of man
but of God himself.
The Word was made flesh,
he lived among us,
and we saw his glory,
the glory that is his as the only Son of the Father,
full of grace and truth.◀

John appears as his witness. He proclaims:
'This is the one of whom I said:
He who comes after me
ranks before me
because he existed before me.'

Indeed, from his fullness we have, all of us, received—
yes, grace in return for grace,
since, though the Law was given through Moses,
grace and truth have come through Jesus Christ.
No one has ever seen God;
it is the only Son, who is nearest to the Father's heart,
who has made him known.

　▶This is the Gospel of the Lord.◀

PROFESSION OF FAITH — *pages 15-16*

PRAYER OVER THE GIFTS

Lord,
make holy these gifts
through the coming of your Son,
who shows us the way of truth
and promises the life of your kingdom.

PREFACE OF CHRISTMAS I-III — *page 19*

COMMUNION ANTIPHON (Jn 1:12)

He gave to all who accepted him the power to become children of God.

PRAYER AFTER COMMUNION

Lord,
hear our prayers.
By this eucharist free us from sin
and keep us faithful to your word.

SOLEMN BLESSING — *pages 394-395*

REFLECTION

God's Son has become a human being with the conception
and birth of Jesus. But this truth is not just an abstract one.
It has a meaning for the human race. It was to show God's
love for every human being that God's Son was born and
the proclamation of this truth to the nations of the earth, in
the persons of the Magi, at an early stage after his birth, is to
underline this aspect of the incarnation.

6 JANUARY

THE EPIPHANY OF THE LORD

(Celebrated in Ireland today)

The title of today's feast means *the showing*. It originally
referred to the self-disclosure of Jesus which took place at
his baptism when the public side of his mission began.
Later it became associated with the manifestation of Jesus to
the Gentiles in the persons of the wise men or Magi in the
Western Church, although it retains its original baptismal
character in the Orthodox Church. A third event connected
with this theme is also associated with today's feast, namely,
when Jesus changed water into wine at the wedding feast at
Cana as the first of the signs which would show who he was.

ENTRANCE ANTIPHON (cf. Ml 3:1; 1 Ch 19:12)

**The Lord and ruler is coming; kingship is his,
and government and power.**

GREETING, PENITENTIAL RITE, GLORIA — *pages 7-14*

OPENING PRAYER

Let us pray
      [that we will be guided by the light of faith]

Father, you revealed your Son to the nations
by the guidance of a star.
Lead us to your glory in heaven
by the light of faith.

or

Let us pray
      [grateful for the glory revealed today
      through God made man]

Father of light, unchanging God,
today you reveal to men of faith
the resplendent fact of the Word made flesh.

Your light is strong,
your love is near;
draw us beyond the limits which this world imposes,
to the life where your Spirit makes all life complete.

FIRST READING   *(Is 60:1-6)*

A reading from the prophet Isaiah.

Above you the glory of the Lord appears.

Arise, shine out Jerusalem, for your light has come,
the glory of the Lord is rising on you,
though night still covers the earth
and darkness the peoples.

Above you the Lord now rises
and above you his glory appears.
The nations come to your light
and kings to your dawning brightness.

Lift up your eyes and look round:
all are assembling and coming towards you,
your sons from far away
and daughters being tenderly carried.

At this sight you will grow radiant,
your heart throbbing and full;
since the riches of the sea will flow to you;
the wealth of the nations come to you;

camels in throngs will cover you,
and dromedaries of Midian and Ephah;
everyone in Sheba will come,

bringing gold and incense
and singing the praise of the Lord.

This is the word of the Lord.

RESPONSORIAL PSALM *(Ps 71:1-2.7-8.10-13)*

℟ **All nations shall fall prostrate before you, O Lord.**

1. O God, give your judgement to the king,
   to a king's son your justice,
   that he may judge your people in justice
   and your poor in right judgement. ℟

2. In his days justice shall flourish
   and peace till the moon fails.
   He shall rule from sea to sea,
   from the Great River to earth's bounds. ℟

3. The kings of Tarshish and the sea coasts
   shall pay him tribute.
   The kings of Sheba and Seba
   shall bring him gifts.
   Before him all kings shall fall prostrate,
   all nations shall serve him. ℟

4. For he shall save the poor when they cry
   and the needy who are helpless.
   He will have pity on the weak
   and save the lives of the poor. ℟

SECOND READING *(Eph 3:2-3.5-6)*

A reading from the letter of St Paul to the Ephesians.

It has now been revealed that pagans share the same inheritance.

You have probably heard how I have been entrusted by God
with the grace he meant for you, and that it was by a revelation
that I was given the knowledge of the mystery. This mystery that
has now been revealed through the Spirit to his holy apostles
and prophets was unknown to any men in past generations; it
means that pagans now share the same inheritance, that they
are parts of the same body, and that the same promise has been
made to them, in Christ Jesus, through the gospel.

This is the word of the Lord.

GOSPEL ACCLAMATION   *(Mt 2:2)*

Alleluia, alleluia!
We saw his star as it rose
and have come to do the Lord homage.
Alleluia!

GOSPEL   *(Mt 2:1-12)*

A reading from the holy Gospel according to Matthew.
We saw his star and have come to do the king homage.

After Jesus had been born at Bethlehem in Judaea during the reign of King Herod, some wise men came to Jerusalem from the east. 'Where is the infant king of the Jews?' they asked. 'We saw his star as it rose and have come to do him homage.' When King Herod heard this he was perturbed, and so was the whole of Jerusalem. He called together all the chief priests and the scribes of the people, and enquired of them where the Christ was to be born. 'At Bethlehem in Judaea', they told him 'for this is what the prophet wrote:

And you, Bethlehem, in the land of Judah,
you are by no means least among the leaders of Judah,
for out of you will come a leader
who will shepherd my people Israel.'

Then Herod summoned the wise men to see him privately. He asked them the exact date on which the star had appeared, and sent them on to Bethlehem. 'Go and find out all about the child', he said 'and when you have found him, let me know, so that I too may go and do him homage.' Having listened to what the king had to say, they set out. And there in front of them was the star they had seen rising; it went forward and halted over the place where the child was. The sight of the star filled them with delight, and going into the house they saw the child with his mother Mary, and falling to their knees they did him homage. Then, opening their treasures, they offered him gifts of gold and frankincense and myrrh. But they were warned in a dream not to go back to Herod, and returned to their own country by a different way.

This is the Gospel of the Lord.

PROFESSION OF FAITH — *pages 15-16*

PRAYER OVER THE GIFTS

Lord,
accept the offerings of your Church,
not gold, frankincense and myrrh,

but the sacrifice and food they symbolise:
Jesus Christ, who is Lord for ever and ever.

PREFACE OF THE EPIPHANY

Father, all-powerful and ever-living God,
we do well always and everywhere to give you thanks.

Today you revealed in Christ your eternal plan of salvation
and showed him as the light of all peoples.
Now that his glory has shone among us
you have renewed humanity in his immortal image.

Now, with angels and archangels,
and the whole company of heaven,
we sing the unending hymn of your praise:
Holy, holy, holy…

COMMUNION ANTIPHON *(cf. Mt 2:2)*

**We have seen his star in the east, and have come with gifts to
adore the Lord.**

PRAYER AFTER COMMUNION

Father, guide us with your light.
Help us to recognise Christ in this eucharist
and welcome him with love,
for he is Lord for ever and ever.

SOLEMN BLESSING

God has called you out of darkness,
into his wonderful light.
May you experience his kindness and blessings,
and be strong in faith, in hope, and in love.
Amen.

Because you are followers of Christ,
who appeared on this day as a light shining in darkness,
may he make you a light to all your sisters and brothers.
Amen.

The wise men followed the star,
and found Christ who is light from light.
May you too find the Lord
when your pilgrimage is ended.
Amen.

May almighty God bless you,
the Father, and the Son, ✠ and the Holy Spirit.
Amen.

REFLECTION

Christianity has been described as a revealed religion. This idea suggests that God has acted in history and so certain historical events have a deeper significance. This is true of the three events which we remember today: the arrival of the wise men, the baptism of the Lord in the Jordan and the wedding feast at Cana. Each of these events has its place in the overall design of God that God's loving plan for humanity would be made known and responded to.

---

11 JANUARY

THE BAPTISM OF THE LORD

Today the Church celebrates that point in Jesus' life when he went public, so to speak. He began to reveal who he was. There is another revelation in today's liturgy. It is that God is Trinity. At his baptism when Jesus the Son came up out of the water the Spirit descended on him and the voice of the Father declared that Jesus was his Son.

ENTRANCE ANTIPHON   *(cf. Mt 3:16-17)*

When the Lord had been baptised, the heavens opened, and the Spirit came down like a dove to rest on him. Then the voice of the Father thundered: This is my beloved Son, with him I am well pleased.

GREETING, PENITENTIAL RITE, GLORIA — *pages 7-14*

OPENING PRAYER

Let us pray

[that we will be faithful to our baptism]

Almighty, eternal God,
when the Spirit descended upon Jesus
at his baptism in the Jordan,
you revealed him as your own beloved Son.
Keep us, your children born of water and the Spirit,
faithful to our calling.

or

Father,
your only Son revealed himself to us by becoming man.
May we who share his humanity
come to share his divinity,

for he lives and reigns with you and the Holy Spirit,
one God, for ever and ever.

or

Let us pray
    [as we listen to the voice of God's Spirit]

Father in heaven,
you revealed Christ as your Son
by the voice that spoke over the waters of the Jordan.

May all who share in the sonship of Christ
follow in his path of service to man,
and reflect the glory of his kingdom
even to the ends of the earth,
for he is Lord for ever and ever.

FIRST READING   *(Is 55:1-11)*

A reading from the prophet Isaiah.

Come to the water. Listen, and your soul will live.

Oh, come to the water all you who are thirsty;
though you have no money, come!
Buy corn without money, and eat,
and, at no cost, wine and milk.
Why spend money on what is not bread,
your wages on what fails to satisfy?
Listen, listen to me, and you will have good things to eat
and rich food to enjoy.
Pay attention, come to me;
listen, and your soul will live.

With you I will make an everlasting covenant
out of the favours promised to David.
See, I have made of you a witness to the peoples,
a leader and a master of the nations.
See, you will summon a nation you never knew,
those unknown will come hurrying to you,
for the sake of the Lord your God,
of the Holy One of Israel who will glorify you.

Seek the Lord while he is still to be found,
call to him while he is still near.
Let the wicked man abandon his way,
the evil man his thoughts.
Let him turn back to the Lord who will take pity on him,
to our God who is rich in forgiving;
for my thoughts are not your thoughts,

my ways not your ways — it is the Lord who speaks.
Yes, the heavens are as high above earth
as my ways are above your ways,
my thoughts above your thoughts.

Yes, as the rain and the snow come down from the heavens and
do not return without watering the earth, making it yield and
giving growth to provide seed for the sower and bread for the
eating, so the word that goes from my mouth does not return to
me empty, without carrying out my will and succeeding in what
it was sent to do.

This is the word of the Lord.

RESPONSORIAL PSALM   (Is 12:2-6)

℟   **With joy you will draw water**
    from the wells of salvation.

1.   Truly, God is my salvation,
     I trust, I shall not fear.
     For the Lord is my strength, my song,
     he became my saviour.
     With joy you will draw water
     from the wells of salvation. ℟

2.   Give thanks to the Lord, give praise to his name!
     Make his mighty deeds known to the peoples!
     Declare the greatness of his name. ℟

3.   Sing a psalm to the Lord
     for he has done glorious deeds,
     make them known to all the earth!
     People of Zion, sing and shout for joy
     for great in your midst is the Holy One of Israel. ℟

SECOND READING   (1 Jn 5:1-9)

A reading from the first letter of St John.

The Spirit and water and blood.

Whoever believes that Jesus is the Christ
has been begotten by God;
and whoever loves the Father that begot him
loves the child whom he begets.
We can be sure that we love God's children
if we love God himself and do what he has commanded us;
this is what loving God is —
keeping his commandments;

and his commandments are not difficult,
because anyone who has been begotten by God
has already overcome the world;
this is the victory over the world —
our faith.
Who can overcome the world?
Only the man who believes that Jesus is the Son of God:
Jesus Christ who came by water and blood,
not with water only,
but with water and blood;
with the Spirit as another witness —
since the Spirit is the truth —
so that there are three witnesses,
the Spirit, the water and the blood,
and all three of them agree.
We accept the testimony of human witnesses,
but God's testimony is much greater,
and this is God's testimony,
given as evidence for his Son.

This is the word of the Lord.

GOSPEL ACCLAMATION *(cf. Jn 1:29)*
Alleluia, alleluia!
John saw Jesus coming towards him, and said:
This is the Lamb of God who takes away the sin of the world.
Alleluia!

GOSPEL *(Mk 1:7-11)*
A reading from the holy Gospel according to Mark.
You are my Son, the Beloved; my favour rests on you.
In the course of his preaching John the Baptist said, 'Someone is following me, someone who is more powerful than I am, and I am not fit to kneel down and undo the strap of his sandals. I have baptised you with water, but he will baptise you with the Holy Spirit.'

It was at this time that Jesus came from Nazareth in Galilee and was baptised in the Jordan by John. No sooner had he come up out of the water than he saw the heavens torn apart and the Spirit, like a dove, descending on him. And a voice came from heaven, 'You are my Son, the Beloved; my favour rests on you.'

This is the Gospel of the Lord.

PROFESSION OF FAITH — *pages 15-16*

PRAYER OVER THE GIFTS

Lord,
we celebrate the revelation of Christ your Son
who takes away the sins of the world.
Accept our gifts
and let them become one with his sacrifice,
for he is Lord for ever and ever.

PREFACE OF THE BAPTISM OF THE LORD

Father,
all-powerful and ever-living God,
we do well always and everywhere to give you thanks.

You celebrated your new gift of baptism
by signs and wonders at the Jordan.
Your voice was heard from heaven
to awaken faith in the presence among us
of the Word made man.

Your Spirit was seen as a dove,
revealing Jesus as your servant,
and anointing him with joy as the Christ,
sent to bring to the poor
the good news of salvation.

In our unending joy we echo on earth
the song of the angels in heaven
as they praise your glory for ever:
Holy, holy, holy...

COMMUNION ANTIPHON   *(Jn 1:32.34)*

This is he of whom John said: I have seen and have given witness that this is the Son of God.

PRAYER AFTER COMMUNION

Lord,
you feed us with bread from heaven.
May we hear your Son with faith
and become your children in name and in fact.

SOLEMN BLESSING — *pages 57-58*

REFLECTION

> The Trinity which is revealed in today's feast is what is unique
> about Christianity and the point at which it differs most from
> Judaism from which it sprang. The revelation of God in the

history of the chosen people took a significant leap forward with the birth of Jesus because now God is most clearly revealed for who God is: Father, Son and Spirit. This is the God who comes to live with us at our baptism and from that time onwards.

— 18 JANUARY —

2nd SUNDAY IN ORDINARY TIME

The Sundays of the year outside of the various seasons are occasions for celebrating the resurrection of the Lord and for considering one or more of the aspects of the Lord's person, life and role which the Church sometimes terms the mysteries of Christ. In a three-year cycle the gospels of Matthew, Mark and Luke are read respectively on a yearly basis. Occasionally this sequence is interrupted as it is today, for instance, when the gospel proclaimed is that of John.

ENTRANCE ANTIPHON   *(Ps 65:4)*

May all the earth give you worship and praise, and break into song to your name, O God, Most High.

GREETING, PENITENTIAL RITE, GLORIA — *pages 7-14*

OPENING PRAYER

Let us pray
    [to our Father for the gift of peace]

Father of heaven and earth,
hear our prayers,
and show us the way to peace in the world.

or

Let us pray
    [for the gift of peace]

Almighty and ever-present Father,
your watchful care reaches from end to end
and orders all things in such power
that even the tensions and the tragedies of sin
cannot frustrate your loving plans.

Help us to embrace your will,
give us the strength to follow your call,
so that your truth may live in our hearts
and reflect peace to those who believe in your love.

FIRST READING   *(1 Sam 3:3-10.19)*

A reading from the first book of Samuel.

Speak, Lord, your servant is listening.

Samuel was lying in the sanctuary of the Lord where the ark of
God was, when the Lord called, 'Samuel! Samuel!' He answered,
'Here I am.' Then he ran to Eli and said, 'Here I am, since you
called me.' Eli said, 'I did not call. Go back and lie down.' So
he went and lay down. Once again the Lord called, 'Samuel!
Samuel!' Samuel got up and went to Eli and said, 'Here I am,
since you called me.' He replied, 'I did not call you, my son;
go back and lie down.' Samuel had as yet no knowledge of the
Lord and the word of the Lord had not yet been revealed to
him. Once again the Lord called, the third time. He got up and
went to Eli and said, 'Here I am, since you called me.' Eli then
understood that it was the Lord who was calling the boy, and
he said to Samuel, 'Go and lie down, and if someone calls say,
"Speak, Lord, your servant is listening".' So Samuel went and lay
down in his place.

The Lord then came and stood by, calling as he had done
before, 'Samuel! Samuel!' Samuel answered, 'Speak, Lord, your
servant is listening.'

Samuel grew up and the Lord was with him and let no word
of his fall to the ground.

This is the word of the Lord.

RESPONSORIAL PSALM   *(Ps 39:2.4.7-10)*

℟   **Here I am, Lord!**
    I come to do your will.

1. I waited, I waited for the Lord
    and he stooped down to me;
    he heard my cry.
    He put a new song into my mouth,
    praise of our God. ℟

2. You do not ask for sacrifice and offerings,
    but an open ear.
    You do not ask for holocaust and victim.
    Instead, here am I. ℟

3. In the scroll of the book it stands written
    that I should do your will.
    My God, I delight in your law
    in the depth of my heart. ℟

4. Your justice I have proclaimed
   in the great assembly.
   My lips I have not sealed;
   you know it, O Lord. ℞

SECOND READING   *(1 Cor 6:13-15.17-20)*

A reading from the first letter of St Paul to the Corinthians.

Your bodies are members making up the body of Christ.

The body is not meant for fornication; it is for the Lord, and the Lord for the body. God who raised the Lord from the dead, will by his power raise us up too.

You know, surely, that your bodies are members making up the body of Christ; anyone who is joined to the Lord is one spirit with him.

Keep away from fornication. All the other sins are committed outside the body; but to fornicate is to sin against your own body. Your body, you know, is the temple of the Holy Spirit, who is in you since you received him from God. You are not your own property; you have been bought and paid for. That is why you should use your body for the glory of God.

This is the word of the Lord.

GOSPEL ACCLAMATION   *(1 Sam 3:9; Jn 6:68)*

Alleluia, alleluia!
Speak, Lord, your servant is listening:
you have the message of eternal life.
Alleluia!

or   *(Jn 1:41.17)*

Alleluia, alleluia!
We have found the Messiah — which means the Christ —
grace and truth have come through him.
Alleluia!

GOSPEL   *(Jn 1:35-42)*

A reading from the holy Gospel according to John.

They saw where he lived, and stayed with him.

As John stood with two of his disciples, Jesus passed, and John stared hard at him and said, 'Look, there is the lamb of God.' Hearing this, the two disciples followed Jesus. Jesus turned round, saw them following and said, 'What do you want?' They answered, 'Rabbi' — which means Teacher — 'where do you live?' 'Come and see' he replied; so they went and saw where he lived, and stayed with him the rest of that day. It was about the tenth hour.

One of these two who became followers of Jesus after hearing what John had said was Andrew, the brother of Simon Peter. Early next morning, Andrew met his brother and said to him, 'We have found the Messiah' — which means the Christ — and he took Simon to Jesus. Jesus looked hard at him and said, 'You are Simon son of John; you are to be called Cephas' — meaning Rock.

This is the Gospel of the Lord.

PROFESSION OF FAITH — *pages 15-16*

PRAYER OVER THE GIFTS
Father,
may we celebrate the eucharist
with reverence and love,
for when we proclaim the death of the Lord
you continue the work of his redemption,
who is Lord for ever and ever.

PREFACE OF SUNDAYS IN ORDINARY TIME I-VIII — *pages 22-25*

COMMUNION ANTIPHON   *(Ps 22:5)*
The Lord has prepared a feast for me: given wine in plenty for me to drink.
or   *(1 Jn 4:16)*
We know and believe in God's love for us.

PRAYER AFTER COMMUNION
Lord,
you have nourished us with bread from heaven.
Fill us with your Spirit,
and make us one in peace and love.

SOLEMN BLESSING — *pages 57-58*

REFLECTION
Today's liturgy focuses on the beginning of Jesus' public ministry and the beginning of the year is an appropriate place to do so. We hear of the way in which Jesus attracted his earliest disciples. The word 'disciple' means a learner and suggests a relationship of teaching and learning between Jesus and those whom he attracts. This is not a bad image to describe the interaction between Jesus and us who are his disciples in this generation.

25 JANUARY

3rd SUNDAY IN ORDINARY TIME

Today we begin to read from the gospel of Mark and this will continue until the end of November apart from Lent and Eastertide. Mark is the shortest gospel and considered by most to be the first one. The passages are selected from the gospel of Mark in the order in which they occur so that come November we shall have worked our way through Mark.

ENTRANCE ANTIPHON   *(Ps 95:1.6)*

Sing a new song to the Lord! Sing to the Lord, all the earth. Truth and beauty surround him, he lives in holiness and glory.

GREETING, PENITENTIAL RITE, GLORIA — *pages 7-14*

OPENING PRAYER

Let us pray
    [for unity and peace]

All-powerful and ever-living God,
direct your love that is within us,
that our efforts in the name of your Son
may bring mankind to unity and peace.

or

Let us pray
    [pleading that our vision
    may overcome our weakness]

Almighty Father,
the love you offer
always exceeds the furthest expression of our human longing,
for you are greater than the human heart.

Direct each thought, each effort of our life,
so that the limits of our faults and weaknesses
may not obscure the vision of your glory
or keep us from the peace you have promised.

FIRST READING   *(Jon 3:1-5.10)*

A reading from the prophet Jonah.

The people of Nineveh renounce their evil behaviour.

The word of the Lord was addressed to Jonah: 'Up!' he said 'Go to Nineveh, the great city, and preach to them as I told you to.' Jonah set out and went to Nineveh in obedience to the word

of the Lord. Now Nineveh was a city great beyond compare: it took three days to cross it. Jonah went on into the city, making a day's journey. He preached in these words, 'Only forty days more and Nineveh is going to be destroyed.' And the people of Nineveh believed in God; they proclaimed a fast and put on sackcloth, from the greatest to the least.

God saw their efforts to renounce their evil behaviour. And God relented: he did not inflict on them the disaster which he had threatened.

This is the word of the Lord.

RESPONSORIAL PSALM   *(Ps 24:4-9)*

℟ **Lord, make me know your ways.**

1. Lord, make me know your ways.
    Lord, teach me your paths.
    Make me walk in your truth, and teach me:
    for you are God my saviour. ℟

2. Remember your mercy, Lord,
    and the love you have shown from of old.
    In your love remember me,
    because of your goodness, O Lord. ℟

3. The Lord is good and upright.
    He shows the path to those who stray,
    he guides the humble in the right path;
    he teaches his way to the poor. ℟

SECOND READING   *(1 Cor 7:29-31)*

A reading from the first letter of St Paul to the Corinthians.

The world as we know it is passing away.

Brothers, our time is growing short. Those who have wives should live as though they had none, and those who mourn should live as though they had nothing to mourn for; those who are enjoying life should live as though there were nothing to laugh about; those whose life is buying things should live as though they had nothing of their own; and those who have to deal with the world should not become engrossed in it. I say this because the world as we know it is passing away.

This is the word of the Lord.

GOSPEL ACCLAMATION   *(Mk 1:15)*

Alleluia, Alleluia!
The kingdom of God is close at hand;

believe the Good News.
Alleluia!

GOSPEL *(Mk 1:14-20)*

A reading from the holy Gospel according to Mark.
Repent, and believe the Good News.

After John had been arrested, Jesus went into Galilee. There he proclaimed the Good News from God. 'The time has come' he said 'and the kingdom of God is close at hand. Repent, and believe the Good News.'

As he was walking along by the Sea of Galilee he saw Simon and his brother Andrew casting a net in the lake — for they were fishermen. And Jesus said to them, 'Follow me and I will make you into fishers of men.' And at once they left their nets and followed him.

Going on a little further, he saw James son of Zebedee and his brother John; they too were in their boat, mending their nets. He called them at once and, leaving their father Zebedee in the boat with the men he employed, they went after him.

This is the Gospel of the Lord.

PROFESSION OF FAITH — *pages 15-16*

PRAYER OVER THE GIFTS

Lord,
receive our gifts.
Let our offerings make us holy
and bring us salvation.

PREFACE OF SUNDAYS IN ORDINARY TIME I-VIII — *pages 22-25*

COMMUNION ANTIPHON *(Ps 33:6)*

Look up at the Lord with gladness and smile; your face will never be ashamed.
or *(Jn 8:12)*

I am the light of the world, says the Lord; the man who follows me will have the light of life.

PRAYER AFTER COMMUNION

God, all-powerful Father,
may the new life you give us increase our love
and keep us in the joy of your kingdom.

SOLEMN BLESSING — *pages 57-58*

REFLECTION

It is interesting to note that the proclamation of the nearness of the Kingdom of God is nearly always accompanied by the command to repent. When put into the mouth of Jesus what he is saying is that the Kingdom of God has practical significance for all. The Kingdom of God is a metaphor to describe all that Jesus was about. When individuals and societies take God as the Lord of their life, it is at hand. The root meaning of the word 'repent' means a change of attitude. That is the next step which all may take to further the coming of the Kingdom.

—————— 1 FEBRUARY ——————
4th SUNDAY IN ORDINARY TIME

In the Hebrew Scriptures, a prophet is not primarily a person who predicts the future. Rather the heart of his role is that he or she speak the word of God for today. Many of the great prophets took on their role with great reluctance. What drove them on was the power of the word of the LORD which they had been urged to proclaim. In many cases also it meant adopting an unpopular stance, particularly at a time when things were going well. In times of crisis, however, it frequently involved giving the people a word of consolation.

ENTRANCE ANTIPHON   (Ps 105:47)

Save us, Lord our God, and gather us together from the nations, that we may proclaim your holy name and glory in your praise.

GREETING, PENITENTIAL RITE, GLORIA — *pages 7-14*

OPENING PRAYER

Let us pray
[for a greater love of God
and of our fellow men]

Lord our God,
help us to love you with all our hearts
and to love all as you love them.

or

Let us pray
[joining in the praise of the living God
for we are his people]

Father in heaven,
from the days of Abraham and Moses
until this gathering of your Church in prayer,
you have formed a people in the image of your Son.

Bless his people with the gift of your kingdom.
May we serve you with our every desire
and show love for one another
even as you have loved us.

FIRST READING   *(Dt 18:15-20)*

A reading from the book of Deuteronomy.

I will raise up a prophet and I will put my words into his mouth.

Moses said to the people: 'Your God will raise up for you a prophet like myself, from among yourselves, from your own brothers; to him you must listen. This is what you yourselves asked of the Lord your God at Horeb on the day of the Assembly. "Do not let me hear again" you said "the voice of the Lord my God, nor look any longer on this great fire, or I shall die"; and the Lord said to me, "All they have spoken is well said. I will raise up a prophet like yourself for them from their own brothers; I will put my words into his mouth and he shall tell them all I command him. The man who does not listen to my words that he speaks in my name, shall be held answerable to me for it. But the prophet who presumes to say in my name a thing I have not commanded him to say, or who speaks in the name of other gods, that prophet shall die."'

This is the word of the Lord.

RESPONSORIAL PSALM   *(Ps 94:1-2.6-9)*

℟ **O that today you would listen to his voice!**
   Harden not your hearts.

1. Come, ring out our joy to the Lord;
   hail the rock who saves us.
   Let us come before him, giving thanks,
   with songs let us hail the Lord. ℟

2. Come in; let us kneel and bend low;
   let us kneel before the God who made us
   for he is our God and we
   the people who belong to his pasture,
   the flock that is led by his hand. ℟

(continued)

3.   O that today you would listen to his voice!
      'Harden not your hearts as at Meribah,
      as on that day at Massah in the desert
      when your fathers put me to the test;
      when they tried me, though they saw my work.' ℞
℞   **O that today you would listen to his voice!**
      Harden not your hearts.

SECOND READING   *(1 Cor 7:32-35)*

A reading from the first letter of St Paul to the Corinthians.

An unmarried woman can devote herself to the Lord's affairs; all she need worry about is being holy.

I would like to see you free from all worry. An unmarried man can devote himself to the Lord's affairs, all he need worry about is pleasing the Lord; but a married man has to bother about the world's affairs and devote himself to pleasing his wife: he is torn two ways. In the same way an unmarried woman, like a young girl, can devote herself to the Lord's affairs; all she need worry about is being holy in body and spirit. The married woman, on the other hand, has to worry about the world's affairs and devote herself to pleasing her husband. I say this only to help you, not to put a halter round your necks, but simply to make sure that everything is as it should be, and that you give your undivided attention to the Lord.

      This is the word of the Lord.

GOSPEL ACCLAMATION   *(cf. Mt 11:25)*

Alleluia, alleluia!
Blessed are you, Father,
Lord of heaven and earth,
for revealing the mysteries of the kingdom
to mere children.
Alleluia!

or   *(Mt 4:16)*

Alleluia, alleluia!
The people that lived in darkness
has seen a great light;
on those who dwell in the land and shadow of death
a light has dawned.
Alleluia!

GOSPEL *(Mk 1:21-28)*

A reading from the holy Gospel according to Mark.

He taught them with authority.

Jesus and his followers went as far as Capernaum, and as soon as the sabbath came Jesus went to the synagogue and began to teach. And his teaching made a deep impression on them because, unlike the scribes, he taught them with authority.

In their synagogue just then there was a man possessed by an unclean spirit, and it shouted, 'What do you want with us, Jesus of Nazareth? Have you come to destroy us? I know who you are: the Holy One of God.' But Jesus said sharply, 'Be quiet! Come out of him!' And the unclean spirit threw the man into convulsions and with a loud cry went out of him. The people were so astonished that they started asking each other what it all meant. 'Here is a teaching that is new' they said 'and with authority behind it: he gives orders even to unclean spirits and they obey him.' And his reputation rapidly spread everywhere, through all the surrounding Galilean countryside.

This is the Gospel of the Lord.

PROFESSION OF FAITH — *pages 15-16*

PRAYER OVER THE GIFTS

Lord,
be pleased with the gifts we bring to your altar,
and make them the sacrament of our salvation.

PREFACE OF SUNDAYS IN ORDINARY TIME I-VIII — *pages 22-25*

COMMUNION ANTIPHON *(Ps 30:17-18)*

Let your face shine on your servant, and save me by your love. Lord, keep me from shame, for I have called to you.

or *(Mt 5:3-4)*

Happy are the poor in spirit; the kingdom of heaven is theirs! Happy are the lowly; they shall inherit the land.

PRAYER AFTER COMMUNION

Lord,
you invigorate us with this help to our salvation.
By this eucharist give the true faith continued growth
throughout the world.

SOLEMN BLESSING — *pages 57-58*

REFLECTION

After his death the near identity that existed between God and Jesus was only gradually recognised by Jesus' disciples. This was a unity which would only with time be expressed in terms of Trinity. But in the meantime the closeness of Jesus' relationship with the Father was expressed by the exercise by him of power which was usually reserved for God alone. One such quality was the authority to cast out unclean spirits.

=== 8 FEBRUARY ===

5th SUNDAY IN ORDINARY TIME

The first reading each Sunday is chosen because of a connection with the gospel of the day. Sometimes an incident occurring in the gospel is seen to be foreshadowed by an earlier event in the Hebrew Scriptures. Other times they will both contain a similar theme. However, before rushing to see how the first reading is fulfilled in the gospel, it is advisable to try to find out what the first reading meant in its own day. A second step can then be to see how both readings enlighten each other.

ENTRANCE ANTIPHON   *(Ps 94:6-7)*

Come, let us worship the Lord. Let us bow down in the presence of our maker, for he is the Lord our God.

GREETING, PENITENTIAL RITE, GLORIA — *pages 7-14*

OPENING PRAYER

Let us pray
[that God will watch over us and protect us]

Father,
watch over your family
and keep us safe in your care,
for all our hope is in you.

or

Let us pray
[with reverence in the presence of the living God]

In faith and love we ask you, Father,
to watch over your family gathered here.
In your mercy and loving kindness
no thought of ours is left unguarded,
no tear unheeded, no joy unnoticed.

Through the prayer of Jesus
may the blessings promised to the poor in spirit
lead us to the treasures of your heavenly kingdom.

FIRST READING *(Jb 7:1-4.6-7)*

A reading from the book of Job.

Restlessly I fret till twilight falls.

Job began to speak:

Is not man's life on earth nothing more than pressed
service,
his time no better than hired drudgery?
Like the slave, sighing for the shade,
or the workman with no thought but his wages,
months of delusion I have assigned to me,
nothing for my own but nights of grief.
Lying in bed I wonder, 'When will it be day?'
Risen I think, 'How slowly evening comes!'
Restlessly I fret till twilight falls.
Swifter than a weaver's shuttle my days have passed,
and vanished, leaving no hope behind.
Remember that my life is but a breath,
and that my eyes will never again see joy.

This is the word of the Lord.

RESPONSORIAL PSALM *(Ps 146:1-6)*

℞   **Praise the Lord who heals the broken-hearted.**

or   **Alleluia!**

1.   Praise the Lord for he is good;
sing to our God for he is loving:
to him our praise is due.   ℞

2.   The Lord builds up Jerusalem
and brings back Israel's exiles,
he heals the broken-hearted,
he binds up all their wounds.
He fixes the number of the stars;
he calls each one by its name.   ℞

3.   Our Lord is great and almighty;
his wisdom can never be measured.
The Lord raises the lowly;
he humbles the wicked to the dust.   ℞

SECOND READING *(1 Cor 9:16-19.22-23)*

A reading from the first letter of St Paul to the Corinthians.

I should be punished if I did not preach the Gospel.

I do not boast of preaching the gospel, since it is a duty which has been laid on me; I should be punished if I did not preach it! If I had chosen this work myself, I might have been paid for it, but as I have not, it is a responsibility which has been put into my hands. Do you know what my reward is? It is this: in my preaching, to be able to offer the Good News free, and not insist on the rights which the gospel gives me.

So though I am not a slave of any man I have made myself the slave of everyone so as to win as many as I could. For the weak I made myself weak. I made myself all things to all men in order to save some at any cost; and I still do this, for the sake of the gospel, to have a share in its blessing.

This is the word of the Lord.

GOSPEL ACCLAMATION *(Jn 8:12)*

Alleluia, alleluia!
I am the light of the world, says the Lord,
anyone who follows me
will have the light of life.
Alleluia!

or *(Mt 8:17)*

Alleluia, alleluia!
He took our sicknesses away,
and carried our diseases for us.
Alleluia!

GOSPEL *(Mk 1:29-39)*

A reading from the holy Gospel according to Mark.

He cured many who suffered from diseases of one kind or another.

On leaving the synagogue, Jesus went with James and John straight to the house of Simon and Andrew. Now Simon's mother-in-law had gone to bed with fever, and they told him about her straightaway. He went to her, took her by the hand and helped her up. And the fever left her and she began to wait on them.

That evening, after sunset, they brought to him all who were sick and those who were possessed by devils. The whole town came crowding round the door, and he cured many who were suffering from diseases of one kind or another; he also cast out many devils, but he would not allow them to speak, because they knew who he was.

In the morning, long before dawn, he got up and left the house, and went off to a lonely place and prayed there. Simon and his companions set out in search of him, and when they found him they said, 'Everybody is looking for you.' He answered, 'Let us go elsewhere, to the neighbouring country towns, so that I can preach there too, because that is why I came.' And he went all through Galilee, preaching in their synagogues and casting out devils.

This is the Gospel of the Lord.

PROFESSION OF FAITH — *pages 15-16*

PRAYER OVER THE GIFTS
Lord our God,
may the bread and wine
you give us for our nourishment on earth
become the sacrament of our eternal life.

PREFACE OF SUNDAYS IN ORDINARY TIME I-VIII — *pages 22-25*

COMMUNION ANTIPHON   *(Ps 106:8-9)*
Give praise to the Lord for his kindness, for his wonderful deeds towards men. He has filled the hungry with good things, he has satisfied the thirsty.

or   *(Mt 5:5-6)*
Happy are the sorrowing; they shall be consoled. Happy those who hunger and thirst for what is right; they shall be satisfied.

PRAYER AFTER COMMUNION
God our Father,
you give us a share in the one bread and the one cup
and make us one in Christ.
Help us to bring your salvation and joy
to all the world.

SOLEMN BLESSING — *pages 57-58*

REFLECTION
Brokenness and healing are to the fore in today's liturgy. There are very few lives which are not touched by sickness, whether of body, mind or spirit. This has always been so and presumably will continue thus. Jesus is the one who is presented as offering hope to those so affected, a light at the end of the tunnel. Those involved in the alleviation of suffering of whatever kind are carrying out the mission of Jesus in their own generation.

15 FEBRUARY
6th SUNDAY IN ORDINARY TIME

Here again the portrayal of Jesus as healing the person who
is sick with leprosy is basically the gospel-writer asking the
question: 'Who is this man, Jesus?' and inviting the hearer to
reply. The close bond that was seen to exist between God and
Jesus, in a dramatic way after his death, meant that Jesus like
God had the power to heal those who were sick in any way.

ENTRANCE ANTIPHON   *(Ps 30:3-4)*

**Lord, be my rock of safety, the stronghold that saves me. For
the honour of your name, lead me and guide me.**

GREETING, PENITENTIAL RITE, GLORIA — *pages 7-14*

OPENING PRAYER

Let us pray
   [that everything we do
   will be guided by God's law of love]
God our Father,
you have promised to remain for ever
with those who do what is just and right.
Help us to live in your presence.

or

Let us pray
   [for the wisdom that is greater than human words]
Father in heaven,
the loving plan of your wisdom took flesh in Jesus Christ,
and changed mankind's history
by his command of perfect love.

May our fulfilment of his command reflect your wisdom
and bring your salvation to the ends of the earth.

FIRST READING   *(Lv 13:1-2.44-46)*

A reading from the book of Leviticus.

The leper must live apart: he must live outside the camp.

The Lord said to Moses and Aaron, 'If a swelling or scab or shiny
spot appears on a man's skin, a case of leprosy of the skin is to
be suspected. The man must be taken to Aaron, the priest, or to
one of the priests who are his sons.

'The man is leprous: he is unclean. The priest must declare
him unclean; he is suffering from leprosy of the head. A man

infected with leprosy must wear his clothing torn and his hair disordered; he must shield his upper lip and cry, "Unclean, unclean". As long as the disease lasts he must be unclean; and therefore he must live apart; he must live outside the camp.'

This is the word of the Lord

RESPONSORIAL PSALM *(Ps 31:1-2.5.11)*

℟ **You are my refuge, O Lord;**
you fill me with the joy of salvation.

1. Happy the man whose offence is forgiven,
   whose sin is remitted.
   O happy the man to whom the Lord
   imputes no guilt,
   in whose spirit is no guile. ℟

2. But now I have acknowledged my sins;
   my guilt I did not hide.
   I said: 'I will confess
   my offence to the Lord.'
   And you, Lord, have forgiven
   the guilt of my sin. ℟

3. Rejoice, rejoice in the Lord,
   exult, you just!
   O come, ring out your joy,
   all you upright of heart. ℟

SECOND READING *(1 Cor 10:31–11:1)*

A reading from the first letter of St Paul to the Corinthians.
Take me for your model, as I take Christ.

Whatever you eat, whatever you drink, whatever you do at all, do it for the glory of God. Never do anything offensive to anyone — to Jews or Greeks or to the Church of God; just as I try to be helpful to everyone at all times, not anxious for my own advantage but for the advantage of everybody else, so that they may be saved.

Take me for your model, as I take Christ.

This is the word of the Lord.

GOSPEL ACCLAMATION *(cf. Eph 1:17.18)*

Alleluia, alleluia!
May the Father of our Lord Jesus Christ
enlighten the eyes of our mind,
so that we can see what hope his call holds for us. Alleluia!

or   *(Lk 7:16)*
Alleluia, alleluia!
A great prophet has appeared among us;
God has visited his people.
Alleluia!

GOSPEL   *(Mk 1:40-45)*
A reading from the holy Gospel according to Mark.
The leprosy left him at once and he was cured.

A leper came to Jesus and pleaded on his knees: 'If you want to'
he said 'you can cure me.' Feeling sorry for him, Jesus stretched
out his hand and touched him. 'Of course I want to!' he said. 'Be
cured!' And the leprosy left him at once and he was cured. Jesus
immediately sent him away and sternly ordered him, 'Mind you
say nothing to anyone, but go and show yourself to the priest,
and make the offering for your healing prescribed by Moses as
evidence of your recovery.' The man went away, but then started
talking about it freely and telling the story everywhere, so that
Jesus could no longer go openly into any town, but had to stay
outside in places where nobody lived. Even so, people from all
around would come to him.

This is the Gospel of the Lord.

PROFESSION OF FAITH — *pages 15-16*

PRAYER OVER THE GIFTS
Lord,
we make this offering in obedience to your word.
May it cleanse and renew us,
and lead us to our eternal reward.

PREFACE OF SUNDAYS IN ORDINARY TIME I-VIII — *pages 22-25*

COMMUNION ANTIPHON   *(Ps 77:29-30)*
They ate and were filled; the Lord gave them what they wanted:
they were not deprived of their desire.

or   *(Jn 3:16)*
God loved the world so much, he gave his only Son, that all who
believe in him might not perish, but might have eternal life.

PRAYER AFTER COMMUNION
Lord,
you give us food from heaven.
May we always hunger
for the bread of life.

SOLEMN BLESSING — *pages 57-58*

REFLECTION

Jesus is portrayed as reluctant to bask in the fame which his miraculous healing has brought him. Instead, he is presented as actually avoiding situations which would bring him attention. Jesus as healer has as much to do with the recognition of who Jesus really was, a recognition which came only gradually and not until after his death, as it had with the ministry of Jesus during the public years of his life.

—————— 22 FEBRUARY ——————

7th SUNDAY IN ORDINARY TIME

Who is Jesus? This is the question which the earliest Christian communities desperately sought to answer after his death when he was experienced by them as being alive in an utterly new way, when 'he was seen' as the gospels put it. And this is the question which today's reading from Mark seeks to answer. Only God can forgive sins. By linking the healing of the paralysed person with the forgiving of his sins the gospel-writer is declaring that Jesus and God are part of a unique relationship.

ENTRANCE ANTIPHON

Lord, your mercy is my hope, my heart rejoices in your saving power. I will sing to the Lord for his goodness to me.

GREETING, PENITENTIAL RITE, GLORIA — *pages 7-14*

OPENING PRAYER

Let us pray

[that God will make us more like Christ, his Son]

Father,

keep before us the wisdom and love

you have revealed in your Son.

Help us to be like him

in word and deed,

for he lives and reigns with you and the Holy Spirit,

one God, for ever and ever.

or

Let us pray
    [to the God of power and might,
    for his mercy is our hope]

Almighty God,
Father of our Lord Jesus Christ,
faith in your word is the way to wisdom,
and to ponder your divine plan is to grow in the truth.
Open our eyes to your deeds,
our ears to the sound of your call,
so that our every act may increase our sharing
in the life you have offered us.

FIRST READING   *(Is 43:18-19.21-22.24-25)*

A reading from the book of Isaiah.

I it is who must blot out everything.

Thus says the Lord:
    No need to recall the past,
    no need to think about what was done before.
    See, I am doing a new deed,
    even now it comes to light; can you not see it?
    Yes, I am making a road in the wilderness,
    paths in the wilds.
    The people I have formed for myself
    will sing my praises.
    Jacob, you have not invoked me,
    you have not troubled yourself, Israel, on my behalf.
    Instead you have burdened me with your sins,
    troubled me with your iniquities.
    I it is, I it is, who must blot out everything
    and not remember your sins.
    This is the word of the Lord

RESPONSORIAL PSALM   *(Ps 40:2-5.13-14)*

℞   **Heal my soul for I have sinned against you.**

1. Happy the man who considers the poor and the weak.
    The Lord will save him in the day of evil,
    will guard him, give him life, make him happy in the land
    and will not give him up to the will of his foes. ℞

2. The Lord will help him on his bed of pain,
    he will bring him back from sickness to health.
    As for me, I said: 'Lord, have mercy on me,
    heal my soul for I have sinned against you.' ℞

3.   If you uphold me I shall be unharmed
and set in your presence for evermore.
Blessed be the Lord, the God of Israel
from age to age. Amen. Amen. ℞

SECOND READING   *(2 Cor 1:18-22)*

A reading from the second letter of St Paul to the Corinthians.

Jesus was never Yes and No: with him it was always Yes.

I swear by God's truth, there is no Yes and No about what we say to you. The Son of God, the Christ Jesus that we proclaimed among you — I mean Silvanus and Timothy and I — was never Yes and No: with him it was always Yes, and however many the promises God made, the Yes to them all is in him. That is why it is 'through him' that we answer Amen to the praise of God. Remember it is God himself who assures us all, and you, of our standing in Christ, and has anointed us, marking us with his seal and giving us the pledge, the Spirit, that we carry in our hearts.

    This is the word of the Lord.

GOSPEL ACCLAMATION   *(Jn 1:14.12)*

Alleluia, alleluia!
The Word was made flesh and lived among us;
to all who did accept him
he gave power to become children of God.
Alleluia!

or   *(cf. Lk 4:18)*

Alleluia, alleluia!
The Lord has sent me to bring the good news to the poor,
to proclaim liberty to captives.
Alleluia!

GOSPEL   *(Mk 2:1-12)*

A reading from the holy Gospel according to Mark.

The Son of Man has authority on earth to forgive sins.

When Jesus returned to Capernaum, word went round that he was back; and so many people collected that there was no room left, even in front of the door. He was preaching the word to them when some people came bringing him a paralytic carried by four men, but as the crowds made it impossible to get the man to him, they stripped the roof over the place where Jesus was; and when they had made an opening, they lowered the stretcher on which the paralytic lay. Seeing their faith, Jesus said to the paralytic, 'My child, your sins are forgiven.' Now some scribes were sitting there, and they thought to themselves, 'How can this man talk like that? He is blaspheming. Who can forgive sins but God?' Jesus, inwardly aware that this was what they were thinking, said to them, 'Why do you have these thoughts in your hearts? Which of these is easier: to say to the paralytic, "Your sins are forgiven" or to say, "Get up, pick up your stretcher and walk?" But to prove to you that the Son of Man has authority on earth to forgive sins,' — he said to the paralytic — 'I order you: get up, pick up your stretcher, and go off home.' And the man got up, picked up his stretcher at once and walked out in front of everyone, so that they were all astounded and praised God saying, 'We have never seen anything like this.'

This is the Gospel of the Lord.

PROFESSION OF FAITH — *pages 15-16*

PRAYER OVER THE GIFTS

Lord, as we make this offering,
may our worship in Spirit and truth
bring us salvation

PREFACE OF SUNDAYS IN ORDINARY TIME I-VIII — *pages 22-25*

COMMUNION ANTIPHON   *(Ps 9:2-3)*

I will tell all your marvellous works. I will rejoice and be glad in you, and sing to your name, Most High.

or   *(Jn 11:27)*

Lord, I believe that you are the Christ, the Son of God, who was to come into this world.

PRAYER AFTER COMMUNION

Almighty God,
help us to live the example of love
we celebrate in this eucharist,
that we may come to its fulfilment in your presence.

SOLEMN BLESSING — *pages 57-58*

REFLECTION

The reality of Jesus is that he is human and he is divine. These are two sides of his person. At various times in the history of Christianity, one side has tended to be emphasised at the expense of the other. But when this happens something is wrong. The tradition of the Church in its great early Councils has insisted that both are essential to understand the whole Jesus.

25 FEBRUARY

ASH WEDNESDAY

The season of Lent begins today. It will continue for five and a half weeks, forty days traditionally, and will be followed by Holy Week and then by Eastertide which will last for seven weeks ending on the fiftieth day, Pentecost. Today is one of the two days in the year that we are required to fast and abstain. Fasting was encouraged by the Lord by both word and example and was coupled by him with prayer.

ENTRANCE ANTIPHON *(cf. Ws 11:24-25.27)*

Lord, you are merciful to all, and hate nothing you have created. You overlook the sins of men to bring them to repentance. You are the Lord our God.

(The penitential rite is replaced by the giving of ashes — see below. The Gloria is omitted.)

OPENING PRAYER

Let us pray
 [for the grace to keep Lent faithfully]
Lord,
protect us in our struggle against evil.
As we begin the discipline of Lent,
make this season holy by our self-denial.
or
Let us pray
 [in quiet remembrance of our need for redemption]
Father in heaven,
the light of your truth bestows sight
to the darkness of sinful eyes.
May this season of repentance
bring us the blessing of your forgiveness
and the gift of your light.

FIRST READING *(Joel 2:12-18)*

A reading from the prophet Joel.
Let your hearts be broken, not your garments torn.

'Now, now — it is the Lord who speaks —
come back to me with all your heart,
fasting, weeping, mourning.'
Let your hearts be broken not your garments torn,

turn to the Lord your God again,
for he is all tenderness and compassion,
slow to anger, rich in graciousness,
and ready to relent.
Who knows if he will not turn again, will not relent,
will not leave a blessing as he passes,
oblation and libation
for the Lord your God?
Sound the trumpet in Zion!
Order a fast,
proclaim a solemn assembly,
call the people together,
summon the community,
assemble the elders,
gather the children,
even the infants at the breast.
Let the bridegroom leave his bedroom
and the bride her alcove.
Between vestibule and altar let the priests,
the ministers of the Lord, lament.
Let them say,
'Spare your people, Lord!
Do not make your heritage a thing of shame,
a byword for the nations.
Why should it be said among the nations,
"Where is their God?" '
Then the Lord, jealous on behalf of his land,
took pity on his people.

> This is the word of the Lord.

RESPONSORIAL PSALM   (Ps 50:3-6.12-14.17)

℟ **Have mercy on us, O Lord, for we have sinned.**

1. Have mercy on me, God, in your kindness.
    In your compassion blot out my offence.
    O wash me more and more from my guilt
    and cleanse me from my sin. ℟

2. My offences truly I know them;
    my sin is always before me.
    Against you, you alone, have I sinned:
    what is evil in your sight I have done. ℟

3. A pure heart create for me, O God,
    put a steadfast spirit within me.

Do not cast me away from your presence,
nor deprive me of your holy spirit. ℟

4. Give me again the joy of your help;
with a spirit of fervour sustain me.
O Lord, open my lips
and my mouth shall declare your praise. ℟

SECOND READING   *(2 Cor 5:20–6:2)*

A reading from the second letter of St Paul to the Corinthians.

Be reconciled to God… now is the favourable time.

We are ambassadors for Christ; it is as though God were
appealing through us, and the appeal that we make in Christ's
name is: be reconciled to God. For our sake God made the
sinless one into sin, so that in him we might become the
goodness of God. As his fellow workers, we beg you once again
not to neglect the grace of God that you have received. For he
says: At the favourable time, I have listened to you; on the day
of salvation I came to your help. Well, now is the favourable
time; this is the day of salvation.

This is the word of the Lord.

GOSPEL ACCLAMATION   *(Ps 50:12.14)*

Praise to you, O Christ, king of eternal glory!
A pure heart create for me, O God,
and give me again the joy of your help.
Praise to you, O Christ, king of eternal glory!

or   *(cf. Ps 94:8)*

Praise to you, O Christ, king of eternal glory!
Harden not your hearts today,
but listen to the voice of the Lord.
Praise to you, O Christ, King of eternal glory!

GOSPEL   *(Mt 6:1-6.16-18)*

A reading from the holy Gospel according to Matthew.

Your Father, who sees all that is done in secret, will reward you.

Jesus said to his disciples:

'Be careful not to parade your good deeds before men to
attract their notice; by doing this you will lose all reward from
your Father in heaven. So when you give alms, do not have it
trumpeted before you; this is what the hypocrites do in the
synagogues and in the streets to win men's admiration. I tell
you solemnly, they have had their reward. But when you give

alms, your left hand must not know what your right is doing;
your almsgiving must be secret, and your Father who sees all
that is done in secret will reward you.

'And when you pray, do not imitate the hypocrites: they
love to say their prayers standing up in the synagogues and at
the street corners for people to see them. I tell you solemnly,
they have had their reward. But when you pray go to your
private room and, when you have shut your door, pray to your
Father who is in that secret place, and your Father who sees all
that is done in secret will reward you.

'When you fast do not put on a gloomy look as the
hypocrites do: they pull long faces to let men know they are
fasting. I tell you solemnly, they have had their reward. But
when you fast, put oil on your head and wash your face, so that
no one will know you are fasting except your Father who sees all
that is done in secret; and your Father who sees all that is done
in secret will reward you.'

This is the Gospel of the Lord.

CEREMONY OF ASHES

In the Bible to cover one's head with ashes, to wear sackcloth
and to fast are penitential signs; they express the sinner's repentance
imploring the divine mercy.

So, our reception of ashes at the beginning of Lent means
we recognise ourselves as sinners. We ask God's pardon for his
Church and show our sincere desire to change our ways. Faith
in the Lord's word makes us pass with him from death to life.

BLESSING AND GIVING OF ASHES

After the homily the priest joins his hands and says:

Dear friends in Christ,
let us ask our Father
to bless these ashes
which we will use
as the mark of our repentance.

Silent prayer

Lord,
bless the sinner who asks for your forgiveness
and bless ✠ all those who receive these ashes.
May they keep this lenten season
in preparation for the joy of Easter.

or

Lord,
bless these ashes ✠
by which we show that we are dust.
Pardon our sins
and keep us faithful to the discipline of Lent,
for you do not want sinners to die
but to live with the risen Christ,
who reigns with you for ever and ever.

He sprinkles the ashes with holy water in silence. The priest then places ashes on those who come forward, saying to each:

Turn away from sin and be faithful to the gospel.

or

Remember, you are dust
and to dust you will return.

Meanwhile some of the following antiphons or other appropriate songs are sung.

ANTIPHON 1   *(cf. Joel 2:13)*

Come back to the Lord with all your heart;
leave the past in ashes,
and turn to God with tears and fasting,
for he is slow to anger and ready to forgive.

ANTIPHON 2   *(cf. Joel 2:17; Est 13:17)*

Let the priests and ministers of the Lord
lament before his altar, and say:
Spare us, Lord; spare your people!
Do not let us die for we are crying out to you.

ANTIPHON 3   *(Ps 50:3)*

Lord, take away our wickedness.

These may be repeated after each verse of Psalm 50, 'Have mercy on me, God' (page 104).

RESPONSORY   *(cf. Ba 3:5; Ps 78:9)*

Direct our hearts to better things, O Lord;
heal our sin and ignorance.
Lord, do not face us suddenly with death,
but give us time to repent.

℟   **Turn to us with mercy, Lord; we have sinned against you.**
℣   **Help us, God our Saviour, rescue us for the honour of**
          your name.
℟   **Turn to us with mercy, Lord; we have sinned against you.**

The rite concludes with the Prayer of the Faithful. *The* Profession of Faith *is not said.*

PRAYER OVER THE GIFTS

Lord,
help us to resist temptation
by our lenten works of charity and penance.
By this sacrifice
may we be prepared to celebrate
the death and resurrection of Christ our Saviour
and be cleansed from sin and renewed in spirit.

PREFACE OF LENT IV

Father, all-powerful and ever-living God,
we do well always and everywhere to give you thanks.

Through our observance of Lent
you correct our faults and raise our minds to you,
you help us grow in holiness,
and offer us the reward of everlasting life
through Jesus Christ our Lord.

Through him the angels and all the choirs of heaven
worship in awe before your presence.
May our voices be one with theirs
as they sing with joy the hymn of your glory:
Holy, holy, holy...

COMMUNION ANTIPHON   *(Ps 1:2-3)*

**The man who meditates day and night on the law of the Lord
will yield fruit in due season.**

PRAYER AFTER COMMUNION

Lord,
through this communion
may our lenten penance give you glory
and bring us your protection.

REFLECTION

As a penitential practice, fasting was observed from different motives. Some of the common reasons today for fasting are to be in solidarity with those who are hungry, to deny oneself so that another may have something, to facilitate the process of repentance which means a change of heart or attitude. And so each moment of awareness of hunger becomes an opportunity to double our resolve to embark on the road we have chosen.

1 MARCH

FIRST SUNDAY OF LENT

Lent coincides with springtime and in fact the word itself probably comes from the Old English *lencten,* meaning the lengthening of the days that occurs in spring. And indeed spring is not a bad image for Lent. Spring is the time of new life when the long nights of winter become a thing of the past. It is a time when the hearts of many people lift. Lent offers the possibility to renew and reawaken the life of the spirit and so is a season of joy.

ENTRANCE ANTIPHON   *(Ps 90:15-16)*
When he calls to me, I will answer; I will rescue him and give him honour. Long life and contentment will be his.

GREETING, PENITENTIAL RITE — *pages 7-13*
The Gloria *is omitted.*
OPENING PRAYER
Let us pray
[that this Lent will help us reproduce in our lives
the self-sacrificing love of Christ]
Father,
through our observance of Lent,
help us to understand the meaning
of your Son's death and resurrection,
and teach us to reflect it in our lives.
or
Let us pray
[at the beginning of Lent
for the spirit of repentance]
Lord our God,
you formed man from the clay of the earth
and breathed into him the spirit of life,
but he turned from your face and sinned.

In this time of repentance
we call out for your mercy.
Bring us back to you
and to the life your Son won for us
by his death on the cross
for he lives and reigns for ever and ever.

FIRST READING   *(Gen 9:8-15)*

A reading from the book of Genesis.

God's covenant with Noah after he had saved him from the waters of the flood.

God spoke to Noah and his sons, 'See, I establish my Covenant with you, and with your descendants after you; also with every living creature to be found with you, birds, cattle and every wild beast with you: everything that came out of the ark, everything that lives on the earth. I establish my Covenant with you: no thing of flesh shall be swept away again by the waters of the flood. There shall be no flood to destroy the earth again.'

God said, 'Here is the sign of the Covenant I make between myself and you and every living creature with you for all generations: I set my bow in the clouds and it shall be a sign of the Covenant between me and the earth. When I gather the clouds over the earth and the bow appears in the clouds, I will recall the Covenant between myself and you and every living creature of every kind. And so the waters shall never again become a flood to destroy all things of flesh.'

This is the word of the Lord.

RESPONSORIAL PSALM   *(Ps 24:4-9)*

℞   **Your ways, Lord, are faithfulness and love**
     for those who keep your covenant.

1.   Lord, make me know your ways.
     Lord, teach me your paths.
     Make me walk in your truth, and teach me:
     for you are God my saviour. ℞

2.   Remember your mercy, Lord,
     and the love you have shown from of old.
     In your love remember me,
     because of your goodness, O Lord. ℞

3.   The Lord is good and upright.
     He shows the path to those who stray,
     he guides the humble in the right path;
     he teaches his way to the poor. ℞

SECOND READING   *(1 Pt 3:18-22)*

A reading from the first letter of St Peter.

That water is a type of the baptism which saves you now.

Christ himself, innocent though he was, died once for sins, died for the guilty, to lead us to God. In the body he was put to death, in the spirit he was raised to life, and, in the spirit, he went to preach to the spirits in prison. Now it was long ago, when Noah was still building that ark which saved only a small group of eight people 'by water', and when God was still waiting patiently, that these spirits refused to believe. That water is a type of the baptism which saves you now, and which is not the washing off of physical dirt but a pledge made to God from a good conscience, through the resurrection of Jesus Christ, who has entered heaven and is at God's right hand, now that he has made the angels and Dominations and Powers his subjects.

This is the word of the Lord.

GOSPEL ACCLAMATION *(Mt 4:4)*

Praise to you, O Christ, king of eternal glory!
Man does not live on bread alone,
but on every word that comes from the mouth of God.
Praise to you, O Christ, king of eternal glory!

GOSPEL *(Mk 1:12-15)*

A reading from the holy Gospel according to Mark.

Jesus was tempted by Satan, and the angels looked after him.

The Spirit drove Jesus out into the wilderness and he remained there for forty days, and was tempted by Satan. He was with the wild beasts, and the angels looked after him.

After John had been arrested, Jesus went into Galilee. There he proclaimed the Good News from God. 'The time has come' he said 'and the kingdom of God is close at hand. Repent, and believe the Good News.'

This is the Gospel of the Lord.

PROFESSION OF FAITH — *pages 15-16*

PRAYER OVER THE GIFTS

Lord,
make us worthy to bring you these gifts.
May this sacrifice
help to change our lives.

PREFACE OF THE FIRST SUNDAY OF LENT

Father, all-powerful and ever-living God,
we do well always and everywhere to give you thanks
through Jesus Christ our Lord.

His fast of forty days
makes this a holy season of self-denial.

By rejecting the devil's temptations
he has taught us
to rid ourselves of the hidden corruption of evil,
and so to share his paschal meal in purity of heart,
until we come to its fulfilment
in the promised land of heaven.

Now we join the angels and the saints
as they sing their unending hymn of praise:
Holy, holy, holy…

COMMUNION ANTIPHON   *(Mt 4:4)*

Man does not live on bread alone, but on every word that comes from the mouth of God.

or   *(Ps 90:4)*

The Lord will overshadow you, and you will find refuge under his wings.

PRAYER AFTER COMMUNION

Father,
you increase our faith and hope,
you deepen our love in this communion.
Help us to live by your words
and to seek Christ, our bread of life,
who is Lord for ever and ever.

REFLECTION

> If repentance means a change of attitude or of heart what
> attitude is good to adopt? Is it that frame of mind and spirit
> which recognises that conversion is a daily and a life's project?
> Is it the insight which accepts that what God is inviting us to
> will always surprise us, will never be the merely predictable?
> Is it the grace to believe that God is on our side? If so, this is
> the springtime of the year and the seeds of new life contained
> in these and similar interpretations of the word 'repent' may
> usefully be sown.

2 MARCH

ST DAVID

(Patron of Wales — transferred from the Sunday)

The celebration of the patron of a particular area is an opportunity to consider that history has an important place in bringing forth the kingdom of God. In the Hebrew Scriptures God acted through the events of history. Since the birth of the Church the spreading of the kingdom of God depends on his disciples being willing to act in history. The gospel will not be proclaimed unless there is someone to proclaim it.

ENTRANCE ANTIPHON *(Is 59:21; 56:7)*

My teaching, which I have put in your mouth, will never fail, says the Lord; the gifts which you offered on my altar will be accepted.

or *(Ps 15:5-6)*

You, Lord, are my portion and cup, you restore my inheritance to me; the way of life you marked out for me has made my heritage glorious.

GREETING, PENITENTIAL RITE, GLORIA — *pages 7-14*

OPENING PRAYER

God our Father,
you gave the bishop David to the Welsh Church
to uphold the faith
and to be an example of Christian perfection.
In this changing world
may he help us to hold fast to the values
which bring eternal life.

FIRST READING *(Ph 3:8-14)*

A reading from the letter of St Paul to the Philippians.

I am racing for the finish, for the prize to which God calls us upwards to receive in Christ Jesus.

I believe nothing can happen that will outweigh the supreme advantage of knowing Christ Jesus my Lord. For him I have accepted the loss of everything, and I look on everything as so much rubbish if only I can have Christ and be given a place in him. I am no longer trying for perfection by my own efforts, the perfection that comes from the Law, but I want only the perfection that comes through faith in Christ, and is from God and based on faith. All I want is to know Christ and the power of his resurrection and to share his sufferings by reproducing the pattern of his death. That is the way I can hope to take my place in the resurrection of the dead. Not that I have become perfect yet: I have not yet won, but I am still running, trying to capture the prize for which Christ Jesus captured me. I can assure you my brothers, I am far from thinking that I have already won. All I can say is that I forget the past and I strain ahead for what is still to come; I am racing for the finish, for the prize to which God calls us upwards to receive in Christ Jesus.

This is the word of the Lord.

RESPONSORIAL PSALM   *(Ps 1:1-4.6)*

℟ **Happy the man who has placed**
   his trust in the Lord.

1. Happy indeed is the man
    who follows not the counsel of the wicked,
    nor lingers in the way of sinners
    nor sits in the company of scorners,
    but whose delight is the law of the Lord
    and who ponders his law day and night. ℟

2. He is like a tree that is planted
    beside the flowing waters,
    that yields its fruit in due season
    and whose leaves shall never fade;
    and all that he does shall prosper.

3. Not so are the wicked, not so!
    For they like winnowed chaff
    shall be driven away by the wind;
    for the Lord guards the way of the just
    but the way of the wicked leads to doom. ℟

GOSPEL ACCLAMATION   *(Jn 8:31-32)*
Glory to you, O Christ, you are the word of God.
If you make my word your home
you will indeed be my disciples,
and you will learn the truth, says the Lord.
Glory to you, O Christ, you are the word of God.

GOSPEL   *(Mt 5:13-16)*
A reading from the holy Gospel according to Matthew.
You are the light of the world.
Jesus said to his disciples: 'You are the salt of the earth. But if salt becomes tasteless, what can make it salty again? It is

good for nothing, and can only be thrown out to be trampled underfoot by men.

'You are the light of the world. A city built on a hill-top cannot be hidden. No one lights a lamp to put it under a tub; they put it on the lamp-stand where it shines for everyone in the house. In the same way your light must shine in the sight of men, so that, seeing your good works, they may give the praise to your Father in heaven.'

This is the Gospel of the Lord.

PROFESSION OF FAITH — *pages 15-16*

PRAYER OVER THE GIFTS

Lord,
accept the gifts we bring
on the feast of Saint David.
We offer them to win your forgiveness
and to give honour to your name.

PREFACE OF HOLY MEN AND WOMEN I

Father, all-powerful and ever-living God,
we do well always and everywhere to give you thanks.

You are glorified in your saints,
for their glory is the crowning of your gifts.
In their lives on earth
you give us an example.
In our communion with them,
you give us their friendship.
In their prayer for the Church
you give us strength and protection.
This great company of witnesses spurs us on to victory,
to share their prize of everlasting glory,
through Jesus Christ our Lord.

With angels and archangels
and the whole company of saints
we sing our unending hymn of praise:
Holy, holy, holy…

COMMUNION ANTIPHON (Mk 10:45)

The Son of Man came to give his life as a ransom for all.

or (cf. Mt 19:27.29)

I assure you who left all and followed me: you will receive a hundredfold in return and inherit eternal life.

PRAYER AFTER COMMUNION
All-powerful God,
you have strengthened us with this sacrament.
May we learn from Saint David's example
to seek you above all things,
and to live always as new men in Christ,
who lives and reigns for ever and ever.

REFLECTION

> Each generation has its role to play in the handing on of the
> faith. If the chain of faith is to be complete each link matters.
> There are many people who have not had the faith preached
> to them. The missionary character of the Church means that
> faith is not intended merely to be kept but to be handed on.
> This is what St David did. And this is what the women and
> men who have gone before us bequeathed to us.

=========== 8 MARCH ===========

SECOND SUNDAY OF LENT

As Lent progresses, the shadow of the cross begins to loom.
Even though the gospel narrates the account of the transfiguration
of Jesus in glory it is in the light of his death and resurrection
that this scene is to be viewed. The last sentence makes this clear.
The obedience of Jesus is seen to be prefigured in that of Abraham
who offered his only son, and through him his hope of descendants,
to God when commanded to do so. God's promise to Abraham
subsequently is also seen to have been fulfilled in a manner
beyond all expectation by his raising of Jesus from death.

ENTRANCE ANTIPHON   (Ps 24:6.3.22)
**Remember your mercies, Lord, your tenderness from ages
past. Do not let our enemies triumph over us; O God, deliver
Israel from all her distress.**

or   (Ps 26:8-9)
**My heart has prompted me to seek your face; I seek it, Lord;
do not hide from me.**

GREETING, PENITENTIAL RITE — *pages 7-13*

The Gloria is omitted.

OPENING PRAYER

Let us pray
[for the grace to respond to the Word of God]
God our Father,
help us to hear your Son.
Enlighten us with your word,
that we may find the way to your glory.
or

Let us pray
[in this season of Lent for the gift of integrity]
Father of light,
in you is found no shadow of change
but only the fullness of life and limitless truth.

Open our hearts to the voice of your Word
and free us from the original darkness that shadows our vision.
Restore our sight that we may look upon your Son
who calls us to repentance and a change of heart,
for he lives and reigns with you for ever and ever.

FIRST READING   *(Gen 22:1-2.9-13.15-18)*

A reading from the book of Genesis.
The sacrifice of Abraham, our father in faith.

God put Abraham to the test. 'Abraham, Abraham' he called.
'Here I am' he replied. 'Take your son', God said 'your only child
Isaac, whom you love, and go to the land of Moriah. There you
shall offer him as a burnt offering, on a mountain I will point
out to you.'

When they arrived at the place God had pointed out to
him, Abraham built an altar there and arranged the wood. Then
he stretched out his hand and seized the knife to kill his son.

But the angel of the Lord called to him from heaven.
'Abraham, Abraham' he said. 'I am here' he replied. 'Do not
raise your hand against the boy' the angel said. 'Do not harm
him, for now I know you fear God. You have not refused me
your son, your only son.' Then looking up, Abraham saw a
ram caught by its horns in a bush. Abraham took the ram and
offered it as a burnt-offering in place of his son.

The angel of the Lord called Abraham a second time from
heaven. 'I swear by my own self — it is the Lord who speaks
— because you have done this, because you have not refused
me your son, your only son, I will shower blessings on you, I
will make your descendants as many as the stars of heaven and

the grains of sand on the seashore. Your descendants shall gain possession of the gates of their enemies. All the nations of the earth shall bless themselves by your descendants, as a reward for your obedience.'

This is the word of the Lord.

RESPONSORIAL PSALM   *(Ps 115:10.15-19)*

℟   **I will walk in the presence of the Lord**
    in the land of the living.

1.   I trusted, even when I said:
     'I am sorely afflicted.'
     O precious in the eyes of the Lord
     is the death of his faithful. ℟

2.   Your servant, Lord, your servant am I;
     you have loosened my bonds.
     A thanksgiving sacrifice I make:
     I will call on the Lord's name. ℟

3.   My vows to the Lord I will fulfil
     before all his people,
     in the courts of the house of the Lord,
     in your midst, O Jerusalem.

SECOND READING   *(Rm 8:31-34)*
A reading from the letter of St Paul to the Romans.
God did not spare his own Son.

With God on our side who can be against us? Since God did not spare his own Son, but gave him up to benefit us all, we may be certain, after such a gift, that he will not refuse anything he can give. Could anyone accuse those that God has chosen? When God acquits, could anyone condemn? Could Christ Jesus? No! He not only died for us — he rose from the dead, and there at God's right hand he stands and pleads for us.

This is the word of the Lord.

GOSPEL ACCLAMATION   *(Mt 17:5)*
Glory and praise to you, O Christ!
From the bright cloud the Father's voice was heard:
'This is my Son, the Beloved. Listen to him!'
Glory and praise to you, O Christ!

GOSPEL   *(Mk 9:2-10)*

A reading from the holy Gospel according to Mark.

This is my Son, the Beloved.

Jesus took with him Peter and James and John and led them up a high mountain where they could be alone by themselves. There in their presence he was transfigured: his clothes became dazzlingly white, whiter than any earthly bleacher could make them. Elijah appeared to them with Moses; and they were talking with Jesus. Then Peter spoke to Jesus. 'Rabbi', he said 'it is wonderful for us to be here; so let us make three tents, one for you, one for Moses and one for Elijah'. He did not know what to say; they were so frightened. And a cloud came, covering them in shadow; and there came a voice from the cloud, 'This is my Son, the Beloved. Listen to him'. Then suddenly, when they looked round, they saw no one with them any more but only Jesus.

As they came down the mountain he warned them to tell no one what they had seen, until after the Son of Man had risen from the dead. They observed the warning faithfully, though among themselves they discussed what 'rising from the dead' could mean.

This is the Gospel of the Lord.

PROFESSION OF FAITH — *pages 15-16*

PRAYER OVER THE GIFTS

Lord, make us holy.
May this eucharist take away our sins
that we may be prepared
to celebrate the resurrection.

PREFACE OF THE SECOND SUNDAY OF LENT

Father, all-powerful and ever-living God,
we do well always and everywhere to give you thanks
through Jesus Christ our Lord.

On your holy mountain he revealed himself in glory
in the presence of his disciples.
He had already prepared them for his approaching death.
He wanted to teach them through the Law and the Prophets
that the promised Christ had first to suffer
and so come to the glory of his resurrection.

In our unending joy we echo on earth
the song of the angels in heaven
as they praise your glory for ever:
Holy, holy, holy…

COMMUNION ANTIPHON   (Mt 17:5)

This is my Son, my beloved, in whom is all my delight: listen to him.

PRAYER AFTER COMMUNION

Lord, we give thanks for these holy mysteries
which bring to us here on earth a share in the life to come,
through Christ our Lord.

REFLECTION

Just as, for a greater good, Abraham is prepared to do the
unthinkable, so the Father, because he loved the world so
much, gave his only Son, that the people of the world might
believe in him. We need to consider this aspect of the suffering
and death of Jesus as an antidote to the sometimes vengeful
image put forward of a God who demands the death of his
Son for the redemption of the world.

--------------- 15 MARCH ---------------

THIRD SUNDAY OF LENT

As Lent moves on, the cross comes into clear focus. Today the
story of the cleansing of the temple is recounted for us. What
was at issue for the Jews was the authority by which Jesus could
claim to do this. The answer is found in the phrase 'and when
Jesus rose from the dead'. John, the writer, interprets the death
and resurrection of Jesus as the basis for his authority. This
idea is paralleled in the first reading where the ten commandments
are given their authority by being spoken by the mouth of God.

ENTRANCE ANTIPHON   (Ps 24:15-16)

**My eyes are ever fixed on the Lord, for he releases my feet from
the snare. O look at me and be merciful, for I am wretched
and alone.**

or   (Ezk 36:23-26)

**I will prove my holiness through you. I will gather you from
the ends of the earth; I will pour clean water on you and
wash away all your sins. I will give you a new spirit within
you, says the Lord.**

GREETING, PENITENTIAL RITE — *pages 7-13*

The Gloria *is omitted.*

OPENING PRAYER

Let us pray
> [for confidence in the love of God
> and the strength to overcome all our weakness]

Father,
you have taught us to overcome our sins
by prayer, fasting and works of mercy.
When we are discouraged by our weakness,
give us confidence in your love.

or

Let us pray
> [to the Father and ask him
> to form a new heart within us]

God of all compassion,
Father of all goodness,
to heal the wounds our sins and selfishness bring upon us
you bid us turn to fasting, prayer, and sharing with our brothers.
We acknowledge our sinfulness, our guilt is ever before us:
when our weakness causes discouragement,
let your compassion fill us with hope
and lead us through a Lent of repentance to the beauty of
> Easter joy.

FIRST READING   *(Ex 20:1-17)*

(For Shorter Form, *read between* ▶ ◀*)*

A reading from the book of Exodus.

The Law was given through Moses.

▶God spoke all these words. He said, 'I am the Lord your God who brought you out of the land of Egypt, out of the house of slavery.

'You shall have no gods except me.◀

'You shall not make yourself a carved image or any likeness of anything in heaven or on earth beneath or in the waters under the earth; you shall not bow down to them or serve them. For I, the Lord your God, am a jealous God and I punish the father's fault in the sons, the grandsons, and the great-grandsons of those who hate me; but I show kindness to thousands of those who love me and keep my commandments.

▶'You shall not utter the name of the Lord your God to misuse it, for the Lord will not leave unpunished the man who utters his name to misuse it.

'Remember the sabbath day and keep it holy.◆ For six days you shall labour and do all your work, but the seventh day is a sabbath for the Lord your God. You shall do no work that day, neither you nor your son nor your daughter nor your servants, men or women, nor your animals nor the stranger who lives with you. For in six days the Lord made the heavens and the earth and the sea and all that these hold, but on the seventh day he rested; that is why the Lord has blessed the sabbath day and made it sacred.

◆'Honour your father and your mother so that you may have a long life in the land that the Lord your God has given to you.

'You shall not kill.

'You shall not commit adultery.

'You shall not steal.

'You shall not bear false witness against your neighbour.

'You shall not covet your neighbour's house. You shall not covet your neighbour's wife, or his servant, man or woman, or his ox, or his donkey, or anything that is his.'

This is the word of the Lord.◆

RESPONSORIAL PSALM   (Ps 18:8-11)

℟ **You, Lord, have the message of eternal life.**

1. The law of the Lord is perfect,
    it revives the soul.
    The rule of the Lord is to be trusted,
    it gives wisdom to the simple. ℟

2. The precepts of the Lord are right,
    they gladden the heart.
    The command of the Lord is clear,
    it gives light to the eyes. ℟

3. The fear of the Lord is holy,
    abiding for ever.
    The decrees of the Lord are truth
    and all of them just. ℟

4. They are more to be desired than gold,
    than the purest of gold
    and sweeter are they than honey,
    than honey from the comb. ℟

SECOND READING *(1 Cor 1:22-25)*

A reading from the first letter of St Paul to the Corinthians.

Here we are preaching a crucified Christ, an obstacle to men, but to those who are called, the wisdom of God.

While the Jews demand miracles and the Greeks look for wisdom, here are we preaching a crucified Christ; to the Jews an obstacle that they cannot get over, to the pagans madness, but to those who have been called, whether they are Jews or Greeks, a Christ who is the power and the wisdom of God. For God's foolishness is wiser than human wisdom, and God's weakness is stronger than human strength.

This is the word of the Lord.

GOSPEL ACCLAMATION *(Jn 11:25.26)*

Praise to you, O Christ, king of eternal glory!
I am the resurrection and the life, says the Lord,
whoever believes in me will never die.
Praise to you, O Christ, king of eternal glory!

or *(Jn 3:16)*

Praise to you, O Christ, king of eternal glory!
God loved the world so much that he gave his only Son;
everyone who believes in him has eternal life.
Praise to you, O Christ, king of eternal glory!

GOSPEL *(Jn 2:13-25)*

A reading from the holy Gospel according to John.

Destroy this sanctuary, and in three days I will raise it up.

Just before the Jewish Passover Jesus went up to Jerusalem, and in the Temple he found people selling cattle and sheep and pigeons, and the money changers sitting at their counters there. Making a whip out of some cord, he drove them all out of the Temple, cattle and sheep as well, scattered the money changers' coins, knocked their tables over and said to the pigeon-sellers, 'Take all this out of here and stop turning my Father's house into a market.' Then his disciples remembered the words of scripture: Zeal for your house will devour me. The Jews intervened and said, 'What sign can you show us to justify what you have done?' Jesus answered, 'Destroy this sanctuary, and in three days I will raise it up'. The Jews replied, 'It has taken forty-six years to build this sanctuary: are you going to raise it up in three days?' But he was speaking of the sanctuary that was his body, and when Jesus rose from the dead, his disciples remembered that he had said this, and they believed the scripture and the words he had said.

During his stay in Jerusalem for the Passover many believed in his name when they saw the signs that he gave, but Jesus knew them all and did not trust himself to them; he never needed evidence about any man; he could tell what a man had in him.

This is the Gospel of the Lord.

PROFESSION OF FAITH — *pages 15-16*

PRAYER OVER THE GIFTS
Lord,
by the grace of this sacrifice
may we who ask forgiveness
be ready to forgive one another.

PREFACE OF LENT I or II — *page 20*

COMMUNION ANTIPHON   *(Ps 83:3-4)*
The sparrow even finds a home, the swallow finds a nest wherein to place her young, near to your altars, Lord of hosts, my King, my God! How happy they who dwell in your house! For ever they are praising you.

PRAYER AFTER COMMUNION
Lord,
in sharing this sacrament
may we receive your forgiveness
and be brought together in unity and peace.

REFLECTION
The New Testament speaks of God's raising Jesus from the dead and of Jesus' rising from the dead. In today's gospel it is the latter phrase that is used by John. The technique of having hearers misunderstand a saying of Jesus is one familiar to the fourth gospel. The correct understanding always follows as here. The result of the signs which Jesus worked, and his rising from the dead, was the greatest of these, namely, belief. The effectiveness of all the signs portrayed is measured by whether or not they bring about the belief of the hearers or onlookers.

17 MARCH

ST PATRICK
(Patron of Ireland)

God's plan for salvation took root in a particular race over a long period of time. On the face of it these people were a most unlikely choice in that they were never one of the great military powers of their day. Over the course of the centuries prophetic figures moved to indicate that God's plan was not just for the Jewish people but would embrace all of humankind. The outward movement of the early Church of the Acts of the Apostles confirmed this direction. We attribute the forging of the link between this development of Jewish and Christian origins and Ireland to a particular person at a particular time in history. The time: the mid-fifth century, the person: Patrick.

ENTRANCE ANTIPHON   *(Gen 12:1-2)*

Go from your country and your kindred and your father's house to the land that I will show you; and I will make you the father of a great people.

GREETING, PENITENTIAL RITE, GLORIA — *pages 7-14*

OPENING PRAYER

Lord,
through the work of Saint Patrick in Ireland
we have come to acknowledge the mystery of the one true God
and give thanks for our salvation in Christ;
grant by his prayers
that we who celebrate this festival
may keep alive the fire of faith he kindled.
Through our Lord Jesus Christ, your Son,
who lives and reigns with you and the Holy Spirit,
one God, for ever and ever.

FIRST READING   *(Jr 1:4-9)*

A reading from the prophet Jeremiah.
You shall go to all to whom I send you..

The word of the Lord was addressed to me, saying,
'Before I formed you in the womb I knew you;
before you came to birth I consecrated you;
I have appointed you as prophet to the nations.
I said, 'Ah, Lord God; look, I do not know how to speak: I am a child!'

But the Lord replied,

> 'Do not say, "I am a child."
> Go now to those to whom I send you
> and say whatever I command you.
> Do not be afraid of them,
> for I am with you to protect you —
> it is the Lord who speaks!'

Then the Lord put out his hand and touched my mouth and said to me:

> 'There! I am putting my words into your mouth.'

This is the word of the Lord.

RESPONSORIAL PSALM   *(Ps 116. R/. Mk 16:15)*

℞   **Go out to the whole world:**
    proclaim the Good News.

1.   O praise the Lord, all you nations,
     acclaim him all you peoples. ℞

2.   Strong is his love for us;
     he is faithful for ever. ℞

SECOND READING   *(Roms 10:9-18)*
A reading from the letter of St Paul to the Romans.

Faith comes from what is heard, through the Word Christ.

If your lips confess that Jesus is Lord and if you believe in your heart that God raised him from the dead, then you will be saved. By believing from the heart you are made righteous; by confessing with your lips you are saved. When scripture says: those who believe in him will have no cause for shame, it makes no distinction between Jew and Greek: all belong to the same Lord who is rich enough, however many ask his help, for everyone who calls on the name of the Lord will be saved.

But they will not ask his help unless they believe in him, and they will not believe in him unless they have heard of him, and they will not hear of him unless they get a preacher, and they will never have a preacher unless one is sent, but as scripture says: The footsteps of those who bring good news are a welcome sound. Not everyone, of course, listens to the Good News. As Isaiah says: Lord, how many believed what we proclaimed? So faith comes from what is preached, and what is preached comes from the word of Christ.

Let me put the question: is it possible that they did not hear? Indeed they did; in the words of the psalm, their voice has gone out through all the earth, and their message to the ends of the world.

This is the word of the Lord.

GOSPEL ACCLAMATION   *(Mt 28:19-20)*

Glory to you, O Christ, you are the Word of God!
Go, make disciples of all nations, says the Lord;
I am with you always, yes, to the end of time.
Glory to you, O Christ, you are the Word of God!

GOSPEL   *(Mk 16:15-20)*

A reading from the holy Gospel according to Mark.

They went out and proclaimed the good news everywhere.

Jesus showed himself to the Eleven, and he said to them, 'Go out to the whole world; proclaim the Good News to all creation. He who believes and is baptised will be saved; he who does not believe will be condemned. These are the signs that will be associated with believers: in my name they will cast out devils; they will have the gift of tongues; they will pick up snakes in their hands, and be unharmed should they drink deadly poison; they will lay their hands on the sick, who will recover.'

And so the Lord Jesus, after he had spoken to them, was taken up into heaven: there at the right hand of God he took his place, while they, going out, preached everywhere, the Lord working with them and confirming the word by the signs that accompanied it.

This is the Gospel of the Lord.

PROFESSION OF FAITH — *pages 15-16*

PRAYER OVER THE GIFTS

Lord,
accept this pure sacrifice
which, through the labours of Saint Patrick,
your grateful people make
to the glory of your name.
Through Christ our Lord.

PREFACE

It is truly right and just, our duty and our salvation,
always and everwhere to give you thanks,
Lord, holy Father, almighty and eternal God,
and to offer you fitting praise
as we honour Saint Patrick.

For you drew him through daily prayer
in captivity and hardship
to know you as a loving father.

You chose him out of all the world
to return to the land of his captors,
that they might acknowledge Jesus Christ, their Redeemer.

In the power of your Spirit you directed his paths
to win the sons and daughters of the Irish
to the service of the Triune God.

With joyful hearts we echo on earth
the song of the angels in heaven
as they praise your glory without end:
Holy, holy, holy…

COMMUNION ANTIPHON   *(cf. Mt 8:11)*
**Many will come from east and west and sit down with
Abraham, Isaac and Jacob at the feast in the kingdom of
heaven, says the Lord.**

PRAYER AFTER COMMUNION
Strengthen us, O Lord, by this sacrament
so that we may profess the faith taught by Saint Patrick
an proclaim it in our way of living.
Through Christ our Lord.

SOLEMN BLESSING
May God the Father, who called us together
to celebrate this feast of Saint Patrick,
bless you, protect you and keep you faithful.
Amen.

May Christ the Lord, the High King of Heaven,
be near you at all times and shield you from evil.
Amen.

May the Holy Spirit, who is the source of all holiness,
make you rich in the love of God's people.
Amen.

And may the blessing of almighty God,
the Father, and the Son, ✠ and the Holy Spirit,
come down on you and remain for ever.
Amen.

REFLECTION

> The word which connects the prophetic figures of the Jewish people, of the missioners of the early Church and of Patrick and the other people who spread the Good News to Ireland and elsewhere is 'inclusive'. God's plan for the human race is inclusive of all. This fact will inspire those who seek to eliminate all forms of prejudice and racism and who strive for equality in all areas of the Church's life.

— 22 MARCH —

FOURTH SUNDAY OF LENT

> Today's passage from John's gospel contains one of the most well known sentences of all scripture, the one which declares that God loved the world so much that he sent his only Son. So in human terms, God's motive for sending Jesus among us is love. In other words, all God's actions towards us and his dealings with us are inspired by love. This is good news and if we didn't know it before now, now is the time to take this insight on board and to let it begin to change us.

ENTRANCE ANTIPHON   *(cf Is 66:10-11)*

Rejoice, Jerusalem! Be glad for her, you who love her; rejoice with her, you who mourned for her, and you will find contentment at her consoling breasts.

GREETING, PENITENTIAL RITE — *pages 7-13*

The Gloria *is omitted.*

OPENING PRAYER

Let us pray
    [for a greater faith and love]
Father of peace,
we are joyful in your Word,
your Son Jesus Christ,
who reconciles us to you.
Let us hasten towards Easter
with the eagerness of faith and love.
or

Let us pray
[that by growing in love this lenten season
we may bring the peace of Christ to our world]

God our Father,
your Word, Jesus Christ, spoke peace to a sinful world
and brought mankind the gift of reconciliation
by the suffering and death he endured.

Teach us, the people who bear his name,
to follow the example he gave us:
may our faith, hope, and charity
turn hatred to love, conflict to peace, death to eternal life.

FIRST READING   *(2 Ch 36:14-16.19-23)*

A reading from the second book of Chronicles.

*The wrath and mercy of God are revealed in the exile and in the release
of his people.*

All the heads of the priesthood, and the people too, added
infidelity to infidelity, copying all the shameful practices of the
nations and defiling the Temple that the Lord had consecrated
for himself in Jerusalem. The Lord, the God of their ancestors,
tirelessly sent them messenger after messenger, since he wished
to spare his people and his house. But they ridiculed the
messengers of God, they despised his words, they laughed at his
prophets, until at last the wrath of the Lord rose so high against
his people that there was no further remedy.

Their enemies burned down the Temple of God, demolished
the walls of Jerusalem, set fire to all its palaces, and destroyed
everything of value in it. The survivors were deported by
Nebuchadnezzar to Babylon; they were to serve him and his sons
until the kingdom of Persia came to power. This is how the word
of the Lord was fulfilled that he spoke through Jeremiah, 'Until
this land has enjoyed its sabbath rest, until seventy years have
gone by, it will keep sabbath throughout the days of its desolation.'

And in the first year of Cyrus king of Persia, to fulfil the
word of the Lord that was spoken through Jeremiah, the Lord
roused the spirit of Cyrus king of Persia to issue a proclamation
and to have it publicly displayed throughout his kingdom: 'Thus
speaks Cyrus king of Persia, "The Lord, the God of heaven, has
given me all the kingdoms of the earth; he has ordered me to build
him a Temple in Jerusalem, in Judah. Whoever there is among
you of all his people, may his God be with him! Let him go up"'.

This is the word of the Lord.

RESPONSORIAL PSALM   *(Ps 136:1-6)*

℟ **O let my tongue cleave to my mouth
   if I remember you not!**

1. By the rivers of Babylon
    there we sat and wept,
    remembering Zion:
    on the poplars that grew there
    we hung our harps. ℟

2. For it was there that they asked us,
    our captors, for songs,
    our oppressors, for joy.
    'Sing to us,' they said,
    'one of Zion's songs.' ℟

3. O how could we sing
    the song of the Lord
    on alien soil?
    If I forget you, Jerusalem,
    let my right hand wither! ℟

4. O let my tongue
    cleave to my mouth
    if I remember you not,
    if I prize not Jerusalem
    above all my joys! ℟

SECOND READING   *(Eph 2:4-10)*

A reading from the letter of St Paul to the Ephesians.

You who were dead through your sins have been saved through grace.

God loved us with so much love that he was generous with his
mercy: when we were dead through our sins, he brought us to
life with Christ — it is through grace that you have been saved
— and raised us up with him and gave us a place with him in
heaven, in Christ Jesus.

   This was to show for all ages to come, through his goodness
towards us in Christ Jesus, how infinitely rich he is in grace.
Because it is by grace that you have been saved, through faith;
not by anything of your own, but by a gift from God; not by
anything that you have done, so that nobody can claim the
credit. We are God's work of art, created in Christ Jesus to live
the good life as from the beginning he has meant us to live it.

   This is the word of the Lord.

GOSPEL ACCLAMATION   *(Jn 3:16)*

Glory and praise to you, O Christ!
God loved the world so much that he gave his only Son;
everyone who believes in him has eternal life.
Glory and praise to you, O Christ!

GOSPEL   *(Jn 3:14-21)*

A reading from the holy Gospel according to John.

God sent his Son so that through him the world might be saved.

Jesus said to Nicodemus:

'The Son of Man must be lifted up
as Moses lifted up the serpent in the desert,
so that everyone who believes may have eternal life in him.
Yes, God loved the world so much
that he gave his only Son,
so that everyone who believes in him may not be lost
but may have eternal life.
For God sent his Son into the world
not to condemn the world,
but so that through him the world might be saved.
No one who believes in him will be condemned;
but whoever refuses to believe is condemned already,
because he has refused to believe
in the name of God's only Son.
On these grounds is sentence pronounced:
that though the light has come into the world
men have shown they prefer
darkness to the light
because their deeds were evil.
And indeed, everybody who does wrong
hates the light and avoids it,
for fear his actions should be exposed;
but the man who lives by the truth
comes out into the light,
so that it may be plainly seen that what he does
    is done in God.'

This is the Gospel of the Lord.

PROFESSION OF FAITH — *pages 15-16*

PRAYER OVER THE GIFTS

Lord,
we offer you these gifts
which bring us peace and joy.

Increase our reverence by this eucharist,
and bring salvation to the world.

PREFACE OF LENT I or II — *page 20*

COMMUNION ANTIPHON *(Ps 121:3-4)*

To Jerusalem, that binds them together in unity, the tribes of the Lord go up to give him praise.

PRAYER AFTER COMMUNION

Father,
you enlighten all who come into the world.
Fill our hearts with the light of your gospel,
that our thoughts may please you,
and our love be sincere.

REFLECTION

Salvation, not being lost, and having eternal life are ideas
which belong together. They are part of the way that our
Christian tradition has tried to explain a fundamental insight
into human nature, namely, that even before we commit
individual acts of wrong doing, by our very nature as human
beings, we are in need of a saviour. This need has been
recognised by God and he has acted accordingly.

— 29 March —

FIFTH SUNDAY OF LENT

Today's first reading speaks of a new covenant. Jeremiah's
ministry spanned the period at the end of the Seventh and
the beginning of the Sixth Century before Christ. He justifies
the notion of a new covenant on the grounds that the earlier
covenant made between God and Israel at the time of the
exodus from Egypt was broken by the people. He interprets all
the mishaps that befell Israel in the meantime as God's attempt
to bring them back to their senses and ultimately to him.

ENTRANCE ANTIPHON *(Ps 42:1-2)*

Give me justice, O God, and defend my cause against the wicked; rescue me from deceitful and unjust men. You, O God, are my refuge.

GREETING, PENITENTIAL RITE — *pages 7-13*
The Gloria is omitted.

OPENING PRAYER

Let us pray
    [for the courage to follow Christ]

Father,
help us to be like Christ your Son,
who loved the world and died for our salvation.
Inspire us by his love,
guide us by his example,
who lives and reigns with you and the Holy Spirit,
one God, for ever and ever.

or

Let us pray
    [for the courage to embrace the world
    in the name of Christ]

Father in heaven,
the love of your Son led him to accept the suffering of the cross
that his brothers might glory in new life.

Change our selfishness into self-giving.
Help us to embrace the world you have given us,
that we may transform the darkness of its pain
into the life and joy of Easter.

FIRST READING   *(Jr 31:31-34)*

A reading from the prophet Jeremiah.

I will make a new covenant and never call their sin to mind.

See, the days are coming — it is the Lord who speaks — when
I will make a new covenant with the House of Israel and the
House of Judah, but not a covenant like the one I made with
their ancestors on the day I took them by the hand to bring
them out of the land of Egypt. They broke that covenant of
mine, so I had to show them who was master. It is the Lord
who speaks. No, this is the covenant I will make with the House
of Israel when those days arrive — it is the Lord who speaks.
Deep within them I will plant my Law, writing it on their hearts.
Then I will be their God and they shall be my people. There will
be no further need for neighbour to try to teach neighbour, or
brother to say to brother, 'Learn to know the Lord!' No, they
will all know me, the least no less than the greatest — it is the
Lord who speaks — since I will forgive their iniquity and never
call their sin to mind.

        This is the word of the Lord.

RESPONSORIAL PSALM   *(Ps 50:3-4.12-15)*

℟   **A pure heart create for me, O God**.

1.   Have mercy on me, God, in your kindness.
     In your compassion blot out my offence.
     O wash me more and more from my guilt
     and cleanse me from my sin. ℟

2.   A pure heart create for me, O God,
     put a steadfast spirit within me.
     Do not cast me away from your presence,
     nor deprive me of your holy spirit. ℟

3.   Give me again the joy of your help;
     with a spirit of fervour sustain me,
     that I may teach transgressors your ways
     and sinners may return to you. ℟

SECOND READING   *(Heb 5:7-9)*

A reading from the letter to the Hebrews.

He learnt to obey and became for all the source of eternal salvation.

During his life on earth, Christ offered up prayer and entreaty, aloud and in silent tears, to the one who had the power to save him out of death, and he submitted so humbly that his prayer was heard. Although he was Son, he learnt to obey through suffering; but having been made perfect, he became for all who obey him the source of eternal salvation.

This is the word of the Lord.

GOSPEL ACCLAMATION   *(Jn 12:26)*

Glory to you, O Christ, you are the Word of God!
If a man serves me, says the Lord, he must follow me;
wherever I am, my servant will be there too.
Glory to you, O Christ, you are the Word of God!

GOSPEL   *(Jn 12:20-30)*

A reading from the holy Gospel according to John.

If a grain of wheat falls on the ground and dies, it yields a rich harvest.

Among those who went up to worship at the festival were some Greeks. These approached Philip, who came from Bethsaida in Galilee, and put this request to him, 'Sir, we should like to see Jesus'. Philip went to tell Andrew, and Andrew and Philip together went to tell Jesus. Jesus replied to them:

'Now the hour has come
for the Son of Man to be glorified.

I tell you, most solemnly,
unless a wheat grain falls on the ground and dies,
it remains only a single grain;
but if it dies,
it yields a rich harvest.
Anyone who loves his life loses it;
anyone who hates his life in this world
will keep it for the eternal life.
If a man serves me, he must follow me,
wherever I am, my servant will be there too.
If anyone serves me, my Father will honour him.
Now my soul is troubled.
What shall I say:
Father, save me from this hour?
But it was for this very reason that I have come to this hour.
Father, glorify your name!'

A voice came from heaven, I have glorified it, and I will
    glorify it again.'

People standing by, who heard this, said it was a clap
of thunder; others said, 'It was an angel speaking to him.' Jesus
answered, 'It was not for my sake that this voice came, but for
yours.

'Now sentence is being passed on this world;
now the prince of this world is to be overthrown.
And when I am lifted up from the earth,
I shall draw all to myself.'

By these words he indicated the kind of death he would die.

This is the Gospel of the Lord.

PROFESSION OF FAITH — *pages 15-16*

PRAYER OVER THE GIFTS

Almighty God,
may the sacrifice we offer
take away the sins of those
whom you enlighten with the Christian faith.

PREFACE OF LENT I or II — *page 20*

COMMUNION ANTIPHON   *(Jn 12:24-25)*

**I tell you solemnly: Unless a grain of wheat falls on the
ground and dies, it remains a single grain; but if it dies, it
yields a rich harvest.**

PRAYER AFTER COMMUNION

Almighty Father,
by this sacrifice
may we always remain one with your Son, Jesus Christ,
whose body and blood we share,
for he is Lord for ever and ever.

REFLECTION

We can be thankful to the prophet Jeremiah for what he has
contributed to the understanding of God which developed
over the centuries of the Hebrew Scriptures. The God of the
earlier covenant on Mount Sinai differs from the God of
the new covenant in Jeremiah in one crucial aspect. God's
response to Israel's failure to keep the first covenant was
punishment. By way of contrast, the God of the New Covenant
will be known as a God who will forgive their iniquity and
never call their sin to mind.

5 APRIL

PASSION (PALM) SUNDAY

Today we hear the account of the passion according to Mark.
On Friday we shall hear John's. Mark's story of the passion is
dominated by two questions: What happens to the disciples?
What happens to Jesus? The disciples who were called to be
with him at the beginning of the Gospel, all forsook him
and fled. And Jesus in this cruel and shocking presentation is
portrayed as one alone, alone in suffering and alone in power
to save.

COMMEMORATION OF THE LORD'S ENTRANCE
INTO JERUSALEM

FIRST FORM: THE PROCESSION

*The congregation assembles in a secondary church or chapel or in some
other suitable place distinct from the church to which the procession will
move. Palm branches are carried.*

*While the priest and ministers go to the place where the people have
assembled, the following antiphon or any other appropriate song is sung.*

ANTIPHON   *(Mt 2:9)*

**Hosanna to the Son of David,
the King of Israel.**

**Blessed is he who comes
in the name of the Lord.
Hosanna in the highest.**

The priest then greets the people in these or similar words:

Dear friends in Christ, for five weeks of Lent we have been preparing, by works of charity and self-sacrifice, for the celebration of our Lord's paschal mystery. Today we come together to begin this solemn celebration in union with the whole Church throughout the world. Christ entered in triumph into his own city, to complete his work as our Messiah: to suffer, to die, and to rise again. Let us remember with devotion this entry which began his saving work and follow him with a lively faith. United with him in his suffering on the cross, may we share his resurrection and new life.

Then the priest says one of the following prayers:

Let us pray.
Almighty God,
we pray you
bless ✠ these branches
and make them holy.
Today we joyfully acclaim Jesus our Messiah and King.
May we reach one day the happiness of the new and
        everlasting Jerusalem
by faithfully following him
who lives and reigns for ever and ever.

or

Let us pray.
Lord,
increase the faith of your people
and listen to our prayers.
Today we honour Christ our triumphant King
by carrying these branches.
May we honour you every day
by living always in him,
for he is Lord for ever and ever.

The priest sprinkles the branches with holy water in silence. The account of the Lord's entrance into Jerusalem is proclaimed.

GOSPEL   *(Mk 11:1-10)*

A reading from the holy Gospel according to Mark.
Blessings on him who comes in the name of the Lord.

When they were approaching Jerusalem, in sight of Bethphage and Bethany, close by the Mount of Olives, Jesus sent two of his disciples and said to them, 'Go off to the village facing you, and as soon as you enter it you will find a tethered colt that no one has yet ridden. Untie it and bring it here. If anyone says to you, "What are you doing?" say, "The Master needs it and will send it back here directly".' They went off and found a colt tethered near a door in the open street. As they untied it, some men standing there said, 'What are you doing, untying that colt?' They gave the answer Jesus had told them, and the men let them go. Then they took the colt to Jesus and threw their cloaks on its back, and he sat on it. Many people spread their cloaks on the road, others greenery which they had cut in the fields. And those who went in front and those who followed were all shouting, 'Hosanna! Blessings on him who comes in the name of the Lord! Blessings on the coming kingdom of our father David! Hosanna in the highest heavens!'

This is the Gospel of the Lord.

PROCESSION

Before the procession begins, the celebrant or suitable minister may address the people in these or similar words:

Let us go forth in peace,
praising Jesus our Messiah,
as did the crowds who welcomed him to Jerusalem.

The procession to the church where Mass will be celebrated then begins. During the procession the following or some other appropriate songs are sung.

ANTIPHON

The children of Jerusalem
welcomed Christ the King.
They carried olive branches
and loudly praised the Lord:
Hosanna in the highest.

(The Antiphon *may be repeated between verses of psalm 23)*

PSALM 23

1.   The Lord's is the earth and its fullness,
     the world and all its peoples.
     It is he who set it on the seas;
     on the waters he made it firm. *(Ant.)*

2. Who shall climb the mountain of the Lord?
    Who shall stand in his holy place?
    The man with clean hands and pure heart,
    who desires not worthless things,
    (who has not sworn so as to deceive his neighbour). *(Ant.)*

3. He shall receive blessings from the Lord
    and reward from the God who saves him.
    Such are the men who seek him,
    seek the face of the God of Jacob. *(Ant.)*

4. O gates, lift high your heads:
    grow higher, ancient doors.
    Let him enter, the king of glory! *(Ant.)*

5. Who is the king of glory?
    The Lord, the mighty, the valiant,
    the Lord, the valiant in war. *(Ant.)*

6. O gates, lift high your heads;
    grow higher, ancient doors.
    Let him enter, the king of glory! *(Ant.)*

7. Who is he, the king of glory?
    He, the Lord of armies,
    he is the king of glory. *(Ant.)*

A hymn in honour of Christ is sung during the procession.

*As the procession enters the church, the following responsory or another
song which refers to the Lord's entrance is sung.*

℞ **The children of Jerusalem
    welcomed Christ the King.
    They proclaimed the resurrection of life,
    and, waving olive branches,
    they loudly praised the Lord:
    Hosanna in the highest.**

℣ **When the people heard that Jesus
    was entering Jerusalem;
    they went to meet him
    and, waving olive branches,
    they loudly praised the Lord:
    Hosanna in the highest.**

The priest goes to the chair and says the Opening Prayer of the Mass,
which concludes the procession. Mass then continues in the usual way.

SECOND FORM: THE SOLEMN ENTRANCE

*If the procession cannot be held outside the church, the commemoration
of the Lord's entrance may be celebrated within the church. The faithful,
carrying palm branches, assemble either in front of the church door or
inside the church.*

THIRD FORM: THE SIMPLE ENTRANCE

*If the solemn entrance is not held, the Lord's entrance is commemorated
with the following simple entrance. While the celebrant goes to the altar,
the entrance antiphon with its psalm (see below) or another song with the
same theme is sung. Mass continues in the usual way.*

ENTRANCE ANTIPHON

**Six days before the solemn passover the Lord came to
Jerusalem, and children waving palm branches ran out to
welcome him. They loudly praised the Lord: Hosanna in the
highest. Blessed are you who have come to us so rich in love
and mercy.**

PSALM   *(Ps 23:9-10)*

Open wide the doors and gates.
Lift high the ancient portals.
The King of glory enters.

Who is the King of glory?
He is God the mighty Lord.

Hosanna in the highest.
Blessed are you who have come to us
so rich in love and mercy.

THE MASS

OPENING PRAYER

Let us pray
[for a closer union with Christ
during this holy season]

Almighty, ever-living God,
you have given the human race Jesus Christ our Saviour
as a model of humility.
He fulfilled your will
by becoming man and giving his life on the cross.
Help us to bear witness to you
by following his example of suffering
and make us worthy to share in his resurrection.

or

Let us pray
      [as we accompany our King to Jerusalem]

Almighty Father of our Lord Jesus Christ,
you sent your Son
to be born of woman and to die on a cross,
so that through the obedience of one man,
estrangement might be dissolved for all men.

Guide our minds by his truth
and strengthen our lives by the example of his death,
that we may live in union with you
in the kingdom of your promise.

FIRST READING   *(Is 50:4-7)*

A reading from the prophet Isaiah.

I did not cover my face against insult — I know I shall not be shamed.

The Lord has given me
a disciple's tongue.
So that I may know how to reply to the wearied,
he provides me with speech.
Each morning he wakes me to hear,
to listen like a disciple.
The Lord has opened my ear.
For my part, I made no resistance,
neither did I turn away.
I offered my back to those who struck me,
my cheeks to those who tore at my beard;
I did not cover my face
against insult and spittle.
The Lord comes to my help,
so that I am untouched by the insults.
So, too, I set my face like flint;
I know I shall not be shamed.

      This is the word of the Lord.

RESPONSORIAL PSALM   *(Ps 21:8-9.17-20.23-24)*

℟   **My God, my God,
      why have you forsaken me?**

1.   All who see me deride me.
      They curl their lips, they toss their heads.
      'He trusted in the Lord, let him save him:
      let him release him if this is his friend.' ℟

2.   Many dogs have surrounded me,
    a band of the wicked beset me.
    They tear holes in my hands and my feet,
    I can count every one of my bones.   ℞

3.   They divide my clothing among them.
    They cast lots for my robe.
    O Lord, do not leave me alone,
    my strength, make haste to help me!   ℞

4.   I will tell of your name to my brethren
    and praise you where they are assembled.
    'You who fear the Lord give him praise;
    all sons of Jacob, give him glory.
    Revere him, Israel's sons.'   ℞

SECOND READING   *(Ph 2:6-11)*

A reading from the letter of St Paul to the Philippians.

He humbled himself, but God raised him high.

His state was divine,
yet Christ Jesus did not cling
to his equality with God
but emptied himself
to assume the condition of a slave,
and became as men are;
and being as all men are,
he was humbler yet,
even to accepting death,
death on a cross.
But God raised him high
and gave him the name
which is above all other names
so that all beings
in the heavens, on earth and in the underworld,
should bend the knee at the name of Jesus
and that every tongue should acclaim
Jesus Christ as Lord,
to the glory of God the Father.

    This is the word of the Lord.

GOSPEL ACCLAMATION   *(Ph 2:8-9)*

Praise to you, O Christ, King of eternal glory!
Christ was humbler yet,
even to accepting death,
death on a cross.

But God raised him high
and gave him the name which is above all names.
Praise to you, O Christ, King of eternal glory.

GOSPEL   (Mk 14:1-15:47)

(For Shorter Form, read between ♦ ♦)

(N. Narrator; J. Jesus; O. other individual voices; C. the 'crowd' — bold types)

The passion of our Lord Jesus Christ according to Mark.

N.   It was two days before the Passover and the feast of Unleavened Bread, and the chief priests and the scribes were looking for a way to arrest Jesus by some trick and have him put to death. For they said,

C.   **It must not be during the festivities, or there will be a disturbance among the people.**

N.   Jesus was at Bethany in the house of Simon the leper; he was at dinner when a woman came in with an alabaster jar of very costly ointment, pure nard. She broke the jar and poured the ointment on his head. Some who were there said to one another indignantly,

C.   **Why this waste of ointment? Ointment like this could have been sold for over three hundred denarii and the money given to the poor;**

N.   and they were angry with her. But Jesus said,

J.   Leave her alone. Why are you upsetting her? What she has done for me is one of the good works. You have the poor with you always, and you can be kind to them whenever you wish, but you will not always have me. She has done what was in her power to do; she has anointed my body beforehand for its burial. I tell you solemnly, wherever throughout all the world the Good News is proclaimed, what she has done will be told also, in remembrance of her.

N.   Judas Iscariot, one of the Twelve, approached the chief priests with an offer to hand Jesus over to them. They were delighted to hear it, and promised to give him money; and he looked for a way of betraying him when the opportunity should occur.

       On the first day of Unleavened Bread, when the Passover lamb was sacrificed, his disciples said to him,

C.   **Where do you want us to go and make the preparations for you to eat the Passover?**

N.   So he sent two of his disciples, saying to them,

J.   Go into the city and you will meet a man carrying a pitcher of water. Follow him, and say to the owner of the house which he enters, 'The Master says: Where is my dining room in which I can eat the passover with my disciples?' He will show you a large upper room furnished with couches, all prepared. Make the preparations for us there.

N.   The disciples set out and went to the city and found everything as he had told them, and prepared the Passover.

　　　When evening came he arrived with the Twelve. And while they were at table eating, Jesus said,

J.   I tell you solemnly, one of you is about to betray me, one of you eating with me.

N.   They were distressed and asked him, one after another,

O.   Not I, surely?

N.   He said to them,

J.   It is one of the Twelve, one who is dipping into the same dish with me. Yes, the Son of Man is going to his fate, as the scriptures say he will, but alas for that man by whom the Son of Man is betrayed! Better for that man if he had never been born!

N.   And as they were eating he took some bread, and when he had said the blessing he broke it and gave it to them, saying,

J.   Take it; this is my body.

N.   Then he took a cup, and when he had returned thanks he gave it to them, and all drank from it, and he said to them,

J.   This is my blood, the blood of the covenant, which is to be poured out for many. I tell you solemnly, I shall not drink any more wine until the day I drink the new wine in the kingdom of God.

N.   After psalms had been sung they left for the Mount of Olives. And Jesus said to them,

J.   You will all lose faith, for the scripture says, "I shall strike the shepherd and the sheep will be scattered." However after my resurrection I shall go before you to Galilee.

N.   Peter said,

O.   Even if all lose faith, I will not.

N.   And Jesus said to him,

J.   I tell you solemnly, this day, this very night, before the cock crows twice, you will have disowned me three times.

N.   But he repeated still more earnestly,

O.   If I have to die with you, I will never disown you.

N.   And they all said the same.

They came to a small estate called Gethsemane, and Jesus said to his disciples,

J.   Stay here while I pray.

N.   Then he took Peter and James and John with him. And a sudden fear came over him, and great distress. And he said to them,

J.   My soul is sorrowful to the point of death. Wait here, and keep awake.

N.   And going on a little further he threw himself on the ground and prayed that, if it were possible, this hour might pass him by. He said,

J.   Abba (Father)! Everything is possible for you. Take this cup away from me. But let it be as you, not I, would have it.

N.   He came back and found them sleeping, and he said to Peter,

J.   Simon, are you asleep? Had you not the strength to keep awake one hour? You should be awake, and praying not to be put to the test. The spirit is willing, but the flesh is weak.

N.   Again he went away and prayed, saying the same words. And once more he came back and found them sleeping, their eyes were so heavy; and they could find no answer for him. He came back a third time and said to them,

J.   You can sleep on now and take your rest. It is all over. The hour has come. Now the Son of Man is to be betrayed into the hands of sinners. Get up! Let us go! My betrayer is close at hand already.

N.   Even while he was still speaking, Judas, one of the Twelve, came up with a number of men armed with swords and clubs, sent by the chief priests and the scribes and the elders. Now the traitor had arranged a signal with them. He had said,

O.   The one I kiss, he is the man. Take him in charge, and see he is well guarded when you lead him away.

N.   So when the traitor came, he went straight up to Jesus and said,

O.   Rabbi!

N.   and kissed him. The others seized him and took him in charge. Then one of the bystanders drew his sword and struck out at the high priest's servant, and cut off his ear.

Then Jesus spoke,

J.   Am I a brigand that you had to set out to capture me with swords and clubs? I was among you teaching in the Temple day after day and you never laid hands on me. But this is to fulfil the scriptures.

N.   And they all deserted him and ran away. A young man who followed him had nothing on but a linen cloth. They caught hold of him, but he left the cloth in their hands and ran away naked.

They led Jesus off to the high priest; and all the chief priests and the elders and the scribes assembled there. Peter had followed him at a distance, right into the high priest's palace, and was sitting with the attendants warming himself at the fire.

The chief priests and the whole Sanhedrin were looking for evidence against Jesus on which they might pass the death-sentence. But they could not find any. Several, indeed, brought false evidence against him, but their evidence was conflicting. Some stood up and submitted this false evidence against him,

C.   **We heard him say, "I am going to destroy this Temple made by human hands, and in three days build another, not made by human hands".**

N.   But even on this point their evidence was conflicting. The high priest then stood up before the whole assembly and put this question to Jesus,

O.   Have you no answer to that? What is this evidence these men are bringing against you?

N.   But he was silent and made no answer at all. The high priest put a second question to him,

O.   Are you the Christ, the Son of the Blessed One?

N.   Jesus said,

J. I am, and you will see the Son of Man seated at the right hand of the Power and coming with the clouds of heaven.

N. The high priest tore his robes, and said,

O. What need of witnesses have we now? You heard the blasphemy. What is your finding?

N. And they all gave their verdict: he deserved to die. Some of them started spitting at him and, blindfolding him, began hitting him with their fists and shouting,

C. **Play the prophet!**

N. And the attendants rained blows on him.

While Peter was down below in the courtyard, one of the high priest's servant-girls came up. She saw Peter warming himself there, stared at him and said,

O. You too were with Jesus, the man from Nazareth.

N. But he denied it, saying,

O. I do not know, I do not understand what you are talking about.

N. And he went out into the forecourt. The servant-girl saw him and again started telling the bystanders,

O. This fellow is one of them.

N. But he again denied it. A little later the bystanders themselves said to Peter,

C. **You are one of them for sure! Why, you are a Galilean.**

N. But he started calling curses on himself and swearing,

O. I do not know the man you speak of.

N. At that moment the cock crew for the second time, and Peter recalled how Jesus had said to him, 'Before the cock crows twice, you will have disowned me three times.' And he burst into tears.

▶First thing in the morning, the chief priests together with the elders and scribes, in short the whole Sanhedrin, had their plan ready. They had Jesus bound and took him away and handed him over to Pilate.

Pilate questioned him,

O. Are you the king of the Jews?

N. He answered,

J. It is you who say it.

N. And the chief priests brought many accusations against him. Pilate questioned him again,

O.   Have you no reply at all? See how many accusations they are bringing against you!

N.   But to Pilate's amazement, Jesus made no further reply.

At festival time Pilate used to release a prisoner for them, anyone they asked for. Now a man called Barabbas was then in prison with the rioters who had committed murder during the uprising. When the crowd went up and began to ask Pilate the customary favour, Pilate answered them,

O.   Do you want me to release for you the king of the Jews?

N.   For he realised it was out of jealousy that the chief priests had handed Jesus over. The chief priests, however, had incited the crowd to demand that he should release Barabbas for them instead. Then Pilate spoke again,

O.   But in that case, what am I to do with the man you call king of the Jews?

N.   They shouted back,

C.   **Crucify him!**

N.   Pilate asked them,

O.   Why? What harm has he done?

N.   But they shouted all the louder,

C.   **Crucify him!**

N.   So Pilate, anxious to placate the crowd, released Barabbas for them and, having ordered Jesus to be scourged, handed him over to be crucified.

The soldiers led him away to the inner part of the palace, that is, the Praetorium, and called the whole cohort together. They dressed him up in purple, twisted some thorns into a crown and put it on him. And they began saluting him,

C.   **Hail, king of the Jews!**

N.   They struck his head with a reed and spat on him; and they went down on their knees to do him homage. And when they had finished making fun of him, they took off the purple and dressed him in his own clothes.

They led him out to crucify him. They enlisted a passer-by, Simon of Cyrene, father of Alexander and Rufus, who was coming in from the country, to carry his cross. They brought Jesus to the place called Golgotha, which means the place of the skull.

They offered him wine mixed with myrrh, but he refused it. Then they crucified him, and shared out his clothing, casting lots to decide what each should get. It was the third hour when they crucified him. The inscription giving the charge against him read: 'The King of the Jews.' And they crucified two robbers with him, one on his right and one on his left.

The passers-by jeered at him; they shook their heads and said,

C.   **Aha! So you would destroy the Temple and rebuild it in three days! Then save yourself: come down from the cross!**

N.   The chief priests and the scribes mocked him among themselves in the same way. They said,

C.   **He saved others, he cannot save himself. Let the Christ, the king of Israel, come down from the cross now, for us to see it and believe.**

N.   Even those who were crucified with him taunted him.

When the sixth hour came there was darkness over the whole land until the ninth hour. And at the ninth hour Jesus cried out in a loud voice,

J.   Eloi, Eloi, lama sabachthani?

N.   This means 'My God, my God, why have you deserted me?' When some of those who stood by heard this they said,

C.   **Listen, he is calling on Elijah.**

N.   Someone ran and soaked a sponge in vinegar and, putting it on a reed, gave it him to drink saying,

O.   Wait and see if Elijah will come to take him down.

N.   But Jesus gave a loud cry and breathed his last.

(All kneel and pause a moment)

And the veil of the Temple was torn in two from top to bottom. The centurion, who was standing in front of him, had seen how he had died, and he said,

O.   In truth this man was a son of God.

N.   There were some women watching from a distance. Among them were Mary of Magdala, Mary who was the mother of James the younger and Joset, and Salome. These used to follow him and look after him when he was in Galilee.

And there were many other women there who had come up to Jerusalem with him.

It was now evening, and since it was Preparation Day (that is, the vigil of the sabbath), there came Joseph of Arimathaea, a prominent member of the Council, who himself lived in the hope of seeing the kingdom of God, and he boldly went to Pilate and asked for the body of Jesus. Pilate, astonished that he should have died so soon, summoned the centurion and enquired if he was already dead. Having been assured of this by the centurion, he granted the corpse to Joseph who brought a shroud, took Jesus down from the cross, wrapped him in the shroud and laid him in a tomb which had been hewn out of the rock. He then rolled a stone against the entrance to the tomb. Mary of Magdala and Mary the mother of Joset were watching and took note of where he was laid.

PROFESSION OF FAITH — *pages 15-16*

PRAYER OVER THE GIFTS

Lord,
may the suffering and death of Jesus, your only Son,
make us pleasing to you.
Alone we can do nothing,
but may this perfect sacrifice win
us mercy and love.

PREFACE OF PASSION (PALM) SUNDAY

Father, all-powerful and ever-living God,
we do well always and everywhere to give you thanks
through Jesus Christ our Lord.

Though he was sinless, he suffered willingly for sinners.
Though innocent, he accepted death to save the guilty.
By his dying, he has destroyed our sins.
By his rising, he has raised us up to holiness of life.

We praise you, Lord, with all the angels and saints
in their song of joy:
Holy, holy, holy...

COMMUNION ANTIPHON   *(Mt 26:42)*

Father, if this cup may not pass, but I must drink it, then your will be done.

PRAYER AFTER COMMUNION

Lord,
you have satisfied our hunger with this eucharistic food.
The death of your Son gives us hope and strengthens our faith.
May his resurrection give us perseverance
and lead us to salvation.

SOLEMN BLESSING

The Father of mercies has given us an example of unselfish love
in the sufferings of his only Son.
Through your service of God and neighbour
may you receive his countless blessings.
Amen

You believe that by his dying
Christ destroyed death for ever.
May he give you everlasting life.
Amen.

He humbled himself for our sakes.
May you follow his example
and share in his resurrection.
Amen.

May almighty God bless you,
the Father, and the Son, ✠ and the Holy Spirit.
Amen.

REFLECTION

> In Mark's gospel, to be a disciple of Jesus is to set out on a
> journey with him. At the death of Jesus in this gospel, there is
> no representative of the chosen disciples. But there is a reference
> to many other women who came up from Galilee to Jerusalem
> with him. They made the journey. They are the true disciples.

9 APRIL

HOLY THURSDAY

EVENING MASS OF THE LORD'S SUPPER

This evening we celebrate the institution of the Eucharist and of the priesthood. At the end of the account of institution there is the phrase: 'Do this as a memorial of me.' Literally, 'Do this for my memorial.' While it is usually translated in the way it is here, it has been suggested that it could mean: Do this so that the Father may remember me.

ENTRANCE ANTIPHON *(Ga 6:14)*

We should glory in the cross of our Lord Jesus Christ, for he is our salvation, our life and our resurrection; through him we are saved and made free.

GREETING, PENITENTIAL RITE, GLORIA — *pages 7-14*

OPENING PRAYER

Let us pray.
God our Father,
we are gathered here to share in the supper
which your only Son left to his Church to reveal his love.
He gave it to us when he was about to die
and commanded us to celebrate it as the new and eternal sacrifice.
We pray that in this eucharist
we may find the fullness of love and life.

FIRST READING *(Ex 12:1-8.11-14)*

A reading from the book of Exodus.

Instructions concerning the Passover meal.

The Lord said to Moses and Aaron in the land of Egypt, 'This month is to be the first of all the others for you, the first month of your year. Speak to the whole community of Israel and say, "On the tenth day of this month each man must take an animal from the flock, one for each family: one animal for each household. If the household is too small to eat the animal, a man must join with his neighbour, the nearest to his house, as the number of persons requires. You must take into account what each can eat in deciding the number for the animal. It must be an animal without blemish, a male one year old; you may take it from either sheep or goats. You must keep it till the fourteenth day of the month when the whole assembly of the community of Israel shall slaughter it between the two evenings. Some of the blood must then be taken and put on the two doorposts and the lintel of the houses where it is eaten. That night, the flesh is to be eaten, roasted over the fire; it must be eaten with unleavened bread and bitter herbs. You shall eat it like this: with a girdle round your waist, sandals on your feet, a staff in your hand. You shall eat it hastily: it is a passover in honour of the Lord. That night, I will go through the land of Egypt and strike down all the first-born in the land of Egypt, man and beast alike, and I shall deal out punishment to all the gods of Egypt, I am the Lord. The blood shall serve to mark the houses that you live in. When I see the blood I will pass over you and you shall escape the destroying plague when I strike the land of Egypt. This day is to be a day of remembrance for you, and you must celebrate it as a feast in the Lord's honour. For all generations you are to declare it a day of festival, for ever'".

This is the word of the Lord.

RESPONSORIAL PSALM   *(Ps 115:12-13.15-18)*

℟ **The blessing-cup that we bless**
   is a communion with the blood of Christ.

1. How can I repay the Lord
   for his goodness to me?
   The cup of salvation I will raise;
   I will call on the Lord's name. ℟

2. O precious in the eyes of the Lord
   is the death of his faithful.
   Your servant, Lord, your servant am I;
   you have loosened my bonds. ℟

3. A thanksgiving sacrifice I make:
   I will call on the Lord's name.
   My vows to the Lord I will fulfil
   before all his people. ℟

SECOND READING   *(1 Cor 11:23-26)*

A reading from the first letter of St Paul to the Corinthians.

Every time you eat this bread and drink this cup, you are proclaiming the death of the Lord.

This is what I received from the Lord, and in turn passed on to you: that on the same night that he was betrayed, the Lord Jesus took some bread, and thanked God for it and broke it, and he said, 'This is my body, which is for you; do this as a memorial of me.' In the same way he took the cup after supper, and said, 'This cup is the new covenant in my blood. Whenever you drink it, do this as a memorial of me.' Until the Lord comes, therefore, every time you eat this bread and drink this cup, you are proclaiming his death.

This is the word of the Lord.

GOSPEL ACCLAMATION   *(Jn 13:34)*
Praise and honour to you, Lord Jesus!
I give you a new commandment:
love one another just as I have loved you, says the Lord.
Praise and honour to you, Lord Jesus!

GOSPEL   *(Jn 13:1-15)*
A reading from the holy Gospel according to John.
Now he showed how perfect his love was.

It was before the festival of the Passover, and Jesus knew that the hour had come for him to pass from this world to the Father. He had always loved those who were his in the world, but now he showed how perfect his love was.

They were at supper, and the devil had already put it into the mind of Judas Iscariot son of Simon, to betray him. Jesus knew that the Father had put everything into his hands, and that he had come from God and was returning to God, and he got up from table, removed his outer garment and, taking a towel, wrapped it round his waist; he then poured water into a basin and began to wash the disciples' feet and to wipe them with the towel he was wearing.

He came to Simon Peter, who said to him, 'Lord, are you going to wash my feet?' Jesus answered, 'At the moment you do not know what I am doing, but later you will understand.' 'Never!' said Peter. 'You shall never wash my feet.' Jesus replied, 'If I do not wash you, you can have nothing in common with me.' 'Then, Lord,' said Simon Peter 'not only my feet, but my hands and my head as well!' Jesus said, 'No one who has taken a bath needs washing, he is clean all over. You too are clean, though not all of you are.' He knew who was going to betray him, that was why he said, 'though not all of you are.'

When he had washed their feet and put on his clothes again he went back to the table. 'Do you understand,' he said, 'what I have done to you? You call me Master and Lord, and rightly; so I am. If I, then, the Lord and Master, have washed your feet, you should wash each other's feet. I have given you an example so that you may copy what I have done to you.'

This is the Gospel of the Lord.

WASHING OF FEET

If the ceremony of the Washing of Feet is conducted, it follows the homily. During the washing of feet the following antiphons or other appropriate hymns are sung.

ANTIPHON 1   *(cf. Jn 13:4.5.15)*

**The Lord Jesus,
when he had eaten with his disciples,
poured water into a basin
and began to wash their feet, saying:
This example I leave you.**

ANTIPHON 2   *(Jn 13:6.7.8)*

**Lord, do you wash my feet?
Jesus said to him:
If I do not wash your feet,
you can have no part with me.**

℣ **So he came to Simon Peter,
who said to him:
Lord, do you wash my feet?**

℣ **Now you do not know what I am doing,
but later you will understand.
Lord, do you wash my feet?**

ANTIPHON 3   *(cf. Jn 13:14)*

**If I, your Lord and Teacher, have washed your feet,
then surely you must wash one another's feet.**

ANTIPHON 4   *(Jn 13:35)*

**If there is this love among you,
all will know that you are my disciples.**

℣ **Jesus said to his disciples:
If there is this love among you,
all will know that you are my disciples.**

ANTIPHON 5   *(Jn 13:34)*

**I give you a new commandment:
love one another as I have loved you, says the Lord.**

ANTIPHON 6 *(1 Cor 13:13)*

Faith, hope, and love,
let these endure among you;
and the greatest of these is love.

The Profession of Faith is not said. Priest introduces the Prayer of the Faithful.

PRAYER OVER THE GIFTS

Lord,
make us worthy to celebrate these mysteries.
Each time we offer this memorial sacrifice,
the work of our redemption is accomplished.

PREFACE OF THE HOLY EUCHARIST I

Father, all-powerful and ever-living God,
we do well always and everywhere to give you thanks
through Jesus Christ our Lord.

He is the true and eternal priest
who established this unending sacrifice.
He offered himself as a victim for our deliverance
and taught us to make this offering in his memory.
As we eat his body which he gave for us,
we grow in strength.
As we drink his blood which he poured out for us,
we are washed clean.

Now, with angels and archangels,
and the whole company of heaven,
we sing the unending hymn of your praise:
Holy, holy, holy…

COMMUNION ANTIPHON *(1 Cor 11:20-21)*

This body will be given for you. This is the cup of the new
covenant in my blood; whenever you receive them, do so in
remembrance of me.

PRAYER AFTER COMMUNION

Almighty God,
we receive new life
from the supper your Son gave us in this world.
May we find full contentment
in the meal we hope to share
in your eternal kingdom.

TRANSFER OF THE HOLY EUCHARIST

After the Prayer after Communion, takes place the solemn transfer of the Blessed Sacrament. During the procession the hymn Pange, lingua *or some other eucharistic song is sung.*

Pange, lingua gloriosi
Corporis mysterium,
Sanguinisque pretiosi,
Quem in mundi pretium
Fructus ventris generosi
Rex effudit gentium.

In supremae nocte coenae,
Recumbens cum fratribus,
Observata lege plene
Cibis in legalibus,
Cibum turbae duodenae
Se dat suis manibus.

Nobis datus, nobis natus
Ex intacta virgine,
Et in mundo conversatus
Sparso verbi semine,
Sui moras incolatus
Miro clausit ordine.

Verbum caro, panem verum,
Verbo carnem efficit:
Fitque sanguis Christi merum:
Et si sensus deficit,
Ad firmandum cor sincerum
Sola fides sufficit.

When the procession reaches the place of reposition, the priest sets the ciborium down. Then he puts incense in the thurible and, kneeling, incenses the Blessed Sacrament, while Tantum ergo sacramentum *is sung. The tabernacle of reposition is then closed.*

Tantum ergo sacramentum
Veneremur cernui:
Et antiquum documentum
Novo cedat ritui;
Praestet fides supplementum
Sensuum defectui.

Genitori, Genitoque
Laus et jubilatio,
Salus, honor, virtus quoque
Sit et benedictio:
Procedenti ab utroque
Compar sit laudatio. Amen.

After a period of silent adoration, the priest and ministers genuflect and return to the sacristy. Then the altar is stripped and, if possible, the crosses are removed from the church. It is desirable to cover any crosses which remain in the church.

The faithful are encouraged to continue adoration before the Blessed Sacrament for a suitable period of time during the night, according to local circumstances, but there should be no solemn adoration after midnight.

REFLECTION

The command of Jesus *'mandatum'* that we should wash one another's feet, that we should copy the example which he has given is so central to this evening's celebration that it gave it its name *'Maundy Thursday'*. All three aspects of today's feast are connected: the institution of the Eucharist, the institution of the priesthood and the Lord's command of sisterly and brotherly love. It is the priesthood which enables the Eucharist

to take place and it is at the Eucharist that we have the principal
reason for loving one another, namely, that we who eat the
one loaf and drink from the one cup are one in the one Lord.

10 APRIL

GOOD FRIDAY

CELEBRATION OF THE LORD'S PASSION

John's account of the passion differs significantly from those
of the other three gospels in this respect that here the death of
Jesus is most clearly presented not as a humiliation or defeat
but as a glorious return to the Father. That Jesus is presented
as being in control throughout his passion is clear from the
answer he gives to those who are seeking him with weapons.
His response 'I am he' is intended to underline his identity
with the God who told Moses that his name was 'I am'. The
response of the crowd in moving back and falling to the
ground is the appropriate one in the presence of God.

All pray silently for a while. Then the priest says:

PRAYER
Lord,
by shedding his blood for us,
your Son, Jesus Christ,
established the paschal mystery.
In your goodness, make us holy
and watch over us always.
or
Lord,
by the suffering of Christ your Son
you have saved us all from the death
we inherited from sinful Adam.
By the law of nature
we have borne the likeness of his manhood.
May the sanctifying power of grace
help us to put on the likeness of our Lord in heaven,
who lives and reigns for ever and ever.

I. LITURGY OF THE WORD

FIRST READING *(Is 52:13–53:12)*

A reading from the prophet Isaiah.

He was pierced through for our faults.

See, my servant will prosper,
he shall be lifted up, exalted, rise to great heights.

As the crowds were appalled on seeing him
— so disfigured did he look
that he seemed no longer human —
so will the crowds be astonished at him,
and kings stand speechless before him;
for they shall see something never told
and witness something never heard before:
'Who could believe what we have heard,
and to whom has the power of the Lord been revealed?'

Like a sapling he grew up in front of us,
like a root in arid ground.
Without beauty, without majesty (we saw him),
no looks to attract our eyes;
a thing despised and rejected by men,
a man of sorrows and familiar with suffering,
a man to make people screen their faces;
he was despised and we took no account of him.

And yet ours were the sufferings he bore,
ours the sorrows he carried.
But we, we thought of him as someone punished,
struck by God, and brought low.
Yet he was pierced through for our faults,
crushed for our sins.
On him lies a punishment that brings us peace,
and through his wounds we are healed.

We had all gone astray like sheep,
each taking his own way,
and the Lord burdened him
with the sins of all of us.
Harshly dealt with, he bore it humbly,
he never opened his mouth,
like a lamb that is led to the slaughter-house,
like a sheep that is dumb before its shearers
never opening its mouth.

By force and by law he was taken;
would anyone plead his cause?
Yes, he was torn away from the land of the living;
for our faults struck down in death.
They gave him a grave with the wicked,
a tomb with the rich,
though he had done no wrong
and there had been no perjury in his mouth.
The Lord has been pleased to crush him with suffering.
If he offers his life in atonement,
he shall see his heirs, he shall have a long life
and through him what the Lord wishes will be done.

His soul's anguish over
he shall see the light and be content.
By his sufferings shall my servant justify many,
taking their faults on himself.

Hence I will grant whole hordes for his tribute,
he shall divide the spoil with the mighty,
for surrendering himself to death
and letting himself be taken for a sinner,
while he was bearing the faults of many
and praying all the time for sinners.

This is the word of the Lord.

RESPONSORIAL PSALM   *(Ps 30:2-6.12-13.15-17.25)*

℟   **Father, into your hands I commend my spirit.**

1.   In you, O Lord, I take refuge.
     Let me never be put to shame.
     In your justice, set me free.
     Into your hands I commend my spirit.
     It is you who will redeem me, Lord. ℟

2.   In the face of all my foes
     I am a reproach,
     an object of scorn to my neighbours
     and of fear to my friends. ℟.

3.   Those who see me in the street
     run far away from me.
     I am like a dead man, forgotten in men's hearts,
     like a thing thrown away. ℟

4.   But as for me, I trust in you, Lord,
     I say: 'You are my God.'

(continued)

My life is in your hands, deliver me
from the hands of those who hate me. ℟

℟ **Father, into your hands I commend my spirit.**

5. Let your face shine on your servant.
   Save me in your love.
   Be strong, let your heart take courage,
   all who hope in the Lord. ℟

SECOND READING   (Heb 4:14-16; 5:7-9)

A reading from the letter to the Hebrews.

*He learnt to obey through suffering and became for all who obey him
the source of eternal salvation.*

Since in Jesus, the Son of God, we have the supreme high priest
who has gone through to the highest heaven, we must never let
go of the faith that we have professed. For it is not as if we had
a high priest who was incapable of feeling our weaknesses with
us; but we have one who has been tempted in every way that
we are, though he is without sin. Let us be confident, then, in
approaching the throne of grace, that we shall have mercy from
him and find grace when we are in need of help.

During his life on earth, he offered up prayer and entreaty,
aloud and in silent tears, to the one who had the power to save
him out of death, and he submitted so humbly that his prayer
was heard. Although he was Son, he learnt to obey through
suffering; but having been made perfect, he became for all who
obey him the source of eternal salvation.

This is the word of the Lord.

GOSPEL ACCLAMATION   (Ph 2:8-9)

Glory and praise to you, O Christ!
Christ was humbler yet,
even to accepting death, death on a cross.
But God raised him high
and gave him the name that is above all names.
Glory and praise to you, O Christ!

GOSPEL   (Jn 18:1–19:42)

*(N. Narrator; J. Jesus; O. other individual voices; C. the 'crowd' — **bold**
types.)*

The passion of our Lord Jesus Christ according to John.

N. Jesus left with his disciples and crossed the Kedron valley.
   There was a garden there, and he went into it with his
   disciples. Judas the traitor knew the place well, since Jesus

had often met his disciples there, and he brought the cohort to this place together with a detachment of guards sent by the chief priests and the Pharisees, all with lanterns and torches and weapons. Knowing everything that was going to happen to him, Jesus then came forward and said,

J. Who are you looking for?

N. They answered,

C. **Jesus the Nazarene.**

N. He said,

J. I am he.

N. Now Judas the traitor was standing among them. When Jesus said, 'I am he', they moved back and fell to the ground. He asked them a second time,

J. Who are you looking for?

N. They said,

C. **Jesus the Nazarene.**

N. Jesus replied,

J. I have told you that I am he. If I am the one you are looking for, let these others go.

N. This was to fulfil the words he had spoken, 'Not one of those you gave me have I lost.'

Simon Peter, who carried a sword, drew it and wounded the high priest's servant, cutting off his right ear. The servant's name was Malchus. Jesus said to Peter,

J. Put your sword back in its scabbard; am I not to drink the cup that the Father has given me?

N. The cohort and its captain and the Jewish guards seized Jesus and bound him. They took him first to Annas, because Annas was the father-in-law of Caiaphas, who was high priest that year. It was Caiaphas who had suggested to the Jews, 'It is better for one man to die for the people.'

Simon Peter, with another disciple, followed Jesus. This disciple, who was known to the high priest, went with Jesus into the high priest's palace, but Peter stayed outside the door. So the other disciple, the one known to the high priest, went out, spoke to the woman who was keeping the door and brought Peter in. The maid on duty at the door said to Peter,

O. Aren't you another of that man's disciples?

N. He answered,

O. I am not.

N. Now it was cold, and the servants and guards had lit a charcoal fire and were standing there warming themselves;

so Peter stood there too, warming himself with the others.

The high priest questioned Jesus about his disciples and his teaching. Jesus answered,

J.   I have spoken openly for all the world to hear; I have always taught in the synagogue and in the Temple where all the Jews meet together: I have said nothing in secret. But why ask me? Ask my hearers what I taught: they know what I said.

N.   At these words, one of the guards standing by gave Jesus a slap in the face, saying.

O.   Is that the way to answer the high priest?

N.   Jesus replied,

J.   If there is something wrong in what I said, point it out; but if there is no offence in it, why do you strike me?

N.   Then Annas sent him, still bound, to Caiaphas the high priest.

As Simon Peter stood there warming himself, someone said to him,

O.   Aren't you another of his disciples?

N.   He denied it saying,

O.   I am not.

N.   One of the high priest's servants, a relation of the man whose ear Peter had cut off, said,

O.   Didn't I see you in the garden with him?

N.   Again Peter denied it; and at once a cock crew.

They then led Jesus from the house of Caiaphas to the Prætorium. It was now morning. They did not go into the Prætorium themselves or they would be defiled and unable to eat the passover. So Pilate came outside to them and said,

O.   What charge do you bring against this man?

N.   They replied,

C.   **If he were not a criminal, we should not be handing him over to you.**

N.   Pilate said,

O.   Take him yourselves, and try him by your own Law.

N.   The Jews answered,

C.   **We are not allowed to put a man to death.**

N.   This was to fulfil the words Jesus had spoken indicating the way he was going to die.

So Pilate went back into the Prætorium and called Jesus to him, and asked,

O.   Are you the king of the Jews?

N. Jesus replied,

J. Do you ask this of your own accord, or have others spoken to you about me?

N. Pilate answered,

O. Am I a Jew? It is your own people and the chief priests who have handed you over to me: what have you done?'

N. Jesus replied,

J. Mine is not a kingdom of this world; if my kingdom were of this world, my men would have fought to prevent my being surrendered to the Jews. But my kingdom is not of this kind.

N. Pilate said,

O. So you are a king then?

N. Jesus answered,

J. It is you who say it. Yes, I am a king. I was born for this, I came into the world for this: to bear witness to the truth; and all who are on the side of truth listen to my voice.

N. Pilate said,

O. Truth? What is that?

N. And with that he went out again to the Jews and said,

O. I find no case against him. But according to a custom of yours I should release one prisoner at the Passover; would you like me, then, to release the king of the Jews?

N. At this they shouted:

C. **Not this man, but Barabbas.**

N. Barabbas was a brigand.

Pilate then had Jesus taken away and scourged; and after this, the soldiers twisted some thorns into a crown and put it on his head, and dressed him in a purple robe. They kept coming up to him and saying,

C. **Hail, king of the Jews!**

N. and they slapped him in the face.

Pilate came outside again and said to them,

O. Look, I am going to bring him out to you to let you see that I find no case.

N. Jesus then came out wearing the crown of thorns and the purple robe. Pilate said,

O. Here is the man.

N. When they saw him the chief priests and the guards shouted,

C. **Crucify him! Crucify him!**

N. Pilate said,

O. Take him yourselves and crucify him: I can find no case against him.

N. The Jews replied,

C. **We have a Law, and according to that Law he ought to die, because he has claimed to be the Son of God.**

N. When Pilate heard them say this his fears increased. Re-entering the Prætorium, he said to Jesus,

O. Where do you come from?

N. But Jesus made no answer. Pilate then said to him,

O. Are you refusing to speak to me? Surely you know I have power to release you and I have power to crucify you?

N. Jesus replied,

J. You would have no power over me if it had not been given you from above; that is why the one who handed me over to you has the greater guilt.

N. From that moment Pilate was anxious to set him free, but the Jews shouted,

C. **If you set him free you are no friend of Caesar's; anyone who makes himself king is defying Caesar.**

N. Hearing these words, Pilate had Jesus brought out, and seated himself on the chair of judgement at a place called the Pavement, in Hebrew Gabbatha. It was Passover Preparation Day, about the sixth hour. Pilate said to the Jews,

O. Here is your king.

N. They said,

C. **Take him away, take him away! Crucify him!**

N. Pilate said,

O. Do you want me to crucify your king?

N. The chief priests answered,

C. **We have no king except Caesar.**

N. So in the end Pilate handed him over to them to be crucified.

     They then took charge of Jesus, and carrying his own cross he went out of the city to the place of the skull or, as it was called in Hebrew, Golgotha, where they crucified him with two others, one on either side with Jesus in the middle. Pilate wrote out a notice and had it fixed to the cross; it ran 'Jesus the Nazarene, King of the Jews'. This notice was read by many of the Jews, because the place where Jesus was crucified was not far from the city, and the writing was in Hebrew, Latin and Greek. So the Jewish chief priests said to Pilate,

C. **You should not write "King of the Jews", but "This man said: I am King of the Jews".**

N. Pilate answered,

O. What I have written, I have written.

N. When the soldiers had finished crucifying Jesus they took his clothing and divided it into four shares, one for each soldier. His undergarment was seamless, woven in one piece from neck to hem; so they said to one another,

C. **Instead of tearing it, let's throw dice to decide who is to have it.**

N. In this way the words of scripture were fulfilled:

'They shared out my clothing among them.
They cast lots for my clothes.'

This is exactly what the soldiers did.

Near the cross of Jesus stood his mother and his mother's sister, Mary the wife of Clopas, and Mary of Magdala. Seeing his mother and the disciple he loved standing near her, Jesus said to his mother,

J. Woman, this is your son.

N. Then to the disciple he said,

J. This is your mother.

N. And from that moment the disciple made a place for her in his home.

After this, Jesus knew that everything had now been completed, and to fulfil the scripture perfectly he said:

J. I am thirsty.

N. A jar full of vinegar stood there, so putting a sponge soaked in vinegar on a hyssop stick they held it up to his mouth. After Jesus had taken the vinegar he said,

J. It is accomplished,

N. and bowing his head he gave up the spirit.

(All kneel and pause a moment)

It was Preparation Day, and to prevent the bodies remaining on the cross during the sabbath — since that sabbath was a day of special solemnity — the Jews asked Pilate to have the legs broken and the bodies taken away. Consequently the soldiers came and broke the legs of the first man who had been crucified with him and then of the other. When they came to Jesus, they found he was already dead, and so instead of breaking his legs one of the soldiers pierced his side with a lance; and immediately there came out blood and water. This is the evidence of one who saw it — trustworthy evidence, and he knows he speaks the truth —

and he gives it so that you may believe as well. Because all
this happened to fulfil the words of scripture:
'Not one bone of his will be broken,'
and again, in another place scripture says:
'They will look on the one whom they have pierced.'
After this, Joseph of Arimathaea, who was a disciple
of Jesus — though a secret one because he was afraid of the
Jews — asked Pilate to let him remove the body of Jesus.
Pilate gave permission, so they came and took it away.
Nicodemus came as well — the same one who had first
come to Jesus at night-time — and he brought a mixture
of myrrh and aloes, weighing about a hundred pounds.
They took the body of Jesus and wrapped it with the spices
in linen cloths, following the Jewish burial custom. At the
place where he had been crucified there was a garden, and
in this garden a new tomb in which no one had yet been
buried. Since it was the Jewish Day of Preparation and the
tomb was near at hand, they laid Jesus there.

GENERAL INTERCESSIONS

1. FOR THE CHURCH

Let us pray, dear friends,
for the holy Church of God throughout the world,
that God the almighty Father
guide it and gather it together
so that we may worship him
in peace and tranquillity.

Silent prayer. Then the priest says:
Almighty and eternal God,
you have shown your glory to all nations in Christ, your Son.
Guide the work of your Church.
Help it to persevere in faith,
proclaim your name,
and bring your salvation to people everywhere.
We ask this through Christ our Lord.
Amen.

2. FOR THE POPE

Let us pray
for our Holy Father, Pope N.,
that God who chose him to be bishop

may give him health and strength
to guide and govern God's holy people.
Silent prayer. Then the priest says:
Almighty and eternal God,
you guide all things by your word,
you govern all Christian people.
In your love protect the Pope you have chosen for us.
Under his leadership deepen our faith
and make us better Christians.
We ask this through Christ our Lord.
Amen.

3. FOR THE CLERGY AND LAITY OF THE CHURCH

Let us pray
for N., our bishop,
for all bishops, priests, and deacons;
for all who have a special ministry
in the Church and for all God's people.
Silent prayer. Then the priest says:
Almighty and eternal God,
your Spirit guides the Church
and makes it holy.
Listen to our prayers
and help each of us
in his own vocation
to do your work more faithfully.
We ask this through Christ our Lord. **Amen**.

4. FOR THOSE PREPARING FOR BAPTISM

Let us pray
for those (among us) preparing for baptism,
that God in his mercy
make them responsive to his love,
forgive their sins through the waters of new birth,
and give them life in Jesus Christ our Lord.
Silent prayer. Then the priest says:
Almighty and eternal God,
you continually bless your Church with new members.
Increase the faith and understanding
of those (among us) preparing for baptism.
Give them a new birth in these living waters
and make them members of your chosen family.
We ask this through Christ our Lord. **Amen**.

5. FOR THE UNITY OF CHRISTIANS

Let us pray
for all our brothers and sisters
who share our faith in Jesus Christ,
that God may gather and keep together in one Church
all those who seek the truth with sincerity.
Silent prayer. Then the priest says:
Almighty and eternal God,
you keep together those you have united.
Look kindly on all who follow Jesus your Son.
We are all consecrated to you by our common baptism.
Make us one in the fullness of faith,
and keep us one in the fellowship of love.
We ask this through Christ our Lord. **Amen**.

6. FOR THE JEWISH PEOPLE

Let us pray
for the Jewish people,
the first to hear the word of God,
that they may continue to grow in the love of his name
and in faithfulness to his covenant.
Silent prayer. Then the priest says:
Almighty and eternal God,
long ago you gave your promise to Abraham and his posterity.
Listen to your Church as we pray
that the people you first made your own
may arrive at the fullness of redemption.
We ask this through Christ our Lord. **Amen**.

7. FOR THOSE WHO DO NOT BELIEVE IN CHRIST

Let us pray
for those who do not believe in Christ,
that the light of the Holy Spirit
may show them the way to salvation.
Silent prayer. Then the priest says:
Almighty and eternal God,
enable those who do not acknowledge Christ
to find the truth
as they walk before you in sincerity of heart.
Help us to grow in love for one another,
to grasp more fully the mystery of your godhead,
and to become more perfect witnesses of your love

in the sight of men.
We ask this through Christ our Lord. **Amen**.

8. FOR THOSE WHO DO NOT BELIEVE IN GOD

Let us pray
for those who do not believe in God,
that they may find him
by sincerely following all that is right.
Silent Prayer. Then the priest says:
Almighty and eternal God,
you created mankind
so that all might long to find you
and have peace when you are found.
Grant that, in spite of the hurtful things
that stand in their way,
they may all recognize in the lives of Christians
the tokens of your love and mercy,
and gladly acknowledge you
as the one true God and Father of us all.
We ask this through Christ our Lord.
Amen.

9. FOR ALL IN PUBLIC OFFICE

Let us pray
for those who serve us in public office,
that God may guide their minds and hearts,
so that all men may live in true peace and freedom.
Silent prayer. Then the priest says:
Almighty and eternal God,
you know the longings of men's hearts
and you protect their rights.
In your goodness
watch over those in authority,
so that people everywhere may enjoy
religious freedom, security, and peace.
We ask this through Christ our Lord.
Amen.

10. FOR THOSE IN SPECIAL NEED

Let us pray, dear friends,
that God the almighty Father
may heal the sick,
comfort the dying,

give safety to travellers,
free those unjustly deprived of liberty,
and rid the world of falsehood,
hunger, and disease.

Silent prayer. Then the priest says:

Almighty, ever-living God,
you give strength to the weary
and new courage to those who have lost heart.
Hear the prayers of all who call on you in any trouble
that they may have the joy of receiving your help in their need.
We ask this through Christ our Lord.
Amen.

II. VENERATION OF THE CROSS

The showing of the Cross takes place in three stages. Three times the priest says:

This is the wood of the cross,
on which hung the Saviour of the world.

All reply:

Come, let us worship.

During the veneration of the Cross, the antiphon, We worship you, Lord, *the Reproaches or other suitable hymns are sung. Numbers 1 and 2 indicate first and second choirs.*

ANTIPHON

1 and 2:   **We worship you, Lord,**
              we venerate your cross,
              we praise your resurrection.
              Through the cross you brought joy to the
              world.

                                                  (Ps 66:2)

1.   May God be gracious and bless us;
             and let his face shed its light upon us.

          (Choirs 1 and 2 repeat Antiphon)

REPROACHES I

1 and 2:   My people, what have I done to you?
             How have I offended you? Answer me!

1:   I led you out of Egypt, from slavery to freedom,
             but you led your Saviour to the cross.

2:   My people, what have I done to you?

	How have I offended you? Answer me!
1:	Holy is God!
2:	Holy and strong!
1:	Holy immortal One, have mercy on us!
1 and 2:	For forty years I led you safely through the desert. I fed you with manna from heaven and brought you to a land of plenty; but you led your Saviour to the cross.
1:	Holy is God!
2:	Holy and strong!
1:	Holy immortal One, have mercy on us!
1 and 2:	What more could I have done for you? I planted you as my fairest vine, but you yielded only bitterness: when I was thirsty you gave me vinegar to drink, and you pierced your Saviour with a lance.
1:	Holy is God!
2:	Holy and strong!
1:	Holy immortal One, have mercy on us!

REPROACHES II

1:	For your sake I scourged your captors and their first born sons, but you brought your scourges down on me.
2:	My people, what have I done to you? How have I offended you? Answer me!
1:	I led you from slavery to freedom and drowned your captors in the sea, but you handed me over to your high priests.
2:	My people, what have I done to you? How have I offended you? Answer me!
1:	I opened the sea before you, but you opened my side with a spear.
2:	My people, what have I done to you? How have I offended you? Answer me!

1: I led you on your way in a pillar of cloud,
but you led me to Pilate's court.

2: My people, what have I done to you?
How have I offended you? Answer me!

1: I bore you up with manna in the desert,
but you struck me down and scourged me.

2: My people, what have I done to you?
How have I offended you? Answer me!

1: I gave you saving water from the rock,
but you gave me gall and vinegar to drink.

2: My people, what have I done to you?
How have I offended you? Answer me!

1: For you I struck down the kings of Canaan,
but you struck my head with a reed.

2: My people, what have I done to you?
How have I offended you? Answer me!

1: I gave you a royal sceptre,
but you gave me a crown of thorns.

2: My people, what have I done to you?
How have I offended you? Answer me!

1: I raised you to the height of majesty,
but you have raised me high on a cross.

2: My people, what have I done to you?
How have I offended you? Answer me!

III. HOLY COMMUNION

The Blessed Sacrament is brought from the place of reposition to the altar.
Then the priest says:
Let us pray with confidence to the Father in the words our
Saviour gave us:

Our Father, who art in heaven,
hallowed be thy name.
Thy kingdom come.
Thy will be done on earth as it is in heaven.
Give us this day our daily bread,
and forgive us our trespasses,
as we forgive those who trespass against us,
and lead us not into temptation,
but deliver us from evil.

Deliver us, Lord, from every evil,
and grant us peace in our day.
In your mercy keep us free from sin
and protect us from all anxiety
as we wait in joyful hope
for the coming of our Saviour, Jesus Christ.
For the kingdom, the power, and the glory are yours, now and for ever.

Lord Jesus Christ, with faith in your love and mercy I eat your body and drink your blood. Let it not bring me condemnation, but health in mind and body.

This is the Lamb of God
who takes away the sins of the world.
Happy are those who are called to his supper.
**Lord, I am not worthy to receive you,
but only say the word and I shall be healed.**

After the Communion a period of silence may be observed. Then the priest says:
Let us pray.
Almighty and eternal God,
you have restored us to life
by the triumphant death and resurrection of Christ.
Continue this healing work within us.
May we who participate in this mystery
never cease to serve you.
We ask this through Christ our Lord.
Amen.

For the dismissal the priest extends his hands towards the people and says the following Prayer over the People.

PRAYER OVER THE PEOPLE
Lord,
send down your abundant blessing,
upon your people who have devoutly recalled the death
    of your Son
in the sure hope of the resurrection.
Grant them pardon; bring them comfort.
May their faith grow stronger
and their eternal salvation be assured.
We ask this through Christ our Lord.
Amen.

REFLECTION

It is not clear from John's account of the passion whether Jesus
is being put to death for religious or political motives. What is
beyond doubt is that no one has taken Jesus' life away from
him. The verb used at his death is 'hands over' (his Spirit). He
has given his life willingly so that God's plan for humankind
would be finished. The account makes clear that a faithful
disciple and a faithful God cannot be separated even in death.

All depart in silence.

---
11 APRIL
THE EASTER VIGIL

The celebration of Holy Thursday, Good Friday and the Easter
Vigil together is the centre of the Church's liturgical life each
year. Tonight's liturgy cannot be separated from its Jewish
background when our fathers and mothers in faith were led
out of slavery at the exodus. This liberation, great as it is in
itself, is an anticipation of, and a means towards, an even
greater one, namely, redemption by Jesus the Christ.

I. THE SERVICE OF LIGHT

*All the lights in the church are put out. Fire is prepared in a suitable place
outside the church. When the people have assembled the priest goes there
with the ministers, one of whom carries the Easter candle. The priest
greets the congregation in these or similar words:*

Dear friends in Christ,
on this most holy night,
when our Lord Jesus Christ passed from death to life,
the Church invites her children throughout the world
to come together in vigil and prayer.
This is the passover of the Lord:
if we honour the memory of his death and resurrection
by hearing his word and celebrating his mysteries,
then we may be confident
that we shall share his victory over death
and live with him for ever in God.
Then the fire is blessed.

Let us pray.
Father,
we share in the light of your glory
through your Son, the light of the world.
Make this new fire ✠ holy, and inflame us with new hope.
Purify our minds by this Easter celebration
and bring us one day to the feast of eternal light.
We ask this through Christ our Lord. **Amen**.

PREPARATION AND LIGHTING OF THE CANDLE

After the blessing of the new fire the Easter candle is brought to the celebrant, who cuts a cross in the wax. Then he traces the Greek letters alpha and omega and numerals of the current year. Meanwhile he says:

1. Christ yesterday and today
2. the beginning and the end
3. Alpha
4. and Omega
5. all time belongs to him
6. and all the ages
7. to him be glory and power
8. through every age for ever. Amen.

Then he may insert five grains of incense into the candle in the form of a cross, saying:

1. By his holy
2. and glorious wounds
3. may Christ our Lord
4. guard us
5. and keep us. Amen.

The priest lights the candle from the new fire, saying:

May the light of Christ, rising in glory,
dispel the darkness of our hearts and minds.

PROCESSION

The deacon (or the priest) takes the Easter candle, lifts high and sings:

Christ our light.

All answer:

Thanks be to God.

At the church door the deacon lifts the candle high and sings a second time:

Christ our light.

All answer:

Thanks be to God.

All light their candles from the Easter candle and continue the procession. When the deacon arrives before the altar, he faces the people and sings a third time:

Christ our light.

All answer:

Thanks be to God.

The lights in the church are put on.

The Easter candle is placed in the middle of the sanctuary. The book and the candle may be incensed. The deacon or the priest now sings the Easter Proclamation. *All stand with their candles lit.*

EASTER PROCLAMATION (EXSULTET)

(Parts given within [ ] *may be omitted)*

Rejoice, heavenly powers! Sing, choirs of angels!
    Exult, all creation around God's throne!
    Jesus Christ, our King, is risen!
    Sound the trumpet of salvation!

Rejoice, O earth, in shining splendour,
    radiant in the brightness of your King!
    Christ has conquered! Glory fills you!
    Darkness vanishes for ever!

Rejoice, O Mother Church! Exult in glory!
    The risen Saviour shines upon you!
    Let this place resound with joy,
    echoing the mighty song of all God's people!

[My dearest friends, standing with me in this holy light,
    join me in asking God for mercy,
    that he may give his unworthy minister
    grace to sing his Easter praises.]

The Lord be with you.
And also with you.
Lift up your hearts.
We lift them up to the Lord.
Let us give thanks to the Lord our Lord.
It is right to give him thanks and praise.

It is truly right
    that with full hearts and minds and voices
    we should praise the unseen God, the all-powerful Father,
    and his only Son, our Lord Jesus Christ.

For Christ has ransomed us with his blood,
    and paid for us the price of Adam's sin
    to our eternal Father!

This is our passover feast,
    when Christ, the true Lamb, is slain,
    whose blood consecrates the homes of all believers.

This is the night when first you saved our fathers:
    you freed the people of Israel from their slavery
    and led them dry-shod through the sea.

[This is the night when the pillar of fire
    destroyed the darkness of sin!]

This is the night when Christians everywhere,
    washed clean of sin
    and freed from all defilement,
    are restored to grace and grow together in holiness.

This is the night when Jesus Christ
    broke the chains of death
    and rose triumphant from the grave.

[What good would life have been to us,
    had Christ not come as our Redeemer?]

Father, how wonderful your care for us!
    How boundless your merciful love!
    To ransom a slave
    you gave away your Son.

O happy fault, O necessary sin of Adam,
    which gained for us so great a Redeemer!
    [Most blessed of all nights, chosen by God
    to see Christ rising from the dead!

Of this night scripture says:
    'The night will be as clear as day:
    it will become my light, my joy.']

The power of this holy night
    dispels all evil, washes guilt away,
    restores lost innocence, brings mourners joy.
    [It casts out hatred, brings us peace, and humbles earthly
        pride.]

Night truly blessed when heaven is wedded to earth
    and man is reconciled with God!

Therefore, heavenly Father, in the joy of this night,
    receive our evening sacrifice of praise,

your Church's solemn offering.

Accept this Easter candle,
   [a flame divided but undimmed,
   a pillar of fire that glows to the honour of God.

Let it mingle with the lights of heaven
   and continue bravely burning]
   to (may it always) dispel the darkness of this night!
   May the Morning Star which never sets find this flame still
      burning:
   Christ, that Morning Star, who came back from the dead,
   and shed his peaceful light on all mankind,
   your Son who lives and reigns for ever and ever. **Amen**.

II. LITURGY OF THE WORD

After the Easter Proclamation *candles are extinguished. The priest gives
an introduction in these or similar words. All sit.*

Dear friends in Christ,
we have begun our solemn vigil.
Let us now listen attentively to the word of God,
recalling how he saved his people throughout history
and, in the fullness of time,
sent his own Son to be our Redeemer.
Through this Easter celebration,
may God bring to perfection
the saving work he has begun in us.

*Nine readings are given. For pastoral reasons the number may be reduced
but one of the readings must always be reading 3 from Exodus.*

*A reader goes to the lectern and proclaims the first reading. Then the
cantor leads the psalm and the people respond. All rise and the priest
sings or says,* Let us pray. *All pray silently for a while and then the priest
sings or says the prayer. Instead of the responsorial psalm a period of
silence may be observed.*

FIRST READING   *(Gen 1:1–2:2)*

(For Shorter Form, *read between* ▶ ◀)
A reading from the book of Genesis.
God saw all he had made, and indeed it was very good.
▶In the beginning God created the heavens and the earth.◀ Now
the earth was a formless void, there was darkness over the deep,
and God's spirit hovered over the water.
    God said, 'Let there be light', and there was light. God saw
that light was good, and God divided light from darkness. God

called light 'day', and darkness he called 'night'. Evening came and morning came: the first day.

God said, 'Let there be a vault in the waters to divide the waters in two.' And so it was. God made the vault, and it divided the waters above the vault from the waters under the vault. God called the vault 'heaven'. Evening came and morning came: the second day.

God said, 'Let the waters under heaven come together into a single mass, and let dry land appear.' And so it was. God called the dry land 'earth' and the mass of waters 'seas', and God saw that it was good.

God said, 'Let the earth produce vegetation: seed-bearing plants, and fruit trees bearing fruit with their seed inside, on the earth.' And so it was. The earth produced vegetation: plants bearing seed in their several kinds, and trees bearing fruit with their seed inside in their several kinds. God saw that it was good. Evening came and morning came: the third day.

God said, 'Let there be lights in the vault of heaven to divide day from night, and let them indicate festivals, days and years. Let them be lights in the vault of heaven to shine on the earth.' And so it was. God made the two great lights: the greater light to govern the day, the smaller light to govern the night, and the stars. God set them in the vault of heaven to shine on the earth, to govern the day and the night and to divide light from darkness. God saw that it was good. Evening came and morning came: the fourth day.

God said, 'Let the waters teem with living creatures, and let birds fly above the earth within the vault of heaven.' And so it was. God created great sea-serpents and every kind of living creature with which the waters teem, and every kind of winged creature. God saw that it was good. God blessed them, saying 'Be fruitful, multiply, and fill the waters of the seas; and let the birds multiply upon the earth.' Evening came and morning came: the fifth day.

God said, 'Let the earth produce every kind of living creature: cattle, reptiles, and every kind of wild beast.' And so it was. God made every kind of wild beast, every kind of cattle, and every kind of land reptile. God saw that it was good.

God said, 'Let us make man in our own image, in the likeness of ourselves, and let them be masters of the fish of the sea, the birds of heaven, the cattle, all the wild beasts and all the reptiles that crawl upon the earth.'

God created man in the image of himself,
in the image of God he created him,
male and female he created them.

God blessed them, saying to them, 'Be fruitful, multiply,
fill the earth and conquer it. Be masters of the fish of the sea,
the birds of heaven and all living animals on the earth.' God
said, 'See, I give you all the seed-bearing plants that are upon
the whole earth, and all the trees with seed-bearing fruit; this
shall be your food. To all wild beasts, all birds of heaven and
all living reptiles on the earth I give all the foliage of plants for
food.' And so it was. God saw all he had made, and indeed it
was very good.◗ Evening came and morning came: the sixth day.

Thus heaven and earth were completed with all their array.
On the seventh day God completed the work he had been
doing. He rested on the seventh day after all the work he had
been doing.

◗This is the word of the Lord.◗

RESPONSORIAL PSALM   *(Ps 103:1-2.5-6.10.12-14.24.35)*

℞   **Send forth your spirit, O Lord,**
    and renew the face of the earth.

1. Bless the Lord, my soul!
    Lord God, how great you are,
    clothed in majesty and glory,
    wrapped in light as in a robe! ℞

2. You founded the earth on its base,
    to stand firm from age to age.
    You wrapped it with the ocean like a cloak:
    the waters stood higher than the mountains. ℞

3. You make springs gush forth in the valleys:
    they flow in between the hills.
    On their banks dwell the birds of heaven;
    from the branches they sing their song. ℞

4. From your dwelling you water the hills;
    earth drinks its fill of your gift.
    You make the grass grow for the cattle
    and the plants to serve man's needs. ℞

5. How many are your works, O Lord!
    In wisdom you have made them all.
    The earth is full of your riches.
    Bless the Lord, my soul! ℞

ALTERNATIVE PSALM   (*Ps 32:4-7.12-13.20.22*)

℟   **The Lord fills the earth with his love.**

1.   The word of the Lord is faithful
      and all his works to be trusted.
      The Lord loves justice and right
      and fills the earth with his love. ℟

2.   By his word the heavens were made,
      by the breath of his mouth all the stars.
      He collects the waves of the ocean;
      he stores up the depths of the sea. ℟

3.   They are happy, whose God is the Lord,
      the people he has chosen as his own.
      From the heavens the Lord looks forth,
      he sees all the children of men. ℟

4.   Our soul is waiting for the Lord.
      The Lord is our help and our shield.
      May your love be upon us, O Lord,
      as we place all our hope in you. ℟

All stand for the prayer.

Let us pray.
Almighty and eternal God,
you created all things in wonderful beauty and order.
Help us now to perceive
how still more wonderful is the new creation
by which in the fullness of time you redeemed your people
through the sacrifice of our passover, Jesus Christ,
who lives and reigns for ever and ever.
Amen.

or

Let us pray.
Lord God,
the creation of man was a wonderful work,
his redemption still more wonderful.
May we persevere in right reason
against all that entices to sin
and so attain to everlasting joy.
We ask this through Christ our Lord.
Amen.

SECOND READING   *(Gen 22:1-18)*

(*For* Shorter Form, *read between* ♦ ♦)

A reading from the book of Genesis.

The sacrifice of Abraham, our father in faith.

♦God put Abraham to the test. 'Abraham, Abraham,' he called. 'Here I am' he replied. 'Take your son,' God said, 'your only child Isaac, whom you love, and go to the land of Moriah. There you shall offer him as a burnt-offering, on a mountain I will point out to you.'♦

Rising early next morning Abraham saddled his ass and took with him two of his servants and his son Isaac. He chopped wood for the burnt-offering and started on his journey to the place God had pointed out to him. On the third day Abraham looked up and saw the place in the distance. Then Abraham said to his servants, 'Stay here with the donkey. The boy and I will go over there; we will worship and come back to you.'

Abraham took the wood for the burnt-offering, loaded it on Isaac, and carried in his own hands the fire and the knife. Then the two of them set out together. Isaac spoke to his father Abraham, 'Father,' he said. 'Yes, my son,' he replied. 'Look,' he said 'here are the fire and the wood, but where is the lamb for the burnt-offering?' Abraham answered, 'My son, God himself will provide the lamb for the burnt-offering.' Then the two of them went on together.

♦When they arrived at the place God had pointed out to him, Abraham built an altar there, and arranged the wood. Then he bound his son Isaac and put him on the altar on top of the wood. Abraham stretched out his hand and seized the knife to kill his son.

But the angel of the Lord called to him from heaven, 'Abraham, Abraham' he said. 'I am here' he replied. 'Do not raise your hand against the boy' the angel said. 'Do not harm him, for now I know you fear God. You have not refused me your son, your only son.' Then looking up, Abraham saw a ram caught by its horns in a bush. Abraham took the ram and offered it as a burnt-offering in place of his son.♦

Abraham called this place 'The Lord provides', and hence the saying today: On the mountain the Lord provides.

♦The angel of the Lord called Abraham a second time from heaven. 'I swear by my own self — it is the Lord who speaks — because you have done this, because you have not refused me your son, your only son, I will shower blessings on you, I will make your descendants as many as the stars of heaven and the grains of sand on the seashore. Your descendants shall gain possession of the gates of their enemies. All the nations of the earth shall bless themselves by your descendants, as a reward for your obedience.'

This is the word of the Lord.

RESPONSORIAL PSALM   *(Ps 15:5.8-11)*

℟   **Preserve me, God, I take refuge in you.**

1.   O Lord, it is you who are my portion and cup;
     it is you yourself who are my prize.
     I keep the Lord ever in my sight:
     since he is at my right hand, I shall stand firm. ℟

2.   And so my heart rejoices, my soul is glad;
     even my body shall rest in safety.
     For you will not leave my soul among the dead,
     nor let your beloved know decay. ℟

3.   You will show me the path of life,
     the fullness of joy in your presence,
     at your right hand happiness for ever. ℟

All stand for the prayer.

Let us pray.
God and Father of all who believe in you,
you promised Abraham that he would become the father of all
        nations,
and through the death and resurrection of Christ
you fulfil that promise:
everywhere throughout the world you increase your chosen
        people.
May we respond to your call
by joyfully accepting your invitation to the new life of grace.
We ask this through Christ our Lord. **Amen.**

(The following reading is obligatory).

THIRD READING   *(Ex 14:15–15:1)*

A reading from the book of Exodus.

The sons of Israel went on dry ground right into the sea.

The Lord said to Moses, 'Why do you cry to me so? Tell sons of Israel to march on. For yourself, raise your staff and stretch out your hand over the sea and part it for the sons of Israel to walk through the sea on dry ground. I for my part will make the heart of the Egyptians so stubborn that they will follow them. So shall I win myself glory at the expense of Pharaoh, of all his army, his chariots, his horsemen. And when I have won glory for myself, at the expense of Pharaoh and his chariots and his army, the Egyptians will learn that I am the Lord.'

Then the angel of the Lord, who marched at the front of the army of Israel, changed station and moved to their rear. The pillar of cloud changed station from the front to the rear of them, and remained there. It came between the camp of the Egyptians and the camp of Israel. The cloud was dark, and the night passed without the armies drawing any closer the whole night long. Moses stretched out his hand over the sea. The Lord drove back the sea with a strong easterly wind all night, and he made dry land of the sea. The waters parted and the sons of Israel went on dry ground right into the sea, walls of water to right and to left of them. The Egyptians gave chase: after them they went, right into the sea, all Pharaoh's horses, his chariots, and his horsemen. In the morning watch, the Lord looked down on the army of the Egyptians from the pillar of fire and of cloud, and threw the army into confusion. He so clogged their chariot wheels that they could scarcely make headway. 'Let us flee from the Israelites,' the Egyptians cried 'the Lord is fighting for them against the Egyptians!' 'Stretch out your hand over the sea,' the Lord said to Moses 'that the waters may flow back on the Egyptians and their chariots and their horsemen.' Moses stretched out his hand over the sea and, as day broke, the sea returned to its bed. The fleeing Egyptians marched right into it, and the Lord overthrew the Egyptians in the very middle of the sea. The returning waters overwhelmed the chariots and the horsemen of Pharaoh's whole army, which had followed the Israelites into the sea; not a single one of them was left. But the sons of Israel had marched through the sea on dry ground, walls of water to right and to left of them. That day, the Lord rescued Israel from the Egyptians, and Israel saw the Egyptians lying dead on the shore. Israel witnessed the great act that the Lord had performed against the Egyptians, and the people venerated the Lord; they put their faith in the Lord and in Moses, his servant.

It was then that Moses and the sons of Israel sang this song in honour of the Lord:

(The Responsorial Psalm follows immediately).

RESPONSORIAL PSALM   *(Ex 15:1-6.17-18)*

℟ **I will sing to the Lord, glorious his triumph!**

1. I will sing to the Lord, glorious his triumph!
    Horse and rider he has thrown into the sea!
    The Lord is my strength, my song, my salvation.
    This is my God and I extol him,
    my father's God and I give him praise. ℟

2. The Lord is a warrior! The Lord is his name.
    The chariots of Pharaoh he hurled into the sea,
    the flower of his army is drowned in the sea.
    The deeps hide them; they sank like a stone. ℟

3. Your right hand, Lord, glorious in its power,
    your right hand, Lord, has shattered the enemy.
    In the greatness of your glory you crushed the foe. ℟

4. You will lead your people and plant them on your mountain,
    the place, O Lord, where you have made your home,
    the sanctuary, Lord, which your hands have made.
    The Lord will reign for ever and ever. ℟

All stand for the prayer.
Let us pray.
Father, even today we see the wonders
of the miracles you worked long ago.
You once saved a single nation from slavery,
and now you offer that salvation to all through baptism.
May the peoples of the world become true sons of Abraham
and prove worthy of the heritage of Israel.
We ask this through Christ our Lord. **Amen.**
or
Let us pray.
Lord God,
in the new covenant
you shed light on the miracles you worked in ancient times:
the Red Sea is a symbol of our baptism,
and the nation you freed from slavery
is a sign of your Christian people.
May every nation
share the faith and privilege of Israel
and come to new birth in the Holy spirit.
We ask this through Christ our Lord. **Amen.**

FOURTH READING   (Is 54:5-14)

A reading from the prophet Isaiah.

With everlasting love the Lord your redeemer has taken pity on you.

Thus says the Lord:

> Now your creator will be your husband,
> his name, the Lord of hosts;
> your redeemer will be the Holy One of Israel,
> he is called the God of the whole earth.
> Yes, like a forsaken wife, distressed in spirit,
> the Lord calls you back.
> Does a man cast off the wife of his youth?
> says your God.

> I did forsake you for a brief moment,
> but with great love will I take you back.
> In excess of anger, for a moment
> I hid my face from you.
> But with everlasting love I have taken pity on you,
> says the Lord, your redeemer.

> I am now as I was in the days of Noah
> when I swore that Noah's waters
> should never flood the world again.
> So now I swear concerning my anger with you
> and the threats I made against you;
> for the mountains may depart,
> the hills be shaken,
> but my love for you will never leave you
> and my covenant of peace with you will never be shaken,
> says the Lord who takes pity on you.

> Unhappy creature, storm-tossed, disconsolate,
> see, I will set your stones on carbuncles
> and your foundations on sapphires.
> I will make rubies your battlements,
> your gates crystal,
> and your entire wall precious stones.
> Your sons will all be taught by the Lord.
> The prosperity of your sons will be great.
> You will be founded on integrity;
> remote from oppression, you will have nothing to fear;
> remote from terror, it will not approach you.

This is the word of the Lord.

(Ps 29:2.4-6.11-13)

℟   **I will praise you, Lord, you have rescued me.**

1.   I will praise you, Lord, you have rescued me
      and have not let my enemies rejoice over me.
      O Lord, you have raised my soul from the dead,
      restored me to life from those who sink into the grave. ℟

2.   Sing psalms to the Lord, you who love him,
      give thanks to his holy name.
      His anger lasts but a moment; his favour through life.
      At night there are tears, but joy comes with dawn. ℟

3.   The Lord listened and had pity.
      The Lord came to my help.
      For me you have changed my mourning into dancing,
      O Lord my God, I will thank you for ever. ℟

All stand for the prayer.
Let us pray.
Almighty and eternal God,
glorify your name by increasing your chosen people
as you promised long ago.
In reward for their trust,
may we see in the Church the fulfilment of your promise.
We ask this through Christ our Lord. **Amen**.

(Is 55:1-11)
A reading from the prophet Isaiah.

Come to me and your soul will live, and I will make an everlasting covenant with you.

Thus says the Lord:

      Oh, come to the water all you who are thirsty;
      though you have no money, come!
      Buy corn without money, and eat,
      and, at no cost, wine and milk.
      Why spend money on what is not bread,
      your wages on what fails to satisfy?
      Listen, listen to me, and you will have good things to eat
      and rich food to enjoy.
      Pay attention, come to me;
      listen, and your soul will live.
      With you I will make an everlasting covenant
      out of the favours promised to David.
      See, I have made of you a witness to the peoples,

a leader and a master of the nations.
See, you will summon a nation you never knew,
those unknown will come hurrying to you,
for the sake of the Lord your God,
of the Holy One of Israel who will glorify you.
Seek the Lord while he is still to be found,
call to him while he is still near.
Let the wicked man abandon his way,
the evil man his thoughts.
Let him turn back to the Lord who will take pity on him,
to our God who is rich in forgiving;
for my thoughts are not your thoughts,
my ways not your ways — it is the Lord who speaks.
Yes, the heavens are as high above earth
as my ways are above your ways,
my thoughts above your thoughts.

Yes, as the rain and the snow come down from the heavens and
do not return without watering the earth, making it yield and
giving growth to provide seed for the sower and bread for the
eating, so the word that goes from my mouth does not return to
me empty, without carrying out my will and succeeding in what
it was sent to do.

This is the word of the Lord.

RESPONSORIAL PSALM   (Is 12:2-6)

℟ **With joy you will draw water**
   from the wells of salvation.

1. Truly God is my salvation,
    I trust, I shall not fear.
    For the Lord is my strength, my song,
    he became my saviour.
    With joy you will draw water
    from the wells of salvation. ℟

2. Give thanks to the Lord, give praise to his name!
    Make his mighty deeds known to the peoples,
    declare the greatness of his name. ℟

3. Sing a psalm to the Lord
    for he has done glorious deeds,
    make them known to all the earth!
    People of Zion, sing and shout for joy
    for great in your midst is the Holy One of Israel. ℟

All stand for the prayer.

Let us pray.
Almighty, ever-living God,
only hope of the world,
by the preaching of the prophets
you proclaimed the mysteries we are celebrating tonight.
Help us to be your faithful people,
for it is by your inspiration alone
that we can grow in goodness.
We ask this through Christ our Lord. **Amen.**

SIXTH READING   *(Ba 3:9-15.32–4:4)*

A reading from the prophet Baruch.

In the radiance of the Lord make your way to light.

Listen, Israel, to commands that bring life;
hear, and learn what knowledge means.
Why, Israel, why are you in the country of your enemies,
growing older and older in an alien land,
sharing defilement with the dead,
reckoned with those who go to Sheol?
Because you have forsaken the fountain of wisdom.
Had you walked in the way of God,
you would have lived in peace for ever.
Learn where knowledge is, where strength,
where understanding, and so learn
where length of days is, where life,
where the light of the eyes and where peace.
But who has found out where she lives,
who has entered her treasure house?
But the One who knows all knows her,
he has grasped her with his own intellect,
he has set the earth firm for ever
and filled it with four-footed beasts,
he sends the light — and it goes,
he recalls it — and trembling it obeys;
the stars shine joyfully at their set times:
when he calls them, they answer, 'Here we are';
they gladly shine for their creator.
It is he who is our God,
no other can compare with him.
He has grasped the whole way of knowledge,
and confided it to his servant Jacob,
to Israel his well-beloved;

so causing her to appear on earth
and move among men.

This is the book of the commandments of God,
the Law that stands for ever;
those who keep her live,
those who desert her die.
Turn back, Jacob, seize her,
in her radiance make your way to light:
do not yield your glory to another,
your privilege to a people not your own.
Israel, blessed are we:
what pleases God has been revealed to us.

This is the word of the Lord.

RESPONSORIAL PSALM   *(Ps 18:8-11)*

℟ **You have the message of eternal life, O Lord.**

1. The law of the Lord is perfect,
    it revives the soul.
    The rule of the Lord is to be trusted,
    it gives wisdom to the simple. ℟

2. The precepts of the Lord are right,
    they gladden the heart.
    The command of the Lord is clear,
    it gives light to the eyes. ℟

3. The fear of the Lord is holy,
    abiding for ever.
    The decrees of the Lord are truth
    and all of them just. ℟

4. They are more to be desired than gold,
    than the purest of gold
    and sweeter are they than honey,
    than honey from the comb. ℟

All stand for the prayer.

Let us pray.
Father,
you increase your Church
by continuing to call all people to salvation.
Listen to our prayers
and always watch over those you cleanse in baptism.
We ask this through Christ our Lord. **Amen**.

SEVENTH READING *(Ezk 36:16-28)*

A reading from the prophet Ezekiel.

I shall pour clean water over you, and I shall give you a new heart.

The word of the Lord was addressed to me as follows: 'Son of man, the members of the House of Israel used to live in their own land, but they defiled it by their conduct and actions. I then discharged my fury at them because of the blood they shed in their land and the idols with which they defiled it. I scattered them among the nations and dispersed them in foreign countries. I sentenced them as their conduct and actions deserved. And now they have profaned my holy name among the nations where they have gone, so that people say of them, "These are the people of the Lord; they have been exiled from his land." But I have been concerned about my holy name, which the House of Israel has profaned among the nations where they have gone. And so, say to the House of Israel, "The Lord says this: I am not doing this for your sake, House of Israel, but for the sake of my holy name, which you have profaned among the nations where you have gone. I mean to display the holiness of my great name, which has been profaned among the nations, which you have profaned among them. And the nations will learn that I am the Lord — it is the Lord who speaks — when I display my holiness for your sake before their eyes. Then I am going to take you from among the nations and gather you together from all the foreign countries, and bring you home to your own land. I shall pour clean water over you and you will be cleansed; I shall cleanse you of all your defilement and all your idols. I shall give you a new heart, and put a new spirit in you; I shall remove the heart of stone from your bodies and give you a heart of flesh instead. I shall put my spirit in you, and make you keep my laws and sincerely respect my observances. You will live in the land which I gave your ancestors. You shall be my people and I will be your God." '

This is the word of the Lord.

RESPONSORIAL PSALM *(Ps 41:3.5; 42:3.4)*

℟ **Like the deer that yearns for running streams,
so my soul is yearning for you, my God.**

1. My soul is thirsting for God,
    the God of my life;
    when can I enter and see
    the face of God? ℟

(continued)

2. These things will I remember
    as I pour out my soul:
    how I would lead the rejoicing crowd
    into the house of God,
    amid cries of gladness and thanksgiving,
    the throng wild with joy. ℞

℞ **Like the deer that yearns for running streams,
    so my soul is yearning for you, my God.**

3. O send forth your light and your truth;
    let these be my guide.
    Let them bring me to your holy mountain
    to the place where you dwell. ℞

4. And I will come to the altar of God,
    the God of my joy.
    My redeemer, I will thank you on the harp,
    O God, my God. ℞

*If a Baptism takes place, the Responsorial Psalm which follows the Fifth
Reading above (page 190) is used or Ps 50 as follows.*

RESPONSORIAL PSALM   *(Ps 50:12-15.18-19)*

℞ **A pure heart create for me, O God.**

1. A pure heart create for me, O God,
    put a steadfast spirit within me.
    Do not cast me away from your presence,
    nor deprive me of your holy spirit. ℞

2. Give me again the joy of your help;
    with a spirit of fervour sustain me,
    that I may teach transgressors your ways
    and sinners may return to you. ℞

3. For in sacrifice you take no delight,
    burnt offering from me you would refuse,
    my sacrifice, a contrite spirit.
    A humbled, contrite heart you will not spurn. ℞

All stand for the prayer.
Let us pray.
God of unchanging power and light,
look with mercy and favour on your entire Church.
Bring lasting salvation to humankind,
so that the world may see

the fallen lifted up,
the old made new,
and all things brought to perfection,
through him who is their origin,
our Lord Jesus Christ,
who lives and reigns for ever and ever.
Amen.

or

Let us pray.
Father,
you teach us in both the Old and the New Testament
to celebrate this passover mystery.
Help us to understand your great love for us.
May the goodness you now show us
confirm our hope in your future mercy.
We ask this through Christ our Lord.
Amen.

or (if there are candidates to be baptised)

Let us pray.
Almighty and eternal God,
be present in this sacrament of your love.
Send your Spirit of adoption
on those to be born again in baptism.
And may the work of our humble ministry
be brought to perfection by your mighty power.
We ask this through Christ our Lord.
Amen.

*After the last reading from the Old Testament with its responsory and
prayer, the altar candles are lighted, and the priest intones the Gloria (see
page 14) which is taken up by all. The church bells are rung, according to
local custom.*

OPENING PRAYER

Let us pray.
Lord God,
you have brightened this night
with the radiance of the risen Christ.
Quicken the spirit of sonship in your Church;
renew us in mind and body
to give you whole-hearted service.

EPISTLE   (Rm 6:3-11)

A reading from the letter of St Paul to the Romans.

Christ, having been raised from the dead, will never die again.

When we were baptized in Christ Jesus we were baptized in his death; in other words, when we were baptized we went into the tomb with him and joined him in death, so that as Christ was raised from the dead by the Father's glory, we too might live a new life.

If in union with Christ we have imitated his death, we shall also imitate him in his resurrection. We must realise that our former selves have been crucified with him to destroy this sinful body and to free us from the slavery of sin. When a man dies, of course, he has finished with sin.

But we believe that having died with Christ we shall return to life with him: Christ, as we know, having been raised from the dead will never die again. Death has no power over him any more. When he died, he died, once for all, to sin, so his life now is life with God; and in that way, you too must consider yourselves to be dead to sin but alive for God in Christ Jesus.

This is the word of the Lord.

After the Epistle all rise. The priest solemnly intones the Alleluia *which is repeated by all.*

RESPONSORIAL PSALM   (Ps 117:1-2.16-17.22-23)

℟ **Alleluia, alleluia, alleluia!**

1.   Give thanks to the Lord for he is good,
     for his love has no end.
     Let the sons of Israel say:
     'His love has no end.' ℟

2.   The Lord's right hand has triumphed;
     his right hand raised me up.
     I shall not die, I shall live
     and recount his deeds. ℟

3.   The stone which the builders rejected
     has become the corner stone.
     This is the work of the Lord,
     a marvel in our eyes. ℟

GOSPEL   (Mk 16:1-7)

A reading from the holy Gospel according to Mark.

Jesus of Nazareth, who was crucified, has risen.

When the sabbath was over, Mary of Magdala, Mary the mother of James, and Salome, bought spices with which to go and anoint him. And very early in the morning on the first day of the week they went to the tomb, just as the sun was rising.

They had been saying to one another, 'Who will roll away the stone for us from the entrance to the tomb?' But when they looked they could see that the stone — which was very big — had already been rolled back. On entering the tomb they saw a young man in a white robe seated on the right-hand side, and they were struck with amazement. But he said to them, 'There is no need for alarm. You are looking for Jesus of Nazareth, who was crucified: he has risen, he is not here. See, here is the place where they laid him. But you must go and tell his disciples and Peter, "He is going before you to Galilee; it is there you will see him, just as he told you." '

This is the Gospel of the Lord.

III. LITURGY OF BAPTISM

The priest goes with the ministers to the baptismal font, if this can be seen by the congregation. Otherwise a vessel of water is placed in the sanctuary.

If there are candidates to be baptised, they are called forward and presented by their godparents. If they are children, the parents and godparents bring them forward in front of the congregation.

Then the priest speaks to the people in these or similar words.

(If there are candidates to be baptised:)
Dear friends in Christ,
as our brothers and sisters approach the waters of rebirth,
let us help them by our prayers
and ask God, our almighty Father,
to support them with his mercy and love.

(If the font is to be blessed, but there is no one to be baptized:)
Dear friends in Christ,
let us ask God, the almighty Father,
to bless this font, that those reborn in it
may be made one with his adopted children in Christ.

All present stand and answer. If there is no one to be baptized and the font is not to be blessed the litany is omitted, and the blessing of water takes place at once.

Lord, have mercy	**Lord, have mercy**
Christ, have mercy	**Christ, have mercy**
Lord, have mercy	**Lord, have mercy**
Holy Mary, Mother of God	**pray for us**
Saint Michael	"
Holy angels of God	"
Saint John the Baptist	"
Saint Joseph	"
Saint Peter and Saint Paul	"
Saint Andrew	"
Saint John	"
Saint Mary Magdalene	"
Saint Stephen	"
Saint Ignatius	"
Saint Lawrence	"
Saint Perpetua and Saint Felicity	"
Saint Agnes	"
Saint Gregory	"
Saint Augustine	"
Saint Athanasius	**pray for**
us	
Saint Basil	"
Saint Martin	"
Saint Benedict	"
Saint Francis and Saint Dominic	"
Saint Francis Xavier	"
Saint John Vianney	"
Saint Catherine	"
Saint Teresa	"
All holy men and women	"
Lord, be merciful	**Lord,**
save your people	
From all evil	"
From every sin	"
From everlasting death	"
By your coming as man	"
By your death and rising to new life	"
By your gift of the Holy Spirit	"
Be merciful to us sinners	**Lord, hear our prayer**

(If there are candidates to be baptized.)

Give new life to these chosen ones by the grace of baptism
                                              Lord, hear our prayer
(If there is no one to be baptized.)
By your grace bless this font where your children will be reborn
                                              Lord, hear our prayer
Jesus, Son of the living God   **Lord, hear our prayer**
Christ, hear us   **Christ, hear us**
Lord Jesus, hear our prayer   **Lord Jesus, hear our prayer**

BLESSING OF BAPTISMAL WATER
The priest then blesses the baptismal water, saying:
Father, you give us grace through sacramental signs,
    which tell us of the wonders of your unseen power.

In baptism we use your gift of water,
    which you have made a rich symbol
    of the grace you give us in this sacrament.

At the very dawn of creation
    your Spirit breathed on the waters,
    making them the wellspring of all holiness.

The waters of the great flood
    you made a sign of the waters of baptism,
    that make an end of sin and a new beginning of goodness.

Through the waters of the Red Sea
    you led Israel out of slavery,
    to be an image of God's holy people,
    set free from sin by baptism.

In the waters of the Jordan
    your Son was baptized by John
    and anointed with the Spirit.

Your Son willed that water and blood
    should flow from his side
    as he hung upon the cross.

After his resurrection he told his disciples:
    'Go out and teach all nations,
    baptizing them in the name of the Father
    and of the Son and of the Holy Spirit.'

Father, look now with love upon your Church,
    and unseal for her the fountain of baptism.

By the power of the Spirit
    give to the water of this font
    the grace of your Son.

You created man in your own likeness:
    cleanse him from sin in a new birth of innocence
    by water and the Spirit.

The priest may lower the Easter candle into the water either once or three times, as he continues:

We ask you, Father, with your Son
    to send the Holy Spirit upon the waters of this font.

He holds the candle in the water:

May all who are buried with Christ
    in the death of baptism
    rise also with him to newness of life.

We ask this through Christ our Lord. **Amen**.

The candle is taken out of the water as the people sing this (or any other appropriate) acclamation:

Springs of water, bless the Lord.
Give him glory and praise for ever.

Those who are to be baptised renounce the devil individually. Then they are questioned about their faith and are baptised. Adults are confirmed immediately after baptism if a bishop, or a priest with the faculty to confirm, is present.

If no one is to be baptized and the font is not to be blessed, the priest blesses the water with the following prayer:

My brothers and sisters,
let us ask the Lord our God
to bless this water he has created,
which we shall use to recall our baptism.
May he renew us
and keep us faithful to the Spirit
we have all received.

All pray silently for a short while. The priest then continues:

Lord our God,
this night your people keep prayerful vigil.
Be with us as we recall the wonder of our creation
and the greater wonder of our redemption.
Bless this water: it makes the seed to grow,
it refreshes us and makes us clean.
You have made of it a servant of your loving kindness:
through water you set your people free,
and quenched their thirst in the desert.
With water the prophets announced a new covenant
that you would make with man.

By water, made holy by Christ in Jordan,
you made our sinful nature new
in the bath that gives rebirth.
Let this water remind us of our baptism;
let us share the joys of our brothers
who are baptized this Easter.
We ask this through Christ our Lord.
Amen.

RENEWAL OF BAPTISMAL PROMISES

*When the rite of baptism (and confirmation) has been completed or, if
there is no baptism, immediately after the blessing of the water, all present
stand with lighted candles and renew their baptismal profession of faith.*

Dear friends,
through the paschal mystery
we have been buried with Christ in baptism,
so that we may rise with him to a new life.
Now that we have completed our lenten observance,
let us renew the promise we made in baptism
when we rejected Satan and his works,
and promised to serve God faithfully
in his holy Catholic Church.
And so:
Do you reject Satan?
I do.
And all his works?
I do.
And all his empty promises?
I do.
or
Do you reject sin, so as to live in the freedom of God's children?
I do.
Do you reject the glamour of evil, and refuse to be mastered by
    sin?
I do.
Do you reject Satan, father of sin and prince of darkness?
I do.
Then the priest continues:
Do you believe in God, the Father almighty,
creator of heaven and earth?
I do.
Do you believe in Jesus Christ, his only Son, our Lord, who was
born of the Virgin Mary, was crucified, died, and was buried,

rose from the dead, and is now seated at the right hand of the Father?
I do.
Do you believe in the Holy Spirit, the holy Catholic Church, the communion of saints, the forgiveness of sins, the resurrection of the body, and life everlasting?
I do.
God, the all-powerful Father of our Lord Jesus Christ,
has given us a new birth by water and the Holy Spirit,
and forgiven all our sins.
May he also keep us faithful to our Lord Jesus Christ for ever
and ever.
Amen.
The priest sprinkles the people with the blessed water, while all sing the following or any other suitable hymn.

I saw water flowing
from the side of the temple, alleluia.
It brought God's life and his salvation,
and the people sang in joyful praise:
alleluia, alleluia.

After the people have been sprinkled, the priest returns to the chair. The Profession of Faith *is omitted, and the priest directs the* Prayer of the Faithful.

IV. LITURGY OF THE EUCHARIST

PRAYER OVER THE GIFTS

Lord, accept the prayers and offerings of your people.
With your help
may this Easter mystery of our redemption
bring to perfection the saving work you have begun in us.

PREFACE OF EASTER I

Father, all-powerful and ever-living God,
we do well always and everywhere to give you thanks
through Jesus Christ our Lord.

We praise you with greater joy than ever
on this Easter night (day),
when Christ became our paschal sacrifice.

He is the true Lamb who took away the sins of the world.
By dying he destroyed our death;
by rising he restored our life.

And so, with all the choirs of angels in heaven
we proclaim your glory
and join in their unending hymn of praise:
Holy, holy, holy...

COMMUNION ANTIPHON   *(1 Cor 5:7-8)*

**Christ has become our paschal sacrifice; let us feast with the
unleavened bread of sincerity and truth, alleluia.**

PRAYER AFTER COMMUNION

Lord, you have nourished us with your Easter sacraments.
Fill us with your Spirit,
and make us one in peace and love.

SOLEMN BLESSING

May almighty God bless you on this solemn feast of Easter,
and may he protect you against all sin.
Amen.

Through the resurrection of his Son
God has granted us healing.
May he fulfil his promises,
and bless you with eternal life.
Amen.

You have mourned for Christ's sufferings;
now you celebrate the joy of his resurrection.
May you come with joy to the feast which lasts for ever.
Amen.

May almighty God bless you,
the Father, and the Son, ✠ and the Holy Spirit.
Amen.

Go in the peace of Christ, alleluia, alleluia.
Thanks be to God, alleluia, alleluia.

REFLECTION

The words 'redeemer' and 'redemption' resonate tonight.
The account of the fall in the Book of Genesis declares that
human beings need salvation and that this need is not just as
a result of individual sin. It is part and parcel of our nature.
The concept of 'redeemer' is the Church's declaration that this
need is met in and through the mystery that is Christ.

12 APRIL

EASTER SUNDAY

Every Sunday is a celebration of Easter Sunday. Every Eucharist is a commemoration and a realisation of the Easter Mystery of the passion, death and resurrection of the Lord. On this day of days the community of the Church shows how seriously it takes the words of Saint Paul that if Christ is not raised from the dead then our faith is in vain. In other words, the resurrection of the Lord is the reason for the existence of Christianity.

ENTRANCE ANTIPHON   *(Ps 138:18.5-6)*

I have risen: I am with you once more; you placed your hand on me to keep me safe. How great is the depth of your wisdom, alleluia!

or   *(Lk 24:34; Rv 1:6)*

The Lord has indeed risen, alleluia. Glory and kingship be his for ever and ever.

GREETING, PENITENTIAL RITE, GLORIA — *pages 7-14*

OPENING PRAYER

Let us pray
    [that the risen Christ will raise us up
    and renew our lives]

God our Father,
by raising Christ your Son
you conquered the power of death
and opened for us the way to eternal life.
Let our celebration today
raise us up and renew our lives
by the Spirit that is within us.

or

Let us pray
    [on this Easter morning for the life
    that never again shall see darkness]

God our Father, creator of all,
today is the day of Easter joy.
This is the morning on which the Lord appeared to men
who had begun to lose hope
and opened their eyes to what the scriptures foretold:
that first he must die, and then he would rise
and ascend into his Father's glorious presence.

May the risen Lord
breathe on our minds and open our eyes
that we may know him in the breaking of bread
and follow him in his risen life.

FIRST READING   *(Acts 10:34.37-43)*

A reading from the Acts of the Apostles.

We have eaten and drunk with him after his resurrection.

Peter addressed Cornelius and his household: 'You must have
heard about the recent happenings in Judaea: about Jesus of
Nazareth and how he began in Galilee, after John had been
preaching baptism. God had anointed him with the Holy
Spirit and with power, and because God was with him, Jesus
went about doing good and curing all who had fallen into the
power of the devil. Now I, and those with me, can witness to
everything he did throughout the country-side of Judaea and
in Jerusalem itself: and also to the fact that they killed him by
hanging him on a tree, yet three days afterwards God raised him
to life and allowed him to be seen, not by the whole people
but only by certain witnesses God had chosen beforehand. Now
we are those witnesses — we have eaten and drunk with him
after his resurrection from the dead — and he has ordered us
to proclaim this to his people and to tell them that God has
appointed him to judge everyone, alive or dead. It is to him that
all the prophets bear this witness: that all who believe in Jesus
will have their sins forgiven through his name.'

This is the word of the Lord.

RESPONSORIAL PSALM   *(Ps 117:1-2.16-17.22-23)*

℟   **This day was made by the Lord;**
    we rejoice and are glad.

or   **Alleluia, alleluia, alleluia!**

1.   Give thanks to the Lord for he is good,
     for his love has no end.
     Let the sons of Israel say:
     'His love has no end.' ℟

2.   The Lord's right hand has triumphed;
     his right hand raised me up.
     I shall not die, I shall live
     and recount his deeds. ℟

(continued)

3.   The stone which the builders rejected
      has become the corner stone.
      This is the work of the Lord,
      a marvel in our eyes. ℞

℞   **This day was made by the Lord;
      we rejoice and are glad.**

or   **Alleluia, alleluia, alleluia!**

SECOND READING   *(Col 3:1-4)*

A reading from the letter of St Paul to the Colossians.

You must look for the things that are in heaven, where Christ is.

Since you have been brought back to true life with Christ, you
must look for the things that are in heaven, where Christ is,
sitting at God's right hand. Let your thoughts be on heavenly
things, not on the things that are on the earth, because you have
died, and now the life you have is hidden with Christ in God.
But when Christ is revealed — and he is your life — you too
will be revealed in all your glory with him.

       This is the word of the Lord.

Alternative Second Reading   *(1 Cor 5:6-8)*

A reading from the first letter of St Paul to the Corinthians.

Get rid of the old yeast, make yourselves into a completely new batch
of bread.

You must know how even a small amount of yeast is enough to
leaven all the dough, so get rid of all the old yeast, and make
yourselves into a completely new batch of bread, unleavened as
you are meant to be. Christ, our passover, has been sacrificed;
let us celebrate the feast, by getting rid of all the old yeast of evil
and wickedness, having only the unleavened bread of sincerity
and truth.

       This is the word of the Lord.

SEQUENCE

**Christians, to the Paschal Victim offer sacrifice and praise.
The sheep are ransomed by the Lamb;
and Christ, the undefiled,
hath sinners to his Father reconciled.
Death with life contended; combat strangely ended!
Life's own Champion, slain, yet lives to reign.
Tell us, Mary: say what thou didst see upon the way.
The tomb the Living did enclose;
I saw Christ's glory as he rose!**

The angels there attesting,
shroud with grave-clothes resting.
Christ, my hope, has risen: he goes before you into Galilee.
That Christ is truly risen from the dead we know.
Victorious king, thy mercy show!

GOSPEL ACCLAMATION   *(1 Cor 5:7-8)*
Alleluia, alleluia!
Christ, our passover, has been sacrificed;
let us celebrate the feast then, in the Lord.
Alleluia!

GOSPEL   *(Jn 20:1-9)*
(Instead of the following Gospel, that of the Easter Vigil may be used.)
A reading from the holy Gospel according to John.
He must rise from the dead.

It was very early on the first day of the week and still dark, when
Mary of Magdala came to the tomb. She saw that the stone had
been moved away from the tomb and came running to Simon
Peter and the other disciple, the one Jesus loved. 'They have
taken the Lord out of the tomb' she said 'and we don't know
where they have put him.'

So Peter set out with the other disciple to go to the tomb.
They ran together, but the other disciple, running faster than
Peter, reached the tomb first; he bent down and saw the linen
cloths lying on the ground, but did not go in. Simon Peter who
was following now came up, went right into the tomb, saw the
linen cloths on the ground, and also the cloth that had been
over his head; this was not with the linen cloths but rolled up
in a place by itself. Then the other disciple who had reached
the tomb first also went in; he saw and he believed. Till this
moment they had failed to understand the teaching of scripture,
that he must rise from the dead.

This is the Gospel of the Lord.

The rite of the Renewal of Baptismal Promises *(page 201) is desirable*
after the homily. The Profession of Faith *is then omitted.*

PRAYER OVER THE GIFTS
Lord,
with Easter joy we offer you the sacrifice
by which your Church is reborn and nourished
through Christ our Lord.

PREFACE OF EASTER I — *page 202*

COMMUNION ANTIPHON   *(1 Cor 5:7-8)*

Christ has become our paschal sacrifice; let us feast with the unleavened bread of sincerity and truth, alleluia.

PRAYER AFTER COMMUNION

Father of love, watch over your Church
and bring us to the glory of the resurrection
promised by this Easter sacrament.

SOLEMN BLESSING — *page 203*

REFLECTION

> Last night we heard the words, 'What good would life have been to us had Christ not come as our Redeemer?' This is not to denigrate the gift of life which we have been given. Rather it directs us where to search if we want to find a meaning to life. It is God who gives us life. It is Christ who gives life its primary significance, namely, the opportunity to embrace discipleship of the Father. Today we celebrate God's vindication of the choice Jesus made. The same choice is also ours.

━━━━━━━━━━━━━━ 19 APRIL ━━━━━━━━━━━━━━

SECOND SUNDAY OF EASTER
(Divine Mercy Sunday)

Eastertide extends from the Easter Vigil until Pentecost and during it the Paschal or Easter candle is lit. It is intended to be a symbol of the risen Lord among his people. His presence is light, shedding this light on the meaning of life. The candle is an invitation to those who seek this light in their lives to search the Scriptures, especially the Gospels, if they wish to embrace the teaching of Jesus found there.

ENTRANCE ANTIPHON   *(1 Pt 2:2)*

Like newborn children you should thirst for milk, on which your spirit can grow to strength, alleluia.

or   *(4 Ezra 2:36-37)*

Rejoice to the full in the glory that is yours, and give thanks to God who called you to his kingdom, alleluia.

GREETING, PENITENTIAL RITE, GLORIA — *pages 7-14*

OPENING PRAYER

Let us pray
    [for a deeper awareness of our Christian baptism]

God of mercy,
you wash away our sins in water,
you give us new birth in the Spirit,
and redeem us in the blood of Christ.
As we celebrate Christ's resurrection
increase our awareness of these blessings,
and renew your gift of life within us.

or

Let us pray
    [as Christians thirsting for the risen life]

Heavenly Father and God of mercy,
we no longer look for Jesus among the dead,
for he is alive and has become the Lord of life.
From the waters of death you raise us with him
and renew your gift of life within us.

Increase in our minds and hearts
the risen life we share with Christ
and help us to grow as your people
toward the fullness of eternal life with you.

FIRST READING   *(Acts 4:32-35)*

A reading from the Acts of the Apostles.

United, heart and soul.

The whole group of believers was united, heart and soul; no one claimed for his own use anything that he had, as everything they owned was held in common.

    The apostles continued to testify to the resurrection of the Lord Jesus with great power, and they were all given great respect.

    None of their members was ever in want, as all those who owned land or houses would sell them, and bring the money from them, to present it to the apostles; it was then distributed to any members who might be in need.

    This is the word of the Lord.

RESPONSORIAL PSALM   *(Ps 117:2-4.15-18.22-24)*

℟ **Give thanks to the Lord for he is good,
for his love has no end.**

or **Alleluia, alleluia, alleluia!**

1. Let the sons of Israel say:
    'His love has no end.'
    Let the sons of Aaron say:
    'His love has no end.'

(continued)

Let those who fear the Lord say:
'His love has no end.' ℟

℟ **Give thanks to the Lord for he is good,
   for his love has no end.**

or **Alleluia, alleluia, alleluia!**

2. The Lord's right hand has triumphed;
    his right hand raised me up.
    I shall not die, I shall live
    and recount his deeds.
    I was punished, I was punished by the Lord,
    but not doomed to die. ℟

3. The stone which the builders rejected
    has become the corner stone.
    This is the work of the Lord,
    a marvel in our eyes.
    This day was made by the Lord;
    we rejoice and are glad. ℟

SECOND READING   *(1 Jn 5:1-6)*

A reading from the first letter of St John.

Anyone who has been begotten by God has already overcome the world.

Whoever believes that Jesus is the Christ
has been begotten by God;
and whoever loves the Father that begot him
loves the child whom he begets.
We can be sure that we love God's children
if we love God himself and do what he has commanded us;
this is what loving God is —
keeping his commandments;
and his commandments are not difficult,
because anyone who has been begotten by God
has already overcome the world;
this is the victory over the world —
our faith.
Who can overcome the world?
Only the man who believes that Jesus is the Son of God;
Jesus Christ who came by water and blood,
not with water only,
but with water and blood;
with the Spirit as another witness —
since the Spirit is the truth.

         This is the word of the Lord.

Alleluia, alleluia!
Jesus said: 'You believe because you can see me.
Happy are those who have not seen and yet believe.'
Alleluia!

GOSPEL   (Jn 20:19-31)

A reading from the holy Gospel according to John.

Eight days later, Jesus came.

In the evening of that same day, the first day of the week, the doors were closed in the room where the disciples were, for fear of the Jews. Jesus came and stood among them. He said to them, 'Peace be with you,' and showed them his hands and his side. The disciples were filled with joy when they saw the Lord, and he said to them again, 'Peace be with you.

'As the Father sent me,
so am I sending you.'

After saying this he breathed on them and said:

'Receive the Holy Spirit.
For those whose sins you forgive,
they are forgiven;
for those whose sins you retain,
they are retained.'

Thomas, called the Twin, who was one of the Twelve, was not with them when Jesus came. When the disciples said, 'We have seen the Lord,' he answered, 'Unless I see the holes that the nails made in his hands and can put my finger into the holes they made, and unless I can put my hand into his side, I refuse to believe.' Eight days later the disciples were in the house again and Thomas was with them. The doors were closed, but Jesus came in and stood among them. 'Peace be with you,' he said. Then he spoke to Thomas, 'Put your finger here; look, here are my hands. Give me your hand; put it into my side. Doubt no longer but believe.' Thomas replied, 'My Lord and my God!' Jesus said to him;

'You believe because you can see me.
Happy are those who have not seen and yet believe.'

There were many other signs that Jesus worked and the disciples saw, but they are not recorded in this book. These are recorded so that you may believe that Jesus is the Christ, the

Son of God, and that believing this you may have life through his name.

This is the Gospel of the Lord.

PROFESSION OF FAITH — *pages 15-16*

PRAYER OVER THE GIFTS

Lord,
through faith and baptism
we have become a new creation.
Accept the offerings of your people
(and of those born again in baptism)
and bring us to eternal happiness.

PREFACE EASTER I — *page 202*

COMMUNION ANTIPHON   *(cf. Jn 20:27)*

Jesus spoke to Thomas: Put your hand here, and see the place of the nails. Doubt no longer, but believe, alleluia.

PRAYER AFTER COMMUNION

Almighty God,
may the Easter sacraments we have received
live for ever in our minds and hearts.

SOLEMN BLESSING — *pages 56-57*

REFLECTION

That the good news of what God has done for humankind in Jesus is intended not just for every race on earth but for every generation and succeeding generation too is clear from today's gospel. We take consolation from the words John attributes to the risen Lord, 'Happy are those who have not seen and yet believe.' The supreme source of this happiness is that God has come to the rescue of humankind by meeting our greatest need, whether it is recognised as such or not, namely, salvation.

23 APRIL

ST GEORGE
(Patron of England)

The patron of England and a martyr, very little is known about the life of George. His historical existence, though it has sometimes been disputed, is now generally accepted. It is likely that he suffered before the time of Constantine in the Fourth Century but it wasn't until the Sixth Century that devotion to him became popular. In 1415 his feast became one of the chief holydays of the year in England. It was around this time that Saint George's arms, a red cross on a white background, became a kind of uniform for soldiers.

ENTRANCE ANTIPHON   *(cf. 4 Ezra 2:35)*

Light for ever will shine on your saints, O Lord, alleluia.

GREETING, PENITENTIAL RITE, GLORIA – *pages 7-14*

OPENING PRAYER

Lord,
hear the prayers of those who praise your mighty power.
As Saint George was ready to follow Christ in suffering and
    death,
so may he be ready to help us in our weakness.

FIRST READING   *(Apo 12:10-12)*

A reading from the book of the Apocalypse.
In the face of death they would not cling to life.

I, John, heard a voice shout from heaven, 'Victory and power and empire for ever have been won by our God, and all authority for his Christ, now that the persecutor, who accused our brothers day and night before our God, has been brought down. They have triumphed over him by the blood of the Lamb and by the witness of their martyrdom, because even in the face of death they would not cling to life. Let the heavens rejoice and all who live there.'

This is the word of the Lord.

RESPONSORIAL PSALM   *(Ps 125)*

℟ **Those who are sowing in tears**
    will sing when they reap.

1. When the Lord delivered Zion from bondage,
    it seemed like a dream.   *(continued)*

Then was our mouth filled with laughter,
on our lips there were songs. ℟

℟ **Those who are sowing in tears**
will sing when they reap.

2. The heathens themselves said:
   'What marvels the Lord worked for them!'
   What marvels the Lord worked for us!
   Indeed we were glad. ℟

3. Deliver us, O Lord, from our bondage
   as streams in dry land.
   Those who are sowing in tears
   will sing when they reap. ℟

4. They go out, they go out, full of tears,
   carrying seed for the sowing;
   they come back, they come back, full of song,
   carrying their sheaves. ℟

GOSPEL ACCLAMATION   (Jm 1:12)

Alleluia, alleluia!
Happy the man who stands firm,
for he has proved himself,
and will win the crown of life.
Alleluia!

GOSPEL   (Jn 15:18-21)

A reading from the holy Gospel according to John.

If they persecuted me, they will persecute you.

Jesus said to his disciples:

'If the world hates you,
remember that it hated me before you.
If you belonged to the world,
the world would love you as its own;
but because you do not belong to the world,
because my choice withdrew you from the world,
therefore the world hates you.
Remember the words I said to you:
A servant is not greater than his master.
If they persecuted me,
they will persecute you too;
if they kept my word,
they will keep yours as well.
But it will be on my account that they will do this,

because they do not know the one who sent me.'
This is the Gospel of the Lord.

PRAYER OVER THE GIFTS

Lord, bless our offerings and make them holy.
May these gifts fill our hearts
with the love which gave Saint George victory
over all his suffering.

PREFACE OF MARTYRS

Father, all powerful and ever-living God,
we do well always and everywhere to give you thanks.

Your holy martyr George followed the example of Christ,
and gave his life for the glory of your name.
His death reveals your power
shining through our human weakness.
You choose the weak and make them strong
in bearing witness to you,
through Jesus Christ our Lord.
In our unending joy we echo on earth
the song of the angels in heaven
as they praise your glory for ever:
Holy, holy, holy…

COMMUNION ANTIPHON   *(Jn 12:24)*

**I tell you solemnly: Unless a grain of wheat falls on the
ground and dies, it remains a single grain; but if it dies,
yields a rich harvest, alleluia.**

PRAYER AFTER COMMUNION

Lord, we receive your gifts from heaven
at this joyful feast.
May we who proclaim at this holy table
the death and resurrection of your Son
come to share his glory with Saint George
and all your holy martyrs.

REFLECTION

The fifty days of Eastertide serve to mark the fact that the
feast of the resurrection of the Lord is the greatest and the
oldest feast of the Christian Church. The spirit of the season is
captured by the word *alleluia* which is an expression of Easter
joy. The word is a combination of two words 'hallelu' and
'Yahweh' meaning 'praise' and 'the Lord' respectively.

26 APRIL

THIRD SUNDAY OF EASTER

In today's gospel Luke describes how fear can lead to faith, joy, wonder and future service. The final section of the gospel echoes a favourite theme of Luke: that Jesus can be known through the interpretation of Scripture.

ENTRANCE ANTIPHON   *(Ps 65:1-2)*

Let all the earth cry out to God with joy; praise the glory of his name; proclaim his glorious praise, alleluia.

GREETING, PENITENTIAL RITE, GLORIA — *pages 7-14*

OPENING PRAYER

Let us pray
    [that Christ will give us
    a share in the glory of his unending life]

God our Father,
may we look forward with hope to our resurrection,
for you have made us your sons and daughters,
and restored the joy of our youth.

or

Let us pray
    [in confident peace and Easter hope]

Father in heaven,
author of all truth,
a people once in darkness has listened to your Word
and followed your Son as he rose from the tomb.

Hear the prayer of this newborn people
and strengthen your Church to answer your call.
May we rise and come forth into the light of day
to stand in your presence until eternity dawns.

FIRST READING   *(Acts 3:13-15.17-19)*

A reading from the Acts of the Apostles.

You killed the prince of life. God, however, raised him from the dead.

Peter said to the people: 'You are Israelites, and it is the God of Abraham, Isaac and Jacob, the God of our ancestors, who has glorified his servant Jesus, the same Jesus you handed over and then disowned in the presence of Pilate, after Pilate had decided to release him. It was you who accused the Holy One, the Just

One, you who demanded the reprieve of a murderer while you killed the prince of life. God, however, raised him from the dead, and to that fact we are the witnesses.

'Now I know, brothers, that neither you nor your leaders had any idea what you were really doing; this was the way God carried out what he had foretold, when he said through all his prophets that his Christ would suffer. Now you must repent and turn to God, so that your sins may be wiped out.'

This is the word of the Lord.

RESPONSORIAL PSALM   *(Ps 4:2.4.7.9)*

℟   **Lift up the light of your face on us, O Lord.**

or   **Alleluia!**

1.   When I call, answer me, O God of justice;
     from anguish you released me,
     have mercy and hear me! ℟

2.   It is the Lord who grants favours to those whom he loves;
     the Lord hears me whenever I call him. ℟

3.   'What can bring us happiness?' many say.
     Lift up the light of your face on us, O Lord. ℟

4.   I will lie down in peace and sleep comes at once,
     for you alone, Lord, make me dwell in safety. ℟

SECOND READING   *(1 Jn 2:1-5)*

A reading from the first letter of St John.

He is the sacrifice that takes our sins away, and not only ours, but the whole world's.

I am writing this, my children,
to stop you sinning;
but if anyone should sin,
we have our advocate with the Father,
Jesus Christ, who is just;
he is the sacrifice that takes our sins away,
and not only ours,
but the whole world's.
We can be sure that we know God
only by keeping his commandments.
Anyone who says, 'I know him',
and does not keep his commandments,
is a liar,
refusing to admit the truth.

But when anyone does obey what he has said,
God's love comes to perfection in him.

This is the word of the Lord.

GOSPEL ACCLAMATION   *(cf. Lk 24:32)*
Alleluia, alleluia!
Lord Jesus, explain the scriptures to us.
Make our hearts burn within us as you talk to us.
Alleluia!

GOSPEL   *(Lk 24:35-48)*
A reading from the holy Gospel according to Luke.

So you see how it is written that the Christ would suffer and on the
third day rise from the dead.

The disciples told their story of what had happened on the road
and how they had recognised Jesus at the breaking of bread.

They were still talking about all this when Jesus himself
stood among them and said to them, 'Peace be with you!' In
a state of alarm and fright, they thought they were seeing a
ghost. But he said, 'Why are you so agitated, and why are these
doubts rising in your hearts? Look at my hands and feet; yes,
it is I indeed. Touch me and see for yourselves; a ghost has no
flesh and bones as you can see I have.' And as he said this he
showed them his hands and feet. Their joy was so great that
they could not believe it, and they stood dumbfounded; so he
said to them, 'Have you anything here to eat?' And they offered
him a piece of grilled fish, which he took and ate before their
eyes.

Then he told them, 'This is what I meant when I said, while
I was still with you, that everything written about me in the Law
of Moses, in the Prophets and in the Psalms, has to be fulfilled.'
He then opened their minds to understand the scriptures, and
he said to them. 'So you see how it is written that the Christ
would suffer and on the third day rise from the dead, and that,
in his name, repentance for the forgiveness of sins would be preached
to all the nations, beginning from Jerusalem. You are witnesses
to this.'

This is the Gospel of the Lord.

PROFESSION OF FAITH — *pages 15-16*

PRAYER OVER THE GIFTS

Lord,
receive these gifts from your Church.
May the great joy you give us
come to perfection in heaven.

PREFACE OF EASTER II-V — *pages 21-22*

COMMUNION ANTIPHON   *(Lk 24:46-47)*

Christ had to suffer and to rise from the dead on the third day. In his name penance for the remission of sins is to be preached to all nations, alleluia.

PRAYER AFTER COMMUNION

Lord,
look on your people with kindness
and by these Easter mysteries
bring us to the glory of the resurrection.

SOLEMN BLESSING — *pages 56-57*

REFLECTION

Luke's account of the death of Jesus emphasised his complete abandonment to God with the words of a psalm, 'Into your hands I commend my spirit.' Today we celebrate God's vindication of him. Jesus explains in today's gospel that the cross has a role in conversion and that resurrection is the outcome. In raising Jesus from the dead, God the Father confirmed the teaching Jesus gave and the life he lived.

3 MAY
FOURTH SUNDAY OF EASTER
Vocation Sunday

The image put before us in today's liturgy to describe the person
and work of Jesus among his disciples is that of shepherd.
It is one which would have been extremely familiar to Jesus'
hearers for whom the sight of an individual leading sheep to
pasture would have been a common one. We are told that in the
Holy Land shepherds lead rather than drive. So sheep follow
rather than are driven. Two aspects of this are important. First,
to follow involves a free choice. Second, to follow someone
means to have confidence in their ability to lead.

ENTRANCE ANTIPHON   *(Ps 32:5-6)*
**The earth is full of the goodness of the Lord; by the word of
the Lord the heavens were made, alleluia.**

GREETING, PENITENTIAL RITE, GLORIA — *pages 7-14*

OPENING PRAYER
Let us pray
    [that Christ our shepherd
    will lead us through the difficulties of this life]

Almighty and ever-living God,
give us new strength
from the courage of Christ our shepherd,
and lead us to join the saints in heaven,
where he lives and reigns with you and the Holy Spirit,
one God, for ever and ever.

or

Let us pray
    [to God our helper in time of distress]

God and Father of our Lord Jesus Christ,
though your people walk in the valley of darkness,
no evil should they fear;
for they follow in faith the call of the shepherd
whom you have sent for their hope and strength.

Attune our minds to the sound of his voice,
lead our steps in the path he has shown,
that we may know the strength of his outstretched arm
and enjoy the light of your presence for ever.

FIRST READING   *(Acts 4:8-12)*

A reading from the Acts of the Apostles.

This is the only name by which we can be saved.

Filled with the Holy Spirit, Peter said: 'Rulers of the people, and elders! If you are questioning us today about an act of kindness to a cripple, and asking us how he was healed, then I am glad to tell you all, and would indeed be glad to tell the whole people of Israel, that it was by the name of Jesus Christ the Nazarene, the one you crucified, whom God raised from the dead, by this name and by no other that this man is able to stand up perfectly healthy, here in your presence today. This is the stone rejected by you the builders, but which has proved to be the keystone. For of all the names in the world given to men, this is the only one by which we can be saved.'

This is the word of the Lord.

RESPONSORIAL PSALM   *(Ps 117:1.8-9.21-23.26.28-29)*

℟   **The stone which the builders rejected
    has become the corner stone.**

or   **Alleluia!**

1.   Give thanks to the Lord for he is good,
     for his love has no end.
     It is better to take refuge in the Lord
     than to trust in men:
     it is better to take refuge in the Lord
     than to trust in princes. ℟

2.   I will thank you for you have given answer
     and you are my saviour.
     The stone which the builders rejected
     has become the corner stone.
     This is the work of the Lord,
     a marvel in our eyes. ℟

3.   Blessed in the name of the Lord
     is he who comes.
     We bless you from the house of the Lord;
     I will thank you for you have given answer
     and you are my saviour.
     Give thanks to the Lord for he is good;
     for his love has no end. ℟

SECOND READING   (1 Jn 3:1-2)

A reading from the first letter of St John.

We shall see God as he really is.

Think of the love that the Father has lavished on us,
by letting us be called God's children;
and that is what we are.
Because the world refused to acknowledge him,
therefore it does not acknowledge us.
My dear people, we are already the children of God
but what we are to be in the future has not yet been revealed;
all we know is, that when it is revealed
we shall be like him
because we shall see him as he really is.

    This is the word of the Lord.

GOSPEL ACCLAMATION   (Jn 10:14)

Alleluia, alleluia!
I am the good shepherd, says the Lord;
I know my own sheep and my own know me.
Alleluia!

GOSPEL   (Jn 10:11-18)

A reading from the holy Gospel according to John.

The good shepherd is one who lays down his life for his sheep.

Jesus said:

    'I am the good shepherd:
    the good shepherd is one who lays down his life for his
        sheep.
    The hired man, since he is not the shepherd
    and the sheep do not belong to him,
    abandons the sheep and runs away
    as soon as he sees a wolf coming,
    and then the wolf attacks and scatters the sheep;
    this is because he is only a hired man
    and has no concern for the sheep.
    I am the good shepherd;
    I know my own
    and my own know me,
    just as the Father knows me
    and I know the Father;
    and I lay down my life for my sheep.
    And there are other sheep I have
    that are not of this fold,

and these I have to lead as well.
They too will listen to my voice,
and there will be only one flock
and one shepherd.
The Father loves me,
because I lay down my life
in order to take it up again.
No one takes it from me;
I lay it down of my own free will,
and as it is in my power to lay it down,
so it is in my power to take it up again;
and this is the command I have been given by my Father.'

This is the Gospel of the Lord.

PROFESSION OF FAITH — *pages 15-16*

PRAYER OVER THE GIFTS
Lord,
restore us by these Easter mysteries.
May the continuing work of our Redeemer
bring us eternal joy.

PREFACE OF EASTER II-V — *pages 21-22*

COMMUNION ANTIPHON
**The Good Shepherd is risen! He who laid down his life for
his sheep, who died for his flock, he is risen, alleluia.**

PRAYER AFTER COMMUNION
Father, eternal shepherd,
watch over the flock redeemed by the blood of Christ
and lead us to the promised land.

SOLEMN BLESSING — *pages 56-57*

REFLECTION
Lord Jesus, today we are invited once again to renew the
choice we have made in becoming and remaining your
disciple. Just as you made the choice to do the Father's will
in freedom so do we realise that it is in freedom that we are
asked to respond. Because the Father has raised you from the
dead we have confidence that the path you chose is also open
to us. You prayed that where you are we may be also. We make
that prayer today. Amen.

10 MAY

FIFTH SUNDAY OF EASTER

Today's gospel offers us an image of what it means to be a
disciple of Jesus. The word literally means one who is
learning, a good attitude to carry throughout life. The way one
learns from another is by observing what they do, by trying to
capture some of the spirit which animates them, in short, by
being with them. And this is precisely what the image of the
vine and the branches is intended to convey, namely, that it is
by keeping company with the Lord, who is forever present in
the Church, that we develop and grow as followers of his.

ENTRANCE ANTIPHON   *(Ps 97:1-2)*

**Sing to the Lord a new song, for he has done marvellous deeds;
he has revealed to the nations his saving power, alleluia.**

GREETING, PENITENTIAL RITE, GLORIA — *pages 7-14*

OPENING PRAYER

Let us pray
    [that we may enjoy true freedom]

God our Father,
look upon us with love.
You redeem us and make us your children in Christ.
Give us true freedom
and bring us to the inheritance you promised.

or

Let us pray
    [in the freedom of the children of God]

Father of our Lord Jesus Christ,
you have revealed to the nations your saving power
and filled all ages with the words of a new song.
Hear the echo of this hymn.
Give us voice to sing your praise
throughout this season of joy.

FIRST READING   *(Acts 9:26-31)*

A reading from the Acts of the Apostles.

Barnabas explained how the Lord had appeared to Saul on his journey.

When Saul got to Jerusalem he tried to join the disciples, but
they were all afraid of him: they could not believe he was really
a disciple. Barnabas, however, took charge of him, introduced

him to the apostles, and explained how the Lord had appeared to Saul and spoken to him on his journey, and how he had preached boldly at Damascus in the name of Jesus. Saul now started to go round with them in Jerusalem, preaching fearlessly in the name of the Lord. But after he had spoken to the Hellenists, and argued with them, they became determined to kill him. When the brothers knew, they took him to Caesarea, and sent him off from there to Tarsus.

The churches throughout Judaea, Galilee and Samaria were now left in peace, building themselves up, living in the fear of the Lord, and filled with the consolation of the Holy Spirit.

This is the word of the Lord.

RESPONSORIAL PSALM   *(Ps 21:26-28.30-32)*

℟   **You, Lord, are my praise in the great assembly.**

or   **Alleluia!**

1.   My vows I will pay before those who fear him.
     The poor shall eat and shall have their fill.
     They shall praise the Lord, those who seek him.
     May their hearts live for ever and ever! ℟

2.   All the earth shall remember and return to the Lord,
     all families of the nations worship before him.
     They shall worship him, all the mighty of the earth;
     before him shall bow all who go down to the dust. ℟

3.   And my soul shall live for him, my children serve him.
     They shall tell of the Lord to generations yet to come,
     declare his faithfulness to peoples yet unborn:
     'These things the Lord has done.' ℟

SECOND READING   *(1 Jn 3:18-24)*

A reading from the first letter of St John.

His commandments are these: that we believe in his Son and that we love one another.

My children,
our love is not to be just words or mere talk,
but something real and active;
only by this can we be certain
that we are the children of the truth
and be able to quieten our conscience in his presence,
whatever accusations it may raise against us,
because God is greater than our conscience and he knows
        everything.

My dear people,
if we cannot be condemned by our conscience,
we need not be afraid in God's presence,
and whatever we ask him,
we shall receive,
because we keep his commandments
and live the kind of life that he wants.
His commandments are these:
that we believe in the name of his Son Jesus Christ
and that we love one another
as he told us to.
Whoever keeps his commandments
lives in God and God lives in him.
We know that he lives in us
by the Spirit that he has given us.

This is the word of the Lord.

GOSPEL ACCLAMATION   (Jn 15:4.5)

Alleluia, alleluia!
Make your home in me, as I make mine in you,
says the Lord.
Whoever remains in me bears fruit in plenty.
Alleluia!

GOSPEL   (Jn 15:1-8)

A reading from the holy Gospel according to John.
Whoever remains in me, with me in him, bears fruit in plenty.

Jesus said to his disciples:

'I am the true vine,
and my Father is the vinedresser.
Every branch in me that bears no fruit
he cuts away,
and every branch that does bear fruit he prunes
to make it bear even more.
You are pruned already,
by means of the word that I have spoken to you.
Make your home in me, as I make mine in you.
As a branch cannot bear fruit all by itself,
but must remain part of the vine,
neither can you unless you remain in me.
I am the vine,
you are the branches.
Whoever remains in me, with me in him,

bears fruit in plenty;
for cut off from me you can do nothing.
Anyone who does not remain in me
is like a branch that has been thrown away
— he withers;
these branches are collected and thrown on the fire,
and they are burnt.
If you remain in me
and my words remain in you,
you may ask what you will
and you shall get it.
It is to the glory of my Father that you should bear much
fruit,
and then you will be my disciples.'
This is the Gospel of the Lord.

PROFESSION OF FAITH — *pages 15-16*

PRAYER OVER THE GIFTS
Lord God,
by this holy exchange of gifts
you share with us your divine life.
Grant that everything we do
may be directed by the knowledge of your truth.

PREFACE OF EASTER II-V — *pages 21-22*

COMMUNION ANTIPHON   *(Jn 15:5)*
**I am the vine and you are the branches, says the Lord; he who
lives in me, and I in him, will bear much fruit, alleluia!**

PRAYER AFTER COMMUNION
Merciful Father,
may these mysteries give us new purpose
and bring us to a new life in you.

SOLEMN BLESSING — *pages 56-57*

REFLECTION
Lord Jesus, we thank you for the many ways that you are
present to your Church: in the assembled congregation, in the
word that is proclaimed, in the person of the minister and
in the holy sacrament. Through these means you invite us to
keep company with you today and throughout our lives.

17 MAY
SIXTH SUNDAY OF EASTER

Love, or charity, has often been described as the primary
Christian virtue. If there were any doubt as to why it should
be so today's gospel would dispel it. The Father's relationship
with Jesus is seen in terms of love. So too is Jesus' relationship
with his disciples. And it is love which Jesus commands his
disciples to have for one another. Saint John puts this demand
of Jesus in the context of his last supper conversation with his
disciples, thus giving it added emphasis. Jesus' laying down
his life for his friends is presented as the highest expression of
love that any human being can have for another.

ENTRANCE ANTIPHON   *(cf. Is 48:20)*

**Speak out with a voice of joy; let it be heard to the ends of
the earth: The Lord has set his people free, alleluia.**

GREETING, PENITENTIAL RITE, GLORIA — *pages 7-14*

OPENING PRAYER

Let us pray
    [that we may practise in our lives
    the faith we profess]

Ever-living God,
help us to celebrate our joy
in the resurrection of the Lord
and to express in our lives
the love we celebrate.
or

Let us pray
    [in silence, reflecting on the joy of Easter]

God our Father, maker of all,
the crown of your creation was the Son of Man,
born of a woman, but without beginning;
he suffered for us but lives for ever.

May our mortal lives be crowned with the ultimate joy
of rising with him,
who is Lord for ever and ever.

FIRST READING   *(Acts 10:25-26.34-35.44-48)*

A reading from the Acts of the Apostles.
The Holy Spirit has been poured out on the pagans too.

As Peter reached the house Cornelius went out to meet him, knelt at his feet and prostrated himself. But Peter helped him up. 'Stand up,' he said 'I am only a man after all!'

Then Peter addressed them: 'The truth I have now come to realise' he said 'is that God does not have favourites, but that anybody of any nationality who fears God and does what is right is acceptable to him.'

While Peter was still speaking the Holy Spirit came down on all the listeners. Jewish believers who had accompanied Peter were all astonished that the gift of the Holy Spirit should be poured out on the pagans too, since they could hear them speaking strange languages and proclaiming the greatness of God. Peter himself then said, 'Could anyone refuse the water of baptism to these people, now they have received the Holy Spirit just as much as we have?' He then gave orders for them to be baptised in the name of Jesus Christ. Afterwards they begged him to stay on for some days.

This is the word of the Lord.

RESPONSORIAL PSALM   *(Ps 97:1-4)*

℟   **The Lord has shown his salvation to the nations.**

or   **Alleluia!**

1.   Sing a new song to the Lord
     for he has worked wonders.
     His right hand and his holy arm
     have brought salvation. ℟

2.   The Lord has made known his salvation;
     has shown his justice to the nations.
     He has remembered his truth and love
     for the house of Israel. ℟

3.   All the ends of the earth have seen
     the salvation of our God.
     Shout to the Lord all the earth,
     ring out your joy. ℟

SECOND READING   *(1 Jn 4:7-10)*

A reading from the first letter of St John.

God is love.

My dear people,
let us love one another
since love comes from God
and everyone who loves is begotten by God and knows God.

Anyone who fails to love can never have known God,
because God is love.
God's love for us was revealed
when God sent into the world his only Son
so that we could have life through him;
this is the love I mean:
not our love for God,
but God's love for us when he sent his Son
to be the sacrifice that takes our sins away.

    This is the word of the Lord.

GOSPEL ACCLAMATION   *(Jn 14:23)*

Alleluia, alleluia!
Jesus said: 'If anyone loves me he will keep my word,
and my Father will love him, and we shall come to him.'
Alleluia!

GOSPEL   *(Jn 15:9-17)*

A reading from the holy Gospel according to John.

A man can have no greater love than to lay down his life for his friends.

Jesus said to his disciples:

    'As the Father has loved me,
    so have I loved you.
    Remain in my love.
    If you keep my commandments
    you will remain in my love,
    just as I have kept my Father's commandments
    and remain in his love.
    I have told you this
    so that my own joy may be in you
    and your joy be complete.
    This is my commandment:
    love one another,
    as I have loved you.
    A man can have no greater love
    than to lay down his life for his friends.
    You are my friends,
    if you do what I command you.
    I shall not call you servants any more,
    because a servant does not know
    his master's business;
    I call you friends,
    because I have made known to you

everything I have learnt from my Father.
You did not choose me,
no, I chose you;
and I commissioned you
to go out and to bear fruit,
fruit that will last;
and then the Father will give you
anything you ask him in my name.
What I command you
is to love one another.'
This is the Gospel of the Lord.

PROFESSION OF FAITH — *pages 15-16*

PRAYER OVER THE GIFTS

Lord,
accept our prayers and offerings.
Make us worthy of your sacraments of love
by granting us your forgiveness.

PREFACE OF EASTER II-V — *pages 21-22*

COMMUNION ANTIPHON   *(Jn 14:15-16)*

**If you love me, keep my commandments, says the Lord. The
Father will send you the Holy Spirit, to be with you for ever,
alleluia.**

PRAYER AFTER COMMUNION

Almighty and ever-living Lord,
you restored us to life
by raising Christ from death.
Strengthen us by this Easter sacrament;
may we feel its saving power in our daily life.

SOLEMN BLESSING — *pages 56-57*

REFLECTION

It is not by accident that the theme of love should emerge
at the same time as the theme of the Spirit in our liturgical
celebration. The call to love one another is both a challenge
and an ideal. We fail in this regard regularly. But it is the Spirit
who helps us in our weakness. The Spirit, who is the Father's
gift to us, has been poured into our hearts at our baptism.
The Spirit is a silent but powerful force sustaining us in our
inadequacies and encouraging and empowering us on our
journey.

24 MAY
THE ASCENSION OF THE LORD

World Communications Day

The Ascension, which is one of the chief feasts of the Church's year, marks the close of the appearances of Jesus which took place after his resurrection and celebrates his exaltation to the Father. It is an essential element of the resurrection of the Lord. It is portrayed as having taken place variously, even by the same author, on the evening of Easter Sunday and forty days later. It underlines the teaching that it is from Heaven that the exalted Christ exercises his power over heaven and earth.

ENTRANCE ANTIPHON   (Acts 1:10)

Men of Galilee, why do you stand looking in the sky? The Lord will return, just as you have seen him ascend, alleluia.

GREETING, PENITENTIAL RITE, GLORIA — *pages 7-14*

OPENING PRAYER

Let us pray
    [that the risen Christ
    will lead us to eternal life]
God our Father,
make us joyful in the ascension of your Son Jesus Christ.
May we follow him into the new creation,
for his ascension is our glory and our hope.

or

Let us pray
    [on this day of Ascension
    as we watch and wait for Jesus' return]

Father in heaven,
our minds were prepared for the coming of your kingdom
when you took Christ beyond our sight
so that we might seek him in his glory.

May we follow where he has led
and find our hope in his glory,
for he is Lord for ever.

FIRST READING   (Acts 1:1-11)

A reading from the Acts of the Apostles.
He was lifted up while they looked on.

In my earlier work, Theophilus, I dealt with everything Jesus had done and taught from the beginning until the day he gave his instructions to the apostles he had chosen through the Holy Spirit, and was taken up to heaven. He had shown himself alive to them after his Passion by many demonstrations: for forty days he had continued to appear to them and tell them about the kingdom of God. When he had been at table with them, he had told them not to leave Jerusalem, but to wait there for what the Father had promised. 'It is,' he had said, 'what you have heard me speak about: John baptised with water but you, not many days from now, will be baptised with the Holy Spirit.'

Now having met together, they asked him, 'Lord, has the time come? Are you going to restore the kingdom to Israel?' He replied, 'It is not for you to know times or dates that the Father has decided by his own authority, but you will receive power when the Holy Spirit comes on you, and then you will be my witnesses not only in Jerusalem but throughout Judaea and Samaria, and indeed to the ends of the earth.'

As he said this he was lifted up while they looked on, and a cloud took him from their sight. They were still staring into the sky when suddenly two men in white were standing near them and they said, 'Why are you men from Galilee standing here looking into the sky? Jesus who has been taken up from you into heaven, this same Jesus will come back in the same way as you have seen him go there.'

This is the word of the Lord.

RESPONSORIAL PSALM   (Ps 46:2-3.6-9)

℟   **God goes up with shouts of joy;**
      the Lord goes up with trumpet blast.

or   **Alleluia!**

1.   All peoples, clap your hands,
       cry to God with shouts of joy!
       For the Lord, the Most High, we must fear,
       great king over all the earth. ℟

2.   God goes up with shouts of joy;
       the Lord goes up with trumpet blast.
       Sing praise for God, sing praise,
       sing praise to our king, sing praise. ℟

3.   God is king of all the earth.
       Sing praise with all your skill.
       God is king over the nations;
       God reigns on his holy throne. ℟

SECOND READING   *(Eph 4:1-13)*

A reading from the letter of St Paul to the Ephesians.

Fully mature with the fullness of Christ.

I, the prisoner in the Lord, implore you to lead a life worthy of your vocation. Bear with one another charitably, in complete selflessness, gentleness and patience. Do all you can to preserve the unity of the Spirit by the peace that binds you together. There is one Body, one Spirit, just as you were all called into one and the same hope when you were called. There is one Lord, one faith, one baptism, and one God who is Father of all, over all, through all and within all.

Each one of us, however, has been given his own share of grace, given as Christ allotted it. It was said that he would:

When he ascended to the height, he captured prisoners,
he gave gifts to men.

When it says, 'he ascended', what can it mean if not that he descended right down to the lower regions of the earth? The one who rose higher than all the heavens to fill all things is none other than the one who descended. And to some, his gift was that they should be apostles; to some, prophets; to some, evangelists; to some, pastors and teachers; so that the saints together make a unity in the work of service, building up the body of Christ. In this way we are all to come to unity in our faith and in our knowledge of the Son of God, until we become the perfect Man, fully mature with the fullness of Christ himself.

This is the word of the Lord.

(The following Second Reading of Year A, Eph 1:17-23, may be used instead of the above.)

A reading from the letter of St Paul to the Ephesians.

He made him sit at his right hand in heaven.

May the God of our Lord Jesus Christ, the Father of glory, give you a spirit of wisdom and perception of what is revealed, to bring you to full knowledge of him. May he enlighten the eyes of your mind so that you can see what hope his call holds for you, what rich glories he has promised the saints will inherit and how infinitely great is the power that he has exercised for us believers. This you can tell from the strength of his power at work in Christ, when he used it to raise him from the dead and to make him sit at his right hand, in heaven, far above every Sovereignty, Authority, Power, or Domination, or any other name that can be named, not only in this age, but also in the age to come. He has put all things under his feet, and made him as the ruler of everything, the head of the Church; which is his body, the fullness of him who fills the whole creation.

This is the word of the Lord.

GOSPEL ACCLAMATION   (Mt 28:19.20)

Alleluia, alleluia!
Go, make disciples of all the nations;
I am with you always; yes, to the end of time.
Alleluia!

GOSPEL   (Mk 16:15-20)

A reading from the holy Gospel according to Mark.

He was taken up into heaven: there at the right hand of God he took his place.

Jesus showed himself to the Eleven, and said to them, 'Go out to the whole world; proclaim the Good News to all creation. He who believes and is baptised will be saved; he who does not believe will be condemned. These are the signs that will be associated with believers: in my name they will cast out devils; they will have the gift of tongues; they will pick up snakes in their hands, and be unharmed should they drink deadly poison; they will lay their hands on the sick, who will recover.'

And so the Lord Jesus, after he had spoken to them, was taken up into heaven: there at the right hand of God he took his place, while they, going out, preached everywhere, the Lord working with them and confirming the word by the signs that accompanied it.

This is the Gospel of the Lord.

PROFESSION OF FAITH — *pages 15-16*

PRAYER OVER THE GIFTS

Lord, receive our offering
as we celebrate the ascension of Christ your Son.
May his gifts help us rise with him
to the joys of heaven,
where he lives and reigns for ever and ever.

PREFACE OF THE ASCENSION I

Father, all-powerful and ever-living God,
we do well always and everywhere to give you thanks.

[Today] the Lord Jesus, the King of glory,
the conqueror of sin and death,
ascended to heaven while the angels sang his praises.

Christ, the mediator between God and man,
judge of the world and Lord of all,
has passed beyond our sight,
not to abandon us but to be our hope.
Christ is the beginning, the head of the Church;
where he has gone, we hope to follow.

The joy of the resurrection and ascension renews the whole world,
while the choirs of heaven sing for ever to your glory:
Holy, holy, holy…

COMMUNION ANTIPHON   *(Mt 28:20)*

**I, the Lord, am with you always, until the end of the world,
alleluia.**

PRAYER AFTER COMMUNION

Father, in this eucharist
we touch the divine life you give to the world.
Help us to follow Christ with love
to eternal life where he is Lord for ever and ever.

SOLEMN BLESSING

May almighty God bless you on this day
when his only Son ascended into heaven
to prepare a place for you. **Amen.**

After his resurrection, Christ was seen by his disciples.
When he appears as judge
may you be pleasing for ever in his sight. **Amen**.

You believe that Jesus has taken his seat in majesty
at the right hand of the Father.
May you have the joy of experiencing
that he is also with you to the end of time,
according to his promise. **Amen**.

May almighty God bless you,
the Father, and the Son, ✠ and the Holy Spirit. **Amen**.

REFLECTION

The Lord linked his Ascension into Heaven with the sending
of the Holy Spirit, making one a condition of the other. The
Ascension marks the transition from Jesus' visible presence
to his Church to his invisible dwelling among us until the
end of time. That is why the Ascension is not a departure but
an arrival. It is a celebration of the presence of the risen Lord
throughout the world wherever two or three are gathered in
his name.

31 MAY

PENTECOST SUNDAY

VIGIL MASS

"Come, Holy Spirit!" Where truth, love, goodness, peace, kindness, wisdom, courage, patience, and many others of his fruits are present, there the Spirit is active. In so many different ways, the Spirit reminds the world of the Gospel.

ENTRANCE ANTIPHON   *(cf Rm 5:5; 8:11)*

The love of God has been poured into our hearts by his Spirit living in us, alleluia.

GREETING, PENITENTIAL RITE, GLORIA — *pages 7-14*

OPENING PRAYER

Let us pray
[that the Holy Spirit
may bring peace and unity to all humankind]

Almighty and ever-living God,
you fulfilled the Easter promise
by sending us your Holy Spirit.
May that Spirit unite the races and nations on earth
to proclaim your glory.

or

God our Father,
you have given us new birth.
Strengthen us with your Holy Spirit
and fill us with your light.

or

Let us pray
[that the flame of the Spirit will descend upon us]

Father in heaven,
fifty days have celebrated the fullness
of the mystery of your revealed love.

See your people gathered in prayer,
open to receive the Spirit's flame.
May it come to rest in our hearts
and dispense the divisions of word and tongue.
With one voice and one song
may we praise your name in joy and thanksgiving.

FIRST READING *(Gen 11:1-9)*

A reading from the book of Genesis.

It was named Babel because there the language of the whole earth was confused.

Throughout the earth men spoke the same language, with the same vocabulary. Now as they moved eastwards they found a plain in the land of Shinar where they settled. They said to one another, 'Come, let us make bricks and bake them in the fire.' — For stone they used bricks, and for mortar they used bitumen. — 'Come,' they said, 'let us build ourselves a town and a tower with its top reaching heaven. Let us make a name for ourselves, so that we may not be scattered about the whole earth.'

Now the Lord came down to see the town and the tower that the sons of man had built. 'So they are all a single people with a single language!' said the Lord. 'This is but the start of their undertakings! There will be nothing too hard for them to do. Come, let us go down and confuse their language on the spot so that they can no longer understand one another.' The Lord scattered them thence over the whole face of the earth, and they stopped building the town. It was named Babel therefore, because there the Lord confused the language of the whole earth. It was from there that the Lord scattered them over the whole face of the earth.

This is the word of the Lord.

RESPONSORIAL PSALM *(Ps 103:1-2.24.27-30.35)*

℟ **Send forth your Spirit, O Lord,
and renew the face of the earth.**

or **Alleluia!**

1. Bless the Lord, my soul!
   Lord God, how great you are,
   clothed in majesty and glory,
   wrapped in light as in a robe! ℟

2. How many are your works, O Lord!
   In wisdom you have made them all.
   The earth is full of your riches.
   Bless the Lord, my soul. ℟

3. All of these look to you
   to give them their food in due season.
   You give it, they gather it up:
   you open your hand, they have their fill. ℟

4. You take back your spirit, they die,
    returning to the dust from which they came.
    You send forth your spirit, they are created;
    and you renew the face of the earth. ℞

SECOND READING   *(Rm 8:22-27)*

A reading from the letter of St Paul to the Romans.

The Spirit himself expresses our plea in a way that could never be put
into words.

From the beginning till now the entire creation, as we know,
has been groaning in one great act of giving birth; and not only
creation, but all of us who possess the first-fruits of the Spirit,
we too groan inwardly as we wait for our bodies to be set free.
For we must be content to hope that we shall be saved — our
salvation is not in sight, we should not have to be hoping for it
if it were — but, as I say, we must hope to be saved since we are
not saved yet — it is something we must wait for with patience.

   The Spirit too comes to help us in our weakness. For when
we cannot choose words in order to pray properly, the Spirit
himself expresses our plea in a way that could never be put into
words, and God who knows everything in our hearts knows
perfectly well what he means, and that the pleas of the saints
expressed by the Spirit are according to the mind of God.

   This is the word of the Lord.

GOSPEL ACCLAMATION

Alleluia, alleluia!
Come, Holy Spirit, fill the hearts of your faithful
and kindle in them the fire of your love.
Alleluia!

GOSPEL   *(Jn 7:37-39)*

A reading from the holy Gospel according to John.

From his breast shall flow fountains of living water.

On the last day and greatest day of the festival, Jesus stood there
and cried out:

   'If any man is thirsty, let him come to me!
   Let the man come and drink who believes in me!'

As scripture says: From his breast shall flow fountains of living water.

   He was speaking of the Spirit which those who believed in
him were to receive; for there was no Spirit as yet because Jesus
had not yet been glorified.

   This is the Gospel of the Lord.

PROFESSION OF FAITH — *pages 15-16*

PRAYER OVER THE GIFTS

Lord,
send your Spirit on these gifts
and through them help the Church you love
to show your salvation to all the world.

PREFACE OF PENTECOST — *page 245*

COMMUNION ANTIPHON   *(Jn 7:37)*

On the last day of the festival, Jesus stood and cried aloud: If anyone is thirsty, let him come to me and drink, alleluia.

PRAYER AFTER COMMUNION

Lord,
through this eucharist,
send the Holy Spirit of Pentecost into our hearts
to keep us always in your love.

SOLEMN BLESSING — *page 246*

REFLECTION

Pentecost, the second feast in rank of the Jews, means the "fiftieth day" after Passover. For the Christians it is celebrated ten days after the Ascension, to commemorate the descent of the Spirit and the beginning of the Church.

MASS DURING THE DAY

The word 'Pentecost' meaning 'fiftieth day' was the name given to the Feast of Weeks in the Jewish calendar because it fell on the fiftieth day after Passover. In the Christian tradition it was applied to the feast of the descent of the Holy Spirit because this event is portrayed as occurring fifty days after Easter Sunday. After Easter it has been described as the second festival of the Church. Pentecost Sunday marks the close of Eastertide.

ENTRANCE ANTIPHON   *(Ws 1:7)*

The Spirit of the Lord fills the whole world. It holds all things together and knows every word spoken by man, alleluia.
or   *(cf. Rm 5:5; 8:11)*
The love of God has been poured into our hearts by his Spirit living in us, alleluia.

GREETING, PENITENTIAL RITE, GLORIA — *pages 7-14*

OPENING PRAYER

Let us pray
[that the Spirit will work through our lives
to bring Christ to the world]

God our Father,
let the Spirit you sent on your Church
to begin the teaching of the gospel
continue to work in the world
through the hearts of all who believe.

or

Let us pray
[in the Spirit who dwells within us]

Father of light, from whom every good gift comes,
send your Spirit into our lives
with the power of a mighty wind,
and by the flame of your wisdom
open the horizons of our minds.

Loosen our tongues to sing your praise
in words beyond the power of speech,
for without your Spirit
man could never raise his voice in words of peace
or announce the truth that Jesus is Lord,
who lives and reigns with you and the Holy Spirit,
one God, for ever and ever.

FIRST READING   *(Acts 2:1-11)*

A reading from the Acts of the Apostles.

They were all filled with the Holy Spirit and began to speak.

When Pentecost day came round, the apostles had all met in one room, when suddenly they heard what sounded like a powerful wind from heaven, the noise of which filled the entire house in which they were sitting; and something appeared to them that seemed like tongues of fire; these separated and came to rest on the head of each of them. They were all filled with the Holy Spirit, and began to speak foreign languages as the Spirit gave them the gift of speech.

Now there were devout men living in Jerusalem from every nation under heaven, and at this sound they all assembled, each one bewildered to hear these men speaking his own language. They were amazed and astonished. 'Surely' they said 'all these men speaking are Galileans? How does it happen that each of us hears them in his own native language? Parthians, Medes and

Elamites; people from Mesopotamia, Judaea and Cappadocia, Pontus and Asia, Phrygia and Pamphylia, Egypt and the parts of Libya round Cyrene; as well as visitors from Rome — Jews and proselytes alike — Cretans and Arabs; we hear them preaching in our own language about the marvels of God.'

This is the word of the Lord.

RESPONSORIAL PSALM   *(Ps 103:1.24.29-31.34)*

℟   **Send forth your Spirit, O Lord,
      and renew the face of the earth.**

or   **Alleluia!**

1.   Bless the Lord, my soul!
      Lord God, how great you are!
      How many are your works, O Lord!
      The earth is full of your riches. ℟

2.   You take back your spirit, they die,
      returning to the dust from which they came.
      You send forth your spirit, they are created;
      and you renew the face of the earth. ℟

3.   May the glory of the Lord last for ever!
      May the Lord rejoice in his works!
      May my thoughts be pleasing to him.
      I find my joy in the Lord. ℟

SECOND READING   *(Gal 5:16-25)*

A reading from the letter of St Paul to the Galatians.
The fruit of the Spirit.

If you are guided by the Spirit you will be in no danger of yielding to self-indulgence, since self-indulgence is the opposite of the Spirit, the Spirit is totally against such a thing, and it is precisely because the two are so opposed that you do not always carry out your good intentions. If you are led by the Spirit, no law can touch you. When self-indulgence is at work the results are obvious: fornication, gross indecency and sexual irresponsibility; idolatry and sorcery; feuds and wrangling, jealousy, bad temper and quarrels; disagreements, factions, envy; drunkenness, orgies and similar things. I warn you now, as I warned you before: those who behave like this will not inherit the kingdom of God. What the Spirit brings is very different: love, joy, peace, patience, kindness, goodness, trustfulness, gentleness and self-control. There can be no law against things like that, of course. You cannot belong to Christ Jesus unless you crucify all self-indulgent passions and desires.

Since the Spirit is our life, let us be directed by the Spirit.

This is the word of the Lord.

(The following Second Reading of Year A, 1 Cor 12:3-7.12-13, may be used instead of the above.)

A reading from the first letter of St Paul to the Corinthians.
In the one Spirit we were all baptised.

No one can say, 'Jesus is Lord' unless he is under the influence of the Holy Spirit.

There is a variety of gifts but always the same Spirit; there are all sorts of service to be done, but always to the same Lord; working in all sorts of different ways in different people, it is the same God who is working in all of them. The particular way in which the Spirit is given to each person is for a good purpose.

Just as a human body, though it is made up of many parts, is a single unit because all these parts, though many, make one body, so it is with Christ. In the one Spirit we were all baptised, Jews as well as Greeks, slaves as well as citizens, and one Spirit was given to us all to drink.

This is the word of the Lord.

SEQUENCE
(The Sequence may be said or sung.)

Holy Spirit, Lord of light,
From the clear celestial height
Thy pure beaming radiance give.

Come, thou Father of the poor,
Come with treasures which endure;
Come, thou light of all that live!

Thou, of all consolers best,
Thou, the soul's delightful guest,
Dost refreshing peace bestow.

Thou in toil art comfort sweet;
Pleasant coolness in the heat;
Solace in the midst of woe.

Light immortal, light divine,
Visit thou these hearts of thine,
And our inmost being fill:

If thou take thy grace away,
Nothing pure in man will stay;
All his good is turned to ill.

Heal our wounds, our strength renew;
On our dryness pour thy dew;
Wash the stains of guilt away:

Bend the stubborn heart and will;
Melt the frozen, warm the chill;
Guide the steps that go astray.

Thou, on us who evermore
Thee confess and thee adore,
With thy sevenfold gifts descend:

Give us comfort when we die;
Give us life with thee on high;
Give us joys that never end.

GOSPEL ACCLAMATION

Alleluia, alleluia!
Come, Holy Spirit, fill the hearts of your faithful
and kindle in them the fire of your love.
Alleluia!

GOSPEL   *(Jn 15:26-27; 16:12-15)*

A reading from the holy Gospel according to John.
The Spirit of truth will lead you to the complete truth.

Jesus said to his disciples:

'When the Advocate comes,
    whom I shall send to you from the Father,
    the Spirit of truth who issues from the Father,
    he will be my witness.
And you too will be witnesses,
    because you have been with me from the outset.

I still have many things to say to you
    but they would be too much for you now.
But when the Spirit of truth comes
    he will lead you to the complete truth,
    since he will not be speaking as from himself
    but will say only what he has learnt;
    and he will tell you of the things to come.
He will glorify me,
    since all he tells you
    will be taken from what is mine.
Everything the Father has is mine;
    that is why I said:

All he tells you
will be taken from what is mine.'
This is the Gospel of the Lord.

(The following Gospel of Year A, Jn 20:19-23, may be used instead of the above.)

A reading from the holy Gospel according to John.

As the Father sent me, so am I sending you: receive the Holy Spirit.

In the evening of the first day of the week, the doors were closed in the room where the disciples were, for fear of the Jews. Jesus came and stood among them. He said to them, 'Peace be with you,' and showed them his hands and his side. The disciples were filled with joy when they saw the Lord, and he said to them again, 'Peace be with you'.

'As the Father sent me,
so am I sending you.'

After saying this he breathed on them and said:

'Receive the Holy Spirit.
For those whose sins you forgive,
they are forgiven;
for those whose sins you retain,
they are retained.'

This is the Gospel of the Lord

PROFESSION OF FAITH — *pages 15-16*

PRAYER OVER THE GIFTS

Lord,
may the Spirit you promised
lead us into all truth
and reveal to us the full meaning of this sacrifice.

PREFACE OF PENTECOST

Father, all-powerful and ever-living God,
we do well always and everywhere to give you thanks.

Today you sent the Holy Spirit
on those marked out to be your children
by sharing the life of your only Son,
and so you brought the paschal mystery to its completion.

Today we celebrate the great beginning of your Church
when the Holy Spirit made known to all peoples
    the one true God,

and created from the many languages of man
one voice to profess one faith.

The joy of the resurrection renews the whole world,
while the choirs of heaven sing for ever to your glory:
Holy, holy, holy…

COMMUNION ANTIPHON   *(Acts 2:4, 11)*

**They were all filled with the Holy Spirit, and they spoke of
the great things God had done, alleluia.**

PRAYER AFTER COMMUNION

Father, may the food we receive in the eucharist
help our eternal redemption.
Keep within us the vigour of your Spirit
and protect the gifts you have given to your Church.

SOLEMN BLESSING

[This day] the Father of light
has enlightened the minds of the disciples
by the outpouring of the Holy Spirit.
May he bless you
and give you the gifts of the Spirit for ever.
Amen.

May that fire which hovered over the disciples
as tongues of flame
burn out all evil from your hearts
and make them glow with pure light.
Amen.

God inspired speech in different tongues
to proclaim one faith.
May he strengthen your faith
and fulfil your hope of seeing him face to face.
Amen.

May almighty God bless you,
the Father, and the Son, ✠ and the Holy Spirit.
Amen.

REFLECTION

The words of Jesus, 'Receive the Holy Spirit' are addressed to
the whole group of believers. The Spirit empowers us to forgive
those who have offended us. This is not an impossible task. In
fact, to forgive another is a very practical exercise of opening
oneself to the Spirit.

7 JUNE

THE MOST HOLY TRINITY

The Christian teaching on the Most Holy Trinity is based on what has been revealed of God in the life, death and resurrection of Jesus of Nazareth. It is Christianity's answer to the question: who is God? The Jewish people knew God only as one. With the proclamation of Jesus as divine this question took on a fresh urgency. Jesus the Christ reveals God fully. This God is Father, Son and Holy Spirit.

ENTRANCE ANTIPHON

Blessed be God the Father and his only-begotten Son and the Holy Spirit: for he has shown that he loves us.

GREETING, PENITENTIAL RITE, GLORIA — *pages 7-14*

OPENING PRAYER

Let us pray
    [to the one God, Father, Son and Spirit,
    that our lives may bear witness to our faith]

Father,
you sent your Word to bring us truth
and your Spirit to make us holy.
Through them we come to know the mystery of your life.
Help us to worship you, one God in three Persons,
by proclaiming and living our faith in you.

or

Let us pray
    [to our God who is Father, Son, and Holy Spirit]

God, we praise you:
Father all-powerful, Christ Lord and Saviour, Spirit of love.
You reveal yourself in the depths of our being,
drawing us to share in your life and your love.
One God, three Persons,
be near to the people formed in your image,
close to the world your love brings to life.
We ask you this, Father, Son, and Holy Spirit,
one God, true and living, for ever and ever.

FIRST READING   (Dt 4:32-34.39-40)

A reading from the book of Deuteronomy.

The Lord is God indeed, in heaven above as on earth beneath, he and no
other.

Moses said to the people: 'Put this question to the ages that
are past, that went before you, from the time God created man
on earth: Was there ever a word so majestic, from one end of
heaven to the other? Was anything ever heard? Did ever a people
hear the voice of the living God speaking from the heart of the
fire, as you heard it, and remain alive? Has any god ventured
to take to himself one nation from the midst of another by
ordeals, signs, wonders, war with mighty hand and outstretched
arm, by fearsome terrors — all this that the Lord your God did
for you before your eyes in Egypt?

   'Understand this today, therefore, and take it to heart: The
Lord is God indeed, in heaven above as on earth beneath, he
and no other. Keep his laws and commandments as I give them
to you today so that you and your children may prosper and
live long in the land that the Lord your God gives you for ever.'

   This is the word of the Lord.

RESPONSORIAL PSALM   (Ps 32:4-6.9.18-20.22)

℟ **Happy the people the Lord has chosen as his own.**

1. The word of the Lord is faithful
    and all his works to be trusted.
    The Lord loves justice and right
    and fills the earth with his love. ℟

2. By his word the heavens were made,
    by the breath of his mouth all the stars.
    He spoke; and they came to be.
    He commanded; they sprang into being. ℟

3. The Lord looks on those who revere him,
    on those who hope in his love,
    to rescue their souls from death,
    to keep them alive in famine. ℟

4. Our soul is waiting for the Lord.
    The Lord is our help and our shield.
    May your love be upon us, O Lord,
    as we place all our hope in you. ℟

SECOND READING   *(Rm 8:14-17)*

A reading from the letter of St Paul to the Romans.

You received the spirit of sons, and it makes us cry out, 'Abba, Father!'

Everyone moved by the Spirit is a son of God. The spirit you received is not the spirit of slaves bringing fear into your lives again; it is the spirit of sons, and it makes us cry out, 'Abba, Father!' The Spirit himself and our spirit bear united witness that we are children of God. And if we are children we are heirs as well: heirs of God and coheirs with Christ, sharing his sufferings so as to share his glory.

This is the word of the Lord.

GOSPEL ACCLAMATION   *(cf. Rv 1:8)*

Alleluia, alleluia!
Glory be to the Father, and to the Son, and to the Holy Spirit,
the God who is, who was, and who is to come.
Alleluia.

GOSPEL   *(Mt 28:16-20)*

A reading from the holy Gospel according to Matthew.

Baptise them in the name of the Father and of the Son and of the Holy Spirit.

The eleven disciples set out for Galilee, to the mountain where Jesus had arranged to meet them. When they saw him they fell down before him, though some hesitated. Jesus came up and spoke to them. He said, 'All authority in heaven and on earth has been given to me. Go therefore, make disciples of all the nations; baptise them in the name of the Father and of the Son and of the Holy Spirit, and teach them to observe all the commands I gave you. And know that I am with you always; yes, to the end of time.'

This is the Gospel of the Lord.

PROFESSION OF FAITH — *pages 15-16*

PRAYER OVER THE GIFTS

Lord our God,
make these gifts holy,
and through them
make us a perfect offering to you.

PREFACE OF THE HOLY TRINITY

Father, all-powerful and ever-living God,
we do well always and everywhere to give you thanks.

We joyfully proclaim our faith
in the mystery of your Godhead.
You have revealed your glory
as the glory also of your Son
and of the Holy Spirit:
three Persons equal in majesty,
undivided in splendour,
yet one Lord, one God,
ever to be adored in your everlasting glory.

And so, with all the choirs of angels in heaven
we proclaim your glory
and join in their unending hymn of praise:
Holy, holy, holy…

COMMUNION ANTIPHON *(Gal 4:6)*

You are the sons of God, so God has given you the Spirit of his Son to form your hearts and make you cry out: Abba, Father.

PRAYER AFTER COMMUNION

Lord God,
we worship you, a Trinity of Persons, one eternal God.
May our faith and the sacrament we receive
bring us health of mind and body.

REFLECTION

From the earliest times the public prayer of the Church has addressed God as Father, Son and Spirit. This lived experience helped the Church to understand its own faith even before this faith was expressed in the form of doctrine. To begin prayer with the traditional formula, 'In the name of the Father and of the Son and of the Holy Spirit' is to confess the faith of the Church. This short phrase is a proclamation of one of the central aspects of the Christian faith.

14 JUNE

THE BODY AND BLOOD OF CHRIST
(CORPUS CHRISTI)

This feast has been celebrated universally throughout the Western Church since the Fourteenth Century. It commemorates the gift that God has presented to humanity in the Eucharist. Holy Thursday is the natural day to commemorate this alongside the celebration of the passion and death of Jesus on Good Friday and the resurrection at the Easter vigil. On this day the Church singles out the Eucharist to be the focus of attention and contemplation.

ENTRANCE ANTIPHON   *(Ps 80:17)*

The Lord fed his people with the finest wheat and honey; their hunger was satisfied.

GREETING, PENITENTIAL RITE, GLORIA — *pages 7-14*

OPENING PRAYER

Let us pray
   [to the Lord who gives himself in the eucharist,
   that this sacrament may bring us salvation and peace]

Lord Jesus Christ, you gave us the eucharist
as the memorial of your suffering and death.
May our worship of this sacrament of your body and blood
help us to experience the salvation you won for us
and the peace of the kingdom
where you live with the Father and the Holy Spirit,
one God, for ever and ever.

or

Let us pray
   [for the willingness to make present in our world
   the love of Christ shown to us in the eucharist]

Lord Jesus Christ, we worship you living among us
in the sacrament of your body and blood.
May we offer to our Father in heaven
a solemn pledge of undivided love.
May we offer to our brothers and sisters
a life poured out in loving service of that kingdom
where you live with the Father and the Holy Spirit,
one God, for ever and ever.

FIRST READING   (*Ex 24:3-8*)

A reading from the book of Exodus.

This is the blood of the Covenant that the Lord has made with you.

Moses went and told the people all the commands of the Lord and all the ordinances. In answer, all the people said with one voice, 'We will observe all the commands that the Lord has decreed.' Moses put all the commands of the Lord into writing, and early next morning he built an altar at the foot of the mountain, with twelve standing-stones for the twelve tribes of Israel. Then he directed certain young Israelites to offer holocausts and to immolate bullocks to the Lord as communion sacrifices. Half of the blood Moses took up and put into basins, the other half he cast on the altar. And taking the Book of the Covenant he read it to the listening people, and they said, 'We will observe all that the Lord has decreed; we will obey.' Then Moses took the blood and cast it towards the people. 'This' he said 'is the blood of the Covenant that the Lord has made with you, containing all these rules.'

This is the word of the Lord.

RESPONSORIAL PSALM   (*Ps 115:12-13.15-18*)

℟   **The cup of salvation I will raise;**
     I will call on the Lord's name.

or   **Alleluia!**

1.   How can I repay the Lord
     for his goodness to me?
     The cup of salvation I will raise;
     I will call on the Lord's name. ℟

2.   O precious in the eyes of the Lord
     is the death of his faithful.
     Your servant, Lord, your servant am I;
     you have loosened my bonds. ℟

3.   A thanksgiving sacrifice I make:
     I will call on the Lord's name.
     My vows to the Lord I will fulfil
     before all his people. ℟

SECOND READING   (*Heb 9:11-15*)

A reading from the letter to the Hebrews.

The blood of Christ can purify our inner self from dead actions.

Now Christ has come, as the high priest of all the blessings which were to come. He has passed through the greater, the more perfect tent, which is better than one made by men's hands because it is not of this created order; and he has entered the sanctuary once and for all, taking with him not the blood of goats and bull calves, but his own blood, having won an eternal redemption for us. The blood of goats and bulls and the ashes of a heifer are sprinkled on those who have incurred defilement and they restore the holiness of their outward lives; how much more effectively the blood of Christ, who offered himself as the perfect sacrifice to God through the eternal Spirit, can purify our inner self from dead actions so that we do our service to the living God.

He brings a new covenant, as the mediator, only so that the people who were called to an eternal inheritance may actually receive what was promised: his death took place to cancel the sins that infringed the earlier covenant.

This is the word of the Lord.

SEQUENCE *(Shorter Form)*
(The Sequence *may be said or sung.)*

Behold the bread of angels, sent
For pilgrims in their banishment,
The bread for God's true children meant,
    That may not unto dogs be given:

Oft in the olden types foreshadowed;
In Isaac on the altar bowed,
And in the ancient paschal food,
    And in the manna sent from heaven.

Come then, good shepherd, bread divine,
Still show to us thy mercy sign;
Oh, feed us still, still keep us thine;
So may we see thy glories shine
    In fields of immortality;

O thou, the wisest, mightiest, best,
Our present food, our future rest,
Come, make us each thy chosen guest,
Co-heirs of thine, and comrades blest
    With saints whose dwelling is with thee.

(Jn 6:51-52)

Alleluia, alleluia!
I am the living bread which has come down from heaven,
says the Lord.
Anyone who eats this bread will live for ever.
Alleluia!

GOSPEL   *(Mk 14:12-16.22-26)*

A reading from the holy Gospel according to Mark.

This is my body. This is my blood.

On the first day of Unleavened Bread, when the Passover lamb
was sacrificed, his disciples said to Jesus, 'Where do you want us
to go and make the preparations for you to eat the passover?'
So he sent two of his disciples, saying to them, 'Go into the city
and you will meet a man carrying a pitcher of water. Follow
him, and say to the owner of the house which he enters, "The
Master says: Where is my dining room in which I can eat the
passover with my disciples?" He will show you a large upper room
furnished with couches, all prepared. Make the preparations for
us there.' The disciples set out and went to the city and found
everything as he had told them, and prepared the Passover.

     And as they were eating he took some bread, and when he
had said the blessing he broke it and gave it to them. 'Take it,'
he said 'this is my body.' Then he took a cup, and when he had
returned thanks he gave it to them, and all drank from it, and he
said to them, 'This is my blood, the blood of the covenant, which
is to be poured out for many. I tell you solemnly, I shall not
drink any more wine until the day I drink the new wine in the
kingdom of God.'

     After psalms had been sung they left for the Mount of
Olives.

     This is the Gospel of the Lord.

PROFESSION OF FAITH — *pages 15-16*

PRAYER OVER THE GIFTS

Lord,
may the bread and cup we offer
bring your Church the unity and peace they signify.

PREFACE OF THE HOLY EUCHARIST I

Father, all-powerful and ever-living God,
we do well always and everywhere to give you thanks

through Jesus Christ our Lord.

He is the true and eternal priest
who established this unending sacrifice.
He offered himself as a victim for our deliverance
and taught us to make this offering in his memory.
As we eat his body which he gave for us,
we grow in strength.
As we drink his blood which he poured out for us,
we are washed clean.

Now, with angels and archangels,
and the whole company of heaven,
we sing the unending hymn of your praise:
Holy, holy, holy…

COMMUNION ANTIPHON   *(Jn 6:57)*

**Whoever eats my flesh and drinks my blood will live in me
and I in him, says the Lord.**

PRAYER AFTER COMMUNION

Lord Jesus Christ,
you give us your body and blood in the eucharist
as a sign that even now we share your life.
May we come to possess it completely in the kingdom
where you live for ever and ever.

REFLECTION

The practice of reserving the consecrated bread mostly, but
occasionally wine also in a tabernacle, is universal. A good
appreciation of this practice will involve connecting it with the
celebration of the Eucharist where the four-fold action of the
Lord: taking, blessing, breaking and giving is commemorated.
His body and blood are given to his Church for the nourishment
of his people. With this in mind the sacred elements are
reserved for the veneration of the Church and when the
occasion requires for the communion of those who are sick.

21 JUNE
12th SUNDAY IN ORDINARY TIME

Bread and wine are central to our celebration of the Eucharist.
Yet the early Christians didn't stress these material objects originally
at a time when pagan religions were using many material things
such as a lamb and blood. In contrast the early Christians stressed
the spiritual aspect of the things they used at the Eucharist.
Later on, to counter an opinion which maintained that creation
was evil the Christians emphasised the goodness of creation
by focusing again on the material objects of bread and wine.

ENTRANCE ANTIPHON   *(Ps 27:8-9)*

**God is the strength of his people. In him, we his chosen live
in safety. Save us, Lord, who share in your life, and give us
your blessing; be our shepherd for ever.**

GREETING, PENITENTIAL RITE, GLORIA — *pages 7-14*

OPENING PRAYER

Let us pray
      [that we may grow in the love of God]

Father, guide and protector of your people,
grant us an unfailing respect for your name,
and keep us always in your love.

or

Let us pray
      [to God whose fatherly love keeps us safe]

God of the universe,
we worship you as Lord.
God, ever close to us,
we rejoice to call you Father.
From this world's uncertainty we look to your covenant.
Keep us one in your peace, secure in your love.

FIRST READING   *(Job 3:1.8-11)*

A reading from the book of Job.

Here your proud waves shall break.

From the heart of the tempest the Lord gave Job his answer. He
said:
      Who pent up the sea behind closed doors
      when it leapt tumultuous out of the womb,
      when I wrapped it in a robe of mist

and made black clouds its swaddling bands;
when I marked the bounds it was not to cross
and made it fast with a bolted gate?
Come thus far, I said, and no farther:
here your proud waves shall break.

This is the word of the Lord.

RESPONSORIAL PSALM   *(Ps 106:23-26.28-31)*

℟   **O give thanks to the Lord,**
    for his love endures for ever.

or **Alleluia!**

1. Some sailed to the sea in ships
    to trade on the mighty waters.
    These men have seen the Lord's deeds,
    the wonders he does in the deep. ℟

2. For he spoke; he summoned the gale,
    tossing the waves of the sea
    up to heaven and back into the deep;
    their soul melted away in their distress. ℟

3. Then they cried to the Lord in their need
    and he rescued them from their distress.
    He stilled the storm to a whisper:
    all the waves of the sea were hushed. ℟

4. They rejoiced because of the calm
    and he led them to the haven they desired.
    Let them thank the Lord for his love,
    the wonders he does for men. ℟

SECOND READING   *(2 Cor 5:14-17)*

A reading from the second letter of St Paul to the Corinthians.
Now the new creation is here.

The love of Christ overwhelms us when we reflect that if one man
has died for all, then all men should be dead; and the reason
he died for all was so that living men should live no longer for
themselves, but for him who died and was raised to life for them.

From now onwards, therefore, we do not judge anyone by
the standards of the flesh. Even if we did once know Christ in
the flesh, that is not how we know him now. And for anyone
who is in Christ, there is a new creation; the old creation has
gone, and now the new one is here.

This is the word of the Lord.

GOSPEL ACCLAMATION   *(cf. Eph 1:17.8)*

Alleluia, alleluia!
May the Father of our Lord Jesus Christ
enlighten the eyes of our mind,
so that we can see what hope his call holds for us.
Alleluia!

or   *(Lk 7:16)*

Alleluia, alleluia!
A great prophet has appeared among us;
God has visited his people.
Alleluia!

GOSPEL   *(Mk 4:35-41)*

A reading from the holy Gospel according to Mark.

Who can this be? Even the wind and the sea obey him.

With the coming of evening, Jesus said to his disciples, 'Let us cross over to the other side.' And leaving the crowd behind they took him, just as he was, in the boat; and there were other boats with him. Then it began to blow a gale and the waves were breaking into the boat so that it was almost swamped. But he was in the stern, his head on the cushion, asleep. They woke him and said to him, 'Master, do you not care? We are going down!' And he woke up and rebuked the wind and said to the sea, 'Quiet now! Be calm!' And the wind dropped, and all was calm again. Then he said to them, 'Why are you so frightened? How is it that you have no faith?' They were filled with awe and said to one another, 'Who can this be? Even the wind and the sea obey him.'

This is the Gospel of the Lord.

PROFESSION OF FAITH — *pages 15-16*

PRAYER OVER THE GIFTS

Lord, receive our offering,
and may this sacrifice of praise
purify us in mind and heart
and make us always eager to serve you.

PREFACE OF SUNDAYS IN ORDINARY TIME I-VIII — *pages 22-25*

COMMUNION ANTIPHON   *(Ps 114:15)*

The eyes of all look to you, O Lord, and you give them food in due season.

or   *(Jn 10:11.15)*

I am the Good Shepherd; I give my life for my sheep, says the Lord.

PRAYER AFTER COMMUNION

Lord, you give us the body and blood of your Son
to renew your life within us.
In your mercy, assure our redemption
and bring us to the eternal life
we celebrate in the eucharist.

SOLEMN BLESSING — *pages 57-58*

REFLECTION

An interesting aspect of today's gospel is that the word here
translated as 'awe' and in other places as 'fear' is attributed by
Mark to the disciples when the storm has died down. Could it
be that there is a different 'fear' intended here. When Jesus is
recognised for who he is, namely, the Son of God, the appropriate
response is one of awe and reverence.

---

28 JUNE

13th SUNDAY IN ORDINARY TIME

The last sentence of today's gospel makes it clear how the story
is not to be interpreted. It is a mistake to see Jesus as someone
who during his public ministry wished to prove something by
the use of his supernatural powers. The reluctance of Jesus to
have this incident kept quiet is indication of that. Rather today's gospel is first an invitation to its original hearers to have
faith. That same invitation is extended to us here and now by
the christian community.

ENTRANCE ANTIPHON   *(Ps 46:2)*

All nations, clap your hands. Shout with a voice of joy to God.

GREETING, PENITENTIAL RITE, GLORIA — *pages 7-14*

OPENING PRAYER

Let us pray
     [that Christ may be our light]
Father, you call your children
to walk in the light of Christ.
Free us from darkness
and keep us in the radiance of your truth.
or
Let us pray
     [for the strength to reject the darkness of sin]

Father in heaven,
the light of Jesus
has scattered the darkness of hatred and sin.
Called to that light
we ask for your guidance.
Form our lives in your truth, our hearts in your love.

FIRST READING   *(Ws 1:13-15; 2:23-24)*

A reading from the book of Wisdom.

It was the devil's envy that brought death into the world.

Death was not God's doing,
he takes no pleasure in the extinction of the living.
To be — for this he created all;
the world's created things have health in them,
in them no fatal poison can be found,
and Hades holds no power on earth;
for virtue is undying.
Yet God did make man imperishable,
he made him in the image of his own nature;
it was the devil's envy that brought death into the world,
as those who are his partners will discover.

　　　This is the word of the Lord.

RESPONSORIAL PSALM   *(Ps 29:2.4-6.11-13)*

℟   **I will praise you, Lord, you have rescued me.**

1.   I will praise you, Lord, you have rescued me
　　and have not let my enemies rejoice over me.
　　O Lord, you have raised my soul from the dead,
　　restored me to life from those who sink into the grave. ℟

2.   Sing psalms to the Lord, you who love him,
　　give thanks to his holy name.
　　His anger lasts but a moment; his favour through life.
　　At night there are tears, but joy comes with dawn. ℟

3.   The Lord listened and had pity.
　　The Lord came to my help.
　　For me you have changed my mourning into dancing,
　　O Lord my God, I will thank you for ever. ℟

SECOND READING   *(2 Cor 8:7.9.13-15)*

A reading from the second letter of St Paul to the Corinthians.

In giving relief to others, balance what happens to be your surplus now against their present need.

You always have the most of everything — of faith, of eloquence, of understanding, of keenness for any cause, and the biggest share of our affection — so we expect you to put the most into this work of mercy too. Remember how generous the Lord Jesus was: he was rich, but he became poor for your sake, to make you rich out of his poverty. This does not mean that to give relief to others you ought to make things difficult for yourselves: it is a question of balancing what happens to be your surplus now against their present need, and one day they may have something to spare that will supply your own need. That is how we strike a balance: as scripture says: The man who gathered much had none too much, the man who gathered little did not go short.

This is the word of the Lord.

GOSPEL ACCLAMATION   *(cf. Jn 6:63.68)*
Alleluia, alleluia!
Your words are spirit, Lord,
and they are life:
you have the message of eternal life. Alleluia!
or
Alleluia, alleluia!   *(cf. 2 Tm 1:10)*
Our Saviour Christ Jesus abolished death,
and he has proclaimed life through the Good News. Alleluia!

GOSPEL   *(Mk 5:21-43)*
(For Shorter Form, *read between* ◆◆*)*
A reading from the holy Gospel according to Mark.
Little girl, I tell you to get up.

◆When Jesus had crossed in the boat to the other side, a large crowd gathered round him and he stayed by the lakeside. Then one of the synagogue officials came up, Jairus by name, and seeing him, fell at his feet and pleaded with him earnestly, saying, 'My little daughter is desperately sick. Do come and lay your hands on her to make her better and save her life.' Jesus went with him and a large crowd followed him; they were pressing all round him.◆

Now there was a woman who had suffered from a haemorrhage for twelve years; after long and painful treatment under various doctors, she had spent all she had without being any the better for it, in fact, she was getting worse. She had heard about Jesus, and she came up behind him through the crowd and touched his cloak. 'If I can touch even his clothes,' she had told herself 'I shall be well again.' And the source of the bleeding dried up instantly, and she felt in herself that she was cured of her complaint. Immediately aware that power had gone out from him Jesus turned round in the crowd and said, 'Who touched my clothes?' His disciples said to him, 'You see how the crowd is pressing round you and yet you say, "Who touched me"? ' But he continued to look all round to see who had done it. Then the woman came forward, frightened and trembling because she knew what had happened to her, and she fell at his feet and told him the whole truth. 'My daughter' he said 'your faith has restored you to health; go in peace and be free from your complaint.'

⁕While he was still speaking some people arrived from the house of the synagogue official to say, 'Your daughter is dead: why put the Master to any further trouble?' But Jesus had overheard this remark of theirs and he said to the official, 'Do not be afraid; only have faith.' And he allowed no one to go with him except Peter and James and John the brother of James. So they came to the official's house and Jesus noticed all the commotion, with people weeping and wailing unrestrainedly. He went in and said to them, 'Why all this commotion and crying? The child is not dead, but asleep.' But they laughed at him. So he turned them all out and, taking with him the child's father and mother and his own companions, he went into the place where the child lay. And taking the child by the hand he said to her, 'Talitha, kum!' which means, 'Little girl, I tell you to get up.' The little girl got up at once and began to walk about, for she was twelve years old. At this they were overcome with astonishment, and he ordered them strictly not to let anyone know about it, and told them to give her something to eat.

This is the Gospel of the Lord.⁕

PROFESSION OF FAITH — *page 15-16*

PRAYER OVER THE GIFTS

Lord God, through your sacraments
you give us the power of your grace.
May this eucharist
help us to serve you faithfully.

PREFACE OF SUNDAYS IN ORDINARY TIME I-VIII — *pages 22-25*

COMMUNION ANTIPHON   *(Ps 102:1)*

O bless the Lord, my soul, and all that is within me bless his holy name.

or (*Jn 17:20-21*)

Father, I pray for them: may they be one in us, so that the world may believe it was you who sent me.

PRAYER AFTER COMMUNION

Lord,
may this sacrifice and communion
give us a share in your life
and help us bring your love to the world.

SOLEMN BLESSING — *pages 57-58*

REFLECTION

Jesus is presented in the gospels as having raised three people from the dead. In this he is not unique as other biblical characters are similarly portrayed. Certainly there are echoes of his equality with God as it is God who gives life. Such gospel events point to the new life which Jesus now possesses if only to suggest that his new life is different from that of the people he has raised from the dead. And it is faith in this new life of the Risen Lord that today's hearers are invited to be open to.

29 JUNE

STS PETER AND PAUL, APOSTLES

(Celebrated in England and Wales on Sunday 28th June)

VIGIL MASS

Peter was a humble fisherman. Paul was a persecutor of the first Christians. But they were chosen to become the pillars of our faith, which they sealed with their martyrdom in Rome.

ENTRANCE ANTIPHON

Peter the apostle and Paul the teacher of the Gentiles have brought us to know the law of the Lord.

GREETING, PENITENTIAL RITE, GLORIA — *pages 7-14*

OPENING PRAYER

Let us pray
[that the prayers of the apostles
will lead us to salvation]

Lord our God,
encourage us through the prayers of Saints Peter and Paul.
May the apostles who strengthened the faith of the infant Church
help us on our way of salvation.

or

Let us pray
      [to be true to the faith
      which has come to us through the apostles Peter and Paul]

Father in heaven,
the light of your revelation brought Peter and Paul
the gift of faith in Jesus your Son.

Through their prayers
may we always give thanks for your life
given us in Christ Jesus,
and for having been enriched by him
in all knowledge and love.

FIRST READING   *(Acts 3:1-10)*

A reading from the Acts of the Apostles.

I will give you what I have: in the name of Jesus stand up and walk!

Once, when Peter and John were going up to the Temple for
the prayers at the ninth hour, it happened that there was a man
being carried past. He was a cripple from birth; and they used
to put him down every day near the Temple entrance called
the Beautiful Gate so that he could beg from the people going
in. When this man saw Peter and John on their way into the
Temple he begged from them. Both Peter and John looked
straight at him and said, 'Look at us.' He turned to them
expectantly, hoping to get something from them, but Peter said,
'I have neither silver nor gold, but I will give you what I have: in
the name of Jesus Christ the Nazarene, walk!' Peter then took
him by the hand and helped him to stand up. Instantly his
feet and ankles became firm, he jumped up, stood, and began
to walk, and he went with them into the Temple, walking and
jumping and praising God. Everyone could see him walking and
praising God, and they recognised him as the man who used to
sit begging at the Beautiful Gate of the Temple. They were all
astonished and unable to explain what had happened to him.

      This is the word of the Lord.

RESPONSORIAL PSALM *(Ps 18:2-5)*

℟ **Their word goes forth through all the earth.**

1. The heavens proclaim the glory of God
   and the firmament shows forth the work of his hands.
   Day unto day takes up the story
   and night unto night makes known the message. ℟

2. No speech, no word, no voice is heard
   yet their span extends through all the earth,
   their words to the utmost bounds of the world. ℟

SECOND READING *(Gal 1:11-20)*

A reading from the letter of St Paul to the Galatians.

God specially chose me while I was still in my mother's womb.

The Good News I preached is not a human message that I was given by men, it is something I learnt only through a revelation of Jesus Christ. You must have heard of my career as a practising Jew, how merciless I was in persecuting the Church of God, how much damage I did to it, how I stood out among other Jews of my generation, and how enthusiastic I was for the traditions of my ancestors.

Then God, who had specially chosen me while I was still in my mother's womb, called me through his grace and chose to reveal his Son to me, so that I might preach the Good News about him to the pagans. I did not stop to discuss this with any human being, nor did I go up to Jerusalem to see those who were already apostles before me, but I went off to Arabia at once and later went straight back from there to Damascus. Even when after three years I went up to Jerusalem to visit Cephas and stayed with him for fifteen days, I did not see any of the other apostles; I only saw James, the brother of the Lord, and I swear before God that what I have just written is the literal truth.

This is the word of the Lord.

GOSPEL ACCLAMATION *(Jn 21:17)*

Alleluia, alleluia!
Lord, you know everything;
you know I love you.
Alleluia!

GOSPEL *(Jn 21:15-19)*

A reading from the holy Gospel according to John.

Feed my lambs, feed my sheep.

After Jesus had shown himself to his disciples, and eaten with them, he said to Simon Peter, 'Simon son of John, do you love me more than these others do?' He answered, 'Yes, Lord, you know I love you.' Jesus said to him, 'Feed my lambs,' A second time he said to him, 'Simon son of John, do you love me?' He replied, 'Yes, Lord, you know I love you.' Jesus said to him, 'Look after my sheep.' Then he said to him a third time, 'Simon, son of John, do you love me?' Peter was upset that he asked him the third time, "Do you love me?" and said, 'Lord, you know everything; you know I love you.' Jesus said to him, 'Feed my sheep.

> 'I tell you most solemnly,
> when you were young
> you put on your own belt
> and walked where you liked;
> but when you grow old
> you will stretch out your hands,
> and somebody else will put a belt round you
> and take you where you would rather not go.'

In these words he indicated the kind of death by which Peter would give glory to God. After this he said, 'Follow me.'

This is the Gospel of the Lord.

PROFESSION OF FAITH — *pages 15-16*

PRAYER OVER THE GIFTS
Lord, we present these gifts
on this feast of the apostles Peter and Paul.
Help us to know our own weakness
and to rejoice in your saving power.

PREFACE OF SAINTS PETER AND PAUL — *page 270*

COMMUNION ANTIPHON   *(Jn 21:15.17)*
Simon, son of John, do you love me more than these? Lord, you know all things; you know that I love you.

PRAYER AFTER COMMUNION
Father,
you give us light by the teaching of your apostles.
In this sacrament we have received
fill us with your strength.

SOLEMN BLESSING — *page 271*

REFLECTION

St Clement of Rome recalls how the 'greatest and most righteous pillars were persecuted and engaged in the context unto death.' He exhorts us to have the 'good apostles before our eyes, for they have with many indignities and tortures, provided for us a most noble example.'

MASS DURING THE DAY

Simon Peter the fisherman from Bethsaida was chosen by the Lord to lead the community of believers after Jesus' ascension. He himself had to learn what it meant to be a follower of Jesus and the accounts of him in the Gospels are far from glowing at times. His is a reflection of struggling with failure that is part of discipleship. Saul of Tarsus, whose dramatic call by the Lord is found in the Acts of the Apostles, though not one of the Twelve, is the Apostle of the gentiles. The celebration of their common feast day is a symbol of the inclusive call of God to both Jew and gentile alike.

ENTRANCE ANTIPHON

These men, conquering all human frailty, shed their blood and helped the Church to grow. By sharing the cup of the Lord's suffering, they became the friends of God.

GREETING, PENITENTIAL RITE, GLORIA — *pages 7-14*

OPENING PRAYER

Let us pray
[that we will remain true to the faith of the apostles]
God our Father,
today you give us the joy
of celebrating the feast of the apostles Peter and Paul.
Through them your Church first received the faith.
Keep us true to their teaching.

or

Let us pray
[one with Peter and Paul in our faith
in Christ the Son of the living God]
Praise to you,
the God and Father of our Lord Jesus Christ,
who in your great mercy

have given us new birth and hope
through the power of Christ's resurrection.

Through the prayers of the apostles Peter and Paul
share their joy in following the Lord
to the unfading inheritance
reserved for us in heaven.

FIRST READING   *(Acts 12:1-11)*

A reading from the Acts of the Apostles.

Now I know the Lord really did save me from Herod.

King Herod started persecuting certain members of the Church.
He beheaded James the brother of John, and when he saw that
this pleased the Jews he decided to arrest Peter as well. This
was during the days of Unleavened Bread, and he put Peter in
prison, assigning four squads of four soldiers each to guard him
in turns. Herod meant to try Peter in public after the end of
Passover week. All the time Peter was under guard the Church
prayed to God for him unremittingly.

On the night before Herod was to try him, Peter was sleeping
between two soldiers, fastened with double chains, while guards
kept watch at the main entrance to the prison. Then suddenly
the angel of the Lord stood there, and the cell was filled with
light. He tapped Peter on the side and woke him. 'Get up!' he
said 'Hurry!' — and the chains fell from his hands. The angel
then said, 'Put on your belt and sandals.' After he had done this,
the angel next said, 'Wrap your cloak round you and follow me.'
Peter followed him, but had no idea that what the angel did was
all happening in reality; he thought he was seeing a vision. They
passed through two guard posts one after the other, and reached
the iron gate leading to the city. This opened of its own accord;
they went through it and had walked the whole length of one
street when suddenly the angel left him. It was only then that Peter
came to himself. 'Now I know it is all true,' he said. 'The Lord
really did send his angel and has saved me from Herod and from
all that the Jewish people were so certain would happen to me.'

This is the word of the Lord.

RESPONSORIAL PSALM   *(Ps 33:2-9)*

℟.   **From all my terrors the Lord set me free.**

or   **The angel of the Lord rescues those who revere him.**

1.   I will bless the Lord at all times,
      his praise always on my lips;

in the Lord my soul shall make its boast.
The humble shall hear and be glad. ℟

2. Glorify the Lord with me.
Together let us praise his name.
I sought the Lord and he answered me;
from all my terrors he set me free. ℟

3. Look towards him and be radiant;
let your faces not be abashed.
This poor man called; the Lord heard him
and rescued him from all his distress. ℟

4. The angel of the Lord is encamped
around those who revere him, to rescue them.
Taste and see that the Lord is good.
He is happy who seeks refuge in him. ℟

SECOND READING   *(2 Tm 4:6-8.17-18)*

A reading from the second letter of St Paul to Timothy

All there is to come now is the crown of righteousness reserved for me.

My life is already being poured away as a libation, and the time
has come for me to be gone. I have fought the good fight to the
end; I have run the race to the finish; I have kept the faith; all
there is to come now is the crown of righteousness reserved for
me, which the Lord, the righteous judge, will give to me on that
Day; and not only to me but to all those who have longed for
his Appearing.

The Lord stood by me and gave me power, so that through
me the whole message might be proclaimed for all the pagans
to hear; and so I was rescued from the lion's mouth. The Lord
will rescue me from all evil attempts on me, and bring me safely
to his heavenly kingdom. To him be glory for ever and ever.
Amen.

This is the word of the Lord.

GOSPEL ACCLAMATION   *(Mt 16:18)*

Alleluia, alleluia!
You are Peter and on this rock I will build my Church.
And the gates of the underworld can never hold out against it.
Alleluia!

GOSPEL   *(Mt 16:13-19)*

A reading from the holy Gospel according to Matthew.

You are Peter, and I will give you the keys of the kingdom of heaven.

When Jesus came to the region of Caesarea Philippi he put this question to his disciples, 'Who do people say the Son of Man is?' And they said, 'Some say he is John the Baptist, some Elijah, and others Jeremiah or one of the prophets.' 'But you,' he said 'who do you say I am?' Then Simon Peter spoke up, 'You are the Christ,' he said 'the Son of the living God.' Jesus replied, 'Simon son of Jonah, you are a happy man! Because it was not flesh and blood that revealed this to you but my Father in heaven. So I now say to you: You are Peter and on this rock I will build my Church. And the gates of the underworld can never hold out against it. I will give you the keys of the kingdom of heaven: whatever you bind on earth shall be considered bound in heaven; whatever you loose on earth shall be considered loosed in heaven.'

This is the Gospel of the Lord.

PROFESSION OF FAITH — *pages 15-16*

PRAYER OVER THE GIFTS

Lord,
may your apostles join their prayers to our offering
and help us to celebrate this sacrifice in love and unity.

PREFACE OF SAINTS PETER AND PAUL

Father, all-powerful and ever-living God,
we do well always and everywhere to give you thanks.

You fill our hearts with joy
as we honour your great apostles:
Peter, our leader in the faith,
and Paul, its fearless preacher.

Peter raised up the Church
from the faithful flock of Israel.
Paul brought your call to the nations,
and became the teacher of the world.
Each in his chosen way gathered into unity
the one family of Christ.
Both shared a martyr's death
and are praised throughout the world.

Now, with the apostles and all the angels and saints,
we praise you for ever:
Holy, holy, holy…

COMMUNION ANTIPHON *(Mt 16:16.18)*

Peter said: You are the Christ, the Son of the living God. Jesus answered: You are Peter the rock on which I will build my Church.

PRAYER AFTER COMMUNION

Lord,
renew the life of your Church
with the power of this sacrament.
May the breaking of bread
and the teaching of the apostles
keep us united in your love.

SOLEMN BLESSING

Bow your heads and pray for God's blessing.

The Lord has set you firm within his Church,
which he built upon the rock of Peter's faith.
may he bless you with a faith that never falters.
Amen.

The Lord has given you knowledge of the faith
through the labours and preaching of Saint Paul.
May his example inspire you to lead others to Christ
by the manner of your life.
Amen.

May the keys of Peter, and the words of Paul,
their undying witness and their prayers,
lead you to the joy of that eternal home
which Peter gained by his cross, and Paul by the sword.
Amen.

May almighty God bless you,
the Father, and the Son, ✠ and the Holy Spirit.
Amen.

REFLECTION

Simon Peter was not the most likely one to be called by the Lord to lead the community of the faithful. He was a simple fisherman with no great education who must have seemed destined to live the life of a fisherman. Saul of Tarsus was even a more unlikely candidate because he had actually set his face against the young Church and was even remarkable for the zeal with which he persecuted it. But the call of the Lord knows no limits and God does not see as human beings do.

5 JULY
14th SUNDAY IN ORDINARY TIME

The procession at the Preparation of the Gifts allows for
popular participation in the Liturgy of the Eucharist. The
practice of a procession declined severely after the year 1,000
due to less frequent communion when less material was
needed, and to the change in the bread used. The Church
takes care of what type of bread it uses. With the advent of
the small host there was an increase in the money offered
and a decrease in bread and wine. The restored rite involves the
presentation of ourselves and of gifts with a view towards their
being transformed.

ENTRANCE ANTIPHON   (Ps 47:10-11)

**Within your temple, we ponder your loving kindness, O God.
As your name, so also your praise reaches to the ends of the
earth; your right hand is filled with justice.**

GREETING, PENITENTIAL RITE, GLORIA — *pages 7-14*

OPENING PRAYER

Let us pray
    [for forgiveness through the grace of Jesus Christ]

Father,
through the obedience of Jesus,
your servant and your Son,
you raised a fallen world.
Free us from sin
and bring us the joy that lasts for ever.

or

Let us pray
    [for greater willingness
    to serve God and our fellow men]

Father, in the rising of your Son
death gives birth to new life.
The sufferings he endured restored hope to a fallen world.
Let sin never ensnare us
with empty promises of passing joy.
Make us one with you always,
so that our joy may be holy,
and our love may give life.

FIRST READING *(Ezk 2:2-5)*

A reading from the prophet Ezekiel.

The sons are defiant and obstinate and they shall know that there is a prophet among them.

The spirit came into me and made me stand up, and I heard the Lord speaking to me. He said, 'Son of man, I am sending you to the Israelites, to the rebels who have turned against me. Till now they and their ancestors have been in revolt against me. The sons are defiant and obstinate; I am sending you to them, to say, "The Lord says this." Whether they listen or not, this set of rebels shall know there is a prophet among them.'

This is the word of the Lord.

RESPONSORIAL PSALM *(Ps 122)*

℟ **Our eyes are on the Lord**
 till he show us his mercy.

1. To you have I lifted up my eyes,
   you who dwell in the heavens:
   my eyes, like the eyes of slaves
   on the hand of their lords. ℟

2. Like the eyes of a servant
   on the hand of her mistress,
   so our eyes are on the Lord our God
   till he show us mercy. ℟

3. Have mercy on us, Lord, have mercy.
   We are filled with contempt.
   Indeed all too full is our soul
   with the scorn of the rich,
   with the proud man's disdain. ℟

SECOND READING *(2 Cor 12:7-10)*

A reading from the second letter of St Paul to the Corinthians.

I shall be very happy to make my weaknesses my special boast so that the power of Christ may stay over me.

In view of the extraordinary nature of these revelations, to stop me from getting too proud I was given a thorn in the flesh, an angel of Satan to beat me and stop me from getting too proud! About this thing, I have pleaded with the Lord three times for it to leave me, but he has said, 'My grace is enough for you: my power is at its best in weakness.' So I shall be very happy to make my weaknesses my special boast so that the power of Christ may stay over me, and that is why I am quite content with my weaknesses, and with insults, hardships, persecutions, and the agonies I go through for Christ's sake. For it is when I am weak that I am strong.

This is the word of the Lord.

GOSPEL ACCLAMATION   *(Jn 1:14.12)*

Alleluia, alleluia!
The Word was made flesh and lived among us;
to all who did accept him
he gave power to become children of God.
Alleluia!
or   *(cf. Lk 4:18)*

Alleluia, alleluia!
The Lord has sent me to bring the good news to the poor,
to proclaim liberty to captives.
Alleluia!

GOSPEL   *(Mk 6:1-6)*

A reading from the holy Gospel according to Mark.

A prophet is despised only in his own country.

Jesus went to his home town and his disciples accompanied him. With the coming of the sabbath he began teaching in the synagogue and most of them were astonished when they heard him. They said, 'Where did the man get all this? What is this wisdom that has been granted him, and these miracles that are worked through him? This is the carpenter, surely, the son of Mary, the brother of James and Joset and Jude and Simon? His sisters, too, are they not here with us?' And they would not accept him. And Jesus said to them, 'A prophet is only despised in his own country among his own relations and in his own house'; and he could work no miracle there, though he cured a few sick people by laying his hands on them. He was amazed at their lack of faith.

This is the Gospel of the Lord.

PROFESSION OF FAITH — *pages 15-16*

PRAYER OVER THE GIFTS

Lord,
let this offering to the glory of your name
purify us and bring us closer to eternal life.

PREFACE OF SUNDAYS IN ORDINARY TIME I-VIII — *pages 22-25*

COMMUNION ANTIPHON *(Ps 33:9)*

Taste and see the goodness of the Lord; blessed is he who hopes in God.

or *(Mt 11:28)*

Come to me, all you that labour and are burdened, and I will give you rest, says the Lord.

PRAYER AFTER COMMUNION

Lord,
may we never fail to praise you
for the fullness of life and salvation
you give us in this eucharist.

SOLEMN BLESSING — *pages 57-58*

REFLECTION

Jesus is presented in today's gospel as a prophet. Originally a prophet was someone with a word for their own generation rather than with a future date in mind. A prophet spoke the word that he was inspired to speak whether this word was welcome or not. Speaking out on behalf of God is what the prophet did best. Jesus fulfilled this aspect of a prophet's vocation and the authority of his teaching is attested to by the astonishment with which it was received.

═══════════════ 12 JULY ═══════════════

15th SUNDAY IN ORDINARY TIME

By bringing gifts to the Eucharist, especially bread and wine, the early Christians were sharing in the elements of the original meal and making provision for the poor and the upkeep of the Church.

ENTRANCE ANTIPHON *(Ps 16:15)*

In my justice I shall see your face, O Lord; when your glory appears, my joy will be full.

GREETING, PENITENTIAL RITE, GLORIA — *pages 7-14*

OPENING PRAYER

Let us pray
  [that the gospel may be our rule of life]
God our Father,
your light of truth
guides us to the way of Christ.

May all who follow him
reject what is contrary to the gospel.

or

Let us pray
    [to be faithful to the light we have received,
        to the name we bear]

Father, let the light of your truth
guide us to your kingdom
through a world filled with lights contrary to your own.
Christian is the name and the gospel we glory in.
May your love make us what you have called us to be.

FIRST READING   *(Am 7:12-15)*

A reading from the prophet Amos.
Go, prophesy to my people.

Amaziah, the priest of Bethel, said to Amos, 'Go away, seer;
get back to the land of Judah; earn your bread there, do your
prophesying there. We want no more prophesying in Bethel; this
is the royal sanctuary, the national temple.' 'I was no prophet,
neither did I belong to any of the brotherhoods of prophets,'
Amos replied to Amaziah. 'I was a shepherd, and looked after
sycamores: but it was the Lord who took me from herding the
flock, and the Lord who said, "Go, prophesy to my people Israel".'

This is the word of the Lord.

RESPONSORIAL PSALM   *(Ps 84:9-14)*

℟   **Let us see, O Lord, your mercy
    and give us your saving help.**

1. I will hear what the Lord God has to say,
    a voice that speaks of peace,
    peace for his people.
    His help is near for those who fear him
    and his glory will dwell in our land. ℟

2. Mercy and faithfulness have met;
    justice and peace have embraced.
    Faithfulness shall spring from the earth
    and justice look down from heaven. ℟

3. The Lord will make us prosper
    and our earth shall yield its fruit.
    Justice shall march before him
    and peace shall follow his steps. ℟

SECOND READING   *(Eph 1:3-14)*

(For Shorter Form, read between ▶ ◀)

A reading from the letter of St Paul to the Ephesians.

Before the world was made, God chose us.

▶Blessed be God the Father of our Lord Jesus Christ,
who has blessed us with all the spiritual blessings of heaven in
    Christ.
Before the world was made, he chose us, chose us in Christ,
to be holy and spotless, and to live through love in his presence,
determining that we should become his adopted sons, through
    Jesus Christ,
for his own kind purposes,
to make us praise the glory of his grace,
his free gift to us in the Beloved,
in whom, through his blood, we gain our freedom,
    the forgiveness of our sins.
Such is the richness of the grace
which he has showered on us
in all wisdom and insight.
He has let us know the mystery of his purpose,
the hidden plan he so kindly made in Christ from the
    beginning
to act upon when the times had run their course to the end:
that he would bring everything together under Christ, as head,
everything in the heavens and everything on earth.◀

And it is in him that we were claimed as God's own,
chosen from the beginning,
under the predetermined plan of the one who guides all things
as he decides by his own will;
chosen to be,
for his greater glory,
the people who would put their hopes in Christ before he came.
Now you too, in him,
have heard the message of the truth and the good news of your
    salvation,
and have believed it:
and you too have been stamped with the seal of the Holy Spirit
    of the Promise,
the pledge of our inheritance
which brings freedom for those whom God has taken for his own,
to make his glory praised.

    ▶This is the word of the Lord.◀

GOSPEL ACCLAMATION   *(cf. Jn 6:63.68)*

Alleluia, alleluia!
Your words are spirit, Lord,
and they are life:
you have the message of eternal life.
Alleluia!

or   *(cf. Eph 1:17.18)*

Alleluia, alleluia!
May the Father of our Lord Jesus Christ
enlighten the eyes of our mind,
so that we can see what hope his call holds for us.
Alleluia!

GOSPEL   *(Mk 6:7-13)*

A reading from the holy Gospel according to Mark.

He began to send them out.

Jesus summoned the Twelve and began to send them out in pairs giving them authority over the unclean spirits. And he instructed them to take nothing for the journey except a staff — no bread, no haversack, no coppers for their purses. They were to wear sandals but, he added, 'Do not take a spare tunic.' And he said to them, 'If you enter a house anywhere, stay there until you leave the district. And if any place does not welcome you and people refuse to listen to you, as you walk away shake off the dust from under your feet as a sign to them.' So they set off to preach repentance: and they cast out many devils, and anointed many sick people with oil and cured them.

This is the Gospel of the Lord.

PROFESSION OF FAITH — *pages 15-16*

PRAYER OVER THE GIFTS

Lord,
accept the gifts of your Church.
May this eucharist
help us grow in holiness and faith.

PREFACE OF SUNDAYS IN ORDINARY TIME I-VIII — *pages 22-25*

COMMUNION ANTIPHON   *(Ps 83:4-5)*

The sparrow even finds a home, the swallow finds a nest
wherein to place her young, near to your altars, Lord of hosts,
my King, my God! How happy they who dwell in your house!
For ever they are praising you.

or   *(Jn 6:57)*

Whoever eats my flesh and drinks my blood will live in me and I in him, says the Lord.

PRAYER AFTER COMMUNION

Lord, by our sharing in the mystery of this eucharist,
let your saving love grow within us.

SOLEMN BLESSING — *pages 57-58*

REFLECTION

In today's first reading there is a confrontation between two prophets, one who was the official spokesman at a royal shrine and who was anxious that what was preached there would be politically correct, particularly to the ears of the king. He didn't like the messages of the second prophet and turned his aggression on the messenger. In response Amos admits that he has no formal qualifications for the role he has been given. In fact we get the distinct impression that he is a reluctant prophet. What stands out in this incident is the command of the Lord in taking the initiative and the obedience of Amos in responding.

═══════════ 19 JULY ═══════════

16th SUNDAY IN ORDINARY TIME

The custom of bringing gifts when coming to the Eucharist developed differently in the Eastern Church and in the West. In the East before the Eucharist people brought gifts for the Eucharist itself, for the poor and for the upkeep of the Church, particularly the clergy. The minister took what was necessary for the Eucharist and brought this in solemnly after the liturgy of the word. In the West all the gifts were collected after the liturgy of the word, some used for the Eucharist and the remainder left to one side.

ENTRANCE ANTIPHON   *(Ps 53:6.8)*

God himself is my help. The Lord upholds my life. I will offer you a willing sacrifice; I will praise your name, O Lord, for its goodness.

GREETING, PENITENTIAL RITE, GLORIA — *pages 7-14*

Let us pray
     [to be kept faithful in the service of God]
Lord,
be merciful to your people.
Fill us with your gifts
and make us always eager to serve you
in faith, hope, and love.

or

Let us pray
     [that God will continue to bless us
     with his compassion and love]
Father,
let the gift of your life
continue to grow in us,
drawing us from death to faith, hope, and love.
Keep us alive in Christ Jesus.
Keep us watchful in prayer
and true to his teaching
till your glory is revealed in us.

FIRST READING   *(Jr 23:1-6)*

A reading from the prophet Jeremiah.

The remnant of my flock I will gather and I will raise up shepherds to
look after them.

'Doom for the shepherds who allow the flock of my pasture to
be destroyed and scattered — it is the Lord who speaks! This,
therefore, is what the Lord, the God of Israel says about the
shepherds in charge of my people: You have let my flock be
scattered and go wandering and have not taken care of them.
Right, I will take care of you for your misdeeds — it is the Lord
who speaks! But the remnant of my flock I myself will gather
from all the countries where I have dispersed them, and will
bring them back to their pastures: they shall be fruitful and
increase in numbers. I will raise up shepherds to look after them
and pasture them; no fear, no terror for them any more; not one
shall be lost — it is the Lord who speaks!

     'See, the days are coming — it is the Lord who speaks —
     when I will raise a virtuous Branch for David,
     who will reign as true king and be wise,
     practising honesty and integrity in the land.

In his days Judah will be saved
and Israel dwell in confidence.
And this is the name he will be called:
The Lord-our-integrity.'
This is the word of the Lord.

RESPONSORIAL PSALM *(Ps 22)*

℟ **The Lord is my shepherd;**
there is nothing I shall want.

1. The Lord is my shepherd;
   there is nothing I shall want.
   Fresh and green are the pastures
   where he gives me repose.
   Near restful waters he leads me,
   to revive my drooping spirit. ℟

2. He guides me along the right path;
   he is true to his name.
   If I should walk in the valley of darkness
   no evil would I fear.
   You are there with your crook and your staff;
   with these you give me comfort. ℟

3. You have prepared a banquet for me
   in the sight of my foes.
   My head you have anointed with oil;
   my cup is overflowing. ℟

4. Surely goodness and kindness shall follow me
   all the days of my life.
   In the Lord's own house shall I dwell
   for ever and ever. ℟

SECOND READING *(Eph 2:13-18)*

A reading from the letter of St Paul to the Ephesians.

Christ Jesus is the peace between us, and has made the two into one.

In Christ Jesus, you that used to be so far apart from us
have been brought very close, by the blood of Christ. For he
is the peace between us, and has made the two into one and
broken down the barrier which used to keep them apart,
actually destroying in his own person the hostility caused by
the rules and decrees of the Law. This was to create one single
New Man in himself out of the two of them and by restoring
peace through the cross, to unite them both in a single Body

and reconcile them with God. In his own person he killed the hostility. Later he came to bring the good news of peace, peace to you who were far away and peace to those who were near at hand. Through him, both of us have in the one Spirit our way to come to the Father.

This is the word of the Lord.

GOSPEL ACCLAMATION   *(Jn 10:27)*

Alleluia, alleluia!
The sheep that belong to me listen to my voice,
says the Lord,
I know them and they follow me.
Alleluia!

GOSPEL   *(Mk 6:30-34)*

A reading from the holy Gospel according to Mark.

They were like sheep without a shepherd.

The apostles rejoined Jesus and told him all they had done and taught. Then he said to them, 'You must come away to some lonely place all by yourselves and rest for a while'; for there were so many coming and going that the apostles had no time even to eat. So they went off in a boat to a lonely place where they could be by themselves. But people saw them going, and many could guess where; and from every town they all hurried to the place on foot and reached it before them. So as he stepped ashore he saw a large crowd; and he took pity on them because they were like sheep without a shepherd, and he set himself to teach them at some length.

This is the Gospel of the Lord.

PROFESSION OF FAITH — *pages 15-16*

PRAYER OVER THE GIFTS

Lord,
bring us closer to salvation
through these gifts which we bring in your honour.
Accept the perfect sacrifice you have given us,
bless it as you blessed the gifts of Abel.

PREFACE OF SUNDAYS IN ORDINARY TIME I-VIII — *pages 22-25*

COMMUNION ANTIPHON   *(Ps 110:4-5)*

The Lord keeps in our minds the wonderful things he has done. He is compassion and love; he always provides for his faithful.

or   *(Rv 3:20)*

I stand at the door and knock, says the Lord. If anyone hears my voice and opens the door, I will come in and sit down to supper with him, and he with me.

PRAYER AFTER COMMUNION

Merciful Father,
may these mysteries
give us new purpose
and bring us to a new life in you.

SOLEMN BLESSING — *pages 57-58*

REFLECTION

> Today's readings reflect on the theme of leadership of the people of God. The shortcomings of the leaders of the Jewish people at the time of Jeremiah at the end of the Seventh Century B.C. are condemned. Jesus highlights the plight of the people of his own day who lack credible leadership. Mark underlines Jesus' willingness to make good this deficiency and his authority to do so.

— 26 JULY —

17th SUNDAY IN ORDINARY TIME

> There are three processions included in the Mass: the entrance procession, the procession at the preparation of the gifts and the communion procession. Each is accompanied or followed by a prayer which sums up what the actions express. The prayer over the gifts is a general prayer which does this and which in addition looks forward to a time beyond this particular celebration. In this way life and liturgy are connected.

ENTRANCE ANTIPHON   *(Ps 67:6-7.36)*

God is in his holy dwelling; he will give a home to the lonely, he gives power and strength to his people.

GREETING, PENITENTIAL RITE, GLORIA — *pages 7-14*

OPENING PRAYER

Let us pray
> [that we will make good use of the gifts
> that God has given us]

God our Father and protector,
without you nothing is holy,
nothing has value.
Guide us to everlasting life
by helping us to use wisely
the blessings you have given to the world.

or

Let us pray
     [for the faith to recognise God's presence in our world]

God our Father,
open our eyes to see your hand at work
in the splendour of creation,
in the beauty of human life.
Touched by your hand our world is holy.
Help us to cherish the gifts that surround us,
to share your blessings with our brothers and sisters,
and to experience the joy of life in your presence.

FIRST READING   *(2 Kings 4:42-44)*

A reading from the second book of the Kings.
They will eat and have some left over.

A man came from Baal-shalishah, bringing Elisha, the man of
God, bread from the first-fruits, twenty barley loaves and fresh
grain in the ear. 'Give it to the people to eat,' Elisha said. But his
servant replied, 'How can I serve this to a hundred men?' 'Give
it to the people to eat' he insisted 'for the Lord says this, "They
will eat and have some left over"'. He served them; they ate and
had some over, as the Lord had said.

    This is the word of the Lord.

RESPONSORIAL PSALM   *(Ps 144:10-11.15-18)*

℟ **You open wide your hand, O Lord,**
    and grant our desires.

1.   All your creatures shall thank you, O Lord,
       and your friends shall repeat their blessing.
       They shall speak of the glory of your reign
       and declare your might, O God. ℟

2.   The eyes of all creatures look to you
       and you give them their food in due time.
       You open wide your hand,
       grant the desires of all who live. ℟

3.   The Lord is just in all his ways
      and loving in all his deeds.
      He is close to all who call him,
      who call on him from their hearts.   ℟

SECOND READING   *(Eph 4:1-6)*

A reading from the letter of St Paul to the Ephesians.

One Body, one Lord, one faith, one baptism.

I, the prisoner in the Lord, implore you to lead a life worthy of
your vocation. Bear with one another charitably, in complete
selflessness, gentleness and patience. Do all you can to preserve
the unity of the Spirit by the peace that binds you together. There
is one Body, one Spirit, just as you were all called into one and
the same hope when you were called. There is one Lord, one
faith, one baptism, and one God who is Father of all, through
all and within all.

      This is the word of the Lord.

GOSPEL ACCLAMATION   *(cf. Jn 6:63.68)*

Alleluia, alleluia!
Your words are spirit, Lord, and they are life:
you have the message of eternal life.
Alleluia!

or   *(Lk 7:16)*

Alleluia, alleluia!
A great prophet has appeared among us;
God has visited his people
Alleluia!

GOSPEL   *(Jn 6:1-15)*

A reading from the holy Gospel according to John.

Jesus gave out as much as was wanted to all who were sitting ready.

Jesus went off to the other side of the Sea of Galilee — or of
Tiberias — and a large crowd followed him, impressed by the
signs he gave by curing the sick. Jesus climbed the hillside,
and sat down there with his disciples. It was shortly before the
Jewish feast of Passover.

      Looking up, Jesus saw the crowds approaching and said to
Philip, 'Where can we buy some bread for these people to eat?'
He only said this to test Philip; he himself knew exactly what
he was going to do. Philip answered, 'Two hundred denarii
would only buy enough to give them a small piece each.' One
of his disciples, Andrew, Simon Peter's brother, said, 'There is

a small boy here with five barley loaves and two fish; but what is that between so many?' Jesus said to them, 'Make the people sit down.' There was plenty of grass there, and as many as five thousand men sat down. Then Jesus took the loaves, gave thanks, and gave them out to all who were sitting ready; he then did the same with the fish, giving out as much as was wanted. When they had eaten enough he said to the disciples, 'Pick up the pieces left over, so that nothing gets wasted.' So they picked them up, and filled twelve hampers with scraps left over from the meal of five barley loaves. The people, seeing this sign that he had given, said, 'This really is the prophet who is to come into the world.' Jesus, who could see they were about to come and take him by force and make him king, escaped back to the hills by himself.

This is the Gospel of the Lord.

PROFESSION OF FAITH — *pages 15-16*

PRAYER OVER THE GIFTS

Lord,
receive these offerings
chosen from your many gifts.
May these mysteries make us holy
and lead us to eternal joy.

PREFACE OF SUNDAYS IN ORDINARY TIME I-VIII — *pages 22-25*

COMMUNION ANTIPHON   (Ps 102:2)

O bless the Lord, my soul, and remember all his kindness.
or   (Mt 5:7-8)
**Happy are those who show mercy; mercy shall be theirs.
Happy are the pure of heart, for they shall see God.**

PRAYER AFTER COMMUNION

Lord,
we receive the sacrament
which celebrates the memory
of the death and resurrection of Christ your Son.
May this gift bring us closer to our eternal salvation.

SOLEMN BLESSING — *pages 57-58*

REFLECTION

In today's gospel we heard the account of the miraculous feeding of the crowd with five loaves and two fish. Behind the gospel accounts of such miracles lies the proclamation that in Jesus,

God's power is at work. The gospel of Mark, which we listen to this year, is particularly anxious not to have Jesus appear as just another of the many miracle workers which were common in the literature of that time. God's power at work in Jesus is the focus of attention rather than Jesus as the worker of miracles.

2 AUGUST

18th SUNDAY IN ORDINARY TIME

At the preparation of the gifts the prayers which begin, 'Blessed are you, Lord, God of all creation' are two newly composed ones which reflect a Jewish influence. Bread and wine are symbols of the relationship of collaboration which exists between God and humanity. The prayers bring out clearly what these objects stand for.

ENTRANCE ANTIPHON *(Ps 69:2.6)*

God, come to my help. Lord, quickly give me assistance. You are the one who helps me and sets me free: Lord, do not be long in coming.

GREETING, PENITENTIAL RITE, GLORIA — *pages 7-14*

OPENING PRAYER

Let us pray
    [for the gift of God's forgiveness and love]

Father of everlasting goodness,
our origin and guide,
be close to us
and hear the prayers of all who praise you.
Forgive our sins and restore us to life.
Keep us safe in your love.

or

Let us pray
    [to the Father whose kindness never fails]

God our Father,
gifts without measure flow from your goodness
to bring us your peace.
Our life is your gift.
Guide our life's journey,
for only your love makes us whole.
Keep us strong in your love.

FIRST READING   (Ex 16:2-4.12-15)

A reading from the book of Exodus.

I will rain down bread for you from the heavens.

The whole community of the sons of Israel began to complain against Moses and Aaron in the wilderness and said to them, 'Why did we not die at the Lord's hand in the land of Egypt, when we were able to sit down to pans of meat and could eat bread to our heart's content! As it is, you have brought us to this wilderness to starve this whole company to death!'

Then the Lord said to Moses, 'Now I will rain down bread for you from the heavens. Each day the people are to go out and gather the day's portion; I propose to test them in this way to see whether they will follow my law or not.

'I have heard the complaints of the sons of Israel. Say this to them, "Between the two evenings you shall eat meat, and in the morning you shall have bread to your heart's content. Then you will learn that I, the Lord, am your God"'. And so it came about: quails flew up in the evening, and they covered the camp; in the morning there was a coating of dew all round the camp. When the coating of dew lifted, there on the surface of the desert was a thing delicate, powdery, as fine as hoarfrost on the ground. When they saw this, the sons of Israel said to one another, 'What is that?' not knowing what it was. 'That' said Moses to them 'is the bread the Lord gives you to eat.'

This is the word of the Lord.

RESPONSORIAL PSALM   (Ps 77:3-4.23-25.54)

℟   **The Lord gave them bread from heaven.**

1.   The things we have heard and understood,
     the things our fathers have told us,
     we will tell to the next generation:
     the glories of the Lord and his might. ℟

2.   He commanded the clouds above
     and opened the gates of heaven.
     He rained down manna for their food,
     and gave them bread from heaven. ℟

3.   Mere men ate the bread of angels.
     He sent them abundance of food.
     He brought them to his holy land,
     to the mountain which his right hand had won. ℟

SECOND READING   *(Eph 4:17.20-24)*

A reading from the letter of St Paul to the Ephesians.

Put on the new self that has been created in God's way.

I want to urge you in the name of the Lord, not to go on living the aimless kind of life that pagans live. Now that is hardly the way you have learnt from Christ, unless you failed to hear him properly when you were taught what the truth is in Jesus. You must give up your old way of life; you must put aside your old self, which gets corrupted by following illusory desires. Your mind must be renewed by a spiritual revolution so that you can put on the new self that has been created in God's way, in the goodness and holiness of the truth.

This is the word of the Lord.

GOSPEL ACCLAMATION   *(Jn 14:6)*

Alleluia, alleluia!
I am the Way, the Truth and the Life, says the Lord;
no one can come to the Father except through me.
Alleluia!

or   *(Mt 4:4)*

Alleluia, alleluia!
Man does not live on bread alone,
but on every word that comes from the mouth of God.
Alleluia!

GOSPEL   *(Jn 6:24-35)*

A reading from the holy Gospel according to John.

He who comes to me will never be hungry; he who believes in me will never thirst.

When the people saw that neither Jesus nor his disciples were there, they got into boats and crossed to Capernaum to look for Jesus. When they found him on the other side, they said to him, 'Rabbi, when did you come here?' Jesus answered:

'I tell you most solemnly,
you are not looking for me
because you have seen the signs
but because you had all the bread you wanted to eat.
Do not work for food that cannot last,
but work for food that endures to eternal life,
the kind of food the Son of Man is offering you,
for on him the Father, God himself, has set his seal.'

Then they said to him, 'What must we do if we are to do the works that God wants?' Jesus gave them this answer, 'This is

working for God: you must believe in the one he has sent.' So
they said, 'What sign will you give to show us that we should
believe in you? What work will you do? Our fathers had manna
to eat in the desert; as scripture says: He gave them bread from
heaven to eat.' Jesus answered:

'I tell you most solemnly,
it was not Moses who gave you bread from heaven,
it is my Father who gives you the bread from heaven,
the true bread;
for the bread of God
is that which comes down from heaven
and gives life to the world.'

'Sir,' they said 'give us that bread always.' Jesus answered:

'I am the bread of life.
He who comes to me will never be hungry;
he who believes in me will never thirst.'

This is the Gospel of the Lord.

PROFESSION OF FAITH — *pages 15-16*

PRAYER OVER THE GIFTS

Merciful Lord,
make holy these gifts,
and let our spiritual sacrifice
make us an everlasting gift to you.

PREFACE OF SUNDAYS IN ORDINARY TIME I-VIII — *pages 22-25*

COMMUNION ANTIPHON   *(Ws 16:20)*

**You gave us bread from heaven, Lord: a sweet-tasting bread
that was very good to eat.**

or   *(Jn 6:35)*

**The Lord says: I am the bread of life. A man who comes to me
will not go away hungry, and no one who believes in me will
thirst.**

PRAYER AFTER COMMUNION

Lord,
you give us the strength of new life
by the gift of the eucharist.
Protect us with your love
and prepare us for eternal redemption.

SOLEMN BLESSING — *pages 57-58*

REFLECTION

The gospel for today and for the next three Sundays interrupts the readings from Saint Mark to present us with the Sixth Chapter of Saint John which portrays Jesus as the bread of life. He is presented as the one who comes from heaven with the word of life. The crowd is an unbelieving one and in John's gospel the only sin is the sin of unbelief. Faith and life go together. As the gospel puts it in another place: 'These things are written so that you may believe that Jesus is the Christ, and that believing, you may have life in his name.'

---

9 AUGUST

19th SUNDAY IN ORDINARY TIME

At the preparation of the gifts, wine and a little water are poured into the chalice. Adding a little water to wine was an ancient custom. The prayer which the priest says as he is mixing the water and wine is an ancient Christian prayer. The theme of the prayer is exchange, that we may share Christ's divinity as he humbled himself to share our humanity. This is an important theme of Christmas. Cyprian sees the mingling as a symbol of Christ and the Church.

ENTRANCE ANTIPHON *(Ps 73:20.19.22.23)*

Lord, be true to your covenant, forget not the life of your poor ones for ever. Rise up, O God, and defend your cause; do not ignore the shouts of your enemies.

GREETING, PENITENTIAL RITE, GLORIA — *pages 7-14*

OPENING PRAYER

Let us pray
[in the Spirit
that we may grow in the love of God]

Almighty and ever-living God,
your Spirit made us your children,
confident to call you Father.
Increase your Spirit within us
and bring us to our promised inheritance.

or

Let us pray
[that through us
others may find the way to life in Christ]

Father, we come, reborn in the Spirit,
to celebrate our sonship in the Lord Jesus Christ.
Touch our hearts,
help them grow towards the life you have promised.
Touch our lives,
make them signs of your love for all.

FIRST READING   (1 Kings 19:4-8)

A reading from the first book of Kings.

Strengthened by the food he walked until he reached the mountain of God.

Elijah went into the wilderness, a day's journey, and sitting under a furze bush wished he were dead. 'Lord', he said 'I have had enough. Take my life; I am no better than my ancestors.' Then he lay down and went to sleep. But an angel touched him and said, 'Get up and eat.' He looked round, and there at his head was a scone baked on hot stones, and a jar of water. He ate and drank and then lay down again. But the angel of the Lord came back a second time and touched him and said, 'Get up and eat, or the journey will be too long for you.' So he got up and ate and drank, and strengthened by that food he walked for forty days and forty nights until he reached Horeb, the mountain of God.

This is the word of the Lord.

RESPONSORIAL PSALM   (Ps 33:2-9)

℟ **Taste and see that the Lord is good.**

1. I will bless the Lord at all times,
    his praise always on my lips;
    in the Lord my soul shall make its boast.
    The humble shall hear and be glad. ℟

2. Glorify the Lord with me.
    Together let us praise his name.
    I sought the Lord and he answered me;
    from all my terrors he set me free. ℟

3. Look towards him and be radiant;
    let your faces not be abashed.
    This poor man called; the Lord heard him
    and rescued him from all his distress. ℟

4. The angel of the Lord is encamped
    around those who revere him, to rescue them.
    Taste and see that the Lord is good.
    He is happy who seeks refuge in him. ℟

SECOND READING   *(Eph 4:30-5:2)*

A reading from the letter of St Paul to the Ephesians.

Follow Christ by loving as he loved you.

Do not grieve the Holy Spirit of God who has marked you
with his seal for you to be set free when the day comes. Never
have grudges against others, or lose your temper, or raise your
voice to anybody, or call each other names, or allow any sort of
spitefulness. Be friends with one another, and kind, forgiving
each other as readily as God forgave you in Christ.

Try, then, to imitate God, as children of his that he loves,
and follow Christ by loving as he loved you, giving himself up
in our place as a fragrant offering and a sacrifice to God.

This is the word of the Lord.

GOSPEL ACCLAMATION   *(Jn 14:23)*

Alleluia, alleluia!
If anyone loves me he will keep my word,
and my Father will love him,
and we shall come to him.
Alleluia!

or   *(Jn 6:51)*

Alleluia, alleluia!
I am the living bread which has come down from heaven,
says the Lord.
Anyone who eats this bread will live for ever.
Alleluia!

GOSPEL   *(Jn 6:41-51)*

A reading from the holy Gospel according to John.

I am the living bread which has come down from heaven.

The Jews were complaining to each other about Jesus, because
he had said, 'I am the bread that came down from heaven.'
'Surely this is Jesus son of Joseph' they said. 'We know his father
and mother. How can he now say, "I have come down from
heaven"?' Jesus said in reply, 'Stop complaining to each other.

'No one can come to me
unless he is drawn by the Father who sent me,
and I will raise him up at the last day.
It is written in the prophets:
They will all be taught by God,
and to hear the teaching of the Father,
and learn from it,

is to come to me.
Not that anybody has seen the Father,
except the one who comes from God:
he has seen the Father.
I tell you most solemnly,
everybody who believes has eternal life.
I am the bread of life.
Your fathers ate the manna in the desert
and they are dead;
but this is the bread that comes down from heaven,
so that a man may eat it and not die.
I am the living bread which has come down from heaven.
Anyone who eats this bread will live for ever;
and the bread that I shall give
is my flesh, for the life of the world.'

This is the Gospel of the Lord.

PROFESSION OF FAITH — *pages 15-16*

PRAYER OVER THE GIFTS

God of power,
giver of the gifts we bring,
accept the offering of your Church
and make it the sacrament of our salvation.

PREFACE OF SUNDAYS IN ORDINARY TIME I-VIII — *pages 22-25*

COMMUNION ANTIPHON   *(Ps 147:12.14)*

Praise the Lord, Jerusalem; he feeds you with the finest wheat.
or   *(Jn 6:52)*
**The bread I shall give is my flesh for the life of the world,
says the Lord.**

PRAYER AFTER COMMUNION

Lord, may the eucharist you give us
bring us to salvation
and keep us faithful to the light of your truth.

SOLEMN BLESSING — *pages 57-58*

REFLECTION

In today's gospel the Jews are portrayed as complaining or
murmuring about Jesus. There is an echo of the murmuring of
the generation which came out of Egypt into the wilderness. It
is an expression of disbelief, the only sin according to John's
gospel. Water and manna resulted from the lack of faith in

the wilderness. Here Jesus as the bread of life is the result. At the end of the passage the death which followed the eating of manna in the desert is contrasted with the life that comes through eating the bread from heaven.

---

15 AUGUST

THE ASSUMPTION
OF THE BLESSED VIRGIN MARY

VIGIL MASS

(Celebrated in England and Wales on Sunday 16th August)

'Happy the womb that bore you and the breasts you sucked!' This is a blessing for Mary as a woman by another anonymous woman from the crowd. Womanhood itself has become a blessing in Mary. We all treasure the Word of God — his saving presence — in earthen vessels.

ENTRANCE ANTIPHON

All honour to you, Mary! Today you were raised above the choirs of angels to lasting glory with Christ.

GREETING, PENITENTIAL RITE, GLORIA — *pages 7-14*

OPENING PRAYER

Let us pray
    [that the Virgin Mary will help us
    with her prayers]

Almighty God,
you gave a humble virgin
the privilege of being the mother of your Son,
and crowned her with the glory of heaven.
May the prayers of the Virgin Mary
bring us to the salvation of Christ
and raise us up to eternal life.
or

Let us pray
    [with Mary to the Father,
    in whose presence she now dwells]

Almighty Father of our Lord Jesus Christ,
you have revealed the beauty of your power
by exalting the lowly virgin of Nazareth

and making her the mother of our Saviour.
May the prayers of this woman clothed with the sun
bring Jesus to the waiting world
and fill the void of incompletion
with the presence of her child,
who lives and reigns with you and the Holy Spirit,
one God, for ever and ever.

FIRST READING   *(1 Ch 15:3-4.15-16; 16:1-2)*

A reading from the first book of Chronicles.

They brought in the ark of God and set it inside the tent which David had pitched for it.

David gathered all Israel together in Jerusalem to bring the ark of God up to the place he had prepared for it. David called together the sons of Aaron and the sons of Levi. And the Levites carried the ark of God with the shafts on their shoulders, as Moses had ordered in accordance with the word of the Lord.

David then told the heads of the Levites to assign duties for their kinsmen as cantors, with their various instruments of music, harps and lyres and cymbals, to play joyful tunes. They brought the ark of God in and put it inside the tent that David had pitched for it; and they offered holocausts before God, and communion sacrifices. And when David had finished offering holocausts and communion sacrifices, he blessed the people in the name of the Lord.

This is the word of the Lord.

RESPONSORIAL PSALM   *(Ps 131:6-7.9-10.13-14)*

℟   **Go up, Lord, to the place of your rest,
      you and the ark of your strength.**

1.   At Ephrata we heard of the ark;
      we found it in the plains of Yearim.
      'Let us go to the place of his dwelling;
      let us go to kneel at his footstool.' ℟

2.   Your priests shall be clothed with holiness:
      your faithful shall ring out their joy.
      For the sake of David your servant
      do not reject your anointed. ℟

3.   For the Lord has chosen Zion;
      he has desired it for his dwelling:
      'This is my resting-place for ever,
      here have I chosen to live.' ℟

SECOND READING   *(1 Cor 15:54-57)*

A reading from the first letter of St Paul to the Corinthians.

He gave us victory through our Lord Jesus Christ.

When this perishable nature has put on imperishability, and when this mortal nature has put on immortality, then the words of scripture will come true: Death is swallowed up in victory. Death, where is your victory? Death, where is your sting? Now the sting of death is sin, and sin gets its power from the Law. So let us thank God for giving us the victory through our Lord Jesus Christ.

This is the word of the Lord.

GOSPEL ACCLAMATION   *(Lk 11:28)*

Alleluia, alleluia!
Happy are those who hear the word of God, and keep it.
Alleluia!

GOSPEL   *(Lk 11:27-28)*

A reading from the holy Gospel according to Luke.

Happy the womb that bore you!

As Jesus was speaking, a woman in the crowd raised her voice and said, 'Happy the womb that bore you and the breasts you sucked!' But he replied, 'Still happier those who hear the word of God and keep it!'

This is the Gospel of the Lord.

PROFESSION OF FAITH — *pages 15-16*

PRAYER OVER THE GIFTS

Lord, receive this sacrifice of praise and peace
in honour of the assumption of the Mother of God.
May our offering bring us pardon
and make our lives a thanksgiving to you.

PREFACE OF THE ASSUMPTION — *page 297*

COMMUNION ANTIPHON   *(cf. Lk 11:27)*

Blessed is the womb of the Virgin Mary; she carried the Son of the eternal Father.

PRAYER AFTER COMMUNION

God of mercy,
we rejoice because Mary, the mother of our Lord,
was taken into the glory of heaven.
May the holy food we receive at this table
free us from evil.

SOLEMN BLESSING — *page 298*
REFLECTION

We join St Bernard of Clairvaux in his prayer to the Blessed Virgin: Turn, then, most gracious advocate, your eyes of mercy towards us; and after this exile, show unto us the blessed fruit of your womb, Jesus.

MASS DURING THE DAY

Today's feast celebrates the belief that the Blessed Virgin Mary, when she completed her earthly life, was in body and soul assumed into heavenly glory. Some strands of the tradition record the death of the B.V.M. at Jerusalem, while others attest that she was assumed during her natural life. While the earliest references to this belief date from the Fourth Century it wasn't until 1950 that Pope Pius XII defined it as an article of faith. This date has been observed as a feastday of Mary since the beginning of the Seventh Century.

ENTRANCE ANTIPHON   *(Rv 12:1)*

A great sign appeared in heaven: a woman clothed with the sun, the moon beneath her feet, and a crown of twelve stars on her head.

or

Let us rejoice in the Lord and celebrate this feast in honour of the Virgin Mary, at whose assumption the angels rejoice, giving praise to the Son of God.

GREETING, PENITENTIAL RITE, GLORIA — *pages 7-14*

OPENING PRAYER

Let us pray
[that we will join Mary, the mother of the Lord,
in the glory of heaven]

All-powerful and ever-living God,
you raised the sinless Virgin Mary, mother of your Son,
body and soul to the glory of heaven.
May we see heaven as our final goal
and come to share her glory.

or

Let us pray
[that with the help of Mary's prayers
we too may reach our heavenly home]

Father in heaven,
all creation rightly gives you praise,
for all life and all holiness come from you.

In the plan of your wisdom
she who bore the Christ in her womb
was raised body and soul in glory to be with him in heaven.
May we follow her example in reflecting your holiness
and join in her hymn of endless life and praise.

FIRST READING *(Rv 11:19; 12:1-6.10)*

A reading from the book of the Apocalypse.

A woman adorned with the sun, standing on the moon.

The sanctuary of God in heaven opened, and the ark of the covenant could be seen inside it.

Now a great sign appeared in heaven: a woman, adorned with the sun, standing on the moon, and with the twelve stars on her head for a crown. She was pregnant, and in labour, crying aloud in the pangs of childbirth. Then a second sign appeared in the sky, a huge red dragon which had seven heads and ten horns, and each of the seven heads crowned with a coronet. Its tail dragged a third of the stars from the sky and dropped them to the earth, and the dragon stopped in front of the woman as she was having the child, so that he could eat it as soon as it was born from its mother. The woman brought a male child into the world, the son who was to rule all the nations with an iron sceptre, and the child was taken straight up to God and to his throne, while the woman escaped into the desert, where God had made a place of safety ready. Then I heard a voice shout from heaven, 'Victory and power and empire for ever have been won by our God, and all authority for his Christ.'

This is the word of the Lord.

RESPONSORIAL PSALM *(Ps 44:10-12.16)*

℟ **On your right stands the queen,
in garments of gold.**

1. The daughters of kings are among your loved ones.
   On your right stands the queen in gold of Ophir. *(continued)*

Listen, O daughter, give ear to my words:
forget your own people and your father's house. ℟

℟ **On your right stands the queen,
in garments of gold.**

2. So will the king desire your beauty:
he is your lord, pay homage to him.
They are escorted amid gladness and joy;
they pass within the palace of the king. ℟

SECOND READING   (1 Cor 15:20-26)

A reading from the first letter of St Paul to the Corinthians.

Christ as the first-fruits and then those who belong to him.

Christ has been raised from the dead, the first-fruits of all who
have fallen asleep. Death came through one man and in the
same way the resurrection of the dead has come through one
man. Just as all die in Adam, so all will be brought to life in
Christ; but all of them in their proper order: Christ as the first-
fruits and then, after the coming of Christ, those who belong
to him. After that will come the end, when he hands over the
kingdom to God the Father, having done away with every
sovereignty, authority and power. For he must be king until
he has put all his enemies under his feet and the last of the
enemies to be destroyed is death, for everything is to be put
under his feet.

This is the word of the Lord.

GOSPEL ACCLAMATION

Alleluia, alleluia!
Mary has been taken up into heaven;
all the choirs of angels are rejoicing.
Alleluia!

GOSPEL   (Lk 1:39-56)

A reading from the holy Gospel according to Luke.

The Almighty has done great things for me, he has exalted the lowly.

Mary set out and went as quickly as she could to a town in
the hill country of Judah. She went into Zechariah's house
and greeted Elizabeth. Now as soon as Elizabeth heard Mary's
greeting, the child leapt in her womb and Elizabeth was filled
with the Holy Spirit. She gave a loud cry and said, 'Of all
women you are the most blessed, and blessed is the fruit of your
womb. Why should I be honoured with a visit from the mother

of my Lord? For the moment your greeting reached my ears, the child in my womb leapt for joy. Yes, blessed is she who believed that the promise made to her by the Lord would be fulfilled.'

And Mary said:

'My soul proclaims the greatness of the Lord
and my spirit exults in God my saviour;
because he has looked upon his lowly handmaid.
Yes, from this day forward all generations will call me
    blessed,
for the Almighty has done great things for me.
Holy is his name,
and his mercy reaches from age to age for those who fear
    him.
He has shown the power of his arm,
he has routed the proud of heart.
He has pulled down princes from their thrones and exalted
    the lowly.
The hungry he has filled with good things, the rich sent
    empty away.
He has come to the help of Israel his servant, mindful of
    his mercy
— according to the promise he made to our ancestors —
of his mercy to Abraham and to his descendants for ever.'

Mary stayed with Elizabeth about three months and then went back home.

This is the Gospel of the Lord.

PROFESSION OF FAITH — *pages 15-16*

PRAYER OVER THE GIFTS

Lord, receive this offering of our service.
You raised the Virgin Mary to the glory of heaven.
By her prayers, help us to seek you
and to live in your love.

PREFACE OF THE ASSUMPTION

Father, all-powerful and ever-living God,
we do well always and everywhere to give you thanks,
through Jesus Christ our Lord.

Today the virgin Mother of God was taken up into heaven
to be the beginning and the pattern of the Church in its
    perfection,

and a sign of hope and comfort for your people on their pilgrim
way.
You would not allow decay to touch her body,
for she had given birth to your Son, the Lord of all life,
in the glory of the incarnation.

In our joy we sing to your glory
with all the choirs of angels:
Holy, holy, holy…

COMMUNION ANTIPHON   *(Lk 1:48-49)*

**All generations will call me blessed, for the Almighty has done
great things for me.**

PRAYER AFTER COMMUNION

Lord,
may we who receive this sacrament of salvation
be led to the glory of heaven
by the prayers of the Virgin Mary.

SOLEMN BLESSING

Born of the Blessed Virgin Mary,
the Son of God redeemed mankind.
May he enrich you with his blessings. **Amen**.

You received the author of life through Mary.
May you always rejoice in her loving care. **Amen**.

You have come to rejoice at Mary's feast.
May you be filled with the joys of the Spirit
and the gifts of your eternal home. **Amen**.

May almighty God bless you,
the Father, and the Son, ✠ and the Holy Spirit.
Amen.

REFLECTION

Luke puts the *Magnificat* on the lips of Mary. It describes the
state of 'anawim' of the Hebrew Scriptures – the downtrodden
remnant of Israelites who were left when the mighty and
powerful were carried away into exile. It emphasises a merciful
God's vindication of the faithful weak against the strong. It is a
revolutionary prayer on many levels: moral – scattering the
proud; social – putting down the mighty and exalting the
lowly; and economic – filling the hungry and sending the rich
away empty.

16 AUGUST

20th SUNDAY IN ORDINARY TIME

The eucharistic prayer is the central prayer of the Mass which is frequently referred to as Eucharist. It is a prayer of thanksgiving, praise, confessing, blessing and acknowledging. It is a Jewish type of prayer and has its origins in the two prayers of thanks which were said over the bread and wine. When he was multiplying the loaves the Lord gave thanks to God his Father. This type of thanks is broader than a simple expression of being grateful. It is what Paul has in mind when he recommends his hearers always to give thanks in psalms, hymns and sacred songs.

ENTRANCE ANTIPHON   *(Ps 83:10-11)*

God, our protector, keep us in mind; always give strength to your people. For if we can be with you even one day, it is better than a thousand without you.

GREETING, PENITENTIAL RITE, GLORIA — *pages 7-14*

OPENING PRAYER

Let us pray
    [that the love of God
    may raise us beyond what we see
    to the unseen glory of his kingdom]

God our Father,
may we love you in all things and above all things
and reach the joy you have prepared for us
beyond all our imagining.

or

Let us pray
    [with humility and persistence]

Almighty God, ever-loving Father,
your care extends beyond the boundaries of race and nation
to the hearts of all who live.

May the walls, which prejudice raises between us,
crumble beneath the shadow of your outstretched arm.

FIRST READING   *(Pr 9:1-6)*

A reading from the book of Proverbs.

Eat my bread, drink the wine I have prepared for you.

Wisdom has built herself a house,
she has erected her seven pillars,
she has slaughtered her beasts, prepared her wine,
she has laid her table.
She has despatched her maidservants
and proclaimed from the city's heights:
'Who is ignorant? Let him step this way.'
To the fool she says,
'Come and eat my bread,
drink the wine I have prepared!
Leave your folly and you will live,
walk in the ways of perception.'

This is the word of the Lord.

RESPONSORIAL PSALM   *(Ps 33:2-3.10-15)*

℞   **Taste and see that the Lord is good.**

1.   I will bless the Lord at all times,
     his praise always on my lips;
     in the Lord my soul shall make its boast.
     The humble shall hear and be glad. ℞

2.   Revere the Lord, you his saints.
     They lack nothing, those who revere him.
     Strong lions suffer want and go hungry
     but those who seek the Lord lack no blessing. ℞

3.   Come, children, and hear me
     that I may teach you the fear of the Lord.
     Who is he who longs for life
     and many days, to enjoy his prosperity? ℞

4.   Then keep your tongue from evil
     and your lips from speaking deceit.
     Turn aside from evil and do good;
     seek and strive after peace. ℞

SECOND READING   *(Eph 5:15-20)*
A reading from the letter of St Paul to the Ephesians.
Recognise what is the will of God.

Be very careful about the sort of lives you lead, like intelligent
and not like senseless people. This may be a wicked age, but
your lives should redeem it. And do not be thoughtless but
recognise what is the will of the Lord. Do not drug yourselves
with wine, this is simply dissipation; be filled with the Spirit.
Sing the words and tunes of the psalms and hymns when you

are together, and go on singing and chanting to the Lord in your hearts, so that always and everywhere you are giving thanks to God who is our Father in the name of our Lord Jesus Christ.

This is the word of the Lord.

GOSPEL ACCLAMATION   *(Jn 1:14.12)*

Alleluia, alleluia!
The Word was made flesh and lived among us;
to all who did accept him
he gave power to become children of God.
Alleluia!

or   *(Jn 6:56)*

Alleluia, alleluia!
He who eats my flesh and drink my blood
lives in me, and I live in him,
says the Lord.
Alleluia!

GOSPEL   *(Jn 6:51-58)*

A reading from the holy Gospel according to John.
My flesh is real food and my blood is real drink.

Jesus said to the crowd:

'I am the living bread which has come down from heaven.
Anyone who eats this bread will live for ever;
and the bread that I shall give
is my flesh, for the life of the world.'

Then the Jews started arguing with one another: 'How can this man give us his flesh to eat?' they said. Jesus replied:

'I tell you most solemnly,
if you do not eat the flesh of the Son of Man
and drink his blood,
you will not have life in you.
Anyone who does eat my flesh and drink my blood
has eternal life,
and I shall raise him up on the last day.
For my flesh is real food
and my blood is real drink.
He who eats my flesh and drinks my blood
lives in me
and I live in him.
As I, who am sent by the living Father,
myself draw life from the Father,

so whoever eats me will draw life from me.
This is the bread come down from heaven;
not like the bread our ancestors ate:
they are dead,
but anyone who eats this bread will live for ever.'
This is the Gospel of the Lord.

PROFESSION OF FAITH — *pages 15-16*

PRAYER OVER THE GIFTS

Lord,
accept our sacrifice
as a holy exchange of gifts.
By offering what you have given us
may we receive the gift of yourself.

PREFACE OF SUNDAYS IN ORDINARY TIME I-VIII — *pages 22-25*

COMMUNION ANTIPHON   *(Ps 129:7)*

With the Lord there is mercy, and fullness of redemption.
or   *(Jn 6:51-52)*
**I am the living bread from heaven, says the Lord; if anyone
eats this bread he will live for ever.**

PRAYER AFTER COMMUNION

God of mercy,
by this sacrament you make us one with Christ.
By becoming more like him on earth,
may we come to share his glory in heaven,
where he lives and reigns for ever and ever.

SOLEMN BLESSING — *pages 57-58*

REFLECTION

In today's first reading from the book of Proverbs the terms
'eating' and 'drinking' are used as symbols to mean accepting
the insights and teachings of another. The words that John
attributes to Jesus may be understood in this way also so
that to eat the flesh of the Son of Man and drink his blood in
addition to their usual sacramental meaning include the idea
of accepting Jesus' teaching and trying to put it into practice in
daily living.

23 AUGUST
21st SUNDAY IN ORDINARY TIME

The Eucharistic prayer is a prayer of thanksgiving and praise. One way in which the Jewish people gave thanks was to recount God's deeds, to recall what God has done not simply as a memorial but including the element of proclamation. This is precisely what the eucharistic prayer does. By relating what God has done and in particular what God has done through Jesus within the context of proclamation the eucharistic prayer becomes an expression of thanksgiving.

ENTRANCE ANTIPHON *(Ps 85:1-3)*

Listen, Lord, and answer me. Save your servant who trusts in you. I call to you all day long, have mercy on me, O Lord.

GREETING, PENITENTIAL RITE, GLORIA — *pages 7-14*

OPENING PRAYER

Let us pray
[that God will make us one in mind and heart]

Father,
help us to see the values
that will bring us lasting joy in this changing world.
In our desire for what you promise
make us one in mind and heart.

or

Let us pray
[with minds fixed on eternal truth]

Lord our God,
all truth is from you,
and you alone bring oneness of heart.

Give your people the joy
of hearing your word in every sound
and of longing for your presence more than for life itself.
May all the attractions of a changing world
serve only to bring us
the peace of your kingdom which this world does not give.

FIRST READING *(Jos 24:1-2.15-18)*

A reading from the book of Joshua.
We will serve the Lord, for he is our God.

Joshua gathered all the tribes of Israel together at Shechem; then he called the elders, leaders, judges and scribes of Israel, and they presented themselves before God. Then Joshua said to all the people: 'If you will not serve the Lord, choose today whom you wish to serve, whether the gods that your ancestors served beyond the River, or the gods of the Amorites in whose land you are now living. As for me and my House, we will serve the Lord.'

The people answered, 'We have no intention of deserting the Lord our God and serving other gods! Was it not the Lord our God who brought us and our ancestors out of the land of Egypt, the house of slavery, who worked those great wonders before our eyes and preserved us all along the way we travelled and among all the peoples through whom we journeyed? We too will serve the Lord, for he is our God.'

This is the word of the Lord.

RESPONSORIAL PSALM   *(Ps 33:2-3.16-23)*

℞   **Taste and see that the Lord is good.**

1.   I will bless the Lord at all times,
      his praise always on my lips;
      in the Lord my soul shall make its boast.
      The humble shall hear and be glad.   ℞

2.   The Lord turns his face against the wicked
      to destroy their remembrance from the earth.
      The Lord turns his eyes to the just
      and his ears to their appeal.   ℞

3.   They call and the Lord hears
      and rescues them in all their distress.
      The Lord is close to the broken-hearted;
      those whose spirit is crushed he will save.   ℞

4.   Many are the trials of the just man
      but from them all the Lord will rescue him.
      He will keep guard over all his bones,
      not one of his bones shall be broken.   ℞

5.   Evil brings death to the wicked;
      those who hate the good are doomed.
      The Lord ransoms the souls of his servants.
      Those who hide in him shall not be condemned.   ℞

SECOND READING   *(Eph 5:25-32)*

A reading from the letter of St Paul to the Ephesians.

This mystery has many implications for Christ and his Church.

Husbands should love their wives just as Christ loved the Church and sacrificed himself for her to make her holy. He made her clean by washing her in water with a form of words, so that when he took her to himself she would be glorious, with no speck or wrinkle or anything like that, but holy and faultless. In the same way, husbands must love their wives as they love their own bodies; for a man to love his wife is for him to love himself. A man never hates his own body, but he feeds it and looks after it; and that is the way Christ treats the Church, because it is his body — and we are its living parts. For this reason, a man must leave his father and mother and be joined to his wife, and the two will become one body. This mystery has many implications; but I am saying it applies to Christ and the Church.

This is the word of the Lord.

GOSPEL ACCLAMATION   *(cf. Jn 6:63.68)*

Alleluia, alleluia!
Your words are spirit, Lord,
and they are life:
you have the message of eternal life.
Alleluia!

GOSPEL   *(Jn 6:60-69)*

A reading from the holy Gospel according to John.

Whom shall we go to? You have the message of eternal life.

After hearing his doctrine many of the followers of Jesus said, 'This is intolerable language. How could anyone accept it?' Jesus was aware that his followers were complaining about it and said, 'Does this upset you? What if you should see the Son of Man ascend to where he was before?

'It is the spirit that gives life,
the flesh has nothing to offer.
The words I have spoken to you are spirit
and they are life.

'But there are some of you who do not believe.' For Jesus knew from the outset those who did not believe, and who it was that would betray him. He went on, 'This is why I told you that no one could come to me unless the Father allows him.' After this, many of his disciples left him and stopped going with him.

Then Jesus said to the Twelve, 'What about you, do you want to go away too?' Simon Peter answered, 'Lord, who shall we go to? You have the message of eternal life, and we believe; we know that you are the Holy One of God.'

This is the Gospel of the Lord.

PROFESSION OF FAITH — *pages 15-16*

PRAYER OVER THE GIFTS

Merciful God,
the perfect sacrifice of Jesus Christ
made us your people.
In your love,
grant peace and unity to your Church.

PREFACE OF SUNDAYS IN ORDINARY TIME I-VIII — *pages 22-25*

COMMUNION ANTIPHON   *(Ps 103:13-15)*

Lord, the earth is filled with your gift from heaven; man grows bread from earth, and wine to cheer his heart.

or   *(Jn 6:55)*

The Lord says: The man who eats my flesh and drinks my blood will live for ever; I shall raise him to life on the last day.

PRAYER AFTER COMMUNION

Lord,
may this eucharist increase within us
the healing power of your love.
May it guide and direct our efforts
to please you in all things.

SOLEMN BLESSING — *pages 57-58*

REFLECTION

Today's gospel evokes a scene in the life of Jesus and by implication later on in the life of the community for which John was writing in which there is division. In both cases the division is caused by the departure of some who had previously been disciples. The confession placed on the lips of Peter emphasises that the appropriate response to such situations is to remain a part of the community which celebrates the Eucharist.

30 AUGUST

22nd SUNDAY IN ORDINARY TIME

The First Eucharistic Prayer, sometimes referred to as the Roman Canon, was the only such prayer used in the Roman rite until 1968 when the other three now familiar prayers were made available. Since the participants at the Second Vatican Council didn't envisage the use of the vernacular generally it was as a result of the dynamism which the Council initiated that the number was increased. While no particular eucharistic prayer is perfect each makes its own contribution to an understanding of what such a prayer should be.

ENTRANCE ANTIPHON   *(Ps 85:3,5)*

I call to you all day long, have mercy on me, O Lord. You are good and forgiving, full of love for all who call to you.

GREETING, PENITENTIAL RITE, GLORIA — *pages 7-14*

OPENING PRAYER

Let us pray
    [that God will increase our faith
    and bring to perfection the gifts he has given us]

Almighty God,
every good thing comes from you.
Fill our hearts with love for you,
increase our faith,
and by your constant care
protect the good you have given us.
or

Let us pray
    [to God who forgives all who call upon him]

Lord God of power and might,
nothing is good which is against your will,
and all is of value which comes from your hand.
Place in our hearts a desire to please you
and fill our minds with insight into love,
so that every thought may grow in wisdom
and all our efforts may be filled with your peace.

FIRST READING   *(Dt 4:1-2.6-8)*

A reading from the book of Deuteronomy.

Add nothing to what I command you, keep the commandments of the Lord.

Moses said to the people: 'Now, Israel, take notice of the laws and customs that I teach you today, and observe them, that you may have life and may enter and take possession of the land that the Lord the God of your fathers is giving you. You must add nothing to what I command you, and take nothing from it, but keep the commandments of the Lord your God just as I lay them down for you. Keep them, observe them and they will demonstrate to the peoples your wisdom and understanding. When they come to know of all these laws they will exclaim, "No other people is as wise and prudent as this great nation." And indeed, what great nation is there that has its gods so near as the Lord our God is to us whenever we call to him? And what great nation is there that has laws and customs to match this whole Law that I put before you today?'

This is the word of the Lord.

RESPONSORIAL PSALM   (Ps 14:2-5)

℟ **The just will live in the presence of the Lord.**

1.   Lord, who shall dwell on your holy mountain?
     He who walks without fault;
     he who acts with justice
     and speaks the truth from his heart. ℟

2.   He who does no wrong to his brother,
     who casts no slur on his neighbour,
     who holds the godless in disdain,
     but honours those who fear the Lord. ℟

3.   He who keeps his pledge, come what may;
     who takes no interest on a loan
     and accepts no bribes against the innocent.
     Such a man will stand firm for ever. ℟

SECOND READING   (Jm 1:17-18.21-22.27)
A reading from the letter of St James.
You must do what the word tells you.

It is all that is good, everything that is perfect, which is given us from above; it comes down from the Father of all light; with him there is no such thing as alteration, no shadow of a change. By his own choice he made us his children by the message of the truth so that we should be a sort of first-fruits of all that he had created.

Accept and submit to the word which has been planted in you and can save your souls. But you must do what the word tells you, and not just listen to it and deceive yourselves.

Pure unspoilt religion, in the eyes of God our Father is this: coming to the help of orphans and widows when they need it, and keeping oneself uncontaminated by the world.

This is the word of the Lord.

GOSPEL ACCLAMATION   *(cf. Jn 6:63.68)*

Alleluia, alleluia!
Your words are spirit, Lord,
and they are life:
you have the message of eternal life.
Alleluia!

or   *(Jm 1:18)*

Alleluia, alleluia!
By his own choice the Father made us his children
by the message of the truth,
so that we should be a sort of first-fruits
of all that he created.
Alleluia!

GOSPEL   *(Mk 7:1-8.14-15.21-23)*

A reading from the holy Gospel according to Mark.

You put aside the commandment of God to cling to human traditions.

The Pharisees and some of the scribes who had come from Jerusalem gathered round Jesus, and they noticed that some of his disciples were eating with unclean hands, that is, without washing them. For the Pharisees, and the Jews in general, follow the tradition of the elders and never eat without washing their arms as far as the elbow; and on returning from the market place they never eat without first sprinkling themselves. There are also many other observances which have been handed down to them concerning the washing of cups and pots and bronze dishes. So these Pharisees and scribes asked him, 'Why do your disciples not respect the tradition of the elders but eat their food with unclean hands?' He answered, 'It was of you hypocrites that Isaiah so rightly prophesied in this passage of scripture:

This people honours me only with lip-service,
while their hearts are far from me.
The worship they offer me is worthless,
the doctrines they teach are only human regulations.

You put aside the commandment of God to cling to human traditions.'

He called the people to him again and said, 'Listen to me, all of you, and understand. Nothing that goes into a man from outside can make him unclean; it is the things that come out of a man that make him unclean. For it is from within, from men's hearts, that evil intentions emerge: fornication, theft, murder, adultery, avarice, malice, deceit, indecency, envy, slander, pride, folly. All these evil things come from within and make a man unclean.'

This is the Gospel of the Lord.

PROFESSION OF FAITH — *pages 15-16*

PRAYER OVER THE GIFTS

Lord,
may this holy offering
bring us your blessing
and accomplish within us
its promise of salvation.

PREFACE OF SUNDAYS IN ORDINARY TIME I-VIII — *pages 22-25*

COMMUNION ANTIPHON   *(Ps 30:20)*

O Lord, how great is the depth of the kindness which you have shown to those who love you.

or   *(Mt 5:9-10)*

Happy are the peacemakers; they shall be called children of God. Happy are they who suffer persecution for justice' sake; the kingdom of heaven is theirs.

PRAYER AFTER COMMUNION

Lord,
you renew us at your table with the bread of life.
May this food strengthen us in love
and help us to serve you in each other.

SOLEMN BLESSING — *pages 57-58*

REFLECTION

Today we resume the reading of Mark's gospel which was interrupted for the past four Sundays. The message of today's section is echoed in the first reading, namely, the importance of living God's commandments. In the gospel, Jesus distinguishes between the observance of mere human custom and the keeping of God's law. There is no doubt as to which is the more important. What is recommended is not just outward conformity but an alignment of the heart.

6 SEPTEMBER

23rd SUNDAY IN ORDINARY TIME

The eucharistic prayer is one of the most important of all liturgical texts. In the Eastern Church where it is called an *anaphora* it is remarkable for its unity and no part of it is changed. Eucharistic Prayer Four which was written as a unit is an example of such a prayer. This is why if a proper preface is to be used at Mass this eucharistic prayer is not used. The key to the spirit of the prayer is found in the dialogue which precedes it, namely, thanksgiving in its broadest sense.

ENTRANCE ANTIPHON   *(Ps 118:137.124)*

Lord, you are just, and the judgements you make are right. Show mercy when you judge me, your servant.

GREETING, PENITENTIAL RITE, GLORIA — *pages 7-14*

OPENING PRAYER

Let us pray
  [that we may realise the freedom God has given us
  in making us his sons and daughters]

God our Father,
you redeem us
and make us your children in Christ.
Look upon us,
give us true freedom
and bring us to the inheritance you promised.

or

Let us pray
  [to our just and merciful God]

Lord our God,
in you justice and mercy meet.
With unparalleled love you have saved us from death
and drawn us into the circle of your life.

Open our eyes to the wonders this life sets before us,
that we may serve you free from fear
and address you as God our Father.

FIRST READING   *(Is 35:4-7)*

A reading from the prophet Isaiah.

The ears of the deaf shall be unsealed and the tongues of the dumb shall be loosed.

Say to all faint hearts,
'Courage! Do not be afraid.
'Look, your God is coming,
vengeance is coming,
the retribution of God;
he is coming to save you.'

Then the eyes of the blind shall be opened,
the ears of the deaf unsealed,
then the lame shall leap like a deer
and the tongues of the dumb sing for joy;

for water gushes in the desert,
streams in the wasteland,
the scorched earth becomes a lake,
the parched land springs of water.

    This is the word of the Lord.

RESPONSORIAL PSALM   (Ps 145:7-10)

℟ **My soul, give praise to the Lord.**

or **Alleluia!**

1. It is the Lord who keeps faith for ever,
    who is just to those who are oppressed.
    It is he who gives bread to the hungry,
    the Lord, who sets prisoners free. ℟

2. It is the Lord who gives sight to the blind,
    who raises up those who are bowed down,
    the Lord who loves the just,
    the Lord, who protects the stranger. ℟

3. The Lord upholds the widow and orphan,
    but thwarts the path of the wicked.
    The Lord will reign for ever,
    Zion's God, from age to age. ℟

SECOND READING   (Jm 2:1-5)

A reading from the letter of St James.

God chose the poor to be the heirs to the kingdom.

My brothers, do not try to combine faith in Jesus Christ, our glorified
Lord, with the making of distinctions between classes of people. Now
suppose a man comes into your synagogue, beautifully dressed and
with a gold ring on, and at the same time a poor man comes in,
in shabby clothes, and you take notice of the well-dressed man,

and say, 'Come this way to the best seat'; then you tell the poor man, 'Stand over there' or 'You can sit on the floor by my foot-rest.' Can't you see that you have used two different standards in your mind, and turned yourselves into judges, and corrupt judges at that?

Listen, my dear brothers: it was those who are poor according to the world that God chose, to be rich in faith and to be the heirs to the kingdom which he promised to those who love him.

This is the word of the Lord.

GOSPEL ACCLAMATION   *(1 S 3:9; Jn 6:68)*

Alleluia, alleluia!
Speak, Lord, your servant is listening:
you have the message of eternal life.
Alleluia!
or   *(cf. Mt 4:23)*

Alleluia, alleluia!
Jesus proclaimed the Good News of the kingdom,
and cured all kinds of sickness among the people.
Alleluia

GOSPEL   *(Mk 7:31-37)*

A reading from the holy Gospel according to Mark.

He makes the deaf hear and the dumb speak.

Returning from the district of Tyre, Jesus went by way of Sidon towards the Sea of Galilee, right through the Decapolis region. And they brought him a deaf man who had an impediment in his speech; and they asked him to lay his hand on him. He took him aside in private, away from the crowd, put his fingers into the man's ears and touched his tongue with spittle. Then looking up to heaven he sighed; and he said to him, 'Ephphatha,' that is, 'Be opened.' And his ears were opened, and the ligament of his tongue was loosened and he spoke clearly. And Jesus ordered them to tell no one about it, but the more he insisted, the more widely they published it. Their admiration was unbounded. He has done all things well,' they said 'he makes the deaf hear and the dumb speak.'

This is the Gospel of the Lord.

PROFESSION OF FAITH — *pages 15-16*

PRAYER OVER THE GIFTS

God of peace and love,
may our offering bring you true worship
and make us one with you.

PREFACE OF SUNDAYS IN ORDINARY TIME I-VIII — *pages 22-25*

COMMUNION ANTIPHON   *(Ps 41:2-3)*

**Like a deer that longs for running streams, my soul longs for
you, my God. My soul is thirsting for the living God.**
or   *(Jn 8:12)*
**I am the light of the world, says the Lord; the man who follows
me will have the light of life.**

PRAYER AFTER COMMUNION

Lord,
your word and your sacrament
give us food and life.
May this gift of your Son
lead us to share his life for ever.

SOLEMN BLESSING — *pages 57-58*

REFLECTION

From today's first reading we read that the arrival of God's saving
power on behalf of God's people will be accompanied by such
wonders as the blind seeing and the deaf having their hearing
restored. So when Mark portrays Jesus as one who heals he is making
a statement about who Jesus is, namely, the one sent by God to
bring salvation. The little detail of Jesus' taking the man aside
and of his ordering his hearers not to speak about what happened
is another example of Mark's wish to play down the miraculous
element of Jesus' works and instead to focus on who Jesus is.

13 SEPTEMBER
24th SUNDAY IN ORDINARY TIME

The question 'Who is Jesus?' is the underlying one behind the stories of the Gospel. Today that question is asked explicitly. The answer to the question is one which only gradually emerged in the earliest Christian communities. What gave impetus to this question was the fact that Jesus died, apparently a failure and abandoned by most of those who were his followers and perhaps also by God. His subsequent presence among the group of disciples is described by a number of terms in the New Testament: resurrection, exaltation, glorification. This was interpreted by the first Christian communities as God's vindication of him.

ENTRANCE ANTIPHON   *(cf. Si 36:18)*
Give peace, Lord, to those who wait for you, and your prophets will proclaim you as you deserve. Hear the prayers of your servant and of your people Israel.

GREETING, PENITENTIAL RITE, GLORIA — *pages 7-14*

OPENING PRAYER
Let us pray
    [that God will keep us faithful in his service]
Almighty God,
our creator and guide,
may we serve you with all our heart
and know your forgiveness in our lives.
or
Let us pray
    [for the peace which is born of faith and hope]
Father in heaven,
Creator of all,
look down upon your people in their moments of need,
for you alone are the source of our peace.
Bring us to the dignity which distinguishes the poor in spirit
and show us how great is the call to serve,
that we may share in the peace of Christ
who offered his life in the service of all.

FIRST READING   (Is 50:5-9)

A reading from the prophet Isaiah.
I offered my back to those who struck me.

The Lord has opened my ear.
For my part, I made no resistance,
neither did I turn away.
I offered my back to those who struck me,
my cheeks to those who tore at my beard;
I did not cover my face
against insult and spittle.

The Lord comes to my help,
so that I am untouched by the insults.
So, too, I set my face like flint;
I know I shall not be shamed.

My vindicator is here at hand. Does anyone start proceedings
      against me?
Then let us go to court together.
Who thinks he has a case against me?
Let him approach me.
The Lord is coming to my help,
who dare condemn me?

        This is the word of the Lord.

RESPONSORIAL PSALM   (Ps 114:1-6.8-9)

℞   I will walk in the presence of the Lord,
      in the land of the living.

or   Alleluia!

1.   I love the Lord for he has heard
      the cry of my appeal;
      for he turned his ear to me
      in the day when I called him. ℞

2.   They surrounded me, the snares of death,
      with the anguish of the tomb;
      they caught me, sorrow and distress.
      I called on the Lord's name.
      O Lord my God, deliver me! ℞

3.   How gracious is the Lord, and just;
      our God has compassion.
      The Lord protects the simple hearts;
      I was helpless so he saved me. ℞

4. He has kept my soul from death,
    my eyes from tears
    and my feet from stumbling.
    I will walk in the presence of the Lord
    in the land of the living. ℞

SECOND READING   *(Jm 2:14-18)*

A reading from the letter of St James.

If good works do not go with faith, it is quite dead.

Take the case, my brothers, of someone who has never done a single good act but claims that he has faith. Will that faith save him? If one of the brothers or one of the sisters is in need of clothes and has not enough food to live on, and one of you says to them, 'I wish you well; keep yourself warm and eat plenty,' without giving them these bare necessities of life, then what good is that? Faith is like that: if good works do not go with it, it is quite dead.

This is the way to talk to people of that kind: 'You say you have faith and I have good deeds; I will prove to you that I have faith by showing you my good deeds — now you prove to me that you have faith without any good deeds to show.'

This is the word of the Lord.

GOSPEL ACCLAMATION   *(Jn 14:6)*

Alleluia, alleluia!
I am the Way, the Truth and the Life, says the Lord;
no one can come to the Father except through me.
Alleluia!

or   *(Gal 6:14)*

Alleluia, alleluia!
The only thing I can boast about is the cross of our Lord,
    Jesus Christ,
through whom the world is crucified to me, and I to the
    world.
Alleluia!

GOSPEL   *(Mk 8:27-35)*

A reading from the holy Gospel according to Mark.

You are the Christ. The Son of Man is destined to suffer grievously.

Jesus and his disciples left for the villages round Caesarea Philippi. On the way he put this question to his disciples, 'Who do people say I am?' And they told him. 'John the Baptist,' they said, 'others Elijah; others again, one of the prophets.' 'But you,' he asked 'who do you say I am?' Peter spoke up and said to him, 'You are the Christ.' And he gave them strict orders not to tell anyone about him.

And he began to teach them that the Son of Man was destined to suffer grievously, to be rejected by the elders and the chief priests and the scribes, and to be put to death, and after three days to rise again; and he said all this quite openly. Then, taking him aside, Peter started to remonstrate with him. But, turning and seeing his disciples, he rebuked Peter and said to him, 'Get behind me, Satan! Because the way you think is not God's way but man's.'

He called the people and his disciples to him and said, 'If anyone wants to be a follower of mine, let him renounce himself and take up his cross and follow me. For anyone who wants to save his life will lose it; but anyone who loses his life for my sake, and for the sake of the gospel, will save it.'

This is the Gospel of the Lord.

PROFESSION OF FAITH — *pages 15-16*

PRAYER OVER THE GIFTS
Lord,
hear the prayers of your people
and receive our gifts.
May the worship of each one here
bring salvation to all.

PREFACE OF SUNDAYS IN ORDINARY TIME I-VIII — *pages 22-25*

COMMUNION ANTIPHON   *(Ps 35:8)*
O God, how much we value your mercy! All mankind can gather under your protection.
or   *(cf. 1 Cor 10:16)*
The cup that we bless is a communion with the blood of Christ; and the bread that we break is a communion with the body of the Lord.

PRAYER AFTER COMMUNION
Lord,
may the eucharist you have given us
influence our thoughts and actions.
May your Spirit guide and direct us in your way.

SOLEMN BLESSING — *pages 57-58*

REFLECTION

Saint Paul is given the credit for focussing the attention of the early Christian communities on the death of Jesus. More than anything else he said or did it was Jesus' death which was the most powerful witness to his belief in the Kingdom of God. Similarly, it was his death which more than anything else which would throw the greatest light on who he was because it opened the door to the Father's raising him on high and giving him a name which is above all names.

=== 20 SEPTEMBER ===

25th SUNDAY IN ORDINARY TIME

Though originally not part of the Eucharistic Prayer, the *Sanctus*, or 'Holy, holy, holy Lord' is sung after the preface. It contains echoes of the account of the call of the prophet Isaiah and of the vision of John in the fourth chapter of the Book of Revelation. It is a declaration of God's holiness, God's otherness. All creation is united in heaven and on earth in proclaiming this. It is a high point in the Eucharistic Prayer and this is made clear when it is sung.

ENTRANCE ANTIPHON

I am the Saviour of all people, says the Lord. Whatever their troubles, I will answer their cry, and I will always be their Lord.

GREETING, PENITENTIAL RITE, GLORIA — *pages 7-14*

OPENING PRAYER

Let us pray
[that we will grow in the love of God
and of one another]

Father, guide us, as you guide creation
according to your law of love.
May we love one another
and come to perfection
in the eternal life prepared for us.

or

Let us pray
[to the Lord who is a God of love to all peoples]

Father in heaven,
the perfection of justice is found in your love
and all humankind is in need of your law.

Help us to find this love in each other
that justice may be attained
through obedience to your law.

FIRST READING   (Ws 2:12.17-20)

A reading from the book of Wisdom.

Let us condemn him to a shameful death.

The godless say to themselves,
'Let us lie in wait for the virtuous man, since he annoys us
and opposes our way of life,
reproaches us for our breaches of the law
and accuses us of playing false to our upbringing.
Let us see if what he says is true,
let us observe what kind of end he himself will have.
If the virtuous man is God's son, God will take his part
and rescue him from the clutches of his enemies.
Let us test him with cruelty and with torture,
and thus explore this gentleness of his
and put his endurance to the proof.
Let us condemn him to a shameful death
since he will be looked after — we have his word for it.'

This is the word of the Lord.

RESPONSORIAL PSALM   (Ps 53:3-6.8)

℟ **The Lord upholds my life.**

1. O God, save me by your name;
   by your power, uphold my cause.
   O God, hear my prayer;
   listen to the words of my mouth. ℟

2. For proud men have risen against me,
   ruthless men seek my life.
   They have no regard for God. ℟

3. But I have God for my help.
   The Lord upholds my life.
   I will sacrifice to you with willing heart
   and praise your name for it is good. ℟

SECOND READING   (Jm 3:16-4:3)

A reading from the letter of St James.

Peacemakers, when they work for peace, sow the seeds which will bear fruit in holiness.

Wherever you find jealousy and ambition, you find disharmony, and wicked things of every kind being done; whereas the wisdom that comes down from above is essentially something pure; it also makes for peace, and is kindly and considerate; it is full of compassion and shows itself by doing good; nor is there any trace of partiality or hypocrisy in it. Peacemakers, when they work for peace, sow the seeds which will bear fruit in holiness.

Where do these wars and battles between yourselves first start? Isn't it precisely in the desires fighting inside your own selves? You want something and you haven't got it; so you are prepared to kill. You have an ambition that you cannot satisfy; so you fight to get your way by force. Why you don't have what you want is because you don't pray for it; when you do pray and don't get it, it is because you have not prayed properly, you have prayed for something to indulge your own desires.

This is the word of the Lord.

GOSPEL ACCLAMATION   (Jn 8:12)
Alleluia, alleluia!
I am the light of the world, says the Lord,
anyone who follows me
will have the light of life.
Alleluia!

or   (cf. 2 Thess 2:14)

Alleluia, alleluia!
Through the Good News God called us
to share the glory of our Lord Jesus Christ.
Alleluia!

GOSPEL   (Mk 9:30-37)
A reading from the holy Gospel according to Mark.
The Son of Man will be delivered. If anyone wants to be first, he must make himself servant of all.

After leaving the mountain Jesus and his disciples made their way through Galilee; and he did not want anyone to know, because he was instructing his disciples; he was telling them, 'The Son of Man will be delivered into the hands of men; they will put him to death; and three days after he has been put to death he will rise again.' But they did not understand what he said and were afraid to ask him.

They came to Capernaum, and when he was in the house he asked them, 'What were you arguing about on the road?' They said nothing because they had been arguing which of them was the greatest. So he sat down, called the Twelve to him and said, 'If anyone wants to be first, he must make himself last of all and servant of all.' He then took a little child, set him in front of them, put his arms round him, and said to them, 'Anyone who welcomes one of these little children in my name, welcomes me; and anyone who welcomes me welcomes not me but the one who sent me.'

This is the Gospel of the Lord.

PROFESSION OF FAITH — *pages 15-16*

PRAYER OVER THE GIFTS
Lord,
may these gifts which we now offer
to show our belief and our love
be pleasing to you.
May they become for us
the eucharist of Jesus Christ your Son,
who is Lord for ever and ever.

PREFACE OF SUNDAYS IN ORDINARY TIME I-VIII — *pages 22-25*

COMMUNION ANTIPHON   (Ps 118:4-5)
You have laid down your precepts to be faithfully kept. May my footsteps be firm in keeping your commands.

or   (Jn 10:14)
I am the Good Shepherd, says the Lord; I know my sheep, and mine know me.

PRAYER AFTER COMMUNION
Lord,
help us with your kindness.
Make us strong through the eucharist.
May we put into action
the saving mystery we celebrate.

SOLEMN BLESSING — *pages 57-58*

REFLECTION
Today's gospel contains one of the three so-called predictions of the passion of the Lord found in the Gospel of Mark. They are an indication that the shadow of the cross is never eliminated from the life of Jesus and by implication from the life of a disciple. This message is found very early on in Mark's gospel. It is hinted at as early as the first chapter, where Jesus' public ministry is presented as not starting until John the Baptist has been 'handed over'.

27 SEPTEMBER

26th SUNDAY IN ORDINARY TIME

The Fourth Eucharistic Prayer, newly composed for the revised rite of Mass, is noticeable for its complexity and also for its simplicity. The section after the *Sanctus* and before the words of institution or consecration is remarkably similar to the creed in that it begins by stating the Father's role in creation. It goes on to speak of the Son's work of redemption and finishes with a mention of the Spirit as the one who makes holy. All this is done in a spirit of thanksgiving. It is in fact a proclamation of faith. It is worth noting that the creed came into the Mass when the Eucharistic Prayer became silent.

ENTRANCE ANTIPHON   *(Dn 3:31.29.30.43.42)*

O Lord, you had just cause to judge men as you did: because we sinned against you and disobeyed your will. But now show us your greatness of heart, and treat us with your unbounded kindness.

GREETING, PENITENTIAL RITE, GLORIA — *pages 7-14*

OPENING PRAYER

Let us pray
    [for God's forgiveness
    and for the happiness it brings]

Father,
you show your almighty power
in your mercy and forgiveness.
Continue to fill us with your gifts of love.
Help us to hurry toward the eternal life you promise
and come to share in the joys of your kingdom.

or

Let us pray
    [for the peace of the kingdom
    which we have been promised]

Father of our Lord Jesus Christ,
in your unbounded mercy
you have revealed the beauty of your power
through your constant forgiveness of our sins.
May the power of this love be in our hearts
to bring your pardon and your kingdom to all we meet.

FIRST READING   (Nb 11:25-29)

A reading from the book of Numbers.

Are you jealous on my account? If only the whole people of the Lord were prophets!

The Lord came down in the Cloud. He spoke with Moses, but took some of the spirit that was on him and put it on the seventy elders. When the spirit came on them they prophesied, but not again.

Two men had stayed back in the camp; one was called Eldad and the other Medad. The spirit came down on them; though they had not gone to the Tent, their names were enrolled among the rest. These began to prophesy in the camp. The young man ran to tell this to Moses, 'Look,' he said, 'Eldad and Medad are prophesying in the camp.' Then said Joshua the son of Nun, who had served Moses from his youth, 'My Lord Moses, stop them!' Moses answered him, 'Are you jealous on my account? If only the whole people of the Lord were prophets, and the Lord gave his Spirit to them all!'

This is the word of the Lord.

RESPONSORIAL PSALM   (Ps 18:8.10.12-14)

℟   **The precepts of the Lord gladden the heart.**

1.   The law of the Lord is perfect,
     it revives the soul.
     The rule of the Lord is to be trusted,
     it gives wisdom to the simple. ℟

2.   The fear of the Lord is holy,
     abiding for ever.
     The decrees of the Lord are truth
     and all of them just. ℟

3.   So in them your servant finds instruction;
     great reward is in their keeping.
     But who can detect all his errors?
     From hidden faults acquit me. ℟

4.   From presumption restrain your servant
     and let it not rule me.
     Then shall I be blameless,
     clean from grave sin. ℟

SECOND READING   *(Jm 5:1-6)*

A reading from the letter of St James.

Your wealth is all rotting.

An answer for the rich. Start crying, weep for the miseries that are coming to you. Your wealth is all rotting, your clothes are all eaten up by moths. All your gold and your silver are corroding away, and the same corrosion will be your own sentence, and eat into your body. It was a burning fire that you stored up as your treasure for the last days. Labourers mowed your fields, and you cheated them — listen to the wages that you kept back, calling out; realise that the cries of the reapers have reached the ears of the Lord of hosts. On earth you have had a life of comfort and luxury; in the time of slaughter you went on eating to your heart's content. It was you who condemned the innocent and killed them; they offered you no resistance.

This is the word of the Lord.

GOSPEL ACCLAMATION   *(cf. Jn 17:17)*

Alleluia, alleluia!
Your word is truth, O Lord,
consecrate us in the truth.
Alleluia!

GOSPEL   *(Mk 9:38-43.45.47-48)*

A reading from the holy Gospel according to Mark.

Anyone who is not against us is for us. If your hand should cause you to sin, cut it off.

John said to Jesus, 'Master, we saw a man who is not one of us casting out devils in your name; and because he was not one of us we tried to stop him.' But Jesus said, 'You must not stop him: no one who works a miracle in my name is likely to speak evil of me. Anyone who is not against us is for us.

'If anyone gives you a cup of water to drink just because you belong to Christ, then I tell you solemnly, he will most certainly not lose his reward.

'But anyone who is an obstacle to bring down one of these little ones who have faith, would be better thrown into the sea with a great millstone round his neck. And if your hand should cause you to sin, cut it off; it is better for you to enter into life crippled, than to have two hands and go to hell, into the fire that cannot be put out. And if your foot should cause you to sin, cut it off; it is better for you to enter into life lame, than to have two feet and be thrown into hell. And if your eye should cause you to sin, tear it out; it is better for you to enter into the kingdom of God with one eye, than to have two eyes and be thrown into hell where their worm does not die nor their fire go out.'

This is the Gospel of the Lord.

PROFESSION OF FAITH — *pages 15-16*

PRAYER OVER THE GIFTS
God of mercy,
accept our offering
and make it a source of blessing for us.

PREFACE OF SUNDAYS IN ORDINARY TIME I-VIII — *pages 22-25*

COMMUNION ANTIPHON   *(Ps 118:49-50)*
O Lord, remember the words you spoke to me, your servant, which made me live in hope and consoled me when I was downcast.

or   *(1 Jn 3:16)*
This is how we know what love is: Christ gave up his life for us; and we too must give up our lives for our brothers.

PRAYER AFTER COMMUNION
Lord,
may this eucharist
in which we proclaim the death of Christ
bring us salvation
and make us one with him in glory,
for he is Lord for ever and ever.

SOLEMN BLESSING — *pages 57-58*

REFLECTION
The Holy Spirit is frequently referred to as the Sanctifier, the one who makes holy. What does this mean? Holiness belongs to God and we acknowledge this at the *Sanctus*. Jesus sent the Holy Spirit from the Father to complete his work on earth. In other words, the mystery which was realised in Jesus' life must take place in ours too. The Spirit is also to bring us to the fullness of grace. This is the Spirit as Sanctifier at work. It means to bring all sanctification to its perfection.

4 OCTOBER

27th SUNDAY IN ORDINARY TIME

There is a point during the eucharistic prayer at which the priest prays that the Holy Spirit may make holy the gifts of bread and wine. The Holy Spirit's role is to sanctify. At this point we ask the Spirit to carry out this work. Remembering the great mystery which the Lord left us and thanking God, for it engenders confidence in the present. Therefore this petition is saying to God: what you did then, do now.

ENTRANCE ANTIPHON   (Est 13:9.10-11)

O Lord, you have given everything its place in the world, and no one can make it otherwise. For it is your creation, the heavens and the earth and the stars: you are the Lord of all.

GREETING, PENITENTIAL RITE, GLORIA — *pages 7-14*

OPENING PRAYER

Let us pray
    [that God will forgive our failings
    and bring us peace]

Father, your love for us
surpasses all our hopes and desires.
Forgive our failings,
keep us in your peace
and lead us in the way of salvation.

or

Let us pray
    [before the face of God, in trusting faith]

Almighty and eternal God,
Father of the world to come,
your goodness is beyond what our spirit can touch
and your strength is more than the mind can bear.
Lead us to seek beyond our reach
and give us the courage to stand before your truth.

FIRST READING   (Gen 2:18-24)

A reading from the book of Genesis.

They become one body.

The Lord God said, 'It is not good that the man should be alone. I will make him a helpmate.' So from the soil the Lord God fashioned all the wild beasts and all the birds of heaven. These he brought to the man to see what he would call them; each one was to bear the name the man would give it. The man gave names to all the cattle, all the birds of heaven and all the wild beasts. But no helpmate suitable for man was found for him. So the Lord God made the man fall into a deep sleep. And while he slept, he took one of his ribs and enclosed it in flesh. The Lord built the rib he had taken from the man into a woman, and brought her to the man. The man exclaimed:

'This at last is bone from my bones,
and flesh from my flesh!
This is to be called woman,
for this was taken from man.'

This is why a man leaves his father and mother and joins himself to his wife, and they become one body.

This is the word of the Lord.

RESPONSORIAL PSALM   *(Ps 127)*

℞ **May the Lord bless us
all the days of our life.**

1. O blessed are those who fear the Lord
    and walk in his ways!
    By the labour of your hands you shall eat.
    You will be happy and prosper. ℞

2. Your wife will be like a fruitful vine
    in the heart of your house;
    your children like shoots of the olive,
    around your table. ℞

3. Indeed thus shall be blessed
    the man who fears the Lord.
    May the Lord bless you from Zion
    in a happy Jerusalem
    all the days of your life!
    May you see your children's children.
    On Israel, peace! ℞

SECOND READING   *(Heb 2:9-11)*

A reading from the letter to the Hebrews.

The one who sanctifies, and the ones who are sanctified, are of the same stock.

We see in Jesus one who was for a short while made lower than the angels and is now crowned with glory and splendour because he submitted to death; by God's grace he had to experience death for all mankind.

As it was his purpose to bring a great many of his sons into glory, it was appropriate that God, for whom everything exists and through whom everything exists, should make perfect, through suffering, the leader who would take them to their salvation. For the one who sanctifies, and the ones who are sanctified, are of the same stock; that is why he openly calls them brothers.

This is the word of the Lord.

GOSPEL ACCLAMATION   *(cf. Jn 17:17)*

Alleluia, alleluia!
Your word is truth, O Lord,
consecrate us in the truth.
Alleluia!

or   *(1 Jn 4:12)*

Alleluia, alleluia!
As long as we love one another
God will live in us
and his love will be complete in us.
Alleluia!

GOSPEL   *(Mk 10:2-16)*

(For Shorter Form, read between ◗ ◖*)*

A reading from the holy Gospel according to Mark.

What God has united, man must not divide.

◗Some Pharisees approached Jesus and asked, 'Is it against the law for a man to divorce his wife?' They were testing him. He answered them, 'What did Moses command you?' 'Moses allowed us' they said 'to draw up a writ of dismissal and so to divorce.' Then Jesus said to them, 'It was because you were so unteachable that he wrote this commandment for you. But from the beginning of creation God made them male and female. This is why a man must leave father and mother, and the two become one body. They are no longer two, therefore, but one body. So then, what God has united, man must not divide.' Back in the house the disciples questioned him again about this, and he said to them, 'The man who divorces his wife and marries another is guilty of adultery against her. And if a woman divorces her husband and marries another she is guilty of adultery too.'◖

People were bringing little children to him, for him to touch them. The disciples turned them away, but when Jesus saw this he was indignant and said to them, 'Let the little children come to me; do not stop them; for it is to such as these that the kingdom of God belongs. I tell you solemnly, anyone who does not welcome the kingdom of God like a little child will never enter it.' Then he put his arms round them, laid his hands on them and gave them his blessing.

♦This is the Gospel of the Lord.♦

PROFESSION OF FAITH — *pages 15-16*

PRAYER OVER THE GIFTS

Father,
receive these gifts
which our Lord Jesus Christ
has asked us to offer in his memory.
May our obedient service
bring us to the fullness of your redemption.

PREFACE OF SUNDAYS IN ORDINARY TIME I-VIII — *pages 22-25*

COMMUNION ANTIPHON   *(Lm 3:25)*

The Lord is good to those who hope in him, to those who are searching for his love.

or   *(cf. 1 Cor 10:17)*

Because there is one bread, we, though many, are one body, for we all share in the one loaf and the one cup.

PRAYER AFTER COMMUNION

Almighty God,
let the eucharist we share
fill us with your life.
May the love of Christ
which we celebrate here
touch our lives and lead us to you.

SOLEMN BLESSING — *pages 57-58*

REFLECTION

Today's gospel reading from Mark contains Jesus' teaching on the question of divorce and remarriage. Perhaps because of the connection with family life this passage is followed by an account of Jesus' dealing with children. There is a sharp contrast between the way they are treated by the disciples and the manner in which Jesus relates to them. As with many of his practices we can take it that the respect and love that he showed them was not in keeping with the spirit of his time.

11 OCTOBER
28th SUNDAY IN ORDINARY TIME

The words of consecration are frequently referred to today as the account of the institution of the Eucharist. There is an intended shift of emphasis here and it has a lot to recommend it. The idea is to move away from an automatic understanding of what happens when the words are said by the priest. The reality which such an automatic understanding could easily obscure is that God is always the master of God's own gift. This truth can help us to avoid taking God's gift for granted.

ENTRANCE ANTIPHON *(Ps 129:3-4)*

If you, O Lord, laid bare our guilt, who could endure it? But you are forgiving, God of Israel

GREETING, PENITENTIAL RITE, GLORIA — *pages 7-14*

OPENING PRAYER

Let us pray
[that God will help us to love one another]

Lord,
our help and guide,
make your love the foundation of our lives.
May our love for you express itself
in our eagerness to do good for others.

or

Let us pray
[in quiet for the grace of sincerity]

Father in heaven,
the hand of your loving kindness
powerfully yet gently guides all the moments of our day.

Go before us in our pilgrimage of life,
anticipate our needs and prevent our falling.
Send your Spirit to unite us in faith,
that sharing in your service,
we may rejoice in your presence.

FIRST READING *(Ws 7:7-11)*

A reading from the book of Wisdom.
Compared with wisdom, I held riches as nothing.

I prayed, and understanding was given me;
I entreated, and the spirit of Wisdom came to me.

I esteemed her more than sceptres and thrones;
compared with her, I held riches as nothing.
I reckoned no priceless stone to be her peer,
for compared with her, all gold is a pinch of sand,
and beside her silver ranks as mud.
I loved her more than health or beauty,
preferred her to the light,
since her radiance never sleeps.
In her company all good things came to me,
at her hands riches not to be numbered.

This is the word of the Lord.

RESPONSORIAL PSALM   *(Ps 89:12-17)*

℟ **Fill us with your love that we may rejoice.**

1.   Make us know the shortness of our life
     that we may gain wisdom of heart.
     Lord, relent! Is your anger for ever?
     Show pity to your servants. ℟

2.   In the morning, fill us with your love;
     we shall exult and rejoice all our days.
     Give us joy to balance our affliction
     for the years when we knew misfortune. ℟

3.   Show forth your work to your servants;
     let your glory shine on their children.
     Let the favour of the Lord be upon us:
     give success to the work of our hands. ℟

SECOND READING   *(Heb 4:12-13)*

A reading from the letter to the Hebrews.

The word of God can judge secret emotions and thoughts.

The word of God is something alive and active: it cuts like any
double-edged sword but more finely: it can slip through the
place where the soul is divided from the spirit, or joints from
the marrow; it can judge the secret emotions and thoughts. No
created thing can hide from him; everything is uncovered and
open to the eyes of the one to whom we must give account of
ourselves.

This is the word of the Lord.

GOSPEL ACCLAMATION   *(cf. Mt 11:25)*

Alleluia, alleluia!
Blessed are you, Father,

Lord of heaven and earth,
for revealing the mysteries of the kingdom
to mere children.
Alleluia!
or   *(Mt 5:3)*

Alleluia, alleluia!
How happy are the poor in spirit;
theirs is the kingdom of heaven.
Alleluia!

GOSPEL   *(Mk 10:17-30)*

(For Shorter Form, *read between* ◈ ◈*)*

A reading from the holy Gospel according to Mark.

Go and sell everything you own and follow me.

◈Jesus was setting out on a journey when a man ran up, knelt before him and put this question to him, 'Good master, what must I do to inherit eternal life?' Jesus said to him, 'Why do you call me good? No one is good but God alone. You know the commandments: You must not kill; You must not commit adultery; You must not steal; You must not bring false witness; You must not defraud; Honour your father and mother.' And he said to him, 'Master, I have kept all these from my earliest days.' Jesus looked steadily at him and loved him, and he said, 'There is one thing you lack. Go and sell everything you own and give the money to the poor, and you will have treasure in heaven; then come, follow me.' But his face fell at these words and he went away sad, for he was a man of great wealth.

Jesus looked round and said to his disciples, 'How hard it is for those who have riches to enter the kingdom of God!' The disciples were astounded by these words, but Jesus insisted, 'My children,' he said to them, 'how hard it is to enter the kingdom of God! It is easier for a camel to pass through the eye of a needle than for a rich man to enter the kingdom of God.' They were more astonished than ever. 'In that case' they said to one another 'who can be saved?' Jesus gazed at them. 'For men' he said 'it is impossible, but not for God: because everything is possible for God.'◈

Peter took this up. 'What about us?' he asked him. 'We have left everything and followed you.' Jesus said, 'I tell you solemnly, there is no one who has left house, brothers, sisters, father, children or land for my sake and for the sake of the gospel who will not be repaid a hundred times over, houses, brothers, sisters, mothers, children and land — not without persecutions — now in this present time and, in the world to come, eternal life.'

◆This is the Gospel of the Lord.◆

PROFESSION OF FAITH — *pages 15-16*

PRAYER OVER THE GIFTS

Lord,
accept the prayers and gifts
we offer in faith and love.
May this eucharist bring us to your glory.

PREFACE OF SUNDAYS IN ORDINARY TIME I-VIII — *pages 22-25*

COMMUNION ANTIPHON   *(Ps 33:11)*

The rich suffer want and go hungry, but nothing shall be lacking to those who fear the Lord.
or   *(1 Jn 3:2)*
When the Lord is revealed we shall be like him, for we shall see him as he is.

PRAYER AFTER COMMUNION

Almighty Father,
may the body and blood of your Son
give us a share in his life,
for he is Lord for ever and ever.

SOLEMN BLESSING — *pages 57-58*

REFLECTION

Today's gospel makes two basic points. First, that wealth can be an obstacle to discipleship. It would not be helpful to understand this in a fundamentalist way which, on the one hand, would condemn those people who have wealth at their disposal and, on the other, would glorify poverty. Secondly, Jesus states that the rewards of being a disciple of his are infinitely greater than the sacrifices. It is worth noting that these rewards are not confined to the next life but refer to this life too. In typical fashion Mark adds the phrase 'with persecutions' which indicates Mark's view that the shadow of the cross is never far from the disciple of Jesus.

18 OCTOBER
29th SUNDAY IN ORDINARY TIME
(Mission Sunday)

The words of the account of the institution of the Eucharist are
biblical ones, in particular 'mystery' and 'everlasting covenant'.
Each eucharistic prayer has its own introduction which helps
to give it its own particular emphasis or character. The Fourth
Eucharistic Prayer has 'When the time (literally "hour") came'
and this reflects Saint John's mention of Christ's hour which
at one time he shrunk from and later welcomed.

ENTRANCE ANTIPHON   *(Ps 16:6.8)*

**I call upon you, God, for you will answer me; bend your ear
and hear my prayer. Guard me as the pupil of your eye; hide
me in the shade of your wings.**

GREETING, PENITENTIAL RITE, GLORIA — *pages 7-14*

OPENING PRAYER

Let us pray
   [for the gift of simplicity and joy
   in our service of God and man]

Almighty and ever-living God,
our source of power and inspiration,
give us strength and joy
in serving you as followers of Christ,
who lives and reigns with you and the Holy Spirit,
one God, for ever and ever.

or

Let us pray
   [to the Lord who bends close to hear our prayer]

Lord our God, Father of all,
you guard us under the shadow of your wings
and search into the depths of our hearts.

Remove the blindness that cannot know you
and relieve the fear that would hide us from your sight.

FIRST READING   *(Is 53:10-11)*

A reading from the prophet Isaiah.
If he offers his life in atonement, he shall see his heirs, he shall have a
long life.

**The Lord has been pleased to crush his servant with suffering.
If he offers his life in atonement,**

he shall see his heirs, he shall have a long life
and through him what the Lord wishes will be done.

His soul's anguish over
he shall see the light and be content.
By his sufferings shall my servant justify many,
taking their faults on himself.

This is the word of the Lord.

RESPONSORIAL PSALM   *(Ps 32:4-5.18-20.22)*

℟ **May your love be upon us, O Lord,
as we place all our hope in you.**

1. The word of the Lord is faithful
and all his works to be trusted.
The Lord loves justice and right
and fills the earth with his love. ℟

2. The Lord looks on those who revere him,
on those who hope in his love,
to rescue their souls from death,
to keep them alive in famine. ℟

3. Our soul is waiting for the Lord.
The Lord is our help and our shield.
May your love be upon us, O Lord,
as we place all our hope in you. ℟

SECOND READING   *(Heb 4:14-16)*

A reading from the letter to the Hebrews.
Let us be confident in approaching the throne of grace.

Since in Jesus, the Son of God, we have the supreme high priest
who has gone through to the highest heaven, we must never let
go of the faith that we have professed. For it is not as if we had
a high priest who was incapable of feeling our weaknesses with
us; but we have one who has been tempted in every way that
we are, though he is without sin. Let us be confident, then in
approaching the throne of grace, that we shall have mercy from
him and find grace when we are in need of help.

This is the word of the Lord.

GOSPEL ACCLAMATION   *(Jn 14:6)*

**Alleluia, alleluia!
I am the Way, the Truth and the Life, says the Lord;
no one can come to the Father except through me.
Alleluia!**

or   *(Mk 10:45)*

Alleluia, alleluia!
The Son of Man came to serve,
and to give his life as a ransom for many.
Alleluia!

GOSPEL   *(Mk 10:35-45)*

(For Shorter Form, *read between* ◗ ◖*)*

A reading from the holy Gospel according to Mark.

The Son of Man came to give his life as a ransom for many.

James and John, the sons of Zebedee, approached Jesus. 'Master,' they said to him, 'we want you to do us a favour.' He said to them, 'What is it you want me to do for you?' They said to him, 'Allow us to sit one at your right hand and the other at your left in your glory.' 'You do not know what you are asking' Jesus said to them. 'Can you drink the cup that I must drink, or be baptised with the baptism with which I must be baptised?' They replied, 'We can.' Jesus said to them, 'The cup that I must drink you shall drink, and with the baptism with which I must be baptised you shall be baptised, but as for seats at my right hand or my left, these are not mine to grant; they belong to those to whom they have been allotted.'

When the other ten heard this they began to feel indignant with James and John, so ◗Jesus called them to him and said to them, 'You know that among the pagans their so-called rulers lord it over them, and their great men make their authority felt. This is not to happen among you. No; anyone who wants to become great among you must be your servant, and anyone who wants to be first among you must be slave to all. For the Son of Man himself did not come to be served but to serve, and to give his life as a ransom for many.

This is the Gospel of the Lord.◖

PROFESSION OF FAITH — *pages 15-16*

PRAYER OVER THE GIFTS

Lord God,
may the gifts we offer
bring us your love and forgiveness
and give us freedom to serve you with our lives.

PREFACE OF SUNDAYS IN ORDINARY TIME I-VIII — *pages 22-25*

COMMUNION ANTIPHON   *(Ps 32:18-19)*

See how the eyes of the Lord are on those who fear him, on those who hope in his love, that he may rescue them from death and feed them in time of famine.

or   *(Mk 10:45)*

The Son of Man came to give his life as a ransom for many.

PRAYER AFTER COMMUNION

Lord,
may this eucharist help us to remain faithful.
May it teach us the way to eternal life.

SOLEMN BLESSING — *pages 57-58*

REFLECTION

Today's gospel incident sheds light on the disciples' lack of understanding of what their choice involved. This is a theme with which readers of Mark will be familiar. Jesus makes three points in his reply: a place in the kingdom demands suffering; it is not Jesus' privilege to determine status in the coming kingdom and leadership in Jesus' community means service. He lived this last principle in his own life and summed up in the phrase: 'I am among you as one who serves.'

═══════════════ 25 OCTOBER ═══════════════

30th SUNDAY IN ORDINARY TIME

A feature of the eucharistic prayers we use is the mention of the word 'memorial' immediately after the words of institution, when the essential moments of the Paschal Mystery are recalled. There is a direct link to the words in institution, to the command of the Lord who said: 'Do this in memory of me.' This memorial, sometimes referred to as the *anamnesis* is an essential element of every eucharistic prayer. No eucharistic prayer confines itself to remembering the death of Christ but it is always the death and resurrection, in other words, the Paschal Mystery, which is called to mind.

ENTRANCE ANTIPHON   *(Ps 104:3-4)*

Let hearts rejoice who search for the Lord. Seek the Lord and his strength, seek always the face of the Lord.

GREETING, PENITENTIAL RITE, GLORIA — *pages 7-14*

OPENING PRAYER

Let us pray
[for the strength to do God's will]

Almighty and ever-living God,
strengthen our faith, hope, and love.
May we do with loving hearts
what you ask of us
and come to share the life you promise.

or

Let us pray
[in humble hope for salvation]

Praised be you,
God and Father of our Lord Jesus Christ.
There is no power for good
which does not come from your covenant,
and no promise to hope in
that your love has not offered.
Strengthen our faith to accept your covenant
and give us the love to carry out your command.

FIRST READING   *(Jr 31:7-9)*

A reading from the prophet Jeremiah.

I will comfort the blind and the lame as I lead them back.

The Lord says this:
        Shout with joy for Jacob!
        Hail the chief of nations!
        Proclaim! Praise! Shout:
        'The Lord has saved his people,
        the remnant of Israel!'
        See, I will bring them back
        from the land of the North
        and gather them from the far ends of earth;
        all of them: the blind and the lame,
        women with child, women in labour:
        a great company returning here.
        They had left in tears,
        I will comfort them as I lead them back;
        I will guide them to streams of water,
        by a smooth path where they will not stumble.
        For I am a father to Israel,
        and Ephraim is my first-born son.
                This is the word of the Lord.

RESPONSORIAL PSALM   (Ps 125)

℞ **What marvels the Lord worked for us!**
   Indeed we were glad.

1. When the Lord delivered Zion from bondage,
    it seemed like a dream.
    Then was our mouth filled with laughter,
    on our lips there were songs. ℞

2. The heathens themselves said: 'What marvels
    the Lord worked for them!'
    What marvels the Lord worked for us!
    Indeed we were glad. ℞

3. Deliver us, O Lord, from our bondage
    as streams in dry land.
    Those who are sowing in tears
    will sing when they reap. ℞

4. They go out, they go out, full of tears,
    carrying seed for the sowing:
    they come back, they come back, full of song,
    carrying their sheaves. ℞

SECOND READING   (Heb 5:1-6)

A reading from the letter to the Hebrews.
You are a priest of the order of Melchizedek, and for ever.

Every high priest has been taken out of mankind and is
appointed to act for men in their relations with God, to offer
gifts and sacrifices for sins; and so he can sympathise with
those who are ignorant or uncertain because he too lives in
the limitations of weakness. That is why he has to make sin
offerings for himself as well as for the people. No one takes this
honour on himself, but each one is called by God, as Aaron
was. Nor did Christ give himself the glory of becoming high
priest, but he had it from the one who said to him: You are my
son, today I have become your father, and in another text: You
are a priest of the order of Melchizedek, and for ever.

        This is the word of the Lord.

GOSPEL ACCLAMATION   (Jn 8:12)

Alleluia, alleluia!
I am the light of the world, says the Lord,
anyone who follows me
will have the light of life.
Alleluia!

or   *(cf. 2 Tm 1:10)*

Alleluia, alleluia!
Our Saviour Christ Jesus abolished death,
and he has proclaimed life through the Good News.
Alleluia!

GOSPEL   *(Mk 10:46-52)*

A reading from the holy Gospel according to Mark.

Master, let me see again.

As Jesus left Jericho with his disciples and a large crowd,
Bartimaeus (that is, the son of Timaeus), a blind beggar, was
sitting at the side of the road. When he heard that it was Jesus
of Nazareth, he began to shout and to say, 'Son of David, Jesus,
have pity on me.' And many of them scolded him and told him
to keep quiet, but he only shouted all the louder, 'Son of David,
have pity on me.' Jesus stopped and said, 'Call him here.' So
they called the blind man. 'Courage,' they said, 'get up; he is
calling you.' So throwing off his cloak, he jumped up and went
to Jesus. Then Jesus spoke, 'What do you want me to do for you?'
'Rabbuni,' the blind man said to him, 'Master, let me see again.'
Jesus said to him, 'Go; your faith has saved you.' And immediately
his sight returned and he followed him along the road.

This is the Gospel of the Lord.

PROFESSION OF FAITH — *pages 15-16*

PRAYER OVER THE GIFTS

Lord God of power and might,
receive the gifts we offer
and let our service give you glory.

PREFACE OF SUNDAYS IN ORDINARY TIME I-VIII — *pages 22-25*

COMMUNION ANTIPHON   *(Ps 19:6))*

We will rejoice at the victory of God and make our boast in
his great name.

or   *(Eph 5:2)*

Christ loved us and gave himself up for us as a fragrant
offering to God.

PRAYER AFTER COMMUNION

Lord,
bring to perfection within us
the communion we share in this sacrament.
May our celebration have an effect in our lives.

SOLEMN BLESSING — *pages 57-58*

REFLECTION

Today's first reading declares that the Lord has saved his people and that the result of this action is that many people will be gathered together, brought back from where they had been scattered and among these are blind and lame people. Jeremiah's words date from the end of the Seventh Century B.C. One of Mark's purposes in relating the cure of Bartimaeus here is to indicate that God's saving of his people has arrived in the person of Jesus. Bartimaeus' reaction to Jesus and his willingness to follow him on the way of discipleship contrast with the disciples' misunderstanding and blindness displayed during the journey.

1 NOVEMBER

ALL SAINTS

Today's feast to celebrate all the Christian saints, known and unknown, was originally kept on the first Sunday after Pentecost which is the date on which it is still kept by the Eastern Christian Churches. From the middle of the Eighth Century it has been observed on November 1. The word 'saint' means 'holy one'. To make holy is the work of the Spirit. Those in whose lives this work is completed are saints. The Spirit was sent by Jesus from the Father to complete this work on earth.

ENTRANCE ANTIPHON

Let us all rejoice in the Lord and keep a festival in honour of all the saints. Let us join with the angels in joyful praise to the Son of God.

GREETING, PENITENTIAL RITE, GLORIA — *pages 7-14*

OPENING PRAYER

Let us pray

[that the prayers of all the saints
will bring us forgiveness for our sins]

Father, all-powerful and ever-living God,
today we rejoice in the holy men and women
of every time and place.
May their prayers bring us your forgiveness and love.

or

Let us pray
[as we rejoice and keep festival
in honour of all the saints]

God our Father,
source of all holiness,
the work of your hands is manifest in your saints,
the beauty of your truth is reflected in their faith.

May we who aspire to have part in their joy
be filled with the Spirit that blessed their lives,
so that having shared their faith on earth
we may also know their peace in your kingdom.

FIRST READING   *(Rv 7:2-4.9-14)*

A reading from the book of the Apocalypse.

I saw a huge number, impossible to count, of people from every nation, race, tribe and language.

I, John, saw another angel rising where the sun rises, carrying the seal of the living God; he called in a powerful voice to the four angels whose duty was to devastate land and sea, 'Wait before you do any damage on land or at sea or to the trees, until we have put the seal on the foreheads of the servants of our God.' Then I heard how many were sealed: a hundred and forty-four thousand, out of all the tribes of Israel.

After that I saw a huge number, impossible to count, of people from every nation, race, tribe and language; they were standing in front of the throne and in front of the Lamb, dressed in white robes and holding palms in their hands. They shouted aloud, 'Victory to our God, who sits on the throne, and to the Lamb!' And all the angels who were standing in a circle round the throne, surrounding the elders and the four animals, prostrated themselves before the throne, and touched the grounds with their foreheads, worshipping God with these words: 'Amen. Praise and glory and wisdom and thanksgiving and honour and power and strength to our God for ever and ever. Amen.'

One of the elders then spoke, and asked me, 'Do you know who these people are, dressed in white robes, and where they have come from?' I answered him, 'You can tell me, my Lord.' Then he said, 'These are the people who have been through the great persecution, and they have washed their robes white again in the blood of the Lamb.'

This is the word of the Lord.

RESPONSORIAL PSALM   *(Ps 23:1-6)*

℟   **Such are the men who seek your face, O Lord.**

1.   The Lord's is the earth and its fullness,
      the world and all its peoples.
      It is he who set it on the seas;
      on the waters he made it firm. ℟

2.   Who shall climb the mountain of the Lord?
      Who shall stand in his holy place?
      The man with clean hands and pure heart,
      who desires not worthless things. ℟

3.   He shall receive blessings from the Lord
      and reward from the God who saves him.
      Such are the men who seek him,
      seek the face of the God of Jacob. ℟

SECOND READING   *(1 Jn 3:1-3)*

A reading from the first letter of St John.

We shall see God as he really is.

Think of the love that the Father has lavished on us,
by letting us be called God's children;
and that is what we are.
Because the world refused to acknowledge him,
therefore it does not acknowledge us.
My dear people, we are already the children of God
but what we are to be in the future has not yet been revealed;
all we know is, that when it is revealed
we shall be like him
because we shall see him as he really is.
Surely everyone who entertains this hope
must purify himself, must try to be as pure as Christ.

      This is the word of the Lord.

GOSPEL ACCLAMATION   *(Mt 11:28)*

Alleluia, alleluia!
Come to me, all you who labour and are overburdened,
and I will give you rest, says the Lord.
Alleluia!

GOSPEL   *(Mt 5:1-12)*

A reading from the holy Gospel according to Matthew.

Rejoice and be glad, for your reward will be great in heaven.

Seeing the crowds, Jesus went up the hill. There he sat down and was joined by his disciples. Then he began to speak. This is what he taught them:

'How happy are the poor in spirit;
theirs is the kingdom of heaven.
Happy the gentle:
they shall have the earth for their heritage.
Happy those who mourn:
they shall be comforted.
Happy those who hunger and thirst for what is right:
they shall be satisfied.
Happy the merciful:
they shall have mercy shown them.
Happy the pure in heart:
they shall see God.
Happy the peacemakers:
they shall be called children of God.
Happy those who are persecuted in the cause of right:
theirs is the kingdom of heaven.

'Happy are you when people abuse you and persecute you and speak all kinds of calumny against you on my account. Rejoice and be glad, for your reward will be great in heaven.'

This is the Gospel of the Lord.

PROFESSION OF FAITH — *pages 15-16*

PRAYER OVER THE GIFTS

Lord, receive our gifts in honour of the holy men and women who live with you in glory.
May we always be aware
of their concern to help and save us.

PREFACE OF ALL SAINTS

Father, all-powerful and ever-living God,
we do well always and everywhere to give you thanks.

Today we keep the festival of your holy city,
the heavenly Jerusalem, our mother.
Around your throne
the saints, our brothers and sisters,
sing your praise for ever.
Their glory fills us with joy,
and their communion with us in your Church
gives us inspiration and strength

as we hasten on our pilgrimage of faith,
eager to meet them.

With their great company and all the angels
we praise your glory
as we cry out with one voice:
Holy, holy, holy...

COMMUNION ANTIPHON

(Mt 5:8-10)

Happy are the pure of heart for they shall see God. Happy the peacemakers; they shall be called children of God. Happy are they who suffer persecution for justice' sake; the kingdom of heaven is theirs.

PRAYER AFTER COMMUNION

Father, holy one,
we praise your glory reflected in the saints.
May we who share at this table
be filled with your love
and prepared for the joy of your kingdom,
where Jesus is Lord for ever and ever.

SOLEMN BLESSING

God is the glory and joy of all his saints,
whose memory we celebrate today.
May his blessing be with you always. **Amen.**

May the prayers of the saints deliver you from present evil;
may their example of holy living
turn your thoughts to the service of God and neighbour. **Amen.**

God's holy Church rejoices that her children
are one with the saints in lasting peace.
May you come to share with them
in all the joys of our Father's house. **Amen.**

May almighty God bless you,
the Father, and the Son, ✠ and the Holy Spirit. **Amen.**

REFLECTION

Today's gospel presents what are sometimes termed 'the eight beatitudes'. They have been described as a programme for discipleship. They are a portrayal of the way of life to which Christians are called as distinct from the way of life of their contemporaries. Originally their function was probably catechetical instruction associated with Baptism. To accept the gospel comes before accepting its demands.

32nd SUNDAY IN ORDINARY TIME

What made Israel unique in the eyes of its prophets was the covenant between her and God. It was the covenant rather than any ties of race or neighbourliness which bound the Israelites together. The covenant had vertical as well as horizontal responsibilities. By the former they were to worship the LORD alone. By the latter they were to have particular concern for the marginalised in their society. These were identified above all as the stranger, the widow and the orphan.

ENTRANCE ANTIPHON   *(Ps 87:3)*

Let my prayer come before you, Lord; listen, and answer me.

GREETING, PENITENTIAL RITE, GLORIA — *pages 7-14*

OPENING PRAYER

Let us pray
    [for health of mind and body]

God of power and mercy,
protect us from all harm.
Give us freedom of spirit
and health in mind and body
to do your work on earth.

or

Let us pray
    [that our prayer rise like incense
    in the presence of the Lord]

Almighty Father,
strong is your justice and great is your mercy.
Protect us in the burdens and challenges of life.
Shield our minds from the distortion of pride
and enfold our desire with the beauty of truth.

Help us to become more aware of your loving design
so that we may more willingly give our lives in service to all.

FIRST READING   *(1 Kings 17:10-16)*

A reading from the first book of the Kings.

The widow made a little scone from her meal and brought it to Elijah.

Elijah the Prophet went off to Sidon. And when he reached the city gate, there was a widow gathering sticks; addressing her he said, 'Please bring a little water in a vessel for me to drink.'

She was setting off to bring it when he called after her. 'Please' he said, 'bring me a scrap of bread in your hand.' 'As the Lord your God lives,' she replied, 'I have no baked bread, but only a handful of meal in a jar and a little oil in a jug; I am just gathering a stick or two to go and prepare this for myself and my son to eat, and then we shall die.' But Elijah said to her, 'Do not be afraid, go and do as you have said; but first make a little scone of it for me and bring it to me, and then make some for yourself and for your son. For thus the Lord speaks, the God of Israel:

> "Jar of meal shall not be spent,
> jug of oil shall not be emptied,
> before the day when the Lord sends
> rain on the face of the earth"'.

The woman went and did as Elijah told her and they ate the food, she, himself and her son. The jar of meal was not spent nor the jug of oil emptied, just as the Lord had foretold through Elijah.

This is the word of the Lord.

RESPONSORIAL PSALM   (Ps 145:7-10)

℟   **My soul, give praise to the Lord.**

or   **Alleluia!**

1. It is the Lord who keeps faith for ever,
    who is just to those who are oppressed.
    It is he who gives bread to the hungry,
    the Lord, who sets prisoners free. ℟

2. It is the Lord who gives sight to the blind,
    who raises up those who are bowed down.
    It is the Lord who loves the just,
    the Lord, who protects the stranger. ℟

3. The Lord upholds the widow and orphan
    but thwarts the path of the wicked.
    The Lord will reign for ever,
    Zion's God, from age to age. ℟

SECOND READING   (Heb 9:24-28)

A reading from the letter to the Hebrews.

Christ offers himself only once to take the faults of many on himself.

It is not as though Christ had entered a man-made sanctuary which was only modelled on the real one; but it was heaven itself, so that he could appear in the actual presence of God on our behalf. And he does not have to offer himself again and again, like the high priest going into the sanctuary year after year with the blood that is not his own, or else he would have had to suffer over and over again since the world began. Instead of that, he has made his appearance once and for all, now at the end of the last age, to do away with sin by sacrificing himself. Since men only die once, and after that comes judgement, so Christ, too, offers himself only once to take the faults of many on himself, and when he appears a second time, it will not be to deal with sin but to reward with salvation those who are waiting for him.

This is the word of the Lord.

GOSPEL ACCLAMATION   *(Rv 2:10)*

Alleluia, alleluia!
Even if you have to die, says the Lord,
keep faithful, and I will give you
the crown of life.
Alleluia!

or   *(Mt 5:3)*

Alleluia, alleluia!
How happy are the poor in spirit;
their is the kingdom of heaven.
Alleluia!

GOSPEL   *(Mk 12:38-44)*

(For Shorter Form, read between ♦ ♦*)*

A reading from the holy Gospel according to Mark.

This poor widow has put in more than all.

In his teaching Jesus said, 'Beware of the scribes who like to walk about in long robes, to be greeted obsequiously in the market squares, to take the front seats in the synagogues and the places of honour at banquets; these are the men who swallow the property of widows, while making a show of lengthy prayers. The more severe will be the sentence they receive.'

♦He sat down opposite the treasury and watched the people putting money into the treasury, and many of the rich put in a great deal. A poor widow came and put in two small coins, the equivalent of a penny. Then he called his disciples and said to them, 'I tell you solemnly, this poor widow has put more in than all who have contributed to the treasury; for they have all put in money they had over, but she from the little she had has put in everything she possessed, all she had to live on.'

This is the Gospel of the Lord.*

PROFESSION OF FAITH — *pages 15-16*

PRAYER OVER THE GIFTS

God of mercy,
in this eucharist we proclaim the death of the Lord.
Accept the gifts we present
and help us follow him with love,
for he is Lord for ever and ever.

PREFACE OF SUNDAYS IN ORDINARY TIME I-VIII — *pages 22-25*

COMMUNION ANTIPHON   *(Ps 22:1-2)*

The Lord is my shepherd; there is nothing I shall want. In green pastures he gives me rest, he leads me beside the waters of peace.

or   *(Lk 24:35)*

The disciples recognised the Lord Jesus in the breaking of bread.

PRAYER AFTER COMMUNION

Lord,
we thank you for the nourishment you give us
through your holy gift.
Pour out your Spirit upon us
and in the strength of this food from heaven
keep us single-minded in your service.

SOLEMN BLESSING — *pages 57-58*

REFLECTION

In today's Gospel Jesus is portrayed as overturning the status quo of his day when it came to contributing to the temple. He was not content to accept a system of prestige and social importance which was based on the corruption of those who had and the exploitation of those who had not. The hollowness of respectability based on such practices is exposed by him.

33rd SUNDAY IN ORDINARY TIME

The Fourth Eucharistic Prayer contains the expression 'and looking forward to his coming in glory'. It occurs at the point where what is being recalled is mentioned. It is a clear reference to the second coming of Christ and one which echoes the thoughts of the Church at this time of the year. Many prayers of the Eastern Church list the second coming at the end of the events to be commemorated, and so it is part of the mystery of Christ. In his humanity that mystery has been realised but in the rest of humanity it will only be completed at the second coming or *parousia*.

ENTRANCE ANTIPHON   *(Jr 29:11.12.14)*

The Lord says: my plans for you are peace and not disaster; when you call to me, I will listen to you, and I will bring you back to the place from which I exiled you.

GREETING, PENITENTIAL RITE, GLORIA — *pages 7-14*

OPENING PRAYER

Let us pray
    [that God will help us to be faithful]

Father of all that is good,
keep us faithful in serving you,
for to serve you is our lasting joy.

or

Let us pray
    [with hearts that long for peace]

Father in heaven,
ever-living source of all that is good,
from the beginning of time you promised man salvation
through the future coming of your Son, our Lord Jesus Christ.

Help us to drink of his truth
and expand our hearts with the joy of his promises,
so that we may serve you in faith and in love
and know for ever the joy of your presence.

FIRST READING   *(Dn 12:1- 3)*

A reading from the prophet Daniel.

When that time comes, your own people will be spared.

'At that time Michael will stand up, the great prince who mounts guard over your people. There is going to be a time of great distress, unparalleled since nations first came into existence. When that time comes, your own people will be spared, all those whose names are found written in the Book. Of those who lie sleeping in the dust of the earth many will awake, some to everlasting life, some to shame and everlasting disgrace. The learned will shine as brightly as the vault of heaven, and those who have instructed many in virtue, as bright as stars for all eternity.'

This is the word of the Lord.

RESPONSORIAL PSALM   *(Ps 15:5.8-11)*

℟ **Preserve me, God, I take refuge in you.**

1. O Lord, it is you who are my portion and cup;
    it is you yourself who are my prize.
    I keep the Lord ever in my sight:
    since he is at my right hand, I shall stand firm. ℟

2. And so my heart rejoices, my soul is glad;
    even my body shall rest in safety.
    For you will not leave my soul among the dead,
    nor let your beloved know decay. ℟

3. You will show me the path of life,
    the fullness of joy in your presence,
    at your right hand happiness for ever. ℟

SECOND READING   *(Heb 10:11-14.18)*

A reading from the letter to the Hebrews.

By virtue of one single offering, he has achieved the eternal perfection of all whom he is sanctifying.

All the priests stand at their duties every day, offering over and over again the same sacrifices which are quite incapable of taking sins away. Christ, on the other hand, has offered one single sacrifice for sins, and then taken his place for ever, at the right hand of God, where he is now waiting until his enemies are made into a footstool for him. By virtue of that one single offering, he has achieved the eternal perfection of all whom he is sanctifying. When all sins have been forgiven, there can be no more sin offerings.

This is the word of the Lord.

GOSPEL ACCLAMATION   *(Mt 24:42.44)*

Alleluia, alleluia!
Stay awake and stand ready,

because you do not know the hour
when the Son of Man is coming.
Alleluia!

or   *(Lk 21:36)*

Alleluia, alleluia!
Stay awake, praying at all times
for the strength to stand with confidence
before the Son of Man.
Alleluia!

GOSPEL   *(Mk 13:24-32)*

A reading from the holy Gospel according to Mark.

He will gather his chosen from the four winds.

Jesus said to his disciples: 'In those days, after the time of distress, the sun will be darkened, the moon will lose its brightness, the stars will come falling from heaven and the powers in the heavens will be shaken. And then they will see the Son of Man coming in the clouds with great power and glory; then too he will send the angels to gather his chosen from the four winds, from the ends of the world to the ends of heaven.

'Take the fig tree as a parable: as soon as its twigs grow supple and its leaves come out, you know that summer is near. So with you, when you see these things happening: know that he is near, at the very gates. I tell you solemnly, before this generation has passed away all these things will have taken place. Heaven and earth will pass away, but my words will not pass away.

'But as for that day or hour, nobody knows it, neither the angels of heaven, nor the Son; no one but the Father.

This is the Gospel of the Lord.

PROFESSION OF FAITH — *pages 15-16*

PRAYER OVER THE GIFTS

Lord God,
may the gifts we offer
increase our love for you
and bring us to eternal life.

PREFACE OF SUNDAYS IN ORDINARY TIME I-VIII — *pages 22-25*

COMMUNION ANTIPHON   *(Ps 72:28)*

It is good for me to be with the Lord and to put my hope in him.

or   (Mk 11:23.24)

I tell you solemnly, whatever you ask for in prayer, believe that you have received it, and it will be yours, says the Lord.

PRAYER AFTER COMMUNION

Father,
may we grow in love
by the eucharist we have celebrated
in memory of the Lord Jesus,
who is Lord for ever and ever.

SOLEMN BLESSING — *pages 57-58*

REFLECTION

> In these days as we approach the end of the Church's liturgical year the readings look forward to the end of time. Behind all the imagery of cosmic elements such as sun, moon and stars lies a fundamental truth, namely, that at our death we shall fall into the hands of a God who has cared for us during our life on earth. We may believe that the one who did not abandon us during our earthly life will not fail us in death.

━━━━━━━━━━ 22 NOVEMBER ━━━━━━━━━━

OUR LORD JESUS CHRIST, UNIVERSAL KING

> Today's feast which takes place on the last Sunday of the Church's liturgical year is to celebrate the all embracing authority of Jesus the Christ. It was instituted in 1925 at the close of the Jubilee Year. At his trial Jesus was questioned about his claim to be king. He was then in a most unkinglike state. The enigmatic sentence, 'My kingdom is not of this world' throws the focus on the world of the spirit. Unlike the popular perception of kingship Jesus' kingdom is one of service.

ENTRANCE ANTIPHON   (Rv 5:12; 1:6)

The Lamb who was slain is worthy to receive strength and divinity, wisdom and power and honour: to him be glory and power for ever.

GREETING, PENITENTIAL RITE, GLORIA — *pages 7-14*

OPENING PRAYER

Let us pray
    [that all will acclaim Jesus as Lord]

Almighty and merciful God,
you break the power of evil
and make all things new
in your Son Jesus Christ, the King of the universe.
May all in heaven and earth acclaim your glory
and never cease to praise you.

or

Let us pray
    [that the kingdom of Christ
    may live in our hearts and come to our world]

Father all-powerful,
God of love,
you have raised our Lord Jesus Christ from death to life,
resplendent in glory as King of creation.

Open our hearts, free all the world to rejoice in his peace,
to glory in his justice, to live in his love.
Bring all mankind together in Jesus Christ your Son,
whose kingdom is with you and the Holy Spirit,
one God, for ever and ever.

FIRST READING   *(Dn 7:13-14)*

A reading from the prophet Daniel.

His sovereignty is an eternal sovereignty.

I gazed into the visions of the night.
And I saw, coming on the clouds of heaven,
one like a son of man.
He came to the one of great age
and was led into his presence.
On him was conferred sovereignty,
glory and kingship,
and men of all peoples, nations and languages became his
    servants.
His sovereignty is an eternal sovereignty
which shall never pass away,
nor will his empire ever be destroyed.

    This is the word of the Lord.

RESPONSORIAL PSALM   *(Ps 92:1-2)*

℟ **The Lord is king, with majesty enrobed.**

1. The Lord is king, with majesty enrobed;
   the Lord has robed himself with might,
   he has girded himself with power. ℟

2. The world you made firm, not to be moved;
   your throne has stood firm from of old.
   From all eternity, O Lord, you are. ℟

3. Truly your decrees are to be trusted.
   Holiness is fitting to your house,
   O Lord, until the end of time. ℟

SECOND READING   *(Rv 1:5-8)*

A reading from the book of Apocalypse.

Ruler of the kings of the earth … he made us a line of kings, priests to serve his God.

Jesus Christ is the faithful witness, the First-born from the dead, the Ruler of the kings of the earth. He loves us and has washed away our sins with his blood, and made us a line of kings, priests to serve his God and Father; to him, then, be glory and power for ever and ever. Amen. It is he who is coming on the clouds; everyone will see him, even those who pierced him, and all the races of the earth will mourn over him. This is the truth. Amen. 'I am the Alpha and the Omega' says the Lord God, who is, who was, and who is to come, the Almighty.

   This is the word of the Lord.

GOSPEL ACCLAMATION   *(Mk 11:9.10)*

Alleluia, alleluia!
Blessings on him who comes in the name of the Lord!
Blessings on the coming kingdom of our father David!
Alleluia!

GOSPEL   *(Jn 18:33-37)*

A reading from the holy Gospel according to John.

It is you who say that I am a king.

'Are you the king of the Jews?' Pilate asked. Jesus replied, 'Do you ask this of your own accord, or have others spoken to you about me?' Pilate answered, 'Am I a Jew? It is your own people and the chief priests who have handed you over to me: what have you done?' Jesus replied, 'Mine is not a kingdom of this world; if my kingdom were of this world, my men would have fought to prevent my being surrendered to the Jews. But my kingdom is not of this kind.' 'So you are a king then?' said Pilate. 'It is you who say it' answered Jesus. 'Yes, I am a king. I was born for this, I came into the world for this: to bear witness to the truth; and all who are on the side of truth listen to my voice.'

This is the Gospel of the Lord.

PROFESSION OF FAITH — *pages 15-16*

PRAYER OVER THE GIFTS

Lord,
we offer you the sacrifice
by which your Son reconciles mankind.
May it bring unity and peace to the world.

PREFACE OF CHRIST THE KING

Father, all-powerful and ever-living God,
we do well always and everywhere to give you thanks.

You anointed Jesus Christ, your only Son, with the oil of gladness,
as the eternal priest and universal King.

As priest he offered his life on the altar of the cross
and redeemed the human race
by this one perfect sacrifice of peace.

As King he claims dominion over all creation,
that he may present to you, his almighty Father,
an eternal and universal kingdom:
a kingdom of truth and life,
a kingdom of holiness and grace,
a kingdom of justice, love, and peace.

And so, with all the choirs of angels in heaven
we proclaim your glory
and join in their unending hymn of praise:
Holy, holy, holy...

COMMUNION ANTIPHON   *(Ps 28:10-11)*
The Lord will reign for ever and will give his people the gift of peace.

PRAYER AFTER COMMUNION

Lord, you give us Christ, the King of all creation,
as food for everlasting life.
Help us to live by his gospel
and bring us to the joy of his kingdom,
where he lives and reigns for ever and ever.

REFLECTION

Jesus' exchange with Pilate on the subject of kingship is the last time the word 'truth' is mentioned in the gospel. John's gospel has made it clear that Jesus testifies to the truth and that 'the Jews' have rejected the truth. As is frequently the case, dialogues such as this one between Jesus and an antagonist quickly end by showing the character of Jesus' opponent. Pilate's question 'what is truth?' shows that he is ranked with those who cannot hear Jesus' voice.

---

29 NOVEMBER

FIRST SUNDAY OF ADVENT

'The word 'advent' means 'arrival' or 'coming' and with this season the Church begins another new year. There is a threefold coming of Jesus to which the Church draws our attention in this season. First, Jesus' coming as a human being at Bethlehem; second, his daily coming into the lives of those who open their heart to receive him and third, his glorious coming at the end of time. The use of purple vestments underlines the special character of this season.

ENTRANCE ANTIPHON   *(Ps 24:1-3)*

To you, my God, I lift my soul, I trust in you; let me never come to shame. Do not let my enemies laugh at me. No one who waits for you is ever put to shame.

GREETING, PENITENTIAL RITE — *pages 7-13*

The Gloria *is omitted.*

OPENING PRAYER

Let us pray

[that we may take Christ's coming seriously]

All-powerful God,
increase our strength of will for doing good
that Christ may find an eager welcome at his coming
and call us to his side in the kingdom of heaven
where he lives and reigns with you and the Holy Spirit,
one God for ever and ever.

or

Let us pray
　　[in Advent time with longing and waiting
　　for the coming of the Lord]

Father in heaven,
our hearts desire the warmth of your love
and our minds are searching for the light of your Word.

Increase our longing for Christ our Saviour
and give us the strength to grow in love,
that the dawn of his coming
may find us rejoicing in his presence
and welcoming the light of his truth.

FIRST READING   *(Jr 33:14-16)*

A reading from the prophet Jeremiah.

I will make a virtuous Branch grow for David.

See, the days are coming — it is the Lord who speaks — when I
am going to fulfil the promise I made to the House of Israel and
the House of Judah:

　　'In those days and at that time,
　　I will make a virtuous Branch grow for David,
　　who shall practise honesty and integrity in the land.
　　In those days Judah shall be saved
　　and Israel shall dwell in confidence.
　　And this is the name the city will be called:
　　The Lord-our-integrity.'

　　This is the word of the Lord.

RESPONSORIAL PSALM   *(Ps 24:4-5.8-9.10.14)*

℟　**To you, O Lord, I lift up my soul.**

1.　Lord, make me know your ways.
　　Lord, teach me your paths.
　　Make me walk in your truth, and teach me:
　　for you are God my saviour. ℟

2.　The Lord is good and upright.
　　He shows the path to those who stray,
　　he guides the humble in the right path;
　　he teaches his way to the poor. ℟

3.　His ways are faithfulness and love
　　for those who keep his covenant and will.
　　The Lord's friendship is for those who revere him;
　　to them he reveals his covenant. ℟

SECOND READING   (1 Thess 3:12-4:2)

A reading from the first letter of St Paul to the Thessalonians.

May the Lord confirm your hearts in holiness when Christ comes.

May the Lord be generous in increasing your love and make you love one another and the whole human race as much as we love you. And may he so confirm your hearts in holiness that you may be blameless in the sight of our God and Father when our Lord Jesus Christ comes with all his saints.

Finally, brothers, we urge you and appeal to you in the Lord Jesus to make more and more progress in the kind of life that you are meant to live: the life that God wants, as you learnt from us, and as you are already living it. You have not forgotten the instructions we gave you on the authority of the Lord Jesus.

This is the word of the Lord.

GOSPEL ACCLAMATION   (Ps 84:8)

Alleluia, alleluia!
Let us see, O Lord, your mercy
and give us your saving help.
Alleluia!

GOSPEL   (Lk 21:25-28.34-36)

A reading from the holy Gospel according to Luke.

Your liberation is near at hand.

Jesus said to his disciples: 'There will be signs in the sun and moon and stars; on earth nations in agony, bewildered by the clamour of the ocean and its waves; men dying of fear as they await what menaces the world, for the powers of heaven will be shaken. And then they will see the Son of Man coming in a cloud with power and great glory. When these things begin to take place, stand erect, hold your heads high, because your liberation is near at hand.'

'Watch yourselves, or your hearts will be coarsened with debauchery and drunkenness and the cares of life, and that day will be sprung on you suddenly, like a trap. For it will come down on every living man on the face of the earth. Stay awake, praying at all times for the strength to survive all that is going to happen, and to stand with confidence before the Son of Man.'

This is the Gospel of the Lord.

PROFESSION OF FAITH — *pages 15-16*

PRAYER OVER THE GIFTS

Father,
from all you give us
we present this bread and wine.
As we serve you now,
accept our offering
and sustain us with your promise of eternal life.

PREFACE OF ADVENT I — *page 18*

COMMUNION ANTIPHON   *(Ps 84:13)*

The Lord will shower his gifts, and our land will yield its fruit.

PRAYER AFTER COMMUNION

Father,
may our communion
teach us to love heaven.
May its promise and hope
guide our way on earth.

SOLEMN BLESSING — *page 56*

REFLECTION

During this liturgical year the gospel according to Luke will be
read on Sundays. The thirteenth century Italian poet Dante described
Luke as the scribe of Christ's gentleness. It is the gospel of
mercy and compassion. Luke is anxious to point out how the
life of Jesus ought to be paralleled by the life of the Church.
So he will present the life, destiny and teaching of Jesus as a
pattern for the Christian community for which he was writing.

30 NOVEMBER

SAINT ANDREW, APOSTLE
(Patron of Scotland)

Andrew is the patron saint of Scotland, Russia and Greece.
Andrew was the brother of Simon Peter the fisherman from
Bethsaida and even though not one of the inner circle of three,
several incidents concerning him are recorded in the gospels.
The tradition says that he was connected with the writing of
Saint John's gospel. There is also another tradition about Saint
Andrew's cross, shaped like the letter X but this cannot be
traced back beyond the thirteenth century. The tradition also
has it that he was a martyr.

ENTRANCE ANTIPHON   *(cf. Mt 4:18-19)*

**By the Sea of Galilee the Lord saw two brothers, Peter and
Andrew. He called them: come and follow me, and I will
make you fishers of men.**

GREETING, PENITENTIAL RITE, GLORIA — *pages 7-14*

OPENING PRAYER

Lord,
in your kindness hear our petitions.
You called Andrew the apostle
to preach the gospel and guide your Church in faith.
May he always be our friend in your presence
to help us with his prayers.

FIRST READING   *(Ws 3:1-9)*

A reading from the book of Wisdom.
He accepted them as a holocaust.

The souls of the virtuous are in the hands of God,
no torment shall ever touch them.
In the eyes of the unwise, they did appear to die,
their going looked like a disaster,
their leaving us, like annihilation;
but they are in peace.
If they experienced punishment as men see it,
their hope was rich with immortality;
slight was their affliction, great will their blessings be.
God has put them to the test
and proved them worthy to be with him;

he has tested them like gold in a furnace,
and accepted them as a holocaust.
When the time comes for his visitation they will shine out;
as sparks run through the stubble, so will they.
They shall judge nations, rule over peoples,
and the Lord will be their king for ever.
They who trust in him will understand the truth,
those who are faithful will live with him in love;
for grace and mercy await those he has chosen.

   This is the word of the Lord.

RESPONSORIAL PSALM   *(Ps 30:3-4.6.8.17.21)*

℟ **Into your hands, O Lord,
   I commend my spirit.**

1. Be a rock of refuge for me,
    a mighty stronghold to save me,
    for you are my rock, my stronghold.
    For your name's sake, lead me and guide me. ℟

2. Into your hands I commend my spirit.
    It is you who will redeem me, Lord.
    As for me, I trust in the Lord;
    let me be glad and rejoice in your love. ℟

3. Let your face shine on your servant.
    Save me in your love.
    You hide them in the shelter of your presence
    from the plotting of men. ℟

SECOND READING   *(Rm 10:9-18)*

A reading from the letter of St Paul to the Romans.
Faith comes from what is preached, and what is preached comes from
the word of Christ.

If your lips confess that Jesus is Lord and if you believe in your
heart that God raised him from the dead, then you will be
saved. By believing from the heart you are made righteous; by
confessing with your lips you are saved. When scripture says:
those who believe in him will have no cause for shame, it makes no
distinction between Jew and Greek: all belong to the same Lord
who is rich enough, however many ask his help, for everyone
who calls on the name of the Lord will be saved.

   But they will not ask his help unless they believe in him,
and they will not believe in him unless they have heard of him,

and they will not hear of him unless they get a preacher, and they will never have a preacher unless one is sent, but as scripture says: The footsteps of those who bring good news are a welcome sound. Not everyone, of course, listens to the Good News. As Isaiah says: Lord, how many believed what we proclaimed? So faith comes from what is preached, and what is preached comes from the word of Christ.

Let me put the question: is it possible that they did not hear? Indeed they did; in the words of the psalm, their voice has gone out through all the earth, and their message to the ends of the world.

This is the word of the Lord.

GOSPEL ACCLAMATION   (Mt 4:19)
Alleluia, alleluia!
Follow me, says the Lord,
and I will make you into fishers of men.
Alleluia!

GOSPEL   (Mt 4:18-22)
A reading from the holy Gospel according to Matthew.
And they left their nets at once and followed him.

As Jesus was walking by the Sea of Galilee he saw two brothers, Simon, who was called Peter, and his brother Andrew; they were making a cast in the lake with their net, for they were fishermen. And he said to them, 'Follow me and I will make you fishers of men.' And they left their nets at once and followed him.

Going on from there he saw another pair of brothers, James son of Zebedee and his brother John; they were in their boat with their father Zebedee, mending their nets, and he called them. At once, leaving the boat and their father, they followed him.

This is the Gospel of the Lord.

PROFESSION OF FAITH — *pages 15-16*

PRAYER OVER THE GIFTS
All-powerful God,
may these gifts we bring on the feast of Saint Andrew
be pleasing to you
and give life to all who receive them.

PREFACE OF THE APOSTLES I
Father, all-powerful and ever-living God,
we do well always and everywhere to give you thanks.

You are the eternal Shepherd
who never leaves his flock untended.
Through the apostles
you watch over us and protect us always.
You made them shepherds of the flock
to share in the work of your Son,
and from their place in heaven they guide us still.

And so, with all the choirs of angels in heaven
we proclaim your glory
and join in their unending hymn of praise:
Holy, holy, holy Lord…

COMMUNION ANTIPHON   *(Jn 1:41-42)*

**Andrew told his brother Simon: we have found the Messiah,
the Christ; and he brought him to Jesus.**

PRAYER AFTER COMMUNION

Lord,
may the sacrament we have received give us courage
to follow the example of Andrew the apostle.
By sharing in Christ's suffering
may we live with him for ever in glory,
for he is Lord for ever and ever.

SOLEMN BLESSING

Bow your heads and pray for God's blessing.

May God who founded his Church upon the apostles
bless you through the prayers of Saint Andrew. **Amen.**

May God inspire you to follow the example of the apostles,
and give witness to the truth before all. **Amen.**

The teaching of the apostles has strengthened your faith.
May their prayers lead you
to your true and eternal home. **Amen.**

May almighty God bless you,
the Father, and the Son, ✠ and the Holy Spirit. **Amen.**

REFLECTION

Jesus sent his apostles out on mission to baptise and to make
disciples of all nations. In fact the literal meaning of the
word 'apostle' is one who is sent. Over the past two millennia
Christian missionaries have travelled the earth to carry out Christ's
command and to extend the kingdom of God to every race of
people.

6 DECEMBER
SECOND SUNDAY OF ADVENT
(Bible Sunday)

The season of Advent may be seen as a time of preparation for
the great season of Christmas similar to the way in which Lent
is a time of preparation for the Easter season. During Advent
we hear some of the high points of the Old Testament read,
especially from the prophet Isaiah. The Advent wreath is at the
same time a symbol of the passage of the ages before the birth
of Christ and also a symbol of eternity in which God dwells.

ENTRANCE ANTIPHON   (cf. Is 30:19.30)

**People of Zion, the Lord will come to save all nations, and
your hearts will exult to hear his majestic voice.**

GREETING, PENITENTIAL RITE — *pages 7-13*

The Gloria is omitted.

OPENING PRAYER

Let us pray
    [that nothing may hinder us
    from receiving Christ with joy]

God of power and mercy,
open our hearts in welcome.
Remove the things that hinder us from receiving Christ with joy,
so that we may share his wisdom
and become one with him
when he comes in glory,
for he lives and reigns with you and the Holy Spirit,
one God, for ever and ever.

or

Let us pray
    [in Advent time
    for the coming Saviour to teach us wisdom]

Father in heaven,
the day draws near when the glory of your Son
will make radiant the night of the waiting world.

May the lure of greed not impede us from the joy
which moves the hearts of those who seek him.
May the darkness not blind us
to the vision of wisdom
which fills the minds of those who find him.

FIRST READING   *(Ba 5:1-9)*

A reading from the prophet Baruch.

God means to show your splendour to every nation.

Jerusalem, take off your dress of sorrow and distress,
put on the beauty of the glory of God for ever,
wrap the cloak of the integrity of God around you,
put the diadem of the glory of the Eternal on your head:
since God means to show your splendour to every nation under
    heaven,
since the name God gives you for ever will be,
'Peace through integrity, and honour through devotedness.'
Arise, Jerusalem, stand on the heights
and turn your eyes to the east:
see your sons reassembled from west and east
at the command of the Holy One, jubilant that God has
    remembered them.
Though they left you on foot,
with enemies for an escort,
now God brings them back to you
like royal princes carried back in glory.
For God has decreed the flattening
of each high mountain, of the everlasting hills,
the filling of the valleys to make the ground level
so that Israel can walk in safety under the glory of God.
And the forests and every fragrant tree will provide shade
for Israel at the command of God;
for God will guide Israel in joy by the light of his glory
with his mercy and integrity for escort.

> This is the word of the Lord.

RESPONSORIAL PSALM   *(Ps 125)*

℟ **What marvels the Lord worked for us!**
   Indeed we were glad.

1. When the Lord delivered Zion from bondage,
    it seemed like a dream.
    Then was our mouth filled with laughter,
    on our lips there were songs. ℟

2. The heathens themselves said: 'What marvels
    the Lord worked for them!'
    What marvels the Lord worked for us!
    Indeed we were glad. ℟

(continued)

3.   Deliver us, O Lord, from our bondage
      as streams in dry land.
      Those who are sowing in tears
      will sing when they reap. ℟

℟   **What marvels the Lord worked for us!**
     Indeed we were glad.

4.   They go out, they go out, full of tears
      carrying seed for the sowing:
      they come back, they come back, full of song,
      carrying their sheaves. ℟

SECOND READING   *(Ph 1:4-6.8-11)*

A reading from the letter of St Paul to the Philippians.
Be pure and blameless for the day of Christ.

Every time I pray for all of you, I pray with joy, remembering
how you have helped to spread the Good News from the day
you first heard it right up to the present. I am quite certain that
the One who began this good work in you will see that it is
finished when the Day of Christ Jesus comes. God knows how
much I miss you all, loving you as Christ Jesus loves you. My
prayer is that your love for each other may increase more and
more and never stop improving your knowledge and deepening
your perception so that you can always recognise what is best.
This will help you to become pure and blameless, and prepare
you for the Day of Christ, when you will reach the perfect
goodness which Jesus Christ produces in us for the glory and
praise of God.

      This is the word of the Lord.

GOSPEL ACCLAMATION   *(Lk 3:4.6)*

Alleluia, alleluia!
Prepare a way for the Lord,
make his paths straight,
and all mankind shall see the salvation of God.
Alleluia!

GOSPEL   *(Lk 3:1-6)*

A reading from the holy Gospel according to Luke.
All mankind shall see the salvation of God.

In the fifteenth year of Tiberius Caesar's reign, when Pontius
Pilate was governor of Judaea, Herod tetrarch of Galilee, his
brother Philip tetrarch of the lands of Ituraea and Trachonitis,
Lysanias tetrarch of Abilene, during the pontificate of Annas

and Caiaphas, the word of God came to John son of Zechariah, in the wilderness. He went through the whole Jordan district proclaiming a baptism of repentance for the forgiveness of sins, as it is written in the book of the sayings of the prophet Isaiah:

A voice cries in the wilderness:
Prepare a way for the Lord,
make his paths straight.
Every valley will be filled in,
every mountain and hill be laid low,
winding ways will be straightened
and rough roads made smooth.
And all mankind shall see the salvation of God.

This is the Gospel of the Lord.

PROFESSION OF FAITH — *pages 15-16*

PRAYER OVER THE GIFTS
Lord,
we are nothing without you.
As you sustain us with your mercy,
receive our prayers and offerings.

PREFACE OF ADVENT I — *page 18*

COMMUNION ANTIPHON   *(Ba 5:5; 4:36)*
Rise up, Jerusalem, stand on the heights, and see the joy that is coming to you from God.

PRAYER AFTER COMMUNION
Father, you give us food from heaven.
By our sharing in this mystery,
teach us to judge wisely the things of earth
and to love the things of heaven.

SOLEMN BLESSING — *page 56*

REFLECTION
Today's gospel reading from Saint Luke interprets an earlier passage from the prophet called Second Isaiah who lived at one of the low points of Israel's history, namely, at the time of the exile to Babylon in the sixth century B.C. The filling in of valleys and the lowering of mountains are images for the arrival of the Lord bringing salvation. When Luke puts these words on the lips of John the Baptist what he is saying is that the time of God's saving action has come. Get ready to welcome it.

8 DECEMBER
THE IMMACULATE CONCEPTION OF
THE BLESSED VIRGIN MARY

Today's feast celebrates the teaching that 'from the first moment of her conception, the Blessed Virgin Mary was, by the singular grace and privilege of Almighty God, and in view of the merits of Jesus Christ, Saviour of humankind, kept free from all stain of original sin'. This expression of belief was formulated in 1854. There was a feast of the Conception of Mary in the Eastern Church which was known from the seventh century. Without going into details some eastern writers had praised the perfect sinlessness of Mary as implied in the title 'Mother of God'.

ENTRANCE ANTIPHON   *(Is 61:10)*

I exult for joy in the Lord, my soul rejoices in my God; for he has clothed me in the garment of salvation and robed me in the cloak of justice, like a bride adorned with her jewels.

GREETING, PENITENTIAL RITE, GLORIA — *pages 7-14*

OPENING PRAYER

Let us pray
   [that through the prayers of the sinless Virgin Mary,
   God will free us from our sins]

Father,
you prepared the Virgin Mary
to be the worthy mother of your Son.
You let her share beforehand
in the salvation Christ would bring by his death,
and kept her sinless from the first moment of her conception.
Help us by her prayers
to live in your presence without sin.
   or

Let us pray
   [on this feast of Mary
   who experienced the perfection of God's saving power]

Father,
the image of the Virgin is found in the Church.
Mary had a faith that your Spirit prepared
and a love that never knew sin,
for you kept her sinless from the first moment of her
   conception.

Trace in our actions the lines of her love,
in our hearts her readiness of faith.
Prepare once again a world for your Son
who lives and reigns with you and the Holy Spirit,
one God, for ever and ever.

FIRST READING *(Gen 3:9-15.20)*

A reading from the book of Genesis.

I will make you enemies of each other; your offspring and her offspring.

After Adam had eaten of the tree, the Lord God called to him. 'Where are you?' he asked. 'I heard the sound of you in the garden', he replied. 'I was afraid because I was naked, so I hid.' 'Who told you that you were naked?' he asked. 'Have you been eating of the tree I forbade you to eat?' The man replied, 'It was the woman you put with me; she gave me the fruit, and I ate it.' Then the Lord God asked the woman, 'What is this you have done?' The woman replied, 'The serpent tempted me and I ate.'

Then the Lord God said to the serpent, 'Because you have done this,

'Be accursed beyond all cattle,
all wild beasts.
You shall crawl on your belly and eat dust
every day of your life.
I will make you enemies of each other:
you and the woman,
your offspring and her offspring.
It will crush your head
and you will strike its heel.'

The man named his wife 'Eve' because she was the mother of all those who live.

This is the word of the Lord.

RESPONSORIAL PSALM *(Ps 97:1-4)*

℞ **Sing a new song to the Lord**
   for he has worked wonders.

1. Sing a new song to the Lord
    for he has worked wonders.
    His right hand and his holy arm
    have brought salvation. ℞

2. The Lord has made known his salvation;
    has shown his justice to the nations.
    He has remembered his truth and love
    for the house of Israel. ℞

(continued)

3. All the ends of the earth have seen
    the salvation of our God.
    Shout to the Lord all the earth,
    ring out your joy. ℞

℞   **Sing a new song to the Lord
    for he has worked wonders.**

SECOND READING   *(Eph 1:3-6.11-12)*

A reading from the letter of St Paul to the Ephesians.

Before the world was made, God chose us in Christ.

Blessed be God the Father of our Lord Jesus Christ,
who has blessed us with all the spiritual blessings of heaven in
    Christ.
Before the world was made, he chose us, chose us in Christ,
to be holy and spotless, and to live through love in his presence,
determining that we should become his adopted sons, through
    Jesus Christ
for his own kind purposes,
to make us praise the glory of his grace,
his free gift to us in the Beloved.
And it is in him that we were claimed as God's own,
chosen from the beginning,
under the predetermined plan of the one who guides all things
as he decides by his own will;
chosen to be,
for his greater glory,
the people who would put their hopes in Christ before he came.

    This is the word of the Lord.

GOSPEL ACCLAMATION   *(Lk 1:28)*

**Alleluia, alleluia!
Hail, Mary, full of grace; the Lord is with thee!
Blessed art thou among women.
Alleluia!**

GOSPEL   *(Lk 1:26-38)*

A reading from the holy Gospel according to Luke.

You are to conceive and bear a Son.

The angel Gabriel was sent by God to a town in Galilee called
Nazareth, to a virgin betrothed to a man named Joseph, of the
House of David; and the virgin's name was Mary. He went in
and said to her, 'Rejoice, so highly favoured! The Lord is with
you.' She was deeply disturbed by these words and asked herself

what this greeting could mean, but the angel said to her, 'Mary, do not be afraid; you have won God's favour. Listen! You are to conceive and bear a son, and you must name him Jesus. He will be great and will be called Son of the Most High. The Lord God will give him the throne of his ancestor David; he will rule over the House of Jacob for ever and his reign will have no end.' Mary said to the angel, 'But how can this come about, since I am a virgin?' 'The Holy Spirit will come upon you' the angel answered, 'and the power of the Most High will cover you with its shadow. And so the child will be holy and will be called Son of God. Know this too: your kinswoman Elizabeth has, in her old age, herself conceived a son, and she whom people called barren is now in her sixth month, for nothing is impossible to God.' 'I am the handmaid of the Lord' said Mary, 'let what you have said be done to me.' And the angel left her.

This is the Gospel of the Lord.

PROFESSION OF FAITH — *pages 15-16*

PRAYER OVER THE GIFTS

Lord, accept this sacrifice
on the feast of the sinless Virgin Mary.
You kept her free from sin
from the first moment of her life.
Help us by her prayers,
and free us from our sins.

PREFACE OF THE IMMACULATE CONCEPTION

Father, all-powerful and ever-living God,
we do well always and everywhere to give you thanks.

You allowed no stain of Adam's sin
to touch the Virgin Mary.
Full of grace, she was to be a worthy mother of your Son,
your sign of favour to the Church at its beginning,
and the promise of its perfection as the bride of Christ, radiant
    in beauty.

Purest of virgins, she was to bring forth your Son,
the innocent lamb who takes away our sins.
You chose her from all women to be our advocate with you
and our pattern of holiness.

In our joy we sing to your glory
with all the choirs of angels:
Holy, holy, holy...

COMMUNION ANTIPHON

**All honour to you, Mary! From you arose the sun of justice,
Christ our God.**

PRAYER AFTER COMMUNION

Lord our God,
in your love, you chose the Virgin Mary
and kept her free from sin.
May this sacrament of your love
free us from our sins.

SOLEMN BLESSING

Born of the Blessed Virgin Mary,
the Son of God redeemed humankind.
May he enrich you with his blessings.
Amen.

You received the author of life through Mary.
May you always rejoice in her loving care.
Amen.

You have come to rejoice at Mary's feast.
May you be filled with the joys of the Spirit
and the gifts of your eternal home.
Amen.

May almighty God bless you,
the Father, and the Son, ✠ and the Holy Spirit.
Amen.

REFLECTION

Mary's role in salvation and redemption is unique. It has been
the subject of poetry, painting, polemic and polyphony. At its
core is the fact that this young, simple Jewish girl was given
and accepted a call to fulfil a role that only one human being
down through all the ages of time could fill, namely, to be
the mother of the Saviour. It is not that Mary did not need
salvation but that she in a miraculous way anticipated the merits
of that salvation which was won for her and us by her Son.

13 DECEMBER
THIRD SUNDAY OF ADVENT

Today is often referred to as *'Gaudete'* Sunday, meaning 'rejoice' from the first word of the entrance antiphon. The candle on the Advent wreath may be rose-coloured as also may the vestments at today's liturgy. This is to ensure that the joyful character of the season is seen as an integral part of it, a point which the omission of the Gloria could easily obscure. There is no contradiction between Advent as penitential and joyful since to repent means to change one's attitude. In this case an outlook which will be full of joy at what God has done in Christ.

ENTRANCE ANTIPHON *(Ph 4:4.5)*

Rejoice in the Lord always; again I say, rejoice! The Lord is near.

GREETING, PENITENTIAL RITE — *pages 7-13*

The Gloria is omitted.

OPENING PRAYER

Let us pray
[that God will fill us with joy
at the coming of Christ]

Lord God,
may we, your people,
who look forward to the birthday of Christ
experience the joy of salvation
and celebrate that feast with love and thanksgiving.

or

Let us pray
[this Advent
for joy and hope in the coming Lord]

Father of our Lord Jesus Christ,
ever faithful to your promises
and ever close to your Church:
the earth rejoices in hope of the Saviour's coming
and looks forward with longing
to his return at the end of time.

Prepare our hearts and remove the sadness
that hinders us from feeling the joy and hope
which his presence will bestow,
for he is Lord for ever and ever.

FIRST READING   (Zp 3:14-18)

A reading from the prophet Zephaniah.

The Lord will dance with shouts of joy for you as on a day of festival.

Shout for joy, daughter of Zion,
Israel, shout aloud!
Rejoice, exult with all your heart,
daughter of Jerusalem!
The Lord has repealed your sentence;
he has driven your enemies away.
The Lord, the king of Israel, is in your midst;
you have no more evil to fear.
When that day comes, word will come to Jerusalem:
Zion, have no fear,
do not let your hands fall limp.
The Lord your God is in your midst,
a victorious warrior.
He will exult with joy over you,
he will renew you by his love;
he will dance with shouts of joy for you
as on a day of festival.

    This is the word of the Lord.

RESPONSORIAL PSALM   (Is 12:2-6)

℟ **Sing and shout for joy**
   for great in your midst is the Holy One of Israel.

1.   Truly, God is my salvation,
     I trust, I shall not fear.
     For the Lord is my strength, my song,
     he became my saviour.
     With joy you will draw water
     from the wells of salvation. ℟

2.   Give thanks to the Lord, give praise to his name!
     Make his mighty deeds known to the peoples!
     Declare the greatness of his name. ℟

3.   Sing a psalm to the Lord
     for he has done glorious deeds,
     make them known to all the earth!
     People of Zion, sing and shout for joy
     for great in your midst is the Holy One of Israel. ℟

SECOND READING   *(Ph 4:4-7)*

A reading from the letter of St Paul to the Philippians.
The Lord is very near.

I want you to be happy, always happy in the Lord; I repeat, what I want is your happiness. Let your tolerance be evident to everyone: the Lord is very near. There is no need to worry; but if there is anything you need, pray for it, asking God for it with prayer and thanksgiving, and that peace of God, which is so much greater than we can understand, will guard your hearts and your thoughts, in Christ Jesus.

This is the word of the Lord.

GOSPEL ACCLAMATION   *(Is 61:1; Lk 4:18)*

Alleluia, alleluia!
The spirit of the Lord has been given to me.
He has sent me to bring good news to the poor.
Alleluia!

GOSPEL   *(Lk 3:10-18)*

A reading from the holy Gospel according to Luke.
What must we do?

When all the people asked John, 'What must we do? he answered, 'If anyone has two tunics he must share with the man who has none, and the one with something to eat must do the same.' There were tax collectors too who came for baptism, and these said to him, 'Master, what must we do?' He said to them, 'Exact no more than your rate.' Some soldiers asked him in their turn, 'What must we do?' He said to them, 'No intimidation! No extortion! Be content with your pay!'

A feeling of expectancy had grown among the people, who were beginning to think that John might be the Christ, so John declared before them all, 'I baptize you with water, but someone is coming, someone who is more powerful than I am, and I am not fit to undo the strap of his sandals; he will baptize you with the Holy Spirit and fire. His winnowing-fan is in his hand to clear his threshing-floor and to gather the wheat into his barn; but the chaff he will burn in a fire that will never go out.' As well as this, there were many other things he said to exhort the people and to announce the Good News to them.

This is the Gospel of the Lord.

PROFESSION OF FAITH — *pages 15-16*

PRAYER OVER THE GIFTS

Lord,
may the gift we offer in faith and love
be a continual sacrifice in your honour
and truly become our eucharist and our salvation.

PREFACE OF ADVENT II — *page 18*

COMMUNION ANTIPHON   *(Is 35:4)*

**Say to the anxious: be strong and fear not, our God will come
to save us.**

PRAYER AFTER COMMUNION

God of mercy,
may this eucharist bring us your divine help,
free us from our sins,
and prepare us for the birthday of our Saviour,
who is Lord for ever and ever.

SOLEMN BLESSING — *page 56*

REFLECTION

Today's gospel account makes it clear that it is not the
religious leaders who are willing to repent, to change their
attitude, but the ordinary Jewish people and those who,
at best, are on the margins of Jewish society, namely, tax
collectors and soldiers. These are the same people who will
respond positively to Jesus' preaching. Luke will later remind
the community for which he writes that they should be as
open to finding goodness outside the acceptable ways of life
as John the Baptist and Jesus were. This message is as relevant
for our generation today as it ever was.

20 DECEMBER

FOURTH SUNDAY OF ADVENT

The Fourth Sunday of Advent falls during the second part
of Advent when there is an increase in pace, intensity and
expectation. The use of the O-antiphons on the seven
days preceding Christmas Eve at the Gospel Acclamation
contributes to the heightened sense of waiting. Each of these
titles may be used to refer to Jesus and in fact together they
form a miniature litany: Wisdom from above, Lord, Root of
Jesse, Key of David, Rising Sun, King of nations, Emmanuel.

ENTRANCE ANTIPHON   *(Is 45:8)*

**Let the clouds rain down the Just One, and the earth bring
forth a Saviour.**

GREETING, PENITENTIAL RITE — *pages 7-13*

The Gloria is omitted.

OPENING PRAYER

Let us pray
    [as Advent draws to a close,
    that Christ will truly come into our hearts]

Lord,
fill our hearts with your love,
and as you revealed to us by an angel
the coming of your Son as man,
so lead us through his suffering and death
to the glory of his resurrection,
for he lives and reigns with you and the Holy Spirit,
one God, for ever and ever.

or

Let us pray
    [as Advent draws to a close
    for the faith that opens our lives to the Spirit of God]

Father, all-powerful God,
your eternal Word took flesh on our earth
when the Virgin Mary placed her life
at the service of your plan.

Lift our minds in watchful hope
to hear the voice which announces his glory
and open our minds to receive the Spirit
who prepares us for his coming.

FIRST READING   *(Mi 5:1-4)*

A reading from the prophet Micah.

Out of you will be born the one who is to rule over Israel.

The Lord says this:

> You, Bethlehem Ephrathah,
> the least of the clans of Judah,
> out of you will be born for me
> the one who is to rule over Israel;
> his origin goes back to the distant past,
> to the days of old.
> The Lord is therefore going to abandon them
> till the time when she who is to give birth gives birth.
> Then the remnant of his brothers will come back
> to the sons of Israel.
> He will stand and feed his flock
> with the power of the Lord,
> with the majesty of the name of his God.
> They will live secure, for from then on he will
>   extend his power
> to the ends of the land.
> He himself will be peace.

This is the word of the Lord.

RESPONSORIAL PSALM   *(Ps 79:2-3.15-16.18-19)*

℟ **God of hosts, bring us back;**
   let your face shine on us and we shall be saved.

1. O shepherd of Israel, hear us,
    shine forth from your cherubim throne.
    O Lord, rouse up your might,
    O Lord, come to our help. ℟

2. God of hosts, turn again, we implore,
    look down from heaven and see.
    Visit this vine and protect it,
    the vine your right hand has planted. ℟

3. May your hand be on the man you have chosen,
    the man you have given your strength.
    And we shall never forsake you again:
    give us life that we may call upon your name. ℟

SECOND READING   *(Heb 10:5-10)*

A reading from the letter to the Hebrews.

Here I am! I am coming to obey your will.

This is what Christ said, on coming into the world:

> You who wanted no sacrifice or oblation,
> prepared a body for me.
> You took no pleasure in holocausts or sacrifices for sin;
> then I said,
> just as I was commanded in the scroll of the book,
> 'God, here I am! I am coming to obey your will.'

Notice that he says first: You did not want what the Law lays down as the things to be offered, that is: the sacrifices, the oblations, the holocausts and the sacrifices for sin, and you took no pleasure in them; and then he says: Here I am! I am coming to obey your will. He is abolishing the first sort to replace it with the second. And this will was for us to be made holy by the offering of his body made once and for all by Jesus Christ.

This is the word of the Lord.

GOSPEL ACCLAMATION   *(Lk 1:38)*

Alleluia, alleluia!
I am the handmaid of the Lord:
let what you have said be done to me.
Alleluia!

GOSPEL   *(Lk 1:39-45)*

A reading from the holy Gospel according to Luke.

Why should I be honoured with a visit from the mother of my Lord?

Mary set out and went as quickly as she could to a town in the hill country of Judah. She went into Zechariah's house and greeted Elizabeth. Now as soon as Elizabeth heard Mary's greeting, the child leapt in her womb and Elizabeth was filled with the Holy Spirit. She gave a loud cry and said, 'Of all women you are the most blessed, and blessed is the fruit of your womb. Why should I be honoured with a visit from the mother of my Lord? For the moment your greeting reached my ears, the child in my womb leapt for joy. Yes, blessed is she who believed that the promise made her by the Lord would be fulfilled.'

This is the Gospel of the Lord.

PROFESSION OF FAITH — *pages 15-16*

PRAYER OVER THE GIFTS

Lord,
may the power of the Spirit,
which sanctified Mary the mother of your Son,
make holy the gifts we place upon this altar.

PREFACE OF ADVENT II — *page 18*

COMMUNION ANTIPHON   *(Is 7:14)*

The Virgin is with child, and shall bear a son, and she will call him Emmanuel.

PRAYER AFTER COMMUNION

Lord,
in this sacrament
we receive the promise of salvation;
as Christmas draws near
make us grow in faith and love
to celebrate the coming of Christ our Saviour,
who is Lord for ever and ever.

SOLEMN BLESSING — *page 56*

REFLECTION

Jesus has come once at Bethlehem. He will come again in glory. In the meantime he comes to whoever opens their heart to receive him. He is in the joys and sorrows of each day. He is in his Word, in the sacrament and in his people. He is in the least of his brothers and sisters. He is in the place where he is least expected. He is there beside the one who is suffering in solidarity which comes from the fact that he suffered himself. Come, Lord Jesus, come soon. In this time of your coming, support and console us who trust in your love. Amen.

25 DECEMBER

THE NATIVITY OF OUR LORD

VIGIL MASS

Mary 'will give birth to a son and you – Joseph – must name him Jesus.' Tonight we will realize that this prophecy by a messenger from heaven is fulfilled. God is born of a woman. Jesus is one of us for ever. We can trace his ancestry in the history of Israel. From now on no human being should be named 'Forsaken' or 'Abandoned'. You shall be called 'My Delight' by God.

ENTRANCE ANTIPHON   (cf. Ex 16:6-7)

Today you will know that the Lord is coming to save us, and in the morning you will see his glory.

GREETING, PENITENTIAL RITE, GLORIA — *pages 7-14*

OPENING PRAYER

Let us pray
    [that Christmas morning will find us at peace]

God our Father,
every year we rejoice
as we look forward to this feast of our salvation.
May we welcome Christ as our Redeemer,
and meet him with confidence when he comes to be our judge,
who lives and reigns with you and the Holy Spirit,
one God, for ever and ever.

or

Let us pray
    [and be ready to welcome the Lord]

God of endless ages,
Father of all goodness,
we keep vigil for the dawn of salvation
and the birth of your Son.

With gratitude we recall his humanity,
the life he shared with the sons of men.
May the power of his divinity
help us answer his call to forgiveness and life.

FIRST READING   *(Is 62:1-5)*

A reading from the prophet Isaiah.

The Lord takes delight in you.

About Zion I will not be silent,
about Jerusalem I will not grow weary,
until her integrity shines out like the dawn
and her salvation flames like a torch.

The nations then will see your integrity,
all the kings your glory,
and you will be called by a new name,
one which the mouth of the Lord will confer.
You are to be a crown of splendour in the hand of the Lord,
a princely diadem in the hand of your God;
no longer are you to be named 'Forsaken',
nor your land 'Abandoned',
but you shall be called 'My Delight'
and your land 'The Wedded';
for the Lord takes delight in you
and your land will have its wedding.

Like a young man marrying a virgin,
so will the one who built you wed you,
and as the bridegroom rejoices in his bride,
so will your God rejoice in you.

This is the word of the Lord.

RESPONSORIAL PSALM   *(Ps 88:4-5.16-17.27.29)*

℟   **I will sing for ever of your love, O Lord.**

1.   'I have made a covenant with my chosen one;
     I have sworn to David my servant:
     I will establish your dynasty for ever
     and set up your throne through all ages.' ℟

2.   Happy the people who acclaim such a king,
     who walk, O Lord, in the light of your face,
     who find their joy every day in your name,
     who make your justice the source of their bliss. ℟

3   'He will say to me: "You are my father,
     my God, the rock who saves me."
     I will keep my love for him always;
     for him my covenant shall endure.' ℟

SECOND READING   *(Acts 13:16-17.22-25)*

A reading from the Acts of the Apostles.

Paul's witness to Christ, the son of David.

When Paul reached Antioch in Pisidia, he stood up in the
synagogue, held up a hand for silence and began to speak:

'Men of Israel, and fearers of God, listen! The God of our
nation Israel chose our ancestors, and made our people great
when they were living as foreigners in Egypt; then by divine
power he led them out.

'Then he made David their king, of whom he approved in
these words, "I have selected David son of Jesse, a man after
my own heart, who will carry out my whole purpose." To
keep his promise, God has raised up for Israel one of David's
descendants, Jesus, as Saviour, whose coming was heralded
by John when he proclaimed a baptism of repentance for the
whole people of Israel. Before John ended his career he said, "I
am not the one you imagine me to be; that one is coming after
me and I am not fit to undo his sandal".'

This is the word of the Lord.

GOSPEL ACCLAMATION

Alleluia, alleluia!
Tomorrow there will be an end to the sin of the world
and the saviour of the world will be our king.
Alleluia!

GOSPEL *(Shorter Form)*   *(Mt 1:18-25)*

A reading from the holy Gospel according to Matthew.

Mary will give birth to a son and will name him Jesus.

This is how Jesus Christ came to be born. His mother Mary
was betrothed to Joseph; but before they came to live together
she was found to be with child through the Holy Spirit. Her
husband Joseph, being a man of honour and wanting to spare
her publicity, decided to divorce her informally. He had made
up his mind to do this when the angel of the Lord appeared to
him in a dream and said, 'Joseph son of David, do not be afraid
to take Mary home as your wife, because she has conceived what
is in her by the Holy Spirit. She will give birth to a son and
you must name him Jesus, because he is the one who is to save
his people from their sins.' Now all this took place to fulfil the
words spoken by the Lord through the prophet:

The Virgin will conceive and give birth to a son
and they will call him Emmanuel,

a name which means 'God-is-with-us'. When Joseph woke up he did what the angel of the Lord told him to do: he took his wife to his home and, though he had not had intercourse with her, she gave birth to a son; and he named him Jesus.

This is the Gospel of the Lord.

PROFESSION OF FAITH — *pages 15-16*
(All genuflect at the words, 'and was made man'.*)*

PRAYER OVER THE GIFTS

Lord,
as we keep tonight the vigil of Christmas,
may we celebrate this eucharist
with greater joy than ever
since it marks the beginning of our redemption.

PREFACE OF CHRISTMAS I-III — *page 19*

COMMUNION ANTIPHON   *(cf. Is 40:5)*

The glory of the Lord will be revealed, and all humankind will see the saving power of God.

PRAYER AFTER COMMUNION

Father,
we ask you to give us a new birth
as we celebrate the beginning
of your Son's life on earth.
Strengthen us in spirit
as we take your food and drink.

SOLEMN BLESSING — *pages 394-395*

REFLECTION

At the mixture of wine and water in the preparation of the gifts,
let us join quietly with the priest who says: 'By the mystery of
this water and wine may we come to share in the divinity of
Christ, who humbled himself to share in our humanity.'

MIDNIGHT MASS

'I bring you news of great joy: Today a Saviour has been born to you.' The real motive of our joy and celebration is Jesus. He is one of us, in darkness and poverty, and in our hardships and discomforts.

ENTRANCE ANTIPHON *(Ps 2:7)*

The Lord said to me: You are my Son; this day have I begotten you.

or

Let us all rejoice in the Lord, for our Saviour is born to the world. True peace has descended from heaven.

GREETING, PENITENTIAL RITE, GLORIA — *pages 7-14*

OPENING PRAYER

Let us pray
[in the peace of Christmas midnight
that our joy in the birth of Christ
will last for ever]

Father,
you make this holy night radiant
with the splendour of Jesus Christ our light.
We welcome him as Lord, the true light of the world.
Bring us to eternal joy in the kingdom of heaven,
where he lives and reigns with you and the Holy Spirit,
one God, for ever and ever.

or

Let us pray
[with joy and hope
as we await the dawning of the Father's Word]

Lord our God,
with the birth of your Son,
your glory breaks on the world.

Through the night hours of the darkened earth
we your people watch for the coming of your promised Son.
As we wait, give us a foretaste of the joy that you will grant us
when the fullness of his glory has filled the earth,
who lives and reigns with you for ever and ever.

FIRST READING   *(Is 9:1-7)*

A reading from the prophet Isaiah.

A Son is given to us.

The people that walked in darkness
has seen a great light;
on those who live in a land of deep shadow
a light has shone.
You have made their gladness greater,
you have made their joy increase;
they rejoice in your presence
as men rejoice at harvest time,
as men are happy when they are dividing the spoils.
For the yoke that was weighing on him,
the bar across his shoulders,
the rod of his oppressor,
these you break as on the day of Midian.
For all the footgear of battle,
every cloak rolled in blood,
is burnt, and consumed by fire.
For there is a child born for us,
a son given to us
and dominion is laid on his shoulders;
and this is the name they give him:
Wonder-Counsellor, Mighty-God,
Eternal-Father, Prince-of-Peace.
Wide is his dominion
in a peace that has no end,
for the throne of David
and for his royal power,
which he establishes and makes secure
in justice and integrity.
From this time onwards and for ever,
the jealous love of the Lord of hosts will do this.

This is the word of the Lord.

RESPONSORIAL PSALM   *(Ps 95:1-3.11-13)*

℟   **Today a saviour has been born to us;**
    he is Christ the Lord.

1.   O sing a new song to the Lord,
     sing to the Lord all the earth.
     O sing to the Lord, bless his name.   ℟

2. Proclaim his help day by day,
    tell among the nations his glory
    and his wonders among all the peoples. ℟

3. Let the heavens rejoice and earth be glad,
    let the sea and all within it thunder praise,
    let the land and all it bears rejoice,
    all the trees of the wood shout for joy
    at the presence of the Lord for he comes,
    he comes to rule the earth. ℟

4. With justice he will rule the world,
    he will judge the peoples with his truth. ℟

SECOND READING   (Titus 2:11-14)

A reading from the letter of St Paul to Titus.

God's grace has been revealed to the whole human race.

God's grace has been revealed, and it has made salvation possible for the whole human race and taught us that what we have to do is to give up everything that does not lead to God, and all our worldly ambitions; we must be self-restrained and live good and religious lives here in this present world, while we are waiting in hope for the blessing which will come with the Appearing of the glory of our great God and saviour Christ Jesus. He sacrificed himself for us in order to set us free from all wickedness and to purify a people so that it could be his very own and would have no ambition except to do good.

This is the word of the Lord.

GOSPEL ACCLAMATION   (Lk 2:10-11)

Alleluia, alleluia!
I bring you news of great joy:
today a saviour has been born to us, Christ the Lord.
Alleluia!

GOSPEL   (Lk 2:1-14)

A reading from the holy Gospel according to Luke.

Today a saviour has been born to you.

Caesar Augustus issued a decree for a census of the whole world to be taken. This census — the first — took place while Quirinius was governor of Syria, and everyone went to his own town to be registered. So Joseph set out from the town of Nazareth in Galilee and travelled up to Judaea, to the town of David called Bethlehem, since he was of David's House and line, in order to be registered together with Mary, his betrothed, who was with child. While they were there the time came for her to have her child, and she gave birth to a son, her first-born. She wrapped him in swaddling clothes, and laid him in a manger because there was no room for them at the inn. In the countryside close by there were shepherds who lived in the fields and took it in turns to watch their flocks during the night. The angel of the Lord appeared to them and the glory of the Lord shone round them. They were terrified, but the angel said, 'Do not be afraid. Listen, I bring you news of great joy, a joy to be shared by the whole people. Today in the town of David a saviour has been born to you; he is Christ the Lord. And here is a sign for you: you will find a baby wrapped in swaddling clothes and lying in a manger.' And suddenly with the angel there was a great throng of the heavenly host, praising God and singing:

> 'Glory to God in the highest heaven,
> and peace to men who enjoy his favour.'

This is the Gospel of the Lord.

PROFESSION OF FAITH — *pages 15-16*

(All genuflect at the words, 'and was made man'.)

PRAYER OVER THE GIFTS

Lord,
accept our gifts on this joyful feast of our salvation.
By our communion with God made man,
may we become more like him
who joins our lives to yours,
for he is Lord for ever and ever.

PREFACE OF CHRISTMAS I-III — *page 19*

COMMUNION ANTIPHON   *(Jn 1:14)*

The Word of God became man; we have seen his glory.

PRAYER AFTER COMMUNION

God our Father,
we rejoice in the birth of our Saviour.
May we share his life completely
by living as he has taught.

SOLEMN BLESSING

When he came to us as man,
the Son of God scattered the darkness of this world,
and filled this holy night (day) with his glory.

May the God of infinite goodness
scatter the darkness of sin
and brighten your hearts with holiness. **Amen**.

God sent his angels to shepherds
to herald the great joy of our Saviour's birth.
May he fill you with joy
and make you heralds of his gospel. **Amen**.

When the Word became man,
earth was joined to heaven.
May he give you his peace and good will,
and fellowship with all the heavenly host. **Amen**

May almighty God bless you,
the Father, and the Son, ✠ and the Holy Spirit. **Amen**.

REFLECTION

> The Word of God, we are taught by St Athanasius, rightly presented
> his own body a substitute on behalf of all and fulfilled what
> was due to death. Therefore, since the incorruptible Son
> of God was joined to all on account of this similarity, he
> rightly clothed all with incorruptibility by the promise of the
> resurrection.

DAWN MASS

'They hurried away and found Mary and Joseph, and the baby
lying in the manger.' The shepherds found the Baby Jesus at
the centre of his family. He will live with his parents for thirty
years before his identity will be known to all.

ENTRANCE ANTIPHON   *(cf. Is 9:2,6; Lk 1:33)*

**A light will shine on us this day, the Lord is born for us: he
shall be called Wonderful God, Prince of peace, Father of the
world to come; and his kingship will never end.**

GREETING, PENITENTIAL RITE, GLORIA — *pages 7-14*

OPENING PRAYER

Let us pray
    [that the love of Christ
    will be a light to the world]

Father,
we are filled with the new light
by the coming of your Word among us.

May the light of faith
shine in our words and actions.

or

Let us pray
    [for the peace
    that comes from the Prince of peace]

Almighty God and Father of light,
a child is born for us and a son is given to us.

Your eternal Word leaped down from heaven
in the silent watches of the night,
and now your Church is filled with wonder
at the nearness of her God.

Open our hearts to receive his life
and increase our vision with the rising of dawn,
that our lives may be filled with his glory and his peace,
who lives and reigns for ever and ever.

FIRST READING   *(Is 62:11-12)*

A reading from the prophet Isaiah.

Look, your Saviour comes.

This the Lord proclaims to the ends of the earth:
    Say to the daughter of Zion, 'Look,
    your saviour comes,
    the prize of his victory with him,
    his trophies before him.'
    They shall be called 'The Holy People',
    'The Lord's Redeemed'.
    And you shall be called 'The-sought-after',
    'City-not-forsaken'.

This is the word of the Lord.

RESPONSORIAL PSALM   *(Ps 96:1.6.11-12)*

℟ **This day new light will shine upon the earth:**
    the Lord is born for us.

1.   The Lord is king, let earth rejoice,
    the many coastlands be glad.
    The skies proclaim his justice;
    all peoples see his glory. ℟

2.   Light shines forth for the just
    and joy for the upright of heart.
    Rejoice, you just, in the Lord;
    give glory to his holy name.

SECOND READING   *(Titus 3:4-7)*

A reading from the letter of St Paul to Titus.

It was for no reason except his own compassion that he saved us.

When the kindness and love of God our saviour for mankind were revealed, it was not because he was concerned with any righteous actions we might have done ourselves; it was for no reason except his own compassion that he saved us, by means of the cleansing water of rebirth and by renewing us with the Holy Spirit which he has so generously poured over us through Jesus Christ our Saviour. He did this so that we should be justified by his grace, to become heirs looking forward to inheriting eternal life.

This is the word of the Lord.

GOSPEL ACCLAMATION   *(Lk 2:14)*

Alleluia, alleluia!
Glory to God in the highest heaven,
and peace to men who enjoy his favour.
Alleluia!

GOSPEL   *(Lk 2:15-20)*

A reading from the holy Gospel according to Luke.

The shepherds found Mary and Joseph and the baby.

Now when the angels had gone from them into heaven, the shepherds said to one another, 'Let us go to Bethlehem and see this thing that has happened which the Lord has made known to us.' So they hurried away and found Mary and Joseph, and the baby lying in the manger. When they saw the child they repeated what they had been told about him, and everyone who heard it was astonished at what the shepherds had to say. As for Mary, she treasured all these things and pondered them in her heart. And the shepherds went back glorifying and praising God for all they had heard and seen; it was exactly as they had been told.

This is the Gospel of the Lord.

PROFESSION OF FAITH — *pages 15-16*

(All genuflect at the words, 'and was made man'.)

PRAYER OVER THE GIFTS

Father,
may we follow the example of your Son

who became man and lived among us.
May we receive the gift of divine life
through these offerings here on earth.

PREFACE OF CHRISTMAS I-III — *page 19*

COMMUNION ANTIPHON   *(cf. Zc 9:9)*

**Daughter of Zion, exult; shout aloud, daughter of Jerusalem!
Your King is coming, the Holy One, the Saviour of the world.**

PRAYER AFTER COMMUNION

Lord,
with faith and joy
we celebrate the birthday of your Son.
Increase our understanding and our love
of the riches you have revealed in him,
who is Lord for ever and ever.

SOLEMN BLESSING — *pages 394-395*

REFLECTION

> One who is born by baptism possesses in himself all the
> potentialities of his immortal and incorruptible nature, but
> cannot use or exhibit them until the moment God has ordained
> for us to be born from the dead and attain full enjoyment of
> our freedom from corruption, death, pain and change.

MASS DURING THE DAY

The celebration of the anniversary of the Lord's birth seems
to have been observed since the fourth century. The popular
keeping of the feast has always been marked by joy. Some
writers have written of the threefold birth of Christ: eternally
in the bosom of the Father; at Bethlehem from the womb of
the Virgin Mary and mystically in the soul of each Christian.

ENTRANCE ANTIPHON   *(Is 9:6)*

**A child is born for us, a son given to us; dominion is laid on
his shoulder, and he shall be called Wonderful-Counsellor.**

GREETING, PENITENTIAL RITE, GLORIA — *pages 7-14*

OPENING PRAYER

Let us pray
[for the glory promised by the birth of Christ]

Lord God,
we praise you for creating man,
and still more for restoring him in Christ.
Your Son shared our weakness:
may we share his glory,
for he lives and reigns with you and the Holy Spirit,
one God, for ever and ever.

or

Let us pray
> [in the joy of Christmas
> because the Son of God lives among us]

God of love,
Father of all,
the darkness that covered the earth
has given way to the bright dawn of your Word made flesh.

Make us a people of this light.
Make us faithful to your Word,
that we may bring your life to the waiting world.

FIRST READING   *(Is 52:7-10)*

A reading from the prophet Isaiah.
All the ends of the earth shall see the salvation of our God.
How beautiful on the mountains,
are the feet of one who brings good news,
who heralds peace, brings happiness,
proclaims salvation,
and tells Zion,
'Your God is king!'
Listen! Your watchmen raise their voices,
they shout for joy together,
for they see the Lord face to face,
as he returns to Zion.
Break into shouts of joy together,
you ruins of Jerusalem;
for the Lord is consoling his people,
redeeming Jerusalem.
The Lord bares his holy arm
in the sight of all the nations,
and all the ends of the earth shall see
the salvation of our God.

> This is the word of the Lord.

RESPONSORIAL PSALM   (Ps 97:1-6)

℟   **All the ends of the earth have seen
     the salvation of our God.**

1.   Sing a new song to the Lord
     for he has worked wonders.
     His right hand and his holy arm
     have brought salvation. ℟

2.   The Lord has made known his salvation;
     has shown his justice to the nations.
     He has remembered his truth and love
     for the house of Israel. ℟

3.   All the ends of the earth have seen
     the salvation of our God.
     Shout to the Lord all the earth,
     ring out your joy. ℟

4.   Sing psalms to the Lord with the harp,
     with the sound of music.
     With trumpets and the sound of the horn
     acclaim the King, the Lord. ℟

SECOND READING   (Heb 1:1-6)

A reading from the letter to the Hebrews.

God has spoken to us through his Son.

At various times in the past and in various different ways, God
spoke to our ancestors through the prophets; but in our own
time, the last days, he has spoken to us through his Son, the Son
that he has appointed to inherit everything and through whom
he made everything there is. He is the radiant light of God's glory
and the perfect copy of his nature, sustaining the universe by his
powerful command; and now that he has destroyed the defilement
of sin, he has gone to take his place in heaven at the right hand
of divine Majesty. So he is now as far above the angels as the
title which he has inherited is higher than their own name.

     God has never said to any angel: You are my Son, today I
have become your father, or: I will be a father to him and he a
son to me. Again, when he brings the First-born into the world,
he says: Let all the angels of God worship him.

     This is the word of the Lord.

GOSPEL ACCLAMATION
Alleluia, alleluia!
A hallowed day has dawned upon us.

Come, you nations, worship the Lord,
for today a great light has shone down upon the earth.
Alleluia!

GOSPEL   *(Jn 1:1-18)*

(*For* Shorter Form, *read between* ◗ ◖)

A reading from the holy Gospel according to John.

The Word was made flesh, and lived among us.

◗In the beginning was the Word:
the Word was with God
and the Word was God.
He was with God in the beginning.
Through him all things came to be,
not one thing had its being but through him.
All that came to be had life in him
and that life was the light of men,
a light that shines in the dark,
a light that darkness could not overpower.◖

A man came, sent by God.
His name was John.
He came as a witness,
as a witness to speak for the light,
so that everyone might believe through him.
He was not the light,
only a witness to speak for the light.

◗The Word was the true light
that enlightens all men;
and he was coming into the world.
He was in the world
that had its being through him,
and the world did not know him.
He came to his own domain
and his own people did not accept him.
But to all who did accept him
he gave power to become children of God,
to all who believe in the name of him
who was born not out of human stock
or urge of the flesh
or will of man
but of God himself.
The Word was made flesh,

he lived among us,
and we saw his glory,
the glory that is his as the only Son of the Father,
full of grace and truth.◊

John appears as his witness. He proclaims:
'This is the one of whom I said:
He who comes after me
ranks before me
because he existed before me.'

Indeed, from his fullness we have, all of us, received —
yes, grace in return for grace,
since, though the Law was given through Moses,
grace and truth have come through Jesus Christ.
No one has ever seen God;
it is the only Son, who is nearest to the Father's heart,
who has made him known.

◊This is the Gospel of the Lord.◊

PROFESSION OF FAITH — *pages 15-16*

(All genuflect at the words, 'and was made man'.)

PRAYER OVER THE GIFTS
Almighty God,
the saving work of Christ
made our peace with you.
May our offering today
renew that peace within us
and give you perfect praise.

PREFACE OF CHRISTMAS I-III — *page 19*

COMMUNION ANTIPHON   *(Ps 97:3)*
All the ends of the earth have seen the saving power of God.

PRAYER AFTER COMMUNION
Father,
the child born today is the Saviour of the world.
He made us your children.'
May he welcome us into your kingdom
where he lives and reigns with you for ever and ever.

SOLEMN BLESSING — *pages 394-395*

REFLECTION

The stories about the infancy of Jesus found in the gospel accounts of Matthew and Luke contain echoes of the passion story giving the message that even from the beginning of his life the shadow of the cross is never far away. At his birth and at his death Jesus is presented as being received by gentiles but rejected by Jews, welcomed by strangers but turned away by his own. Lord Jesus, born this day at Bethlehem, be born once again in our hearts. Amen.

---

27 DECEMBER

THE HOLY FAMILY

The first Sunday after Christmas Day is kept as the feast of the Holy Family. This feast became popular in the Seventeenth Century and the theme of today has become the subject of celebrated works of art. An inclusive understanding of the term 'family' recognises that we are all part of one or more groupings of people, that no human being is an island. The child Jesus, his mother Mary and her husband Joseph are a symbol of this.

ENTRANCE ANTIPHON   (Lk 2:16)

The shepherds hastened to Bethlehem, where they found Mary and Joseph, and the baby lying in a manger.

GREETING, PENITENTIAL RITE, GLORIA — *pages 7-14*

OPENING PRAYER

Let us pray
[for peace in our families]

Father,
help us to live as the holy family,
united in respect and love.
Bring us to the joy and peace of your eternal home.

or

Let us pray
[as the family of God,
who share in his life]

Father in heaven, creator of all,
you ordered the earth to bring forth life
and crowned its goodness by creating the family of man.
In history's moment when all was ready,

you sent your Son to dwell in time,
obedient to the laws of life in our world.

Teach us the sanctity of human love,
show us the value of family life,
and help us to live in peace with all
that we may share in your life for ever.

FIRST READING   *(1 Sm 1:20-22.24-28)*

A reading from the first book of Samuel.

Samuel is made over to the Lord for the whole of his life.

Hannah conceived and gave birth to a son, and called him Samuel
'since' she said 'I asked the Lord for him.'

When a year had gone by, the husband Elkanah went up
again with all his family to offer the annual sacrifice to the Lord
and to fulfil his vow. Hannah, however, did not go up, having
said to her husband, 'Not before the child is weaned. Then I will
bring him and present him before the Lord and he shall stay
there for ever.'

When she had weaned him, she took him up with her
together with a three-year old bull, an ephah of flour and a
skin of wine, and she brought him to the temple of the Lord
at Shiloh; and the child was with them. They slaughtered the
bull and the child's mother came to Eli. She said, 'If you please,
my lord. As you live, my lord, I am the woman who stood here
beside you, praying to the Lord. This is the child I prayed for,
and the Lord granted me what I asked him. Now I make him
over to the Lord for the whole of his life. He is made over to the
Lord.' There she left him, for the Lord.

This is the word of the Lord.

RESPONSORIAL PSALM   *(Ps 83:2-3.5-6.9-10)*

℟ **They are happy who dwell in your house, O Lord.**

1. How lovely is your dwelling place,
    Lord, God of hosts.
    My soul is longing and yearning,
    is yearning for the courts of the Lord.
    My heart and my soul ring out their joy
    to God, the living God. ℟

2. They are happy, who dwell in your house,
    for ever singing your praise.
    They are happy, whose strength is in you;
    they walk with ever growing strength. ℟

3.   O Lord, God of hosts, hear my prayer,
      give ear, O God of Jacob.
      Turn your eyes, O God, our shield,
      look on the face of your anointed. ℟

SECOND READING   *(1 Jn 3:1-2.21-24)*

A reading from the first letter of St John.

We are called God's children, and that is what we are.

Think of the love that the Father has lavished on us,
by letting us be called God's children;
and that is what we are.
Because the world refused to acknowledge him,
therefore it does not acknowledge us.
My dear people, we are already the children of God
but what we are to be in the future has not yet been revealed,
all we know is, that when it is revealed
we shall be like him
because we shall see him as he really is.

My dear people,
if we cannot be condemned by our own conscience,
we need not be afraid in God's presence,
and whatever we ask him,
we shall receive,
because we keep his commandments
and live the kind of life that he wants.
His commandments are these:
that we believe in the name of his Son Jesus Christ
and that we love one another
as he told us to.
Whoever keeps his commandments
lives in God and God lives in him.
We know that he lives in us
by the Spirit that he has given us.

      This is the word of the Lord.

GOSPEL ACCLAMATION   *(cf. Acts 16:14)*

Alleluia, alleluia!
Open our heart, O Lord,
to accept the words of your Son.
Alleluia!

GOSPEL   *(Lk 2:41-52)*

A reading from the holy Gospel according to Luke.

Jesus is found by his parents sitting among the doctors.

Every year the parents of Jesus used to go to Jerusalem for the feast of the Passover. When he was twelve years old, they went up for the feast as usual. When they were on their way home after the feast, the boy Jesus stayed behind in Jerusalem without his parents knowing it. They assumed he was with the caravan, and it was only after a day's journey that they went to look for him among their relations and acquaintances. When they failed to find him they went back to Jerusalem looking for him everywhere.

Three days later, they found him in the Temple, sitting among the doctors, listening to them and asking them questions; and all those who heard him were astounded at his intelligence and his replies. They were overcome when they saw him, and his mother said to him, 'My child, why have you done this to us? See how worried your father and I have been, looking for you.' 'Why were you looking for me?' he replied. 'Did you not know that I must be busy with my Father's affairs?' But they did not understand what he meant.

He then went down with them and came to Nazareth and lived under their authority. His mother stored up all these things in her heart. And Jesus increased in wisdom, in stature, and in favour with God and men.

This is the Gospel of the Lord.

PROFESSION OF FAITH — *pages 15-16*

PRAYER OVER THE GIFTS

Lord,
accept this sacrifice
and through the prayers of Mary, the virgin Mother of God,
and of her husband, Joseph,
unite our families in peace and love.

PREFACE OF CHRISTMAS I-III — *page 19*

COMMUNION ANTIPHON   *(Ba 3:38)*

Our God has appeared on earth, and lived among men.

PRAYER AFTER COMMUNION

Eternal Father,
we want to live as Jesus, Mary, and Joseph,
in peace with you and one another.

May this communion strengthen us
to face the troubles of life.

SOLEMN BLESSING — *pages 394-395*

REFLECTION

Today's gospel account is that of the finding of the child Jesus in the Temple. It is noticeable that the first word put into the mouth of Jesus by Luke is to call God his Father. The loss of Jesus for three days has been seen as an image of his three days in the tomb. 'To be about my Father's business' means to complete the work which the Father has sent Jesus to do, namely, the work of our salvation. Mary submits to the call of God, keeping his word in her heart. Her greatness lies in her faith. Augustine has said that Mary is more blessed because she believed in her heart than because she conceived in her womb.

DEVOTIONAL PRAYERS

THANKSGIVING AFTER COMMUNION

Adoration. I adore you present in me, Incarnate Word, only-begotten Son and splendour of the Father, born of Mary. I thank you, sole Master and Truth, for your supreme condescension in coming to me, ignorant and sinful as I am. With Mary I offer you to the Father: through you, with you, in you, may there be eternal praise, thanksgiving and supplication for peace to humankind. Enlighten my mind; make me a docile disciple of the Church; grant that I may live of faith; give me an understanding of the Scriptures. Make me your ardent apostle. Let the light of your Gospel, O Divine Master, shine to the farthest bounds of the world.

Resolution. O Jesus, you are the Way which I must follow; the perfect model which I must imitate. In presenting myself at the judgment I want to be found similar to you.

O divine model of humility and obedience, make me similar to you.

O perfect example of mortification and purity, make me similar to you.

O Jesus, poor and patient, make me similar to you.

O exemplar of charity and ardent zeal, make me similar to you.

Petition. O Jesus, my Life, my joy and source of all good, I love you. Above all, I ask of you that I may love you more and more and the souls redeemed by your Blood.

You are the vine and I am the branch: I want to stay united to you always so as to bring forth many fruits.

You are the source: pour out an ever greater abundance of grace to sanctify my soul.

You are my head; I, your member: communicate to me your Holy Spirit with all his gifts.

May your kingdom come through Mary.

Console and save those dear to me. Free the souls in purgatory.

SPIRITUAL COMMUNION

My Jesus, I believe that you are truly present in the Blessed
Sacrament. I love you above all things and I desire you in
my soul. As I cannot now receive you sacramentally, come at
least spiritually into my heart. I embrace you and unite myself
entirely to you. Do not let me leave you ever.

TO JESUS, THE DIVINE MASTER

Jesus, Divine Master, I adore you as the Word Incarnate sent
by the Father to instruct humankind in life-giving truths. You
are uncreated *Truth,* the only Master. You alone have words of
eternal life. I thank you for having ignited in me the light of
reason and the light of faith, and for having called me to the
light of glory. I believe, submitting my whole mind to you and
to the Church, and I condemn all that the Church condemns.
Master, show me the treasures of your wisdom, let me know the
Father, make me your true disciple. Increase my faith so that I
may attain to the eternal vision in heaven.

PRAYER OF ST FRANCIS

Lord, make me an instrument of your peace:
where there is hatred let me sow love,
where there is injury let me sow pardon,
where there is doubt let me sow faith,
where there is despair let me give hope,
where there is darkness let me give light,
where there is sadness let me give joy.

O Divine Master, grant that I may
not try to be comforted but to comfort,
not try to be understood but to understand,
not try to be loved but to love.

Because it is in giving that we receive,
it is in forgiving that we are forgiven,
and it is in dying that we are born to eternal life.

THE DIVINE PRAISES

Blessed be God.
Blessed be His holy Name.
Blessed be Jesus Christ, true God and true man.
Blessed be the Name of Jesus.
Blessed be His most Sacred Heart.
Blessed be His most precious Blood.
Blessed be Jesus in the most holy Sacrament of the Altar.
Blessed be the Holy Spirit, the Paraclete.
Blessed be the great Mother of God, Mary most holy.
Blessed be her holy and immaculate Conception.
Blessed be her glorious assumption.
Blessed be the name of Mary, Virgin and Mother.
Blessed be St Joseph, her most chaste spouse.
Blessed be God in His angels and in His saints.

SOUL OF CHRIST

Soul of Christ, sanctify me,
Body of Christ, save me.
Blood of Christ, inebriate me.
Water from the side of Christ, wash me.
Passion of Christ, strengthen me.
O good Jesus, hear me.
Within your wounds hide me.
Permit me not to be separated from you.
From the malignant enemy defend me.
In the hour of my death call me
And bid me come to you,
That with your saints I may praise you
For ever and ever. Amen.

CONSECRATION TO THE MOST HOLY TRINITY

O divine Trinity, Father, Son and Holy Spirit, present and active in the Church and the depths of my soul, I adore you, I thank you, I love you! And through the hands of Mary most holy, my Mother, I offer, give, and consecrate myself entirely to You for life and for eternity.

To You, heavenly Father, I offer, give and consecrate myself as Your child.

To You, Jesus Master, I offer, give and consecrate myself as Your brother (sister) and disciple.

To You, Holy Spirit, I offer, give and consecrate myself as "a living temple" to be consecrated and sanctified.

O Mary, Mother of the Church and my Mother, teach me to live, through the liturgy and the sacraments, in ever more intimate union with the three Divine Persons, so that my whole life may be a "glory be to the Father, to the Son and to the Holy Spirit." Amen.

PRAYER TO THE HOLY SPIRIT

O divine Holy Spirit, eternal Love of the Father and of the Son, I adore you, I thank you, I love you, and I ask you pardon for all the times I have grieved you in myself and in my neighbour.

Descend with many graces during the holy ordination of bishops and priests, during the consecration of men and women religious, during the reception of Confirmation by all the faithful; be light, sanctity and zeal.

To you, O Spirit of Truth, I consecrate my mind, imagination and memory; enlighten me. May I know Jesus Christ our Master and understand his Gospel and the teaching of holy Church. Increase in me the gifts of wisdom, knowledge, understanding and right judgment.

To you, O sanctifying Spirit, I consecrate my will. Guide me in your will, sustain me in the observance of the commandments, in the fulfilment of my duties. Grant me the gifts of courage and reverence.

To you, O life-giving Spirit, I consecrate my heart. Guard and increase the divine life in me. Grant me the gift of filial love. Amen.

ACT OF SUBMISSION TO THE WILL OF GOD

My God, I do not know what will happen to me today. I only know that nothing will happen to me that was not foreseen by you and directed to my greater good from all eternity. This is enough for me.

I adore your holy, eternal and unfathomable designs. I submit to them with all my heart for love of you. I make a sacrifice of my whole being to you and join my sacrifice to that of Jesus, my divine Saviour.

In his name and by his infinite merits, I ask you to give me patience in my sufferings and perfect submission, so that everything you want or permit to happen will result in your greater glory and my sanctification. Amen.

INVOCATIONS TO THE DIVINE MASTER

Jesus Master, sanctify my mind and increase my faith.

Jesus, teaching in the Church, draw everyone to your school.

Jesus Master, deliver me from error, from vain thoughts, and from eternal darkness.

O Jesus, Way between the Father and us, I offer you everything and look to you for everything.

O Jesus, Way of sanctity, make me your faithful imitator.

O Jesus Way, render me perfect as the Father who is in heaven.

O Jesus Life, live in me, so that I may live in you.

O Jesus Life, do not permit me to separate myself from you.

O Jesus Life, grant that I may live eternally in the joy of your love.

O Jesus Truth, may I be light for the world.

O Jesus Way, may I be an example and model for others.

O Jesus Life, may my presence bring grace and consolation everywhere.

TO RECALL GOD'S PRESENCE

I believe, my God, that I am in your presence, that you are looking at me and listening to my prayers.

You are so great and so holy: I adore you.

You have given me all: I thank you.

You have been so offended by me: I ask your pardon with all my heart.

You are so merciful: and I ask of you all the graces which you know are beneficial to me.

ACT OF FAITH

O my God, I firmly believe that you are one God in three Divine Persons; Father, Son, and Holy Spirit; I believe that your divine Son became man and died for our sins, and that he will come to judge the living and the dead. I believe these and all truths which the holy catholic Church teaches, because you have revealed them who can neither deceive nor be deceived.

ACT OF HOPE

O my God, relying on your infinite goodness and promises, I hope to obtain pardon of my sins, the help of your grace, and life everlasting, through the merits of Jesus Christ, my Lord and Redeemer.

ACT OF LOVE

O my God, I love you above all things, with my whole heart and soul, because you are all good and worthy of all love. I love my neighbour as myself for the love of you. I forgive all who have injured me and I ask pardon of all whom I have injured.

ACT OF CONTRITION

My God, I am heartily sorry for having offended you, and I detest all my sins, because of your just punishment, but most of all because they offend you, my God, who are all good and deserving of all love. I firmly resolve, with the help of your grace, to sin no more and to avoid the near occasions of sin.

PRAYERS TO OUR LADY

THE ANGELUS

The angel of the Lord declared unto Mary.
And she conceived of the holy Spirit.
Hail Mary….

Behold the handmaid of the Lord.
Be it done unto me according to thy word.
Hail Mary…

And the Word was made flesh,
And dwelt among us.
Hail Mary…

Pray for us, O Holy Mother of God.
That we may be made worthy of the promises of Christ.

Let us pray. Pour forth, we beseech thee, O Lord, thy grace into our hearts, that we, to whom the incarnation of Christ, thy Son, was made known by the message of an angel, may by his passion and cross be brought to the glory of his resurrection. Through the same Christ our Lord. Amen.

REGINA COELI

(This prayer is said instead of the Angelus *from the Easter Vigil until the evening of Pentecost Sunday.)*

O Queen of heaven, rejoice, **alleluia!**
For he whom thou didst merit to bear, **alleluia!**
Has risen, as he said, **alleluia!**
Pray for us to God, **alleluia!**
Rejoice and be glad, O Virgin Mary, **alleluia!**
For the Lord has risen indeed, **alleluia!**

Let us pray. O God, who gavest joy to the world through the resurrection of thy Son our Lord Jesus Christ; grant that we may obtain, through his Virgin Mother, Mary, the joys of everlasting Life. Through the same Christ our Lord. Amen.

THE ROSARY

Joyful Mysteries

The Annunciation
The Visitation
The Nativity
The Presentation in the Temple
The Finding of the Child Jesus
    in the Temple

Luminous Mysteries

Jesus' Baptism in the Jordan
Jesus' Self-manifestation at the
    Wedding Feast of Cana
Jesus' Proclamation of the
    Kingdom of God, with His
    Call to Conversion
The Transfiguration
The Institution of the Holy
    Eucharist

Sorrowful Mysteries

The Agony in the Garden
The Scourging at the Pillar
The Crowning with Thorns
Jesus Carries His Cross
Jesus Dies on the Cross

Glorious Mysteries

The Resurrection
The Ascension
The Coming of the Holy Spirit
The Assumption of Our Lady
    into Heaven
The Coronation of Our Lady
    and the Glory of All the
    Saints

SALVE REGINA

Hail, holy Queen, mother of mercy, hail, our life, our sweetness, and our hope. To you do we cry, poor banished children of Eve. To you do we send up our sighs, mourning and weeping in this vale of tears. Turn then, most gracious advocate, your eyes of mercy towards us, and after this our exile show to us the blessed fruit of your womb, Jesus. O Clement, O loving, O sweet Virgin Mary.

ST BERNARD'S PRAYER

Remember, O most gracious Virgin Mary, that never was it known that anyone who fled to your protection, implored your help or sought your intercession, was left unaided. Inspired with this confidence, I fly to you, O Virgin of virgins, my Mother. To you I come, before you I stand, sinful and sorrowful. O Mother of the Word Incarnate! Despise not my petitions, but in your mercy hear and answer me. Amen.

SONG OF MARY (The Magnificat)

My soul proclaims the greatness of the Lord,
my spirit rejoices in God, my Saviour;
for he has looked with favour on his lowly servant,
and from this day all generations will call me blessed.
The Almighty has done great things for me:
holy is his Name.
He has mercy on those who fear him in every generation.
He has shown the strength of his arm,
he has scattered the proud in their conceit.
He has cast down the mighty from their thrones,
and has lifted up the lowly.
He has filled the hungry with good things,
and has sent the rich away empty.
He has come to the help of his servant Israel
for he has remembered his promise of mercy,
the promise he made to our fathers,
to Abraham and his children for ever.

(ICET translation)

The Way of the Cross

Holy and merciful Father,
grant that we may follow the way of the cross
in faith and love, so that we may share
in Christ's passion and together with him
reach the glory of your Kingdom.
We ask you this through your Son Jesus Christ.

FIRST STATION

JESUS IS CONDEMNED TO DEATH

℣ We adore you, O Christ, and we bless you.
℟ Because by your holy cross you have redeemed the world.

So Pilate, wishing to satisfy the crowd, released for them Barabbas; and having scourged Jesus, he delivered him to be crucified (Mk 15:15).

"He came to his own home, and his own people received him not." The whole world — a world made up of Christians, Jews and non-believers — judges its own Creator and Redeemer. It was a judgement passed on Jesus by a small group among those who had followed him: by Judas who, not finding this Messiah up to his expectations, betrayed him to those who were seeking political power and liberation. Peter denied Jesus, while the other disciples fled.

Lord our God, have mercy on us all who have condemned you to death. Your mercy is already manifest in the sublime freedom with which you have borne our ingratitude and rejection.

All:
Our Father...

At the cross her station keeping
Stood the mournful Mother weeping,
Close to Jesus to the last.

SECOND STATION

JESUS TAKES UP HIS CROSS

℣ We adore you, O Christ, and we bless you.
℟ Because by your holy cross you have redeemed the world.

... Jesus went out, bearing his cross, to the place called 'Place of the Skull', which is called in Hebrew Golgotha (Jn 19:17).

Lord, you accept from humankind the same cross of which from all eternity you told your heavenly Father you were ready to bear in freedom and in love. It was not the human race who placed their sins on your shoulders, making of you a scapegoat, but it was you who had freely taken upon yourself our sins: everything you suffered would have otherwise been in vain.

To impose the burden of one's guilt on another is to disclaim any sort of personal culpability. It was not your Father who placed the burden on your shoulders, but the whole Trinity decreed that you should redeem the world lost in sin. You offered yourself to the Father in the Holy Spirit, in order to bring to completion on the cross the work of creation, and the Father — moved by the same Spirit — accepted your sacrifice.

Welcome, beloved Cross! You are the means by which we can finally and effectively show the world the immensity of God's love.

All:
Our Father...

Through her heart, his sorrow sharing,
All his bitter anguish bearing,
Now at length the sword had passed.

THIRD STATION

JESUS FALLS FOR THE FIRST TIME

℣   We adore you, O Christ, and we bless you.
℟   Because by your holy cross you have redeemed the world.

Unless a grain of wheat falls into the earth and dies, it remains alone; but if it dies it bears much fruit (Jn 12:24).

The Bible mentions neither this fall nor the others. But we must remember that Jesus had undergone the appalling Roman scourging, the pain and exhaustion enough to kill anyone.

With repeated blows of the cudgel, the crown of thorns was driven into his sacred head. It is astonishing how our Lord did not lose consciousness when the heavy weight of the cross was placed on his shoulders. His resources were not totally drained.

People of goodwill can surely help the Redeemer as he carries his cross. There are those who wish to do so, and we shall encounter them as we go along.

Let us now ask our Lord to forgive us, for we too have placed unnecessary burdens on his shoulders.

All:
Our Father...

Oh, how sad and sore distressed
Was that Mother highly blest
Of the sole-begotten one!

FOURTH STATION

JESUS MEETS HIS MOTHER

℣ We adore you, O Christ, and we bless you.
℟ Because by your holy cross you have redeemed the world.

Simeon said to Mary, "This child is set for the fall and rising of many in Israel, and for a sign that is spoken against and a sword will pierce through your own soul also" (Lk 2:34-35).

As Mary, the mother, played an essential role in Jesus' conception and birth, likewise she played an essential part in his passion by sharing in his suffering and death. No one is without a companion or a friend, yet on the cross the two criminals crucified with Jesus were of no comfort to him; he needed the presence of the sinless woman, Mary, the ever-Virgin Mother, whom he would make the mother of his mystical body, the Church.

Jesus entrusts to his sorrowful Mother his beloved disciple, John, who would be spiritually united with Peter, the representative of ecclesial unity. Thus, Mary the Immaculate becomes the Mother of the Petrine Church where — on behalf of all believers — she pleads the Holy Spirit by whom she was overshadowed at Nazareth.

All:
Our Father...

Christ above in torment hangs,
She beneath beholds the pangs
of her dying glorious Son.

FIFTH STATION

SIMON OF CYRENE HELPS JESUS CARRY HIS CROSS

℣ We adore you, O Christ, and we bless you.
℟ Because by your holy cross you have redeemed the world.

And they compelled a passer-by, Simon of Cyrene, who was coming in from the country, the father of Alexander and Rufus, to carry his cross (Mk 15:21).

Mary, in the most profound sorrow, accompanies her son on his way to Calvary. Simon, an ordinary man, is not prepared for anything unusual. He is on his way home from work. The evangelists underline the fact that he had to be forced to carry the cross that is too heavy for Jesus.

Even our most feeble "yes" to suffering — despite our resistance and our being unaware of it — becomes a transforming grace, provided that we accept it from the hands of God. Job, a patient man, uttered bitter words for his undeserved fate and great suffering, nevertheless was able to accept everything as coming from God: "The Lord has given and the Lord has taken away. The Lord's name be praised," — this earned him God's justification.

All:
Our Father...

Is there anyone who would not weep,
Whelmed in miseries so deep,
Christ's dear Mother to behold?

SIXTH STATION

VERONICA WIPES THE FACE OF JESUS

℣ We adore you, O Christ, and we bless you.
℟ Because by your holy cross you have redeemed the world.

He had no form or comeliness that we should look at him, and no beauty to attract us. He was despised and rejected by men as one from whom men hide their faces (Is 53:2-3).

Veronica is not mentioned in the Bible, but several women were present along the way to Calvary: women who wished by their presence, not only to profess their faith in the Lord but also to help him unreservedly.

Women in the Gospel are marked by Christ's preferential love of which John, the beloved disciple, was privileged. The Church, the bride of Christ, is therefore graced by the presence of women. In so far as the Church professes her faith and fidelity in loving humility to the Lord, as Veronica did in a gesture of love, Jesus leaves the imprint of his features on all those who are ready to accept it as a peace-token of his love.

Veronica's linen cloth, bearing the features of Jesus, is a sign and a promise to all believers that he will help them who call upon him.

Lord God, imprint in my spirit the sufferings of your Son Jesus.

All:
Our Father...

Can the human heart refrain
From partaking in her pain,
In that Mother's pain untold?

SEVENTH STATION

JESUS FALLS FOR THE SECOND TIME

℣   We adore you, O Christ, and we bless you.
℞   Because by your holy cross you have redeemed the world.

Jesus said to them, 'My soul is very sorrowful, even to death....' And going a little farther, he fell on the ground and prayed that, if it were possible, this hour might pass from him (Mk 14:34-35).

To know that the Son of God's strength should fail him is indeed terrifying, yet it reminds us of what John (3:16) says of him: "God so loved the world that he gave his only Son..." to take upon himself the weight of man's sins and, as man, succumb under it. Humanly speaking, what would the Father have felt upon seeing his Son's sufferings, who in fulfilment of his Father's will gave himself up to death?

We always want to know why God allows so much suffering in the world. There is no easy answer to this. God can only offer a gesture of fatherly love: he loves the world so much that "he gave his only Son" to fall and be crushed under its massive weight.

We should not dwell so much on our own suffering which is nothing compared to what the Son of God suffered for us. Whenever we are able to share in a small way in Christ's suffering, it is indeed a grace.

All:

Our Father…

Bruised, derided, cursed, defiled
She beheld her tender Child
All with bloody scourges rent.

EIGHTH STATION

JESUS COMFORTS THE WOMEN OF JERUSALEM

℣ We adore you, O Christ, and we bless you.
℟ Because by your holy cross you have redeemed the world.

And there followed him a great multitude of the people, and of women who bewailed and lamented him. But Jesus turning to them said, 'Daughters of Jerusalem, do not weep for me, but weep for yourselves and for your children' (Lk 23:27-28).

In this station we are faced with a gnawing question about the role played by the people of Israel in the Passion of Jesus.

We cannot ignore the fact that Israel not only disowned its long-awaited Messiah, but also condemned him to death; we should nonetheless bear in mind that both pagans and Christians are also guilty of his death. Jesus however would not let himself be comforted by the women of Jerusalem: "…weep not for me but for yourselves and for your children."

He foresees the imminent catastrophe which is to befall Jerusalem, and indeed the whole of Israel. The people of Israel could not give solace to the Son of God while he is being condemned.

All:

Our Father...

Let me share with you his pain
who for all my sins was slain
who for me in torment died.

NINTH STATION

JESUS FALLS FOR THE THIRD TIME

℣ We adore you, O Christ, and we bless you.
℟ Because by your holy cross you have redeemed the world.

*Come to me, all who labour and are heavy-laden, and I will give you
rest. Take my yoke upon you, and learn from me; for I am gentle and
lowly in heart, and you will find rest for your souls. For my yoke is
easy, and my burden is light (Mt 11:28-30).*

It would not be inappropriate to think that this third fall of
Jesus came about to the advantage of the people of Israel. Jesus'
greatest pain was possibly the rejection by his own people who
condemned him to the most atrocious death. We should not
forget that his first mission was to gather together the scattered
sheep of Israel. Not having been recognized as the Messiah was
the most poignant defeat and the greatest humiliation he had
to undergo.

This last burden, surely, must redound to Israel's advantage:
how could it be otherwise? The tears of the daughters of
Jerusalem could undoubtedly mingle with the tears of Jesus over
that city whose destruction was imminent (cf. Lk 19:41).

All:

Our Father...

O my Mother, fount of love,
Touch my spirit from above;
Make my heart with yours accord.

TENTH STATION

JESUS IS STRIPPED OF HIS GARMENTS

℣ We adore you, O Christ, and we bless you.
℟ Because by your holy cross you have redeemed the world.

They divided his garments among them, casting lots for them, to decide what each should take (Mk 15:24).

What do clothes matter to a human body which is about to be crucified? Jesus is stripped of his garments to enable the soldiers to work without being hampered.

Since that time in the Garden of Eden, fallen man has been covering himself with all sorts of clothing: from fig leaves and animal skins to the latest fashion of today. On Calvary everything is cast away: the new Adam stands before the Father as he is, having freely taken upon himself the sins and shame of the old Adam.

On the cross man fully manifests himself, and God restores to him his lost dignity — his most precious gift to mankind. In every eucharistic celebration down the centuries he gives to humanity this unadorned body. "The body of Christ" — says the priest as he gives communion — "who takes away the sins of the world": the body which bears your sins and the wounds inflicted on it.

All:
Our Father...

Make me feel as you have felt,
Make my soul to glow and melt
with the love of Christ my Lord.

ELEVENTH STATION

JESUS IS NAILED TO THE CROSS

℣ We adore you, O Christ, and we bless you.
℟ Because by your holy cross you have redeemed the world.

*It was the third hour, when they crucified him. And the inscription
of the charge against him read, 'The King of the Jews.' And with him
they crucified two robbers, one on his right and one on his left (Mk
15:25-27).*

"They know not what they do" (Lk 23:34). They nailed him to
the cross in order to get rid of him, but in so doing, bonded
him the more firmly to the earth. They nailed him down so that
he could no longer go away but remain with us forever: neither
the Resurrection nor the Ascension could alter this.

No one binds Jesus to sinful humanity; he remains with
us, of his own accord, to the very end. And when he returns
on judgement day the cross, "the sign of the Son of Man, will
appear in heaven" (Mt 24:30).

"All things were created through him and for him" (Col 1:16-
17), that is, for the Son whom the Father allows to be nailed to
the cross of the world.

Overwhelmed by this unfathomable mystery we can only
kneel in grateful adoration.

All:
Our Father...

Holy Mother, pierce me through;
In my heart each wound renew
Of my Saviour crucified.

TWELFTH STATION

JESUS DIES ON THE CROSS

℣ We adore you, O Christ, and we bless you.
℟ Because by your holy cross you have redeemed the world.

And when the sixth hour had come, there was darkness over the whole land until the ninth hour. And at the ninth hour Jesus cried with a loud voice, 'Eloi, Eloi, lama sabachtani?' which means, 'My God, my God, why hast thou forsaken me?' ... And one ran and, filling a sponge full of vinegar, put it on a reed and gave it to him to drink... And Jesus uttered a loud cry, and breathed his last.... And when the centurion, who stood facing him, saw that he thus breathed his last, he said, 'Truly this man was the Son of God' (Mk 15:33-39).

Jesus is suspended between heaven and earth, repudiated by men and forsaken by his Father, thus restoring the unity between them. Extending his arms he reaches out to both the sinner who goes back to him and to the one who turns away from him and yet could not hinder Christ to reach out to him. The vertical beam of the cross bridges the gap between God and man, while the horizontal one embraces the ends of the earth.

Bending his head, Jesus gives up the spirit, the same spirit whom he will breathe on the Church on the day of his Resurrection, and in this way all is truly accomplished.

All:

Our Father...

For the sins of his own nation
She saw him hang in desolation
Till his spirit forth he sent.

THIRTEENTH STATION

JESUS IS TAKEN DOWN FROM THE CROSS

℣ We adore you, O Christ, and we bless you.
℟ Because by your holy cross you have redeemed the world.

Standing by the cross of Jesus were his mother and his mother's sister, Mary the wife of Clopas, and Mary Magdalene... The soldiers came to Jesus and when they saw that he was already dead, they did not break his legs. But one of the soldiers pierced his side with a spear, and at once there came out blood and water. After this Joseph of Arimathea... asked Pilate that he might take away the body of Jesus (Jn 19:25.32-34.38).

Jesus is taken down from the cross and his mother accepting the pain that his Son bore for the sake of the world — is there to receive him in her bosom. Each of the seven swords which transfixed the heart of the mother was Mary's renewed assent to her Son's sufferings. It is beyond human comprehension that a person should say "yes" to everything, even to the most harrowing pain.

In her unconditional "yes" Mary becomes the "redeemed earth", capable of receiving on her lap the dead body of the Redeemer. This scene wrapped in silence reveals that Christ's Passion was not suffered in vain: Mary in this moment of weariness and infinite sorrow, represents humanity who accepts with gratitude heaven's blessings.

All:
Our Father...

Let me mingle tears with you
Mourning him who mourned for me,
All the days that I may live.

FOURTEENTH STATION

JESUS IS LAID IN THE TOMB

℣ We adore you, O Christ, and we bless you.
℟ Because by your holy cross you have redeemed the world.

When Pilate learned from the centurion that Jesus was dead, he granted the body to Joseph. And he bought a linen shroud, and taking him down, wrapped him in the linen shroud, and laid him in a tomb which had been hewn out of the rock; and he rolled a stone against the entrance of the tomb. Mary Magdalene and Mary the mother of Joses saw where he was laid (Mk 15:45-47).

The fact that Jesus' body — wrapped in a linen shroud lay in the tomb for three days, rules out any possibility of apparent death. He died as all people die. A large stone indicates definitiveness: everything that had been lived until then is now decisively in the past.

Nevertheless Jesus' death — a death which is absolutely real — was different from any other. For this unique death was the ultimate expression of God's infinite love, and love is the only living reality that cannot die.

Love is nothing else but perfect self-oblation and abnegation, in order to give oneself completely to the loved one. Is this not a form of death? And when one loves in a Christian way, placing his life completely at the service of his neighbour, is this not a "dying to self"?

All:

Our Father...

While my body here decays,
May my soul your goodness praise,
Safe in paradise with you. Amen.

"He descended to the dead.
On the third day he rose again.
He ascended into heaven,
and is seated at the right hand of the Father..."

— *Apostles' Creed*

HYMNS

ABIDE WITH ME

1. Abide with me, fast falls the eventide;
    the darkness deepens, Lord, with me abide!
    When other helpers fail, and comforts flee,
    help of the helpless, O abide with me.

2. Swift to its close ebbs our life's little day;
    earth's joys grow dim, its glories pass away;
    change and decay in all around I see;
    O thou who changest not, abide with me.

3. I need thy presence every passing hour;
    what but thy grace can foil the tempter's power?
    Who like thyself my guide and stay can be?
    Through cloud and sunshine, O abide with me.

4. I fear no foe with thee at hand to bless;
    ills have no weight, and tears no bitterness.
    Where is death's sting? Where, grave, thy victory?
    I triumph still if thou abide with me.

5. Hold thou thy Cross before my closing eyes;
    shine through the gloom, and point me to the skies;
    heaven's morning breaks, and earth's vain shadows flee;
    in life, in death, O Lord, abide with me!

— H.F. Lyte

AMAZING GRACE

1. Amazing grace! How sweet the sound
    that saved a wretch like me.
    I once was lost, but now I'm found,
    was blind, but now I see.

2. 'Twas grace that taught my heart to fear,
    and grace my fears relieved.
    How precious did that grace appear
    the hour I first believed.

3. Through many dangers, toils and snares
    I have already come.
    'Tis grace hath brought me safe thus far,
    and grace will lead me home.

4.   The Lord has promised good to me;
     his word my hope secures.
     He will my shield and portion be
     as long as life endures.

                              — *John Newton*

CHRIST BE BESIDE ME

1.   Christ be beside me, Christ be before me,
     Christ be behind me, King of my heart.
     Christ be within me, Christ be below me,
     Christ be above me, Never to part.

2.   Christ on my right hand, Christ on my left hand.
     Christ all around me, Shield in the strife.
     Christ in my sleeping, Christ in my sitting,
     Christ in my rising, Light of my life.

3.   Christ be in all hearts Thinking about me,
     Christ be on all tongues Telling of me.
     Christ be the vision In eyes that see me,
     In ears that hear me, Christ ever be.

              — *St Patrick's Breastplate* — *J. Quinn*

NEARER, MY GOD, TO THEE

1.   Nearer, my God, to thee, Nearer to thee!
     E'en though it be a cross that raiseth me,
     Still all my song shall be, nearer my God to thee,
     Nearer my God to thee, nearer to thee.

2.   Though, like the wanderer, the sun gone down,
     Darkness be over me, my rest a stone;
     Yet in my dreams I'd be nearer my God to thee,
     Nearer my God to thee, nearer to thee.

3.   There let the way appear steps unto heav'n;
     All that thou sendest me in mercy giv'n,
     Angels to beckon me nearer my God to thee,
     Nearer my God to thee, nearer to thee.

4.   Deep in thy sacred heart let me abide
     Thou who hast come for me, suffered and died.
     Sweet shall my weeping be, grief surely leading me,
     Nearer my God to thee, nearer to thee.

                              — *S. Adams*

PRAISE TO THE HOLIEST IN THE HEIGHT

1. Praise to the Holiest in the height, And in the depth be praise,
    In all his words most wonderful, most sure in all his ways.

2. O loving wisdom of our God! When all was sin and shame,
    a second Adam to the fight, and to the rescue came.

3. O wisest love! That flesh and blood which did in Adam fail,
    should strive afresh against the foe, should strive and should
    prevail.

4. And that a higher gift than grace should flesh and blood refine,
    God's presence and his very self, and essence all divine.

5. O generous love! that he who smote in man for man the foe,
    the double agony in man for man should undergo.

6. And in the garden secretly, and on the cross on high,
    should teach his brethren, and inspire, to suffer and to die.

7. Praise to the Holiest in the height, and in the depth be praise,
    in all his words most wonderful, most sure in all his ways.

— *John Henry Newman*

PRAISE TO THE LORD, THE ALMIGHTY

1. Praise to the Lord, the Almighty, the King of creation!
    O my soul, praise him, for he is your health and salvation.
    All you who hear, now to his altar draw near,
    join in profound adoration.

2. Praise to the Lord, let us offer our gifts at his altar;
    let not our sins and transgressions, now cause us to falter.
    Christ, the High Priest, bids us all join in his feast;
    victims with him on the altar.

3. Praise to the Lord, oh let all that is in us adore him!
    All that has life and breath, come now in praises before him.
    Let the Amen sound from his people again,
    now as we worship before him.

— *J. Neander – C. Winkworth*

THE LORD'S MY SHEPHERD

1. The Lord's my shepherd, I'll not want.
    He makes me down to lie
    in pastures green. He leadeth me
    the quiet waters by.

2. My soul he doth restore again,
    and me to walk doth make

within the paths of righteousness,
e'en for his own name's sake.

3. Yea, though I walk in death's dark vale,
    yet will I fear no ill.
    For thou art with me, and thy rod
    and staff me comfort still.

4. My table thou hast furnishèd
    in presence of my foes,
    my head thou dost with oil anoint,
    and my cup overflows.

5. Goodness and mercy all my life
    shall surely follow me.
    And in God's house for evermore
    my dwelling place shall be.

— *Ps 22, Scottish Psalter*

TO JESUS CHRIST OUR SOVEREIGN KING

1. To Jesus Christ, our sov'reign King,
    Who is the world's Salvation,
    All praise and homage do we bring,
    And thanks and adoration.

    Christ Jesus, victor. Christ Jesus, ruler.
    Christ Jesus, Lord and Redeemer.

2. Your reign extend, O King benign,
    To ev'ry land and nation;
    For in your kingdom, Lord divine,
    Alone we find salvation.

3. To you and to your Church, great King,
    We pledge our hearts' oblation,
    Until before your throne we sing
    In endless jubilation.

— *M.B. Hellriegel*

WHEN I BEHOLD THE WONDROUS CROSS

1. When I behold the wondrous cross,
    On which the prince of glory died,
    My richest gain I count but loss,
    And pour contempt on all my pride.

2. Forbid it, Lord, that I should boast,
    Save in the death of Christ, my God;
    The vain things that attract me most,
    I sacrifice them to his blood.

3. See, from his dead, his hands, his feet,
    What grief and love flow mingled down;
    Did e'er such love and sorrow meet,
    Or thorns compose so rich a crown?

4. Were all the realm of nature mine,
    It would be offering far too small;
    Love so amazing, so divine,
    Demands my soul, my life, my all.

— I. Watts

PRAISE, MY SOUL, THE KING OF HEAVEN

1. Praise, my soul, the king of heaven!
    To his feet your tribute bring.
    Ransomed, healed, restored, forgiven,
    who am I his praise to sing?

    Praise him! Praise him! (2x)
    Praise the everlasting king!

2. Praise him for his grace and favour
    to our fathers in distress;
    praise him still the same for ever,
    slow to chide and swift to bless.

3. Fatherlike, he tends and spares us;
    well our feeble frame he knows:
    in his hands he gently bears us,
    rescues us from all our foes.

4. Angels, help us to adore him;
    you behold him face to face;
    sun and moon bow down before him,
    ev'rything in time and space.

— H.F. Lyte

SOUL OF MY SAVIOUR

1. Soul of my Saviour, sanctify my breast;
    Body of Christ, be thou my saving guest;
    Blood of my Saviour, bathe me in thy tide,
    wash me ye waters, streaming from thy side.

2. Strength and protection may thy passion be;
    O Blessed Jesus, hear and answer me;
    deep in thy wounds, Lord, hide and shelter me;
    so shall I never, never part from thee.

3. Guard and defend me from the foe malign;
    in death's dread moments make me only thine;
    call me, and bid me come to thee on high,
    where I may praise thee with thy saints for aye.

— *Pope John XXII*

SWEET HEART OF JESUS

1. Sweet Heart of Jesus, fount of love and mercy,
    today we come, thy blessing to implore;
    O touch our hearts, so cold and so ungrateful,
    and make them, Lord, thine own for evermore.

    Sweet Heart of Jesus, we implore,
    O make us love thee more and more.

2. Sweet Heart of Jesus, make us know and love thee,
    unfold to us the treasures of thy grace;
    that so our hearts, from things of earth uplifted,
    may long alone to gaze upon thy face.

3. Sweet Heart of Jesus, make us pure and gentle,
    and teach us how to do thy blessed will;
    to follow close the print of thy dear footsteps,
    and when we fall – Sweet Heart, oh, love us still.

4. Sweet Heart of Jesus, bless all hearts that love thee,
    and may thine own Heart ever blessèd be;
    bless us, dear Lord, and bless the friends we cherish,
    and keep us true to Mary and to thee.

— *Author Unknown*

SWEET SACRAMENT DIVINE

1. Sweet sacrament divine, our shepherd and our king,
    Around your earthly shrine, with grateful hearts we sing.
    Jesus to you our voice we raise, in songs of love and joyful
        praise,
    Sweet sacrament divine, sweet sacrament divine.

2. Sweet sacrament of peace, in you mankind is blessed,
    All pain and sorrows cease, and human hearts find rest.
    Upon your promise we rely: "Who eats this Bread will never
        die",
    Sweet sacrament of peace, sweet sacrament of peace.

— *F. Stanfield*

LORD, ACCEPT THE GIFTS WE OFFER

1. Lord, accept the gifts we offer
    At this Eucharistic feast.
    Bread and wine to be transformed now,
    Through the action of thy priest.
    Take us too Lord, and transform us,
    Be thy grace in us increased.

2. May our souls be pure and spotless
    As this host of wheat so fine,
    May all stain of sin be crushed out,
    Like the grape that forms the wine,
    As we, too, become partakers
    In this sacrifice divine.

3. Take our gifts, almighty Father,
    Living God, eternal, true,
    Which we give, through Christ our Saviour,
    Pleading here for us anew.
    Grant salvation to all present
    And our faith and love renew.

— *Sr M. Teresine*

HAIL! REDEEMER, KING DIVINE!

1. Hail! Redeemer, King divine!
    Priest and lamb, the throne is thine,
    King whose reign shall never cease,
    Prince of everlasting peace.

    > *Angels, saints and nations sing:*
    > *Praised be Jesus Christ, our King:*
    > *Lord of life, earth, sky and sea,*
    > *King of love on Calvary.*

2. Eucharistic King, what love
    Draws thee daily from above,
    Clad in signs of bread and wine,
    Feed us, lead us, keep us thine.

3. King whose name creation thrills,
    Rule our minds, our hearts, our wills,
    Till in peace each nation rings,
    With thy praises, King of kings.

— *P. Brennan*

JESUS CHRIST IS RISEN TODAY

1. Jesus Christ is ris'n today, alleluia.
   Our triumphant holy day, alleluia.
   Who did once upon the cross, alleluia.
   Suffer to redeem our loss, alleluia.

2. Hymns of praise then let us sing, alleluia.
   Unto Christ, our heavenly king, alleluia.
   Who endured the cross and grave, alleluia.
   Sinners to redeem and save, alleluia.

3. But the pain which he endured, alleluia.
   Our salvation has procured; alleluia.
   Now above he reigns as king, alleluia.
   Where the angels ever sing, alleluia.

— *J. Arnold*

COME, HOLY GHOST, CREATOR, COME

1. Come, Holy Ghost, Creator, come
   from thy bright heavenly throne.
   Come, take possession of our souls,
   and make them all thine own.

2. Thou who art called the Paraclete,
   best gift of God above,
   the living spring, the living fire,
   sweet unction and true love.

3. Thou who are seven-fold in thy grace,
   finger of God's right hand;
   his promise, teaching little ones
   to speak and understand.

4. O guide our minds with thy blest light,
   with love our hearts inflame;
   and with thy strength, which ne'er decays,
   confirm our mortal frame.

5. Far from us drive our deadly foe;
   true peace unto us bring;
   and through all perils lead us safe
   beneath thy sacred wing.

6. Through thee may we the Father know,
   through thee th' eternal Son,
   and thee the Spirit of them both,
   thrice-blessed Three in One.

7.   All glory to the Father be,
     with his co-equal Son:
     the same to thee great Paraclete,
     while endless ages run.

— Ascribed to Robanus Maurus

O COME, EMMANUEL

1.   O come, O come, Emmanuel, To free your captive Israel,
     That mourns in lonely exile here, Until the Son of God ap-
          pear.
               Rejoice, rejoice, O Israel,
               To you shall come Emmanuel.

2.   O royal branch of Jesse's tree, Redeem us all from tyranny;
     From pain of hell your people free, And over death win
          victory.

3.   O come, great daystar, radiance bright, And heal us with your
          glorious light.
     Disperse the gloomy clouds of night, And death's dark
          shadows put to flight.

4.   O key of David's city, come And open wide our heav'nly
          home:
     Make safe the way that leads above, Protect us ever by your
          love.

5.   O come, O come, great Lord of might, Who once appeared
          on Sinai's height,
     And gave your faithful people law, In all the splendour we
          adore.

— J.M.Neale

HARK, THE HERALD ANGELS SING

1.   Hark, the herald angels sing, glory to the new-born king;
     peace on earth and mercy mild, God and sinners reconciled:
     joyful all ye nations rise, join the triumph of the skies,
     with the angelic host proclaim, Christ is born in Bethlehem.

               Hark, the herald angels sing,
               Glory to the new-born King.

2.   Christ, by highest heaven adored, Christ, the everlasting Lord,
     late in time behold him come, offspring of a Virgin's womb!
     Veiled in flesh the Godhead see, hail the Incarnate Deity!
     Pleased as man with man to dwell, Jesus, our Emmanuel.

3. Hail the heaven-born Prince of peace! Hail the Son of
   righteousness!
   Light and life to all he brings, risen with healing in his wings;
   mild he lays his glory by, born that man no more may die,
   born to raise the sons of earth, born to give them second
   birth.

— C. Wesley

O COME, ALL YE FAITHFUL

1. O come, all ye faithful, joyful and triumphant,
   O come ye, O come ye to Bethlehem;
   Come and behold him, born the king of angels:
   > *O come, let us adore him (3x)*
   > *Christ the Lord.*

2. Born of the Father, light from light eternal,
   Son of the gentle maid our flesh and blood;
   Honour and praise him with the hosts of angels.

3. Sing, choirs of angels, sing in exultation,
   Sing, all ye citizens of heaven above,
   Glory to God in the highest:

4. Now, Lord, we greet you, born this happy morning,
   Jesus to you be glory given, Word of the Father,
   Now in flesh appearing.

— John Wade, tr F. Oakley

SILENT NIGHT

1. Silent night, holy night, all is calm, all is bright,
   round yon virgin mother and child; holy infant so tender and
   mild:
   sleep in heavenly peace, sleep in heavenly peace.

2. Silent night, holy night. Shepherds quake at the sight,
   glories stream from heaven afar, heavenly hosts sing alleluia:
   Christ the Saviour is born, Christ the Saviour is born.

3. Silent night, holy night. Son of God, love's pure light,
   radiant beams from thy holy face, with the dawn of redeeming grace:
   Jesus, Lord, at thy birth, Jesus, Lord, at thy birth.

— Joseph Mohr, tr J. Young

HAIL, QUEEN OF HEAV'N

1. Hail, Queen of heav'n, the ocean star,
   guide of the wand'rer here below;
   thrown on life's surge, we claim thy care;
   save us from peril and from woe.
   Mother of Christ, star of the sea,
   pray for the wanderer, pray for me.

2. O gentle, chaste and spotless maid,
   we sinners make our prayers through thee;
   remind thy Son that he has paid
   the price of our iniquity.
   Virgin most pure, star of the sea,
   pray for the sinner, pray for me.

3. Sojourners in this vale of tears,
   to thee, blest advocate, we cry;
   pity our sorrows, calm our fears,
   and soothe with hope our misery.
   Refuge in grief, star of the sea,
   pray for the mourner, pray for me.

4. And while to him who reigns above,
   in Godhead One, in Persons Three,
   the source of life, of grace, of love,
   homage we pay on bended knee,
   do thou, bright Queen, star of the sea,
   pray for thy children, pray for me.

— *John Lingard*

I'LL SING A HYMN TO MARY

1. I'll sing a hymn to Mary, the Mother of my God,
   the Virgin of all virgins, of David's royal blood.
   O teach me, holy Mary, a loving song to frame,
   when wicked men blaspheme thee, to love and bless thy
   name.

2. O noble Tower of David, of gold and ivory,
   the Ark of God's own promise, the gate of heav'n to me,
   to live and not to love thee would fill my soul with shame;
   when wicked men blaspheme thee, I'll love and bless thy
   name.

3. The saints are high in glory, with golden crowns so bright;
but brighter far is Mary, upon her throne of light.
O that which God did give thee, let mortal ne'er disclaim;
when wicked men blaspheme thee I'll love and bless thy
name.

4. But in the crown of Mary, there lies a wondrous gem,
as Queen of all the angels, which Mary shares with them:
no sin hath e'er defiled thee, so doth our faith proclaim;
when wicked men blaspheme thee I'll love and bless thy
name.

— *John Wyse*

THE BELLS OF THE ANGELUS

1. The bells of the angelus, Call us to pray
In sweet tones announcing, The sacred Ave.

Ave, Ave, Ave, Maria;
Ave, Ave, Ave, Maria.

2. An angel of mercy, Led Bernadette's feet
Where flows the deep torrent, Our Lady to greet.

3. She prayed to our mother, That God's will be done,
She prayed for his glory, That his kingdom come.

4. Immaculate Mary Your praises we sing
Who reign now with Christ, Our redeemer and king.

5. In heaven the blessed Your glory proclaim,
On earth now your children Invoke your fair name.

HAIL GLORIOUS SAINT PATRICK

1. Hail glorious Saint Patrick, dear saint of our isle,
On us thy poor children bestow a sweet smile,
And now thou art high in the mansions above,
On Erin's green valleys look down in thy love.

2. Ever bless and defend the dear land of our birth,
Where shamrock still blooms as when thou wert on earth,
Our hearts shall still burn wheresoever we roam,
For God and Saint Patrick, and our native home.

— *Sr Agnes*